Two English-Language Translators of *Jin Ping Mei*

Two English-Language Translators of Jin Ping Mei examines English translations of the Ming novel *Jin Ping Mei* by translators from different historical periods within the Anglophone world.

Drawing upon theoretical insights from translation studies, literary criticism, and cultural studies, the book explores the treatment of salient features of the novel within translation, including cultural representation, narratological elements, gender-specific motifs, and (homo)sexual themes. Through literary re-imagining and artistic re-creation, Egerton transforms a complex and sprawling narrative into a popular modern middlebrow novel, making it readily accessible and recognizable within Western genres. Roy's interlinear and annotated translation transcends the mere retelling of a vivid story for its unwavering emphasis on every single detail of the original, becoming a portal to the Ming past. It stands as a testament to the significance of literary translation as a medium for understanding the legacy of the late Ming and the socio-cultural dynamics shaping that period in Chinese history.

This book will be a useful reference for scholars and research students within the fields of literary translation studies and translated Chinese literature, particularly Ming-Qing fiction. The book will also appeal to students and researchers studying *Jin Ping Mei*'s translation and reception in the West.

Shuangjin Xiao received his doctorate in Literary Translation Studies from Victoria University of Wellington. His research interests include translation studies, cultural studies, discourse analysis, and transmediality and popular culture in contemporary China. His articles have appeared in academic journals including the *Journal of Intercultural Communication Research*, the *Compilation and Translation Review*, the *International Journal of Linguistics Studies*, and *Translation Matters*. He also works as a freelance translator and is currently researching literary representations of gender and trauma, focusing on their treatment within translational and transmedial contexts.

Routledge Studies in Chinese Translation
Series Editor: Chris Shei, Swansea University, UK

This series encompasses scholarly works on every possible translation activity and theory involving the use of Chinese language. Putting together an important knowledge base for Chinese and Westerner researchers on translation studies, the series draws on multiple disciplines for essential information and further research that is based on or relevant to Chinese translation.

The Translator's Mirror for the Romantic
Cao Xueqin's *Dream* and David Hawkes' *Stone*
Fan Shengyu

Dialect, Voice, and Identity in Chinese Translation
A Descriptive Study of Chinese Translations of Huckleberry Finn, Tess, and Pygmalion
Jing Yu

A Deaf Take on Non-Equivalence in Written Chinese Translation
Chan Yi Hin

The Works of Lin Yutang
Translation and Recognition
Yangyang Long

Chinese Legal Translation
An Analysis of Conditional Clauses in Hong Kong Bilingual Ordinances
Yan Wang

Two English-Language Translators of *Jin Ping Mei*
From *Lotus* to *Plum*
Shuangjin Xiao

For more information about this series, please visit: https://routledge.com/Routledge-Studies-in-Chinese-Translation/book-series/RSCT

Two English-Language Translators of *Jin Ping Mei*

From *Lotus* to *Plum*

Shuangjin Xiao

LONDON AND NEW YORK

First published 2025
by Routledge
4 Park Square, Milton Park, Abingdon, Oxon OX14 4RN

and by Routledge
605 Third Avenue, New York, NY 10158

Routledge is an imprint of the Taylor & Francis Group, an informa business

British Library Cataloguing-in-Publication Data
A catalogue record for this book is available from the British Library

Library of Congress Cataloging-in-Publication Data
Names: Xiao, Shuangjin, author.
Title: Two English-language translators of Jin Ping Mei :
from lotus to plum / Shuangjin Xiao.
Description: Abingdon, Oxon ; New York, NY : Routledge, 2024. |
Series: Routledge studies in Chinese translation |
Includes bibliographical references and index.
Identifiers: LCCN 2024006795 (print) | LCCN 2024006796 (ebook) |
ISBN 9781032751528 (hardback) | ISBN 9781032751566 (paperback) |
ISBN 9781003472674 (ebook)
Subjects: LCSH: Xiaoxiaosheng. Jin Ping Mei ci hua. |
Xiaoxiaosheng–Translations into English–History and criticism. |
LCGFT: Literary criticism.
Classification: LCC PL2698.H73 C5926 2024 (print) |
LCC PL2698.H73 (ebook) | DDC 895.13/4–dc23/eng/20240316
LC record available at https://lccn.loc.gov/2024006795
LC ebook record available at https://lccn.loc.gov/2024006796

ISBN: 978-1-032-75152-8 (hbk)
ISBN: 978-1-032-75156-6 (pbk)
ISBN: 978-1-003-47267-4 (ebk)

DOI: 10.4324/9781003472674

Typeset in Times New Roman
by Newgen Publishing UK

To my grandma

To the memory of my grandpa

To my father and mother

Contents

Acknowledgments

The writing of this book has taken about four years, making it a journey filled with challenges and adventures. It stems from my doctoral dissertation completed at Victoria University of Wellington. The invaluable assistance of my dissertation supervisors, colleagues, and friends has been instrumental in bringing this project to fruition. I am indebted to Limin Bai for her wonderful guidance, endless support, and her vision for my doctoral project. Her instruction and resourcefulness kept my research consistently on the right route. Her open-mindedness, wisdom, and warm personality made a challenging intellectual pursuit a thoroughly enjoyable experience. I extend sincere gratitude to Richard Millington for his continuous encouragement, patience, insightful comments, and knowledgeable advice throughout the process of writing my dissertation. The unwavering support, constant inspiration, and other crucial assistance provided by both scholars were not only intellectually but also emotionally appreciated. I feel blessed and grateful to have had them in my academic career.

Special thanks go to Duncan Campbell, an inspiring intellectual who has remained a constant source of inspiration. Duncan has consistently offered thoughtful ideas on my conception of Chinese literature and its translation into English. I am deeply indebted to him for his patient guidance, continuous intellectual support, and useful suggestions in revising and improving my work, His advice on reaching out to publishers for the publication of my work has proven particularly beneficial.

I would like to express my heartfelt appreciation and thanks to Lintao Qi and Wayne Wen-chun Liang. Their expertise, critical insights, and thoughtful comments have not only helped me improve my work but will also continue to benefit my academic career. Heartfelt thanks are extended to Shengyu Fan for providing valuable suggestions and comments during the writing process of this book. My deep gratitude goes to Chris Shei and Routledge for showing faith and interest in this work. I am particularly indebted to them for investing their valuable time in editing and shaping it into its final book form. I am very grateful to Francis Norman for his careful editing and proofreading of my manuscript during the production process.

Very heartfelt thanks go to Yuqian Yan from the University of Chicago for her generous assistance in providing access to David Roy's archival material stored in the University of Chicago Library. I am indebted to the Chicago University Library, Special Collections, for granting me permission to access David Roy's archive. I also owe special thanks to the Special Collections at the University of Reading, Routledge and Kegan Paul Archive, for granting permission to refer to archival documents related to Clement Egerton's translation of *Jin Ping Mei*. I am wholeheartedly thankful to David Rolston and Katherine Carlitz for providing valuable information on David Roy's translation of *Jin Ping Mei*.

Acknowledgments are also due to all those who have supported and encouraged me throughout this long, challenging, and valuable journey. I am particularly grateful to my family for their continuous encouragement and emotional support during my research journey. My deepest appreciation goes to my parents and my grandma for their endless moral and spiritual support. I owe them a considerable debt of time and love, and I dedicate this book to them.

1 Introduction

Setting the Scene

1.1 Introduction

This book centers on classical Chinese fiction and its translation into English, with a particular focus on the socially significant and "realistic" novel, *Jin Ping Mei*, and its two English-language translations produced within different historical contexts. It systematically investigates how the practice of (re)translation helps to discover or rediscover *Jin Ping Mei*, a not entirely lost but somewhat neglected literary classic from a remote period in the source culture, to recreate the literary appeal of the novel, and to structure it as a piece of English-language literature accessible to a wider audience. *Jin Ping Mei* offers a unique window onto China's premodern culture and history, providing insights into significant intellectual trends and sociocultural transformations. Widely acclaimed as one of the few classical Chinese novels comparable to its outstanding Western counterparts, it stands out for "its grand scope, exquisite characterization, and ingenious plot design" (Hightower 1953, 120). Translating *Jin Ping Mei* into any language presents challenges due to its generic hybridity, exhaustive narrative style, intricate intertextuality, minute details, and tremendous length. That said, it has appeared in several English versions since the late nineteenth century, serving as a gateway to various aspects of premodern China for English-speaking audiences. *Jin Ping Mei* enters the Anglophone literary system through multiple translations and this makes it an illuminating case for investigating how "Western cultures translated non-Western cultures into Western categories" (Lefevere 1999, 77). Given that translation plays a central role in disseminating *Jin Ping Mei* in the Western world, the novel becomes an ideal object of study for exploring literary translation practice, a most effective means for introducing Chinese literature to Western audiences.

1.2 Introduction to the Source Text: *Jin Ping Mei*

Acclaimed as one of the famed *si da qi shu* 四大奇書 (four masterworks) of China's Ming dynasty (1368–1644),[1] *Jin Ping Mei* appeared sometime in the second half of the sixteenth century, a period of growing material wealth and volatile social changes that came to threaten traditional values. It is a mammoth work running to one hundred chapters, which is at once a reflection and a criticism of contemporary

DOI: 10.4324/9781003472674-1

conditions (Lai 1964, 307; Liu 1966, 234). The novel is roughly dated 1617 but the exact dating remains unknown (Huo 1988, 708; Hegel 1998, 38). It tells the story of the rise and fall of a local merchant's household and the fate of his family members within an imaginary urban setting. The novelist uses the household as a metaphor for the dynasty or the state, to show deep concern about the social ills and moral decay of his day and to express a seeming conviction that stability either at the domestic or state level is hardly possible if Confucian orthodoxy, moral order, and traditions cannot be observed (ibid.). However, due to its explicit content, including its *xiangyan* 香豔 narratives (namely, containing risqué, amorous passages), the novel has acquired a controversial reputation. This controversy, in turn, has greatly influenced its perception and reception. Interestingly, the explicit content, especially the *xiangyan* elements, offers an ideal platform for the novelist to convey his inner conflict. This involves criticizing the moral decay of his society while grappling with nostalgic regret for the vanishing Confucian ethical values. The novel has often been misread as pornography or an erotic classic, leading to frequent government proscriptions. On the other hand, over the centuries, it has also been praised by many readers as an exceptional work. Undisputedly, the author of *Jin Ping Mei* succeeded in creating pointed, vivid, and life-size characters with complexity and insight. This was achieved through the use of simple, living, and straightforward language, skillfully capturing and describing the realistic details of contemporary society.

1.2.1 Title and Authorship

The playful title of the novel can be semantically interpreted as "the plum blossom in the golden vase" or simply "Gold Vase Plum." It consists of a combination of three Chinese characters, representing the names of three female characters in the story: Pan **Jin**lian 潘金蓮, Li **Ping**'er 李瓶兒, and Pang Chun**mei** 龐春梅. The arrangement of these three names indicates their importance to the novel's plot. The novel's author is Xiao Xiao Sheng 笑笑生, or the Scoffing Scholar from Lanling, a place in East China's Shandong province. Xiao Xiao Sheng is a pseudonym. It was common practice for novelists in imperial China to write under pseudonyms. The Chinese novel was a late literary form and often regarded as an indecent genre in comparison to poetry and other high art forms. Hence, it came to be known as "small talks" (*xiaoshuo* 小說) or "unofficial histories" (*yeshi* 野史) (Zeitlin 2007, 250). To avoid courting the contempt of the world, fictional writers chose to conceal their true names, and the author of *Jin Ping Mei* is no exception. In *Wanli yehuo bian* 萬歷野獲編, the late Ming historian Shen Defu 沈德符 (1578–1642) wrote that *Jin Ping Mei*'s author was an outstanding scholar-official of the Ming Jiajing 嘉靖 period (1522–66). However, the genuine identity of the novelist has remained a mystery (Shen 1958, 652; Chang and Owen 2010, 105). In view of its stylistic coherence and unified plot, *Jin Ping Mei* is, as Patrick Hanan (1961, 325) indicates, probably a work written by a single literatus of late Ming. Despite numerous hypotheses about the genuine identity of the novelist, no consensus has been reached due to insufficient evidence. Nevertheless, the undisclosed identity of the novelist does not influence the interpretation of the novel. From a poststructur-alist perspective, it is the finished work itself that becomes the object of criticism and interpretation. The meanings embedded within the text exist independently of, or beyond the control of, the text's author, who is declared to be "dead" (Barthes 1977, 142; Foucault 1977, 131). This viewpoint underscores the liberation of the text from the constraints of authorial intent, emphasizing the reader's participa-tion in a dynamic process that goes beyond the confines of the author's original intentions to contribute to the meaning-making within a text. The "death" of the author, in this context, frees the text from a fixed and singular interpretation, allowing it to evolve and resonate differently with diverse audiences over time.

1.2.2 Recensions

There are three distinct recensions or textual variants regarding the text of *Jin Ping Mei*. The first recension refers to the earliest extant edition of the text published sometime after 1616 (Shinobu 1963, 79). This recension, with two prefaces (one by Xinxinzi 欣欣子 and the other by Nongzhuke from Dongwu 东吴弄珠客 dated 1617) and one colophon by Niangong 廿公, is called *Jin Ping Mei cihua* 金瓶梅 詞話 and was compiled and circulated in the Wanli 萬曆 reign (1573–1620) of the Ming dynasty.[2] Discovered in China's Shanxi province in 1932, it is currently the only version complete with all borrowed material, such as copious verses, *ci*-poetry, jokes, popular songs, drama sequences, and court edicts, woven and incorporated into the text (Hanan 1962; Hanan 1963, 39; Huo 1988, 709; Tian 2002, 347; Wang 2015, 22). It bears the closest resemblance to the *ur*-text (namely, the earliest known text) since it was published much earlier, and the rhetorical techniques are ideally maintained (Roy 1993, xxi; Tian 2002, 351). The second recension, known as *Xinke xiuxiang piping Jin Ping Mei* 新刻繡像批評金瓶梅, dates back to the Chongzhen 崇禎 reign (1628–44) of the Ming dynasty. Also referred to the Chongzhen edition, this second recension was carefully edited, with redundant verse passages and song sequences removed to enhance acceptability, readability and reduce printing costs (Hsia 1968, 168; Rolston 1997, 65).[3] It circulated more widely than the first edition in late imperial China, appealing to a more elite reader-ship (Lu 2008, 181; Tian 2002, 349). It contains the undated preface by Nongzhuke and an anonymous commentary (Tian 2002, 347). It is worth noting that no funda-mental variations exist between the first and second recensions, as there are only clear inconsistencies in chapter titles, chapter divisions, quoted poems, the opening chapter, and chapters fifty-three to fifty-seven (Hsia 1968, 170). Tian Xiaofei notes that the *xiuxiang* recension is aesthetically and ideologically more consistent, pri-marily for "its tighter organization, its subtle characterization, and the greater eth-ical complexity that followed from its more serious engagement with Buddhist values" (2002, 387). The third recension is virtually identical to the second except for the preface and commentary (Roy 1993, xx; Roy 1998, 102; Hsia 1968, 166). This recension, also known as the *di yi qi shu* 第一奇書 (or the best-known work of Ming fiction) edition, came out in 1695, decades later than the previous two editions, and includes an exhaustive commentary by the famous Qing (1644–1911) scholar and critic Zhang Zhupo 張竹坡 (1670–98). While almost identical textually to the second recension, the third was the most popular edition circulating in the Qing dynasty and has influenced the reception and interpretation of *Jin Ping Mei* by later critics and readers (Hegel 1998, 301; Wu 2009; Zhu 2002, 80).[4]

1.2.3 Plot Summary

While ostensibly set in Northern Song China (960–1125), *Jin Ping Mei* reflects the customs, morals, and social activities of the novelist's contemporary Ming dynasty (Liu 1966, 234; Chang and Owen 2010, 107). Unfolding with a unilinear plot, *Jin Ping Mei* meticulously details the intimate relations within a large, polygamous household, weaving together themes of love, lust, and power. Set in Qinghe, a fictional prosperous commercial town in North China, the novel serves as a social critique, vividly portraying the decadence and moral corruption prevalent in the society of that era. It delves into the lives of a diverse cast of characters, exposing their flaws, desires, and the repercussions of their actions.

Aristotle posits that the plot is the cornerstone of narrative, emphasizing the need for a beginning, middle, and end to create engaging stories and derive pleasure from the rhythmic arrangement of events. This principle is evident in *Jin Ping Mei*, where the meticulously crafted plot demonstrates a subtle symmetry. In the first twenty chapters, the narrative recounts the gathering of the main characters within the Ximen family. Ximen Qing 西門慶 amasses a prodigious fortune through various financial dealings and attains an official post in Qinghe through unlawful means. Transitioning from the twenty-first to the seventy-ninth chapter, the plot focuses on the expansion of Ximen Qing's wealth and power, his rising status in officialdom, and his numerous sexual conquests involving various women, including his legal wife Wu Yueniang 吳月娘 and five concubines: Jinlian, Meng Yulou 孟玉樓, Li Ping'er, Li Jiao'er 李嬌兒, and Sun Xue'e 孫雪娥. The narrative culminates in his sudden horrific death during the peak of sexual ecstasy after consuming excessive aphrodisiacs. In the concluding twenty chapters, the downfall of the Ximen household and the destinies of its members unfolds in the narrative. With the climax being already shown, the narrative pace quickens, and the tone adopts a somber hue. In the last chapter, the Song state faces defeat by the Jurchens, leading to the death or displacement of countless civilians. Seeking refuge, Wu Yueniang and her fifteen-year-old son, Xiao Ge, find solace in a Buddhist temple where the monk Pu Jing 普靜 offers sacrifices to all the deceased in Qinghe. Subsequently, all departed souls, including Ximen Qing and Jinlian, embark on the journey to rebirth. Pu Jing informs Wu Yueniang that Xiao Ge must become his disciple, as the boy is the reincarnation of his father Ximen Qing. Finally, Xiao Ge embraces Buddhism, becoming a monk and serving as a commentary to his father's life and death. The novel ends with Buddhist retribution and redemption, aligning with the strong moralist tone established in the preface (by Xinxinzi) to the book (the *cihua* recension).

1.2.4 Merit and Value

Jin Ping Mei stands as a milestone in the history of Chinese fiction. Its emergence in the late sixteenth century revolutionized the world of the Chinese novel (Lai 1964, 309; Yang et al. 1978, 55). Its primary reputation is attributed to its break-through in employing homespun language that approximates street conversation, its rhetorical sophistication, and its unwavering exploration of the lives of ordinary men and women, as well as domestic issues, within a fictional universe.

Several specific aspects of *Jin Ping Mei* distinguish it from earlier Ming novels. Prior to *Jin Ping Mei*, fiction was dominated by heroic figures, historical events, legends, and mythology; however, *Jin Ping Mei* breaks away from these conventions by charting the fate of the common man within a recognizable phys-ical milieu (Yang et al. 1978, 60; Gu 2006, 125; Mair 2001, 637; Zhou 2010, 10; Zhang 2023,336). Unbound by traditional norms, it can incorporate new ideas and develop its own structure (Gu 2006, 125; Mair 2001, 638). The novel is the vision of its author and exists in its own fictitious universe, a supposedly realistic location in Ming China, yet a world viewed through the novelist's imagination.

Jin Ping Mei deals in a realistic fashion with the everyday life of a local merchant-cum-official and thus emerges as the prototype of a very different genre, the novel of manners.[5] The novel consists of a mimesis of Chinese life, manners, and conventions during the author's own times. Its depictions, as Lu Xun 魯迅 (1881–1936) suggests, are "clear yet subtle, penetrating yet highly suggestive, and for the sake of contrast [the author] sometimes portrays two different aspects of life" (Lu 1923, 222). Lu Xun also considers *Jin Ping Mei* to be the greatest novel of manners of the Ming dynasty. This sentiment is echoed by Zheng Zhengduo 鄭振鐸 (1898–1958), a contemporary of Lu Xun, who acclaims the novel as a great realistic work that nakedly and unscrupulously depicts the morbid state of Chinese society, capturing the most absurd scenes of a degenerate fin-de-siècle society (Zheng 2005, 71). In the imaginary world of *Jin Ping Mei*, readers can observe the lives of ordinary individuals from different social strata. Later fiction writers would go on to contribute similarly ambitious works featuring fine-grained descriptions of the daily life of ordinary people in Chinese urban society. Thus, it is no surprise that *Jin Ping Mei* is deemed a transitional work in the development of Chinese fiction owing to its experimental nature in abandoning historicity and turning to pure fic-tionality (Lai 1964, 307; Gu 2006, 125; Huang 2001, 58). It is also for this reason that *Jin Ping Mei* is sometimes described as the first genuine Chinese novel (Hanan 1961, 332). When it was first introduced to the Western audience by scholars and sinologists in the nineteenth century, *Jin Ping Mei*, along with other Chinese novels such as *Haoqiu zhuan* 好逑傳 and *Yujiao li* 玉嬌李, was assessed and compared with European novels regarding literary merits and flaws. For instance, William Frederick Mayers (1831–78) offered close readings of several Chinese novels, including *Jin Ping Mei*. Mayers commented that *Jin Ping Mei*, along with several other romantic novels like *Honglou meng*, was written in the colloquial or ver-nacular language and contained the most realistic descriptions of the characters and daily manners. These qualities approached the standard of modern European romances and could be considered the equal of Giovanni Boccaccio's (1313–75) tales (Mayers 1867, 165).

Indeed, *Jin Ping Mei*'s closeness to social reality makes it an essential source on sixteenth-century Chinese culture. The illuminating details of late imperial Chinese life delineated in the novel are historically grounded, and encompass such elements as food, alcohol, jewelry, clothing, architecture, furniture, rituals, festivals, games, jokes, dialects, business dealings, currency, and religion (Shang 2005, 63–92; Berry 1988, 163; Bai 2015). They are closely tied to the novel's narrative style and characterization. Due to its microscopic representation of the everyday world, *Jin Ping Mei* can even be thought of as an encyclopedia of late Ming society. Due to these very qualities, *Jin Ping Mei*, like other romantic novels mentioned above, was considered to be an ideal source for Western scholars to gain insight into Chinese manners, customs, and culture during the nineteenth and early twentieth centuries.

Jin Ping Mei is also regarded as the first Chinese domestic novel, as most of the activities occur within the confines of the male protagonist's household. No novel prior to *Jin Ping Mei* ever showed Chinese family life so impartially, unsparingly, and adequately (Chang and Owen 2010, 108; Zhou and Wu 2012, 133). The novelist takes great pains to describe family structures, kinship relations, and domestic affairs such as banquets, clothing, birthday parties, gift exchanges, customs, ritual activities, and bed scenes. This contributes to the depth of characterization and anchoring the novelist's point of view.

Noticeably, the novelist persistently focuses on women in their family compounds within an urban setting, which represents a key narrative innovation for *Jin Ping Mei* (Chien 1987; Yang et al. 1978, 57; Wang 2014, 67). As the title of the novel suggests, women play a crucial part in weaving together the entire narrative and their actions contribute to the fortunes of their household. In his portrait of women, the novelist borrows numerous earlier sources like poems, *ci*-lyrics, popular songs, and plays to reveal their state of mind and personality. Some of the female characters are portrayed as complex individuals. Anything represented by female characters, such as clothing, fashion, jealousy, promiscuity, unchastity, and power struggle, is indicative of the central interest of the novel, and it is often linked to domestic politics, ethical morality, patriarchy, and misogyny, which are typical of traditional Chinese households. In a word, *Jin Ping Mei* represents the first Chinese novel to display intense interest in depicting women unjustly, unsparingly, and microscopically, which serves as fine material for perceptions of women in contemporary society (Yang et al.1978, 58; Zeng and Xu 2000, 1–16; Jaivin 2021, 113). No novels prior to *Jin Ping Mei* ever give such a meticulous yet unflattering picture of women in a domestic setting, as it were.

Overall, *Jin Ping Mei*'s radical shift in narrative focus, its preoccupation with ordinary, life-size characters and their everyday life, its perceptible physical setting, and its skillful use of different textual sources make it a milestone of the Chinese novel. For its verisimilitudinous description of compelling characters and daily manners, *Jin Ping Mei* is comparable to modern European romances and its style could be considered "no less a master-piece in Chinese than Boccaccio's Tales are in the Italian language" (Mayers 1867, 165). Not surprisingly, *Jin Ping Mei* "has done extremely well at the hands of western translators and scholars as compared with the other three masterworks of Ming fiction" (Hsia 1968, 165). For instance, Herbert Allen Giles (1845–1935), in his *A History of Chinese Literature*, described *Jin Ping Mei* as a marvelous work attributed to a serious scholar and statesman in the Ming dynasty. He further commented that the novel "is written in a simple, easy style, closely approaching the Peking colloquial" (Giles 1901, 309). Noticeably, the Latin American writer and translator Jorge Luis Borges (1899– 1986) observes that *Jin Ping Mei* is essentially fantastic, and the characters in the novel represent social archetypes, interacting organically in the plot as they are not tied to any specific country and operate independently from any referential space (Hubert 2015, 95). Borges approaches the novel by associating it with his immediate present as a reader. For him, the novel transcends its historical origins to resonate with the nuances of his own time and cultural milieu. Borges actually invites readers to explore the intersections of fiction and reality, encouraging them to question the boundaries between imagination and lived experience. As Ning Zongyi and Lu Derong rightly postulate, "whether one examines the novel by placing it on the abscissas of the Chinese novels of manners or explores it by placing it on the ordinates of novels of similar subject matter in the worldwide context, it will not lose its status as a brilliant masterpiece" (Ning and Lu 1984; Gu 2004, 333). *Jin Ping Mei* exerted a great influence on later works, such as *Xu Jin Ping Mei* 續金瓶梅 (A Sequel to *Jin Ping Mei*), *Xingshi yinyuan zhuan* 醒世姻緣傳 (Marriage Destinies to Awaken the World), and *Honglou meng* 紅樓夢 (Story of the Stone), to name only a few (Wu 1986, 2; Scott 1989; Hu 2004, 75; Lu 2008, 200).[6] It has been translated into numerous languages, including English, French, German, Danish, Russian, Japanese, Thai, and Vietnamese. The next section introduces the English translations of the novel.

1.3 Introduction to English Translations of *Jin Ping Mei*

Jin Ping Mei is one of the few Chinese novels translated into English in the early twentieth century, and there are currently four major English variants available in the English-speaking world.

The earliest attempt to introduce *Jin Ping Mei* to an English-reading audience was an anonymous text titled *The Adventures of Hsi-men Ching*, published by The Library of Facetious Lore in 1927. This highly abridged version condenses the highlights of the one-hundred-chapter novel into eighteen chapters of simple, plain English. The Chinese original text was reorganized and reworked as an erotic story about moral redemption. Despite this effort, the translation has gained little attention from the reading public or scholars (Ye 2000, 733). Until recently, it has rekindled scholarly interest in the field of translation studies.[7]

Another available but equally abridged translation, *Chin Ping Mei: The Adventurous History of Hsi-men and his Six Wives*, was made by Bernard Miall (1876–1953) and published by John Lane in London in 1939. It was printed by Putnam in New York in the following year. Miall's text was translated into simple, lively English from the abridged German version, *King Ping Meh*, made by the sinologist Franz Kuhn (1884–1961) in 1930.[8] Kuhn's version comprises forty-nine chapters tastefully selected from the Chinese original and eschews all erotic passages (France 2000, 233). Chang Su-lee describes Miall's text as a mere rehearsal of the plot of the source work, lacking understanding of its insight, appreciation, and even entrée into a culture that is only possible through excellent translations (Chang 1940, 616). That said, a valuable feature for Miall's text is the short but well-informed introduction written by Arthur Waley (1889–1966), a leading figure in Far Eastern studies at the time. Waley writes of the literary background of *Jin Ping Mei*, its legendary authorship, and its early reception in late imperial China, giving readers deep insight (for example, historical context, authorship, and so forth) into the novel of late Ming China.

Both translations are heavily expurgated and inconsistent with the original text in various ways. This project therefore intends to investigate the two full-length English translations: Clement Egerton's *The Golden Lotus* (1939) and David Tod Roy's *The Plum in the Golden Vase* (1993–2013). For current purposes, full-length translation means that all the chapters of a source work are rendered in a sequential manner, together with a complete cast of characters and a coherent storyline. Yet it does not mean that the translation is free of any deletions, omissions, and transmutations. The rest of this section introduces the two translations and sketches out the two translators' backgrounds and information respecting the genesis and basic features of their translated works.

1.3.1 *Clement Egerton's* The Golden Lotus

Clement Egerton, or Colonel Frederick Clement Christie Egerton (b.1890), was a writer, educationist, and anthropologist. His translation *The Golden Lotus* (hereafter *Lotus*), named after the female protagonist Pan Jinlian, was the first full-length translation (running to a hundred chapters) of *Jin Ping Mei* in a European language. It was first published in four volumes by George Routledge and Sons, Ltd. in 1939 and has since then been reprinted many times in London, New York, Tokyo, and Singapore. About fifteen years in the making and not intended to be scholarly, the translation maintains the staccato terseness of the original and captures the spirit of the Chinese narrative (Berry 1988, 170). Modernist writer William Plomer (1903–73) asserts that when Egerton's translation came out in 1939, readers were obliged to him for making a large and remarkable Chinese novel, unknown except to sinologists, available in English (Plomer 1939). Indeed, Egerton's translation made *Jin Ping Mei* one of the few Chinese novels rendered in a major European language in the early twentieth century, which paved the way for the novel to enter the world literature scene.

Egerton, a prolific writer and translator with broad experience and diverse interests, was well versed in German, French, and Latin. His body of work touches upon a wide array of subjects and genres. He was the author of the travelogue *African Majesty* (1939) and of *Salazar: Rebuilder of Portugal* (1943). Egerton also published several other books on church music and education, such as *A Handbook of Church Music* (1909) and *The Future of Education* (1914). In a review of Egerton's works such as *African Majesty* (1939), the anonymous reviewer maintains that Egerton proved adept at writing in a light and easy manner, allowing his readers easy access to the content of his works (anonymous 1939, 179–180). H. G. Worth, who prefaced Egerton's *A Handbook of Church Music* (a book on musical training for beginners), also points out that Egerton always knew what his readers needed and was adept at making his writing as simple as possible to appeal to the target audience (Egerton 1909, xi). Egerton's prose style can also be observed in *The Future of Education* (1914). Upon reading the book, one would find his prose to be rather laconic, fluent, natural, and easily accessible. This suggests that Egerton's prose implies a smooth and seamless flow of language, creating a narrative that is easy to follow, ensuring readers can navigate the content without unnecessary barriers or disruptions. His prose style can make the text relatable and resonate with readers, mirroring the simplicity and authenticity of everyday communication. By employing easily understood language, he ensures a broad audience can engage with the content. This aligns with his progressive views on education, as an accessible writing style makes the ideas presented in *The Future of Education* more widely available and impactful.

Egerton's reader-centered awareness for his books also manifests in his translation of *Jin Ping Mei*, as will be demonstrated later in this study.

Egerton had multiple identities and was by no means limited to being a writer. He served as the Bishop of Norwich, England, and later joined the army. During World War I, he rose to the rank of lieutenant colonel (Witchard 2012, 72). Additionally, he was once a student of the anthropologist Bronislaw Malinowski (1884–1942), whose writings on culture, civilization, custom, family, community, gender, and sexuality had a great influence on him and later led him to turn to *Jin Ping Mei*, a cultural text rich in folkloric and anthropological value. His anthropological interests took him to West Africa and Japan, where he gained valuable insights into the differences between human cultures and civilizations (Hegel 2011, 16).[9] His interest in social psychology led him to learn Chinese, and he later chose to translate *Jin Ping Mei*, an arduous yet rewarding task that occupied about fifteen years.[10] Egerton settled on *Jin Ping Mei* from among the great Chinese novels primarily due to his appreciation of its cultural value, artistic importance, and originality, stating that it "has something, surely, of the quality of a Greek tragedy in its very ruthlessness" (Egerton 1939, viii). He further maintains that he wanted to introduce the novel to his contemporary readers and decided to give them the same overall reading experience that he himself gets when reading the novel. Another impetus was that Egerton came across the novel in Henri Cordier's (1849–1925) *Bibliotheca Sinica*, where Cordier asserts that the translation of *Jin Ping Mei* would render superfluous any other work on the life and manners of the Chinese (Collier 1944, 345; Egerton 1939, ix).

Egerton's choice of translating *Jin Ping Mei* was also influenced by two German sinologists, Wilhelm Grube (1855–1908) and Berthold Laufer (1874–1934). In *Geschichte Der Chinesischen Literatur*, Grube declares that the author of *Jin Ping*

Mei manifests "a power of observation and description so far above the average that all the remaining novel literature of China put together has nothing to compare with it." In *Skizze Der Manjurischen Literatur*, Laufer claims the novel to be the highest in its class and explains that it is "as little unmoral as any work of Zola or Ibsen, and like them a work of art from the hand of a master, who well understands his fellow men" (Egerton 1939, ix). Notably, Egerton's choice might have been influenced by Bertrand Russell (1872–1970), a philosopher, Bloomsbury associate, and a teacher at Cambridge University. Russell's book, *The Problem of China* (1922), written after the Great War, offered favorable comments on Chinese civilization while critiquing Western industrialism, materialism, capitalism, and imperialism (Lin 2001, 30). Russell's ideas resonated with those of G. L. Dickinson's (1862–1932). He was a sinophile, Christian socialist, and like Russel, a teacher at Cambridge. Dickinson's *Letters from John Chinaman* (1901) similarly critiqued Western civilization as aggressive, industrial, and capitalist while emphasizing Chinese civilization as pastoral, peaceful, harmonious with nature, and morally superior. This was in response to the overwhelmingly negative image of China in the West in the early twentieth century (Xie 2018, 500). Dickinson's work drew on insights from H. A. Giles's *Gems of Chinese Literature* (1884) and Eugène Simon's (1829–1896) *La Cité Chinoise*, both introducing Chinese philosophical, cultural, and social traditions, emphasizing China's spirituality, humanism, harmony, and agrarian values (ibid.). Due to various materials produced by translators and scholars in the late and early twentieth century, the philosophical, cultural, and spiritual importance of China gradually became evident to Westerners, which will be further discussed shortly. In *Lotus*, Egerton mentioned that the novel he chose to translate was from a more developed civilization. This implies that his choice was likely influenced by the favorable treatment of Chinese civilization by contemporary intellectuals. Because of the influences mentioned above, it can be assumed that Egerton held a belief and trust that there was something there in Chinese literature, particularly in the case of *Jin Ping Mei*, that could be translated for contemporary readership. This "initial trust", in George Steiner's (1975, 312) parlance, serves as an important motive for Egerton to spend years carrying out his translation project.

It is noteworthy that from the eighteenth to the early twentieth century, Chinese fictional texts were often considered in Western Europe as the most reliable sources of information about Chinese thought and manners. Publishing such texts in translation was deemed the best way to learn about the authentic situations of Chinese family life and domestic morality within Chinese culture (Lehner 2011, 381; Purdy 2021, 309). Moreover, Western scholars and orientalists like Abel Rémusat (1788–1832) and Johann Wolfgang Goethe (1749–1832) acknowledged that European novels shared several characteristics with Chinese novels. European readers could recognize such similarities and identify or establish emotional ties with fictional characters in Chinese novels (Purdy 2021, 310). These assumptions influenced many translators of Chinese texts in the West during this time. In order to make Chinese novels appear like European novels, they had to be remolded in a way that made this recognition (analogies) prominent or at least possible, thereby fostering European readers' accommodation of the unfamiliar into the already known (ibid.,

311). While translating *Jin Ping Mei*, Egerton mentioned that he became totally absorbed by the book as a work of art rather than as a mere psychological document. He emphasized that a deliberately strictly literal translation equipped with elaborate notes and exegeses would be exceedingly valuable. However, he decided against that approach and instead chose to render the novel in a form that his contemporary readers would gain the same impression (namely, like a novel in the British/European sense) from it that he did himself (Egerton 1939, x). This implies that the primary concern for Egerton was the taste and expectancy of contemporary readers, which in turn defined his translation policy to a large extent. This concept recalls the idea of translation as "refraction," involving the transformation of a foreign work into a different language audience with a view to influencing how that audience reads the work (Lefevere 2000, 235). Of course, it should be admitted that Egerton's translation policy was also influenced by his limited background knowledge of Chinese language and culture, given the restricted knowledge about China in the West during the early twentieth century. His interpretations and understanding of *Jin Ping Mei* were shaped by his "prejudices," as termed by Hans-Georg Gadamer (2003, 270). These prejudices, referred to as pre-existing knowledge, assumptions, and biases, played a significant role in defining his translation approach.

Certainly, one cannot assume that the power of Egerton as a translator of *Jin Ping Mei* derived from an intuitive and dilettante approach, which was Edward Fitzgerald's style. Fitzgerald, renowned for his creative translation of the *Rubáiyát* (1859) from Persian, enacted extreme rewriting of the Persian original but exerted a strong sphere of influence in his day because his translation became so transparent that it did not seem to be translated but written originally in English (Drury 2015, 15; Bubb 2023, 19). Fitzgerald's approach echoed Zhukovsky's translation of *The Odyssey*. Zhukovsky became so invisible as a translator that he served as a clarifying looking glass for the reader, who could only feel that what they read was a transparent text without any unfamiliar linguistic or stylistic peculiarities (Loison-Charles 2022, 132). These sorts of transparent translations, Lawrence Venuti (1995, 1) asserts, are generally deemed acceptable by most publishers and readers because they avoid creating an alien and unnatural reading experience. In his translation of *Jin Ping Mei*, Egerton refashioned the original title, choosing *The Golden Lotus* as the new title. This choice involved drawing parallels and intertextually resonating with the popular novel *The Golden Ass* by Lucius Apuleius (b. A.D. 124), Henry James's (1843-1916) novel, *The Golden Bowl*, and James George Frazer's (1854–1941) *The Golden Bough* in Europe. It demonstrates that the translator consciously or unknowingly picks elements from the receptor literary system and language to facilitate the assimilation of the target text into existing structures within the receptor culture. Besides rewriting the original title, Egerton also recast all the chapter titles of the novel so that each title appears simple and straightforward and captures the essence of the plot in each respective chapter (Xiao 2022, 64). This creative and aesthetic transformation of both the source book title and chapter titles, in accordance with the literary and stylistic norms of his era, represents a "diffractive performance" (Gragnolati 2017, 9). This performance is not intended to faithfully replicate the sacred image of the original but rather seeks to cultivate a distinct critical consciousness and to bring about a reader-friendly effect through the "re-creation," in Gadamer's (2003, 386) parlance, of the original text's meaning in a new language. It anticipates a trend in the deployment of translation strategy, specifically involving the domestication or assimilation of the original into the target literary culture, particularly in its aesthetics. The goal is to cater to the expectations of the domestic lay reader, the non-elite public, or simply middlebrow expectations, as will be demonstrated in the subsequent chapters. This is also connected to the nature of translation, which is inherently a hermeneutic experience entwined with acts of "renunciation" and even "betrayal" (Gadamer 2003, 386; George 2022, 157). As Gadamer cogently postulates, the translator "is always in the position of not really being able to express all the dimensions of [the original] text; he must make a constant renunciation" (2003, 386). Gadamer further demonstrates that "translation, like all interpretation, is a highlighting. A translator must understand that highlighting is part of his task. [...] But since he is always in the position of not really being able to express all the dimensions of his text, he must make a constant renunciation" (ibid., 388). Consequently, translation becomes a compromise activity, necessitating the highlighting of certain meanings or features of the original at the expense of downplaying or entirely suppressing others. Another pragmatic reason is that the literary and aesthetic perception of a reader raised in the traditions of English narrative prose differs significantly from that of a source Chinese-language reader. In the following chapters of this book, it will become evident that Egerton, a prolific writer and translator of a Chinese classic novel, was undoubtedly acutely aware of this dynamic, as demonstrated by his continuous "renunciation" when dealing with salient features of the Chinese original.

It so happened, however, that Egerton met Shu Qingchun 舒慶春 (1899–1966), who later became a renowned novelist (with the pen name Lao She 老舍) in China, in the spring of 1925 at the School of Oriental Studies, University of London (Vohra 1974, 12; Hu 1978, 48). Lao She was then a lecturer in Mandarin and Classical Chinese at the School and got on well with Egerton.[11] Lao She had an English name at that time, Colin, and he was also known as Colin C. Shu, or C. C. Shu, which was mentioned by Egerton in his Translator's Note (Zhang 2010, 59). Lao She had converted to Christianity and became a Christian before leaving for England, and the name, Colin, carries a Christian connotation. This conversion helped strengthen Lao She during a period of deep depression when he had lost faith in everything. It also allowed him to make missionary contacts that eventually led to the opportunity to go to England (Vohra 1974, 12). Lao She and Egerton became great friends and decided to rent a flat together, with Lao She paying the rent and Egerton providing the meals. They lived together for about five years, during which Egerton worked closely with Lao She while translating *Jin Ping Mei* (Gunn 2009, 433; Hegel 2011, 15). Their close collaboration likely enabled them to produce a draft based on their individual understanding of *Jin Ping Mei* and how that understanding informed their translation practice. Egerton then likely went back to this draft to edit and refine it before final publication. As a matter of fact, Lao She not only assisted Egerton in translating *Jin Ping Mei* but also co-translated many other Chinese literary works, including his own, with several other English-language translators. One such example is Ida Pruitt (1888–1985), who co-translated Lao She's *Sishi tongtang* 四世同堂 (The Yellow Storm) with Lao She himself in 1951 (Zhang 2016; Gerber and Qi 2020, 103–115). This practice is reminiscent of the co-translation of Western fiction by Lin Shu 林紓 (1852–1924) and Wei Yi's 魏易 (1880–1933) in early twentieth-century China. During this period, Wei Yi acted as the oral interpreter while Lin Shu, who had little or no knowledge of Western languages, wrote down and elaborated on what Wei Yi interpreted. This dynamic granted Lin considerable room for imagination and creativity to rewrite, adapt, recreate, and embellish his translations. He would add, cut, and embellish bits as needed to address deficits and shortcomings in the original works. Rather than passively engaging with Western literature, Lin adopted a critical and interpretative approach to reading and translating Western literary works. He intentionally selected texts that could be easily sinicized and assimilated to traditional Chinese values and family-centered Confucian ethics (Venuti 1998, 179). Lin's translation endeavors spanned an impressive 180 Western literary works, including those by Sir Henry Rider Haggard (1856–1925), Alexandre Dumas *fils* (1824–1895), Sir Walter Scott (1771–1832), Robert Louis Stevenson (1850–1894), Victor Hugo (1802–1885), and Sir Arthur Conan Doyle (1859–1930), among others, all guided by this translation principle. Far from being a dull and mechanical literal transfer, Lin's translation practice was thoroughly hermeneutic, re-imaginative, and inventive (Qian 1981, 18–52). Accordingly, Lin's writerly, creative translations enabled the Western novels to speak with new meaning for contemporary readers concerned with China's tumultuous social and political changes, and thereby became part of modern Chinese literature in their own right (Lung 2004, 161–184; Qian and Campbell 2014, 139–188; Rojas and Bachner 2016, 647; Hill 2013).

Lin's translation practice brings to mind the co-translation of *Honglou meng* by David Hawkes (1923–2009) and John Minford's in the 1970s.[12] In this collaborative effort, Hawkes initially produced a draft for the translation. Subsequently, he revisited the draft, refining it as needed, ultimately shaping it into what is now known as *The Story of the Stone* (Hawkes 2000; Fan 2022). It is worth noting that, unlike the translators of *Jin Ping Mei* examined in this study, Hawkes did not de facto use a definitive Chinese original (namely, existing printed versions) when translating *Honglou meng*. Given that there were seven recensions of the novel available, he opted to "make an original" of his own before the actual translation practice. In this process, Hawkes selectively picked and chose bits here and there, especially when confronted with illogic or incoherent textual blemishes, as evidenced by his translation notebooks published in Hong Kong in 2000 and, more recently, in Mainland China in 2023 (Hawkes 2000; Fan 2022, 33–40). Thanks to Hawkes's artistic adaptation of the Chinese original, his imaginative re-creation, and his use of flexible, creative translation strategies, *The Story of the Stone* has become a classic novel in its own right in the English-speaking world, appealing to those who are interested in literature (a novel) as literature (a novel) and can find much enjoyment in the story (Fan 2022, xx–xxvii). Hawkes's translation practice attests to Karen Emmerich's observation that some originals are not given but made, emphasizing that translators often actively participate in this making or creative process; this challenges the myth of the fixity of the original (Emmerich 2017, 13). In translating *Honglou meng*, Hawkes ipso facto engaged in *translingual editing*, which affords us a glimpse into how translation is not only a translingual practice but also an editing practice. Both editing and translating, as "mutually implicated interpretative practices," contribute to enriching a given work; Hawkes's translation philosophy centered on presenting the English-reading public with a novel in translation, rather than a text solely for scholars to pore over and dissect (Liu 1996; Emmerich 2017, 8; Fan 2022, xxxi; my emphasis). Producing a translated text, especially a literary work, crafted exclusively for scholarly scrutiny and analysis, might curtail its potential readership, constraining its reception among a broad audience within the target context. This limitation could hinder the text from generating even a minor, if not decisive, influence in that particular cultural setting, particularly within the English-language world. Within the hegemonic English-speaking sphere, translation has often been denigrated as "second-order writing, derivative and adulterated," lacking broad appeal for diverse audiences who have an abundance of choices in fiction written originally in English by authors from culturally diverse countries around the world (Venuti 1998, 187; Ginsburgh et al. 2011, 231). If fiction translated into English fails to evoke the reader's identification or doesn't resonate as a novel, it can needlessly divert the reader's interest from the story. Consequently, it appears that employing transformative and inventive strategies in the selection and translation of foreign texts, especially Chinese works, is considered both desirable and advantageous. This approach could ensure the continued relevance of these works in a region that holds a formidable position in the geopolitical economy.

Turning back to Lao She, he also started writing novels for publication in China in the 1920s. Inspired by Charles Dickens's (1812–70) fiction during his stay in England, Lao She wrote several novels, including *Lao Zhang de zhexue* 老張的哲學 (The Philosophy of Old Zhang) (1926), *Zhao ziyue* 趙子曰 (Thus Spake Master Zhao) (1926), and *Erh ma* 二馬 (Mr. Ma and Son) (1929). Lao She's writing skills matured after he produced these early works of fiction, and he increasingly adopted *baihua*, or the vernacular, in writing fiction (Vohra 1974, 19). After returning to China in 1929, Lao She wrote several more novels and plays, including *Luotuo xiangzi* 駱駝祥子 (Rickshaw Boy) (1936), which became a bestseller in the English-speaking world (translated by Evan King in 1945) and brought him international fame (Kao 1980, 37; Pong and Li 2009, 433–435; Prado-Fonts 2014, 177–215). Another notable work is *Chaguan* 茶館 (Tea House) (1957), which was adapted into a television series in China. In 1962, Lao She, himself a Manchurian, assisted Henry Pu-yi Aisin-Gioro 愛新覺羅溥儀 (1906–67), the last emperor of the Manchu dynasty, in revising and polishing his autobiography *Wo de qian bansheng* 我的前半生 (published in 1964 and translated as *From Emperor to Citizen: The Autobiography of Aisin-Gioro Pu Yi* by W. J. F. Jenner in 1989).[13] Many considered him to be the true author of the book. As one of the most prolific writers, Lao She became the first Chinese writer to receive the honor of "People's

Artist" in the People's Republic of China (PRC) in 1952. As noted by George Kao, Lao She undoubtedly assumed a position at the forefront of the Chinese literary figures who praised the Communist regime (Kao 1980, 34). Unfortunately, and ironically, Lao She became one of the first Chinese writers and intellectuals to end his life in 1966 when the Cultural Revolution (1966–76) began with the massing of Red Guards in Peking.[14] While Lao She mentioned his friend Egerton in a 1936 essay titled "My Several Landlords," he rarely referred to his collaboration with Egerton in translating *Jin Ping Mei* in all his later writings. Nevertheless, Egerton expressed sincere gratitude to him in Translator's Notes contained in the first volume of his published translation. Egerton stated that without "the untiring and generously given help" of Lao She during the first draft of his translation, he "should never have dared to undertake such a task" (Egerton 1939, xi). As some scholars speculate, it is more likely that Lao She provided a rough translation, and Egerton later spent years polishing it into its final form (Hegel 2011, 18). Interesting as this speculation may sound, it still requires robust evidence to address this seemingly tangential issue. Perhaps owing to Lao She and the eminent sinologist Walter Simon (1893–1981), Egerton's text is considered quite fluent, serviceable, and free from serious errors and misinterpretation (Hsia 1968, 165; Birch 1974). As H. Bruce Collier comments:

> No attempt has been made to give a literal translation: idiomatic English is used throughout. As a result some of the flavor of the original is inevitable lost. But on the whole it is a brilliant translation of a great novel, so colorful and realistic that the modern novels of China seem very pallid by comparison.
>
> (Collier 1944, 346)

Collier opines that no literal translation technique is used by Egerton; however, this does not align with the findings of a detailed analysis of the translation, as will be shown later in this study. In fact, among other transferring policies, the mixed use of literal transfer, deletion, and omission can be readily detected in Egerton's translation. This certainly merits serious attention for translation studies scholars, and this study attempts to provide evidence of such practices. Lionel Giles (1875–1958) then gives a different point of view on Egerton's translation and states that:

> Colonel Egerton has aimed at producing a smooth English version without omitting the difficult passages, and at the same time he has tried to preserve the spirit of the Chinese. He has been fairly conscientious, but in spite of his endeavour he leaves out much that is in the original, and it cannot be said that his translation is free from mistakes.
>
> (Giles 1940, 370)

Lionel Giles's observation enables a more critical awareness while reading and especially studying Egerton's text from a "translatological" perspective. Scholar and translator Duncan M. Campbell (2008) expresses similar, if not the same, opinions, commenting that the Egerton translation is characterized by fluency and readability,[15] in keeping with the slapstick humor of the original. Noticeably, Egerton didn't use the allegedly superior Wanli edition of *Jin Ping Mei* as his source text, as this recension was unavailable to him (Ye 2000, 733). Instead, Egerton based his translation on the popular Chongzhen edition.[16]

Importantly, influenced by Victorian practice and the decorum of pre-World War Two Britain, the most pungent of sex-related contents in Egerton's translation were coercively rendered into Latin before publication in 1939. In the 1972 reprinted version, however, the Latin portions of Egerton's text were replaced by plain English, except for a few lines in chapter forty-two that were overlooked (Knechtges 1975, 359; Birch 1974; Yang et al. 1978, 54; Spence 1994; Ye 2000, 733; France 2000, 233; Campbell 2008; Qi 2018, 102). Such a practice of treating scenes of sexual ardor in the original (namely, rendering them in Latin) should hardly be surprising since the Egerton translation simply echoed C. K. Scott Moncrieff's (1889–1930) English translation of Marcel Proust's *À la Recherche du Temps Perdu*, in which explicit sexual scenes were made elusive, enigmatic, and allusive rather than frank and direct (Gopnik 2015). This is primarily because, Adam Gopnik (2015) states, the English aesthetes were characterized by sublimation, delicacy, and euphemism, which differed from the French aesthetes and thus gave Moncrieff's translation a particular poetic tone in the early 1920s. Thanks to Moncrieff's ingenious craft of the *Remembrance of Things Past* (a title borrowed from Shakespeare), a number of ordinary British readers showed enthusiasm in reading Proust (Gopnik 2015). Although one would not assert that the Egerton translation was comparable to Moncrieff's in creativity and inventiveness, the former's avoidance of a mechanical, literal rendering of much of the original showed a similarity to the latter, as can be observed in this study. In any case, neither Egerton nor Moncrieff were particularly expert in their original languages, and perhaps this was to their advantage, allowing them more freedom to be creative in their translations. Chapter 5 provides a detailed discussion on how the Egerton translation treats the various kinds of sexual narratives in *Jin Ping Mei*. Since 1972, *Jin Ping Mei*, or *Lotus*, as Birch (1974) posits, has been accessible to the general English-language readership in a manner that has been, or may never be, the case for their Chinese counterparts. In the PRC, only bowdlerized versions of the original novel are readily available to the general reading public.

The Egerton translation appeared in the 1920s and '30s when East-West literary and cultural exchanges were flourishing, and the reception environment for Chinese literature was generally favorable. The language employed in the Egerton translation and the translation strategies used were closely tied to this particular historical milieu. Any literary text, including a translated one, is crafted with a sense of its potential audience. The language chosen by the writer/translator, as well as the act of writing/translating itself, inherently implies one range of potential audience, or "implied reader," in Wolfgang Iser's terms, as opposed to another (Eagleton 1996, 73). According to Hans Robert Jauss, it is crucial to "situate a literary work within its historical 'horizon,' the context of cultural meanings in which it was produced" (Eagleton 1996, 72). This principle extends to translated works. With historical consciousness, it becomes essential to examine the conditions under which a translated text was produced and understand how it reflects or responds to the concerns of its time. As Antoine Berman (1984, 2) postulates, the practice of translation must be articulated in relation to the practice of literature, languages, and the various intercultural and interlingual exchanges at a given historical moment. Therefore, it is essential to contextualize Egerton's translation within the history of the languages, cultures, and literatures of his time.

In the early twentieth century, there was an increase in contacts and exchanges between Far Eastern countries such as China and Japan and Western European countries like Britain, Germany, and France (Clarke 1997, 95–112; Zhan 2018, 282; Laurence 2013; Witchard 2015). China and Britain maintained relatively stable political and economic relations during the interwar period, fostering cross-cultural contacts between them (Endicott 1975; Bickers and Howlett 2016). This can be attributed to the concurrent political, social, and economic turmoils experienced by both China and Britain in the early decades of the twentieth century – China during the anti-Japanese war of aggression and the civil war, and Britain during the two world wars (Laurence 2013, 14). However, it should be remembered that as early as the seventeenth and eighteenth centuries, Jesuits and missionaries were introducing Chinese civilization to European audiences, aiming to dispel ignorance about China. Their primary goal, though, was to convert unbelievers in non-Christian Asian countries such as China and Japan to the true faith (Clarke 1997, 40; Bai 2013, 193–197). Nevertheless, China was already a subject of lively debate and closely integrated into the European consciousness during this period. It played an important role in European intellectual discourse on religion, philosophy, literature, ethics, art, and even technology. This is primarily because, as D. E. Mungello (2013, 2) posits, China was truly a world power in the period 1500-1800, while Europe was experiencing a low point in its history. This strength and prosperity persisted until 1839 when they began to decline (Kitson 2013, 20).

The Jesuit missionaries, highly educated and cultured, were the first orientalist scholars in the West. They developed a deep appreciation for Chinese civilization, including its Confucian philosophy, literature, and arts. In the 1680s, they translated some of the Confucian classics into Latin, thereby exerting a significant influence on the late seventeenth-century European mind in interpreting the Chinese world view for West European readers (Clarke 1997, 40). The missionary Matteo Ricci (1552–1610), for example, considered China a civilization even older than Europe upon his arrival, providing detailed accounts of various aspects of Chinese philosophy, culture, economy, and world view for European readers; Jean-Baptiste Du Halde's (1674–1743) *The General History of China* (1736) (originally published in French in 1735) was perhaps the most representative account of China (Spence 1984; Clarke 1997, 41). Du Halde went so far as to assess that internal trade within China surpassed the combined trade of all European nations. This assessment later found support from Adam Smith (1723–1790), who, in *The Wealth of Nations* (1776), asserted that China was wealthier than any region in Europe (Kitson 2013, 18). The reports from Jesuit missionaries on the Far East were followed by other European travelers. By the middle eighteenth century, a substantial body of (mostly favorable) literature on Asian civilization had been accumulated, which influenced a number of educated classes in Europe, including notable figures such as Gottfried Wilhelm von Leibniz (1646–1716), François-Marie Voltaire (1694–1778), Montesquieu (1689–1755), and Oliver Goldsmith (1728–74), whose intense interest in Eastern philosophy led them to use it as a mirror with which to examine Europe's inadequacies in the same areas (Zhang 1988, 116; Dawson 1967, 55; Clarke 1997, 42). Notable examples include Goldsmith's *The Citizen of the World* (1762), in which non-Christian China was used as a means of satirizing the problematics of Christian Europe; in addition, Voltaire, along with Gottfried Wilhelm Leibniz (1646–1716), Baron de Montesquieu (1689–1755), and others, who wielded China as a weapon to critique the Catholic Church (Clarke 1997, 42–45; Liu 2023, 117). In one sense, China played a significant role as an ideal exemplar for Europeans during the seventeenth and early eighteenth centuries (Kitson 2013, 9). The use of China by these European elites served the purpose of introspecting the self in the West rather than solely or truly being concerned with China per se.

Moreover, China's impact on Western Europe extended to the realms of arts and artifacts. The enthusiasm in this area was particularly noticeable in European adaptations of Chinese styles, evident in furniture, porcelain, enamels, embroideries, screens, paper-hangings, costumes, wallpaper, textile design, garden design, and watercolor painting (Dawson 1964, 349; Zhang 1988, 117; Clarke 1997, 51; Porter 2010). Concurrently, several men of letters in Britain were involved in producing crucial translations of Chinese literature, including popular novels (such as *The Pleasing History*), drama (especially *The Orphan of China*), and Confucian classics. Notable figures among them include Thomas Percy (1729–1811), John Francis Davis (1795–1890), and George Thomas Staunton (1781–1859), among others (Lehner 2011, 286; Kitson 2013, 4). All these collectively fueled the eighteenth-century fashion for things Chinese in Western Europe. Nevertheless, the widespread enthusiasm for all things Chinese, often referred to as the so-called sinophilia, experienced a significant decline toward the end of the eighteenth century, and the perception of China (for example, the manners and customs of the Chinese) underwent a radical change in nineteenth-century Europe (Dawson 1964, 356; Davis 1983, 545; Lehner 2011, 135; Cao 2020, 4). In *China in the English Literature of the Seventeenth and Eighteenth Centuries*, Qian Zhongshu 錢鍾書 (1910–98) explains that sinophilism reached its peak in seventeenth-century England but had already begun to wane in the early eighteenth century (Qian 1940, 351–384; Qian 1941, 113–152; Campbell 2005, 173–182). Drawing upon many examples from seventeenth- and eighteenth-century English literature, Qian demonstrates how fact and fiction about China became intermingled in the minds of Englishmen. This suggests that English men of letters perceived China as more imaginary than real, viewing it as an unfamiliar place filled with fantasies, Utopian idealizations, mysteries, and philosophical conjectures (Hsia 1998, 29–68; Zhang 1998, 19–54; Liu 2023, 117). This perception persisted because most of them seldom set foot in this distant country. In Daniel Defoe's (1660–1731) novel, *Robinson Crusoe* (1719), for example, Crusoe harbors negative impressions of China because he consistently compares what he observes during his travels in China with that of Europe, only to find that the picture of China starkly contrasts with earlier literature (Zhang 1988,

122; Chen 1998, 218). Whereas Defoe's critique of Chinese civilization, as Chen Shouyi (1998) maintains, was significantly influenced by his religious inclinations, imperialistic interests, and journalistic stance, such negative portrayal of China in British popular literature clearly reflects the waning of sinophilism and the emergence of sinophobia during Defoe's time. Similarly, in his *Travels in China* (1804), Sir John Barrow (1764–1848) expressed unfavorable opinions towards several aspects of China, including the habits and manners of the Chinese (Lehner 2011, 132). The travelogue authors' books were best-sellers during that time and played an important role in shaping British perception of China for decades to come (Liu 2023, 123). By the end of the eighteenth century, China-worship in Western Europe had faded, if not died out. Sinophobia gradually came to dominate the European attitude towards China. China almost lost its spiritual significance for Europe and came to be characterized as a decadent civilization; the eternal immobility, despotic society, and lack of freedom attributed to China, as elucidated in the works of Georg Wilhelm Friedrich Hegel (1770–1831), Johann Gottfried Herder (1744–1803), and other thinkers, became a major obstacle to moral and political progress, an idea that has played a significant role in shaping Westerners' perception of and stereotyping about China since the nineteenth century (Zhang 1988 123; Clarke 1997, 53; Liu 2023, 5). Certain historians in the Anglophone world also contend that, in broad terms, prior to the 1750s, China stood as a global superpower, if not a powerhouse of the global economy (ibid.). Nonetheless, from the 1750s onward, China's allure, along with Chinese taste in all aspects, rapidly diminished and encountered outright antagonism in the Western world. Several factors contributed to the decline of sinomania in Western Europe. One important reason was the revival of Hellenism during this period; another factor was a growing awareness of the unreliability, exaggeration, and the inauthentic or unscientific nature of the writings and accounts of European sinophiles and missionaries about China; this was particularly true for earlier reports on Chinese wisdom, moral philosophy, political institutions, and religious practices, which contradicted the growing number of negative travel accounts about China; and lastly, the rise of European imperialism and national sentiments, coupled with a progressively racialized conception of human difference, and a more practical commercial outlook took center stage in dealing with China (Zhang 1988, 123; Clarke 1997, 52; Zhang 2008, 97–98; Porter 2010; Kitson 2013, 13). It was not until the early twentieth century that sinophilia, or the widespread interest in China, began to revive in the West. However, this revival differed significantly from that of the seventeenth and eighteenth centuries, as European intellectuals tended to adopt a more balanced, if not entirely negative, view of China. This shift illustrates that European representations of China often conveyed very different meanings in different historical contexts, reflecting a pragmatic attitude towards things Chinese.

The social and political changes in the West at the beginning of the twentieth century sparked a renewed interest in the Far East. This era witnessed the emergence of a dynamic society amidst continuous global conflicts, brutal wars, the rise of fascism, technological advancements, class-blurring, and economic recession, and these challenging realities of the modern world demanded the creation of new artistic forms and genres to effectively articulate and represent them (Yao

2013, 212). In response to the cultural and spiritual crisis at the turn of the century, the modernist movement emerged, advocating for a new consciousness or innovative means of representation to supplant the conventions of the earlier period with a new and progressive attitude (Clarke 1997, 101). After being neglected and even despised following its eclipse at the end of the eighteenth century, Oriental ideas, particularly traditional Chinese thought and culture, experienced a revival of interest among European scholars and thinkers. Figures such as Richard Wilhelm (1873–1930), Carl Jung (1875–1961), Herman Hesse (1877–1962), Bertolt Brecht (1898–1956), Marianne Moore (1887–1972), William Butler Yeats (1865–1939), and many others regarded Oriental ideas as a rare source of spirituality and modernity in the first decades of the twentieth century (Clarke 1997, 98; Witchard 2012, 36; Qian 2003; Qian 2017; Bush 2013, 196; Zhan 2018, 282). Evidently, during this period, many Western writers, artists, and intellectuals were keenly aware of East Asia, appreciating its timeless cultural traditions, cultural uniqueness, and contemporary events. Consequently, East Asia became an ideal setting for the Western exploration of new forms of self-expression and thematic interests connected to modernity (Bush 2013, 196). Particularly, Britain demonstrated a revived interest in Oriental culture, especially chinoiserie objects, both before and after the First World War.[17] In modernist circles in London, ancient Chinese wisdom proved useful for reflecting on the spiritual inadequacies of the materialist West. Similar to the sinophilia in seventeenth- and eighteenth-century Europe, various Chinese art forms such as paintings, ceramics, fans, calligraphic scrolls, and other handicrafts circulated widely in British homes and became integral elements of British modernist literature, adding a note of exoticism and alienness (Laurence 2013, 298; Thorpe 2016, 86). British intellectuals and artists, including G. L. Dickinson (1862–1932), I. A. Richards (1893–1979), and Sidney Webb (1859–1947), journeyed to China during this period to explore this distant culture through its chinoiserie art, which had been integrated into British life since the eighteenth century (ibid.). They were particularly drawn to the poetry and paintings found on scrolls and ceramics (Laurence 2013, 15; Li 2016, 33). More significantly, traditional Chinese literature regained popularity through a series of translations featuring China's classical poetry, Confucian writings, and drama and fiction. These translations played a crucial role in helping Western audiences seek "salvation from the soul-destroying, postindustrial world" after the First World War (Clarke 1997, 98; Nylan 2013, 167).

Simultaneously, China experienced growing internationalization during and after the May Fourth Movement (1919). Many Chinese writers and intellectuals were eager to explore the West, seeking to learn its humanism and liberalism from Western literature and art (Laurence 2013, 10). The literary and cultural exchanges between China and Britain during this period were marked by two influential literary communities: the Crescent Moon Group and the Bloomsbury Group. Both shared aesthetic and intellectual interests (Laurence 2013, 11). Chinese writers and intellectuals, including Xu Zhimo 徐志摩 (1897–1931), Chen Xiying 陳西瀅 (1896–1970), Ling Shuhua 凌叔華 (1900–90), Hu Shi 胡適 (1891–1962), Lao She, Chiang Yee, and Xiao Qian 蕭乾 (1910-99), most of whom were members of the Crescent Moon Group, either traveled to or studied in Western countries such as Britain and the United States. They actively engaged in literary exchanges with Western writers, significantly influencing and transforming their own literary creations. The May Fourth Literary Movement in China reignited British interest in (traditional) Chinese literature and its translation into English (Laurence 2013, 14). Translations of Chinese literature and philosophical classics by individuals like Waley, Ezra Pound (1885–1972), and Ernest Fenollosa (1853–1908) had a profound impact on Anglo-American modernism.

Waley, an alumnus of Cambridge and a member of the Bloomsbury Group, was a contemporary and friend of Yeats, Pound, the Woolfs, and many other household names in the British literary circle of the 1920s. He was the most widely known translator of Japanese and Chinese literature at the time, despite never having visited either China or Japan (Laurence 2013, 306). Born in England in 1889 with a Jewish background, Waley's original name was Arthur David Schloss. He was a typical scholar who spent his real life surrounded by countless books and documents, valuing his privacy, and possessing a personality largely unknown to the public; additionally, he was suspected of having homosexual or bisexual tendencies (as quoted in Fitzgerald 1982; Morris 1970, 70; de Gruchy 2003, 46). Waley's emotional life involved two women: the ballet dancer and dance critic Beryl de Zoete (1879–1962), with whom Waley had only a long and loving unmarried relationship; and the writer Alison Grant Robertson, a New Zealander whom Waley married in 1966, the year of his death (ibid.; see also Waley 1982). Despite the mystic and complex nature of Waley's private life, he is best remembered for his artistic and creative translations of East Asian classics. His translations of Far Eastern texts were considered by his contemporaries to be English prose and poetry in their own right. As Ivan Morris asserts, "without Waley's books it is unlikely that the classics of the Far East would have become such an important part of our heritage" (Morris 1970, 67). However, Waley's translations have also been critiqued for being overly liberal and unfaithful, and thus unreliable renderings of the originals (de Gruchy 2003, 2). While working at the British Museum from 1913 to 1929, Waley, encouraged by the poet and translator Laurence Binyon (1869–1943), taught himself Chinese and Japanese to appreciate oriental paintings (Laurence 2013, 309). Waley's interest in Chinese literature and arts was further influenced by the writer and critic Clifford Bax (1886–1962), whose *Twenty Chinese Poems* (1910) inspired him to learn Asian languages. He was also influenced by Lytton Strachey (1880–1932), a member of the Bloomsbury Group, and G. L. Dickinson, who first brought China to Waley's attention in 1907 (as quoted in de Gruchy 2003, 168). Despite never traveling to China or Japan and presenting them only as aesthetic Utopias, Waley, a linguistic genius, could learn more quickly than many others (Morris 1970, 39; Kenner 1971, 118; Witchard 2012, 37). In 1916, Waley privately published his *Chinese Poems*, which circulated among his Bloomsbury peers, including Dickinson, Binyon, T. S. Eliot (1888–1965), and Leonard Woolf (1880–1969). In 1917, Waley published thirty-seven pre-Tang poems, thirty-eight poems by Bai Juyi 白居易 (772–846), a renowned poet of the Tang dynasty (618–907). By the end of the year, he had more than twenty-five other poems, most of which had never been translated before. In 1918, Waley released *A Hundred and Seventy Chinese Poems*, and the following year, he published *More Translations from the Chinese*. These works introduced new landscapes, visual techniques, and poetic ideas to a British public drawn to traditional Chinese art, painting, gardens, and the like (Witchard 2012, 37). In Waley's introduction to his *A Hundred and Seventy Chinese Poems*, he acclaimed Chinese literature for its higher level of tolerance and rationality compared to Western literature. This observation played a crucial role in popularizing Chinese literature, especially poetry, in the Western world during his time (Li 2016, 35). In 1929, Waley resigned from his position at the British Museum, enabling him to work as a private scholar and focus his attention on translation without the disruption of a professional career. As a result, his work continued at an astonishing pace. In addition to translations of classical Chinese poetry, Waley translated the Ming novel *Xiyou ji* (Monkey) and the *Analects of Confucius* into English. He also wrote innumerable books and essays for ordinary readers, composed in plain, lucid prose. These works covered various aspects of the arts, thought, manners, and institutions of ancient China, including *Introduction to the Study of Chinese Painting* (1923), *The Way and its Power* (1934), *Three Ways of Thoughts in Ancient China* (1939), *The Nine Songs* (1955), and *The Real Tripitaka* (1952), among others, the list is endless (Hawkes 1970; Spence 1992, 329–336; see also Johns 1968).

Waley also translated other East Asian classics and narratives into English, including *Noh Plays of Japan* (1921), *The Pillow Book of Sei Shōnagon* (1928), and *Genji monogatari* by Murasaki Shikibu (c. 973–c.1014). His translations were highly regarded by many native speakers of the languages he worked in as excellent re-creations rather than mechanical literal or word-for-word renderings (Henig 1974, 76). One of Waley's notable translations, *Tale of Genji* (1925–33), led the English novelist C. P. Snow (1905–80) to recall that "in the late 1920s most literary young people whom I knew were under [its] spell" (Bush 2013, 200). Sinologist and translator David Hawkes, whose masterful translation of *Honglou meng* might be enlightened by Waley, maintains that "to have translated with delicacy and tact, and sustained these qualities throughout the book's whole great length, so that [*Genji*] emerged in English dress as the great and important work of art it is ... [Waley's translation] was a work of genius" (Hawkes 1970, 49). Waley himself also hoped his *Genji* would be read in the context of British literary modernism, a period marked by trauma, aftershock of war, loss, disillusion, nostalgia. He envisioned it as an English novel in its own right, characterized by minimal scholarly intervention, with few notes and rarely identifying the source of a poem; additionally, he intended it to be a typical Western representation of Far Eastern culture between the wars (de Gruchy 2003, 152). Waley's translation brought Shikibu's *Genji* to international acclaim, enriching English and world literature, and shaping Western perceptions of Japanese civilization (Simon 1967, 269; de Gruchy 2003, 4). His exquisite translations, marked by scholarly precision, plain and laconic prose, and easy accessibility, fostered an extraordinary understanding and empathy for East Asian culture among general readers in the first decades of the twentieth century (Henig 1974, 76; Laurence 2013, 308). It is likely that Waley saw himself primarily as a mediator between Western and Eastern cultures, never neglecting the needs of the general reading public in his time. In the preface to his translation of the *Analects*, he stated that he had never forgotten the claims of the ordinary reader (Johns 1983).

As a matter of fact, Waley consistently claimed to be translating or writing for the average reader rather than the specialist, skillfully combining literature with learning. He frequently emphasized "the needs and interests of the non-specialist reader" (Johns 1983, 182; de Gruchy 2003, 139; Li 2016). It is not surprising that Waley was deemed by countless readers as an excellent storyteller and interpretive artist, seamlessly blending scholarship and artistic innovation (de Gruchy 2003, 8; Cohen 1970, 36; Simon 1967, 271). Waley's contribution to British and European sinology remains central and most significant among the members of the Bloomsbury Group. His translations of Chinese classics played a pivotal role in making the distant and ancient world of China a familiar place that ordinary readers could easily understand (ibid.). Most importantly, Waley's approach to translation – treating it as a literary or aesthetic practice rather than a purely scholarly endeavor – helped dispel deep-seated misconceptions and greatly reshaped Western understanding of Chinese culture and literature; Waley's translations from Chinese, along with those from Japanese, gained immense popularity in the West and left a profound impact on younger generations, including members of the Oxford Wits (Hawkes 1964, 91; de Gruchy 2003, 154; Li 2016, 35). In 1953, in recognition of his brilliant translation of Chinese poetry, Waley was awarded the Queen's Medal for Poetry. His translations can be viewed not only as a contribution to English literature and culture but also as a significant factor in enhancing Western familiarity with East Asian culture and history in the first decades of the twentieth century.

It should be borne in mind that Waley's approach to the translation of Chinese literature, which involved abandoning rhyme and fixed stress counts, was also influenced, albeit to a lesser extent, by his friend Pound, who, despite knowing little or no Chinese, provided contemporary readers with a vivid sense of visual beauty of Chinese literature through his translated poems (Laurence 2013, 309). Pound was a poet, translator, and editor who played a major role in the development of the Anglo-American modernist movement (Rizzo 2011, 396). Born and educated in the United States, Pound left for Europe in 1906, moved to London in 1908, and spent his final years in Italy. During his London years, Pound encountered numerous cultural elites, including Yeats, Ford Madox Ford (1873–1939), and T. E. Hulme (1883–1971), who encouraged him to modernize his conventional literary form by employing simple and economical language (ibid.). Alongside fellow writers like Hilda Doolittle (H. D.) (1886–1961), Richard Aldington (1892–1962), James Joyce (1882–1941), and William Carlos Williams (1883–1963), Pound played a pivotal role in developing imagism. This movement advocated for poetry to convey the direct and unmediated truth through striking imagery, precise diction, and concrete detail; it emphasized the importance of respecting formal rhymes but not being bound by them (ibid.; Lathbury 2008, 898). The imagist doctrine greatly influenced contemporary poets, and it also left its mark on prose writers such as Ernest Hemingway (1899–1961), whose prose style owed a great deal to imagism

(Lathbury 2008, 898). To practice imagism, Pound translated numerous classical Chinese poems, publishing them in 1915 under the umbrella title *Cathay*. Despite his limited knowledge of the Chinese language, Pound's *Cathay* exemplified the imagist method, successfully conveying the brevity, economy, concreteness, and conciseness of the original Chinese poems to a wider contemporary readership. This endeavor partially revolutionized the Anglo-American poetic tradition in the twentieth century (Yao 2013, 214). Importantly, during the modernist period in the early twentieth century, it was not uncommon, even a trend, for many English and other European writers to translate foreign literary works, despite that they knew little about the languages of the texts they were translating. This practice included notable figures such as Yeats, H. D., James Joyce (1882–1941), and Hans Bethge (1876–1946), among others (Yao 2013, 215; Woodsworth 2017; Woodsworth 2018, 369; Larsen 2017, 179). For instance, Bethge, despite having little knowledge of the Chinese language, creatively translated Chinese poetry in a manner deemed fairly contemporary and European. His translation introduced a foreign lyrical mode of expression to Germany, easily understood by his contemporaries, and even served as a source of inspiration for innovative creative efforts (Larsen 2017, 180). *Jin Ping Mei*'s translator, Egerton, was no exception. While translating the Chinese masterpiece into English in the 1920s and '30s, he did not have much knowledge of the Chinese language. Nonetheless, he was keenly aware that he was translating a novel with a plain, colloquial style and captivating themes that would resonate with a broad contemporary audience. His translation, characterized by a compact plot and lively prose as will be demonstrated in this study, can be considered a valuable part of English literature. In reality, literary translation during that time was somewhat of a trend, aiming at aesthetic innovation (Woodsworth 2018, 369). Literature in translation, or translated literature, became a new means of modern creation and expression, no longer confined to a mechanical, literal transfer from one language to another. As discussed earlier, these writer-translators engaged in translation as a literary mode to explore new possibilities of aesthetic expression, emphasizing the generative function of translation--namely, serving the needs and preferences of a particular age--in the host culture (Birsanu 2011, 181). Their willingness to translate a given foreign text was largely unaffected by their limited knowledge of that foreign language, which, as it turned out, was a decided advantage rather than a hindrance. This lack of linguistic expertise allowed them the freedom to manipulate the text for individual aesthetic purposes (Yao 2010, 42; Yao 2013, 220). As the writer and translator Borges aptly points out, not knowing the source language can lead to an unexpected gain by crafting a piece of literature that piques the reader's curiosity about the inherent ambiguity in the languages of the original author, the translator, and the historical period in which it was composed (Waisman 2005, 53). For Borges, translation is not merely the transfer of a text from one language to another; rather, it is the transformation of a text into another form. A source work can be enriched by its translation, which is in no way inferior to its original (Kristal 2002, 32). The purpose of literary translation is not fidelity or alleged accuracy, but the conjuring or re-creation of a literary work that can stand on its own (Kristal 2023, 179). A literal translation, as Borges describes it, attempts to maintain all the details of the original text but ultimately alters the emphasis, including meanings, connotations, associations, and the overall effects of the original work. Consequently, it is considered unfaithful and can lead to "defamations" of a work of art. On the other hand, a recreation may omit certain details while introducing interpolations by drawing out latent possibilities in the original. Therefore, it has the potential to either preserve the emphasis of the original or transform and enhance it in terms of literary interest (Kristal 2002, 33). Borges prioritizes translations with interesting transformations or creative recreations, especially those inspired by significant developments in the target literary context, enabling readers to approach past literature with fresh eyes (Kristal 2002, 34; Kristal 2023, 179). As a writer and translator, Borges's translation philosophy can be summarized as follows: removing words and passages deemed redundant, superfluous, or inconsequential; cutting parts of the content that might distract attention from another aspect he wishes to highlight; adding a major or minor nuance not present in the original; and rewriting a work in light of another, influenced by a post-Nietzschean sensibility (Kristal 2002, 87). Borges regards translation as a long, experimental game of chance, where omissions and emphasis played key roles. He characterizes it as a process of re-creation and re-invention that entails choices, priorities, the element of chance, and a spirit of experimentation (ibid.). In coincidence with George Steiner's observation that a translation can explore potentialities that may be concealed or unrealized in the original, Borges emphasizes that translation can bring forth aspects of the original that might be obscured in the language of the original due to the incommensurables or fundamental gulf between languages and cultures (Kristal 2023, 179). It is the very incommensurability of any two languages that provides endless possibilities for the literary translator to achieve innovation and creativity. By understanding translation as a creative endeavor, Borges suggests that while a poem may resist complete translatability, it can nonetheless excel or shine in translation where the original may have limitations, thereby reshaping and improving the original (ibid.; Kristal 2002, 31). Significantly, Borges's observation on literary translation resonates with that of Marcel Proust, whose development as a writer owed much to his practice of translating the works of the British art critic John Ruskin (1819–1900). Proust treated the act of translation as an opportunity to assimilate, emulate, and even surpass masterful works from the past (Woodsworth 2018, 374). Both Borges and Proust's observations on the practice of literary translation align with the translational philosophies of Waley, Pound, and their fellow contemporary writers. By translating Chinese poetry in a manner distinct from previous eras, Pound, partially influenced by Fenollosa's *On the Chinese Written Character as a Medium for Poetry* (a slim volume containing creative translations of Tang poems), developed the "ideogrammic method" for the renaissance of a new kind of poetry, modernist poetry in English (Laurence 2013, 205; Bush 2013, 199; Xie 2021, 13). Pound paid minimal attention to the textual and technical features of Chinese poetry, focusing solely on the theme, subject matter, or spirit of the original (ibid.). This approach resonates with Gadamer's view on the art of translation, as mentioned above, which underscores the inevitability of highlighting certain features of the original while renouncing or diminishing others. As such, Pound's translations became both inventive and interpretative, yet remained accessible (Xie 2021, 234). In his early phase of translation, Pound, with limited knowledge of Chinese, relied on Fenollosa's desultory notes which were at times inaccurate and led him astray; despite the challenges, this allowed him the freedom to translate and appropriate according to his interests, purposes, and the expressive potential of his own language (Xie 2021, 235). The poems in *Cathay* (1915) were translated within such a context. Instead of rendering the Chinese originals (poems written in the Tang dynasty) in a correspondingly archaic English, the language of *Cathay* was idiomatic, succinct, visualized, and contemporary (ibid.). *Cathay* laid the foundation for Pound's translation philosophy, or guiding principle, asserting that translation should appear contemporary or relevant (by transforming old forms to "make it new") rather than historical or archaic to strike contemporary readers as both familiar and alien (ibid.; Woodsworth 2018, 370). In his introduction to Pound's *Selected Poems*, T. S. Eliot, who dedicated his *The Waste Land* to Pound as Pound contributed significantly to its editing and refining, remarks that "Pound is the inventor of Chinese poetry for our time," and he also views Pound's translations as "translucencies" rather than translations per se, creating a sense that Western readers were brought close to or truly grasped the Chinese original by reading them (Hayot 2012, 24; Hayot 2012, 41; Lathbury 2008, 898). Indeed, Pound's translations of Chinese poetry have garnered mixed criticism, primarily due to being noted more for tone, spirit, and feeling than for semantic accuracy. Positive responses commend Pound for successfully conveying the nuances of Chinese culture and capturing the original spirit of Chinese poetry in translation; on the other hand, negative critiques of *Cathay* focus on Pound's appropriation and mistranslation of various concepts and terms (Hayot 2012, 26; Li 2016). According to Robert Kern, *Cathay* had little to do with the real China and was "largely an event within Anglo-American literature," demonstrating Pound's orientalist position by engaging in a very traditional Western perception of the East through the translation of Chinese poetry (as quoted in Hayot 2012, 29; Hayot 1999, 530). Wai-lim Yip views *Cathay* as a form of re-creation, altering local qualities to suit the English-language audience and deleting some allusions to eliminate the burden of annotations; Gyung-Ryul Jang claims that Pound' translations failed to reproduce the rhythm or musical quality of the Chinese originals but adequately captured their visual features and internal logic (as quoted in Hayot 2012, 58). In Steiner's words, Pound's creative translations "altered the feel of the [English] language and set the pattern of cadence for modern verse" (Hayot et al. 2008, 318). Steiner also observes that Pound's translations have changed "the definition and ideals of verse translation in the twentieth century as surely as Pound's poetry has renewed or subverted English and American poetics" (1966, 33). It appears that Pound's creative and transformative approach has not only made Chinese poetry shine in the receptor culture by imbuing it with new life in a new context but has also invigorated contemporary poetic expression. Like Steiner, Qian Zhaoming argues that it is Pound's translations of Chinese poetry that lend his works their freshness, creativity, spontaneity, and simplicity, underscoring the positive influence of China or the Far East on the growth of Anglo-American modernism or poetic tradition (as quoted in Hayot 2012, 62; Yao 2010, 41; see also Beach 1992). As a matter of fact, Pound's approach to translating Chinese poetry both erases and glamorizes the difference between languages. This tension, at the time, was associated with the way the act of translation served as a tool with which he intervened in the English poetic tradition, with a view to making it new by rejecting the dominant mode of writing in his time (Yeh 2016, 287). Despite any distortions and mistranslations, Pound's works ipso facto contributed to bringing English-language audiences closer to the spirit and essence of Chinese poetry, presenting a China that was more spiritual and authentic than linguistically faithful translations could ever be (Yeh 2016, 286). As a result, Chinese poetry in the hands of Pound has acquired new life in a different language and new forms. His translations, along with Waley's, played a crucial role in capturing Western attention for China during the twentieth century.

Additionally, Pound's *The Cantos*, a collection of lyric poetry published in the 1920s, also created a sensation in the early twentieth century. By drawing on a diverse array of earlier texts, ranging from classical Greek and Chinese poetry to the writings of John Adams (1735–1826), *The Cantos* establishes a continuity between ancient heroic figures and Enlightenment thinkers admired by Pound (Riggs 2013). Through various styles and techniques, the poems articulate Pound's political, ideological, aesthetic, economic, and even racial (namely, anti-Semitic) views (Riggs 2013). In *The Cantos*, Pound creatively conveyed the Taoist sensibility, including Taoism's "mystic reverence for nature," to his intended audience, affirming the influence of Chinese culture on Western modernist enterprise (Qian 2003, 71). Pound also translated several Confucian classics in the 1920s and '30s, such as *Ta Hio: The Great Learning of Confucius* (1928) and *Confucius: Digest of the Analects* (1937) and others in the 1950s (Qian 2008, 17; Hayot 2012). Pound's translations, including *Cathay* and *The Cantos*, have not only influenced Western perceptions of Chinese culture and the Chinese poetic tradition but have also affected the American poetic tradition and American poets of the post-World War Two generation (Qian 2003; Beach 1992). According to Qian Zhaoming, what interested Pound, Fenollosa, and many other translation theorists is "less translations as objects than translation as function; less translation's ontological impossibility than the consequent animation of figuration, myth, tropes, twists and turns in the progresses of translation, including all the ways that the translated original 'sur-vives,' as Jacques Derrida puts it--lives not just longer but more and better, beyond the means of its author" (Qian 2003, 51). In Walter Benjamin's (1892–1940) parlance, the translator seeks to produce not a simulacrum of the foreign text's meaning but a peculiar *echo* of that foreign language so that both source and target languages seem fragments of a third, greater language (ibid., my emphasis). In his seminal essay "The Task of the Translator" ([1923] 2021), Benjamin suggests that a translated text possesses its own dynamic existence separate from the original. The task of the translator, according to Benjamin, is to bring about the *re-creation* of a source work within a new language; in this context, *re-creation* implies that a translated work has its own autonomy and mutability, making it susceptible to the influences from its new literary milieu (Drury 2015, 11; my emphasis). Moreover, the translated work also has the potential to influence that literary sphere. Both Qian's and Benjamin's observations are somewhat similar to Qian Zhongshu's ideas on translation, that is, *hua* 化 (to transform) or *huajing* 化境 (realm of transformation), which suggests that "a translation which manages to change a work in the language of one nation into the language of another whilst not evincing any of the forced or inflexible usages that derive from differences between language habits, and which at the same time preserves intact the flavor of the original work, may be considered to have entered this 'realm of transformation'" (Qian and Campbell 2014, 139; Chang 2020). Entering the "realm of transformation" suggests that the translator, in Benjamin's (2021) sense, successfully breaks through the barriers of his or her own language and liberates the language imprisoned in the original in his or her re-creation of that work, such that his or her translation gives the impression that it was originally written in the target language.

It appears that "to better survive", "to echo," or "to transform" represent the ideal goal for the practice of translation. Not surprisingly, numerous writer-translators in the West embraced translation as a literary practice—a method for developing new ways of representing the modern world around them. In 1916, for instance, Pound acknowledged that the practice of translation played a crucial role in the development of a major literary culture in his time, allowing him to break with traditional Edwardian poetics by incorporating new models, particularly his modernist poetic ideologies, into his writings (Yao 2013, 212; Bancroft 2020, 42). Pound's departure from Edwardian verse tendencies drove him to challenge hegemonic translation models of the past, such as sinological obsessions with accuracy and supposed fidelity, and his approach heralded the kinds of translation that would later emerge from (post)modernism (Bancroft 2020, 43). In the case of Waley, as mentioned earlier, he deliberately eschewed the annotation-style translation that would mar the artistry of the original; he sought to avoid impressing general readers with "pedantry" or "superior erudition," which was not his intention; his primary concern was to recast a Chinese or Japanese text in supple, idiomatic, and vibrant English, breathing life into it in the English language and integrating it into English literature (Teele 1969, 367; Schafer 1971, 117; Morris 1970, 69). In *Madly Singing in the Mountains*, Ivan Morris (1970, 73) asserts that Waley's conscious transformation of a Far Eastern classical text into "modern idiomatic English without sacrificing the sense or the beauty of the original is a remarkable creative accomplishment." Morris contends that Waley's translation could even give the impression to readers that it was originally written in English. Furthermore, Morris adds that Waley, by taking great liberties in translation, succeeded in re-creating the essential qualities (for example tone and mood) of the original as a literary piece. According to Morris (1970, 74), any pedantic or mechanically "accurate" translation, for example, a mock-archaic translationese, would only undermine its characteristics in a more detrimental way, rendering it unnatural and unreadable. Thus, it is safe to say that Waley, Pound, and other writer-translators in the early twentieth century did not aim for translations that were simulacra of the originals. Instead, they strived for creative renderings---referred to as "echoes" or "the transformation of souls," or perhaps *huajing* (Qian and Campbell 2014, 140). These translations not only re-created the feeling, tone, mood, and force perceived in the originals, appealing to the tastes of contemporary readers, but also served their own purposes in the thematic concerns of literary modernism.

In short, there was an intellectual trend in Britain during the early decades of the twentieth century that romanticized and exoticized an antiquated China. This trend significantly influenced Anglo-American artists, writers, poets, and other intellectuals, leaving a profound impact on the development of Anglo-American modernism. Literary translation during this period was not governed by traditional semantic fidelity and the constraints of linguistic knowledge; instead, it opted for artistic transformation, serving as a means to express the aesthetic agenda of individual writers/translators who generally rejected scholarly translation (namely, the provision of extensive notes, glosses, or any of the apparatus) and granted translation a compositional role, seamlessly assimilating it into the target literary culture (Yao 2013, 220; Birsanu 2011, 180). To borrow Steven G. Yao's (2013, 212) terms, the practice of translation by modernist writers such as Pound, Waley, Yeats, H. D., Joyce, Brecht, and many others was an integral part of the modernist enterprise of cultural renewal. It constituted an important mode of (re)writing that differed from the more traditional forms of poetry and prose fiction in Western Europe.

Noticeably, Britain between the wars witnessed rapid growth of popular mass culture. Popular culture, including films, novels, magazines, periodicals, and newspapers, flourished and became immensely attractive to the British public (Grandy 2016, 3). Popular fiction and films featuring heroes, villains, gender roles for men and women, and female love-interests appealed to audiences from different social classes (ibid., 4). However, the presence of East Asian motifs and references was not uncommon in English narrative literature. Representations of China and the Chinese were prevalent in popular culture and literature, from H. G. Wells's (1866–1946) *A Modern Utopia* (1905), Giacomo Puccini's (1858–1924) *Turandot* (1924), the Yellow Peril trope in Jack London's (1876–1916) dystopias,[18] and in Sax Rohmer's (1883–1959) novels and films about Dr Fu Manchu (1910s-30s),[19] to various expressions of "Oriental" wisdom and art, as well as art exhibitions (Prado-Fonts 2018, 178). In the case of popular drama, plays with Chinese themes or presented in the Chinese manner, such as *The Yellow Jacket* (1913), *The Circle of Chalk* (1929), and *Lady Precious Stream* (1933), attracted large numbers of mass audiences and enabled their imaginings and fantasies of the distant Orient (Yeh 2015, 177–180; see also Thorpe 2016, 51–135). In addition, China was also an important setting for many influential novels written in the 1920s and '30s, including Pearl Buck's (1892–1973) novels such as *The Good Earth* (1931) and André Malraux's (1901–76) novels such as *The Temptation of the West* (1926) and *Man's Fate* (1933) (Bush 2013, 200). These and many other forms of popular literature and theatrical performance showed a powerful connection between China, or East Asia, and British, or Euro-American modernity. Furthermore, during this period, book publishers and film producers in Britain were generally market-oriented and responded to the tastes and preferences of the mass audience (Grandy 2016, 7). The Egerton translation was produced in this particular intellectual and cultural environment. It was certainly influenced not only by the contemporary modernist approach to translating

Chinese literature, as discussed above, but also by the commercial climate of the interwar period.

After the Great War, Britain witnessed the expansion of mass popular culture, and the pre-War social classes began to blur. Artists and intellectuals struggled to respond to the new commercial world in a variety of ways (Wilson 2019, 6). The inter-war period saw a significant increase in reading material that appealed to the lower or lower-middle classes, both in the form of books and magazines (James 2013, 27). The social and demographic changes provided a good market for popular fiction, and publishers were always quick to adapt to the reader's needs of the day, producing fiction to meet the realistic and definite demand. To attract a wider reading public, authors were encouraged to write novels that could be appreciated without the need for long reading spells and to create fiction that could be profitable or commercially viable (ibid.). This concept found expression or support in Woolf's seminal essay "The Common Reader" (1925), where she emphasized the nature of reading and the relationship between writers and readers. Most importantly, "The Common Reader" delved into the idea of a common reader, a typical, ordinary person who reads for pleasure rather than for academic or scholarly purposes (Woolf 2002). The essay argued for the significance of this common reader and suggested that literature should be accessible and enjoyable to a broad reading public. So far as Egerton's translation is concerned, the principles guiding his translation strategy reflected his pursuit of plainness, conciseness, simplicity, and high readability, aiming to reach a wide reading public. The language of the Egerton translation was idiomatic, laconic, fluent, and contemporary, remaining accessible to the general reading public of the translator's time. These aspects will be further explored in the following chapters. Moreover, as this study will suggest, the Latinization of some sensitive or embarrassing words and passages regarding the candid treatment of sex in the Egerton translation also reflected a commercial standpoint in its publication. The publisher, wary of taking any risks, aimed to publish it earlier than Miall's version, which also came out in London in 1939. This tension between artistic integrity and mass appeal manifests the broader context of the time. In sum, as will become clear over the course of this study, the Egerton translation followed a commercial rather than a purely scholarly or pedagogical path. It integrated the sixteenth-century Chinese novel of manners into the popular literary canon in inter-war Britain, with a focus on the pleasurable reading of the mass reading public.

1.3.2 *David Tod Roy's* The Plum in the Golden Vase

The latest translation of *Jin Ping Mei*, titled *The Plum in the Golden Vase* (henceforth *Plum*), was made by David Tod Roy (1933–2016), a sinologist and professor emeritus of the University of Chicago. Published over a span of twenty years by Princeton University Press, this monumental work consists of five substantial volumes (the first four released in 1993, 2001, 2006, and 2011, respectively, with the final volume completed and released in 2013). Roy's translation, *Plum*, well over 3,000 pages long, stands as an epic scholarly achievement and a "truly complete" version of the Ming-era masterpiece. The sheer length of the Roy translation presumes that a reader of leisure possesses ample time, the most precious of commodities. In contrast to the Egerton translation, which localizes the Chinese source text to the extent of resembling a British novel from the nineteenth century, the Roy translation firmly anchors it in its Ming cultural context. This involves, as this study shows, retaining culturally specific terms, oral storytelling mode, historical references, and the rich tapestry of literary allusions, quotations, stock phrases, amongst other things. As Alison Hardie (1994, 42) reminds us, The Roy translation has the merit of being complete, exceedingly accurate, and in many ways readable. Jennifer Putin (1995) remarks that Roy successfully introduces the Ming classic to global consciousness, imbuing it with new significance within the Chinese literary heritage. Roy's approach may help update or broaden the initial horizons of English-language readers regarding *Jin Ping Mei* in particular and Ming narrative prose in general.

Roy was born in Nanking, China, in 1933.[20] His parents, Presbyterian missionaries, had arrived in China in 1930. His father, Andrew Tod Roy (1903–2004), well versed in Chinese, served as a philosophy professor at the University of Nanking. During the Sino-Japanese war, the University relocated to China's Southwestern city, Chengdu, and Roy stayed there with his family until 1945. After the war, the family returned to the U.S. and then went back to China again in 1948 during the Civil War. From 1948 to 1950, Roy and his family resided in Shanghai and Nanking, where Roy and his brother J. Stapleton Roy (1935-), later the U.S. ambassador to China from 1991–1995, received their primary education. Roy spent most of his early years in China, learning Chinese and developing an interest in traditional Chinese novels such as *Jin Ping Mei* and *Honglou meng*. One of his tutors was Zhao Yanan 趙亞南, who assisted Pearl S. Buck in translating *Shuihu zhuan* (Roy 2013; Ye 2019). In China, Roy heard about *Jin Ping Mei* and, as a teenager, became intrigued by its reputation for pornography (Abowd 2016; Roy 2013). He read Egerton's 1939 translation stored in the library of Nanking University but was frustrated as well as stimulated by the Latin segments. In 1950, he found an unexpurgated version (*Jin Ping Mei cihua*) in a secondhand bookshop near the Confucian Temple in Nanking, starting his lifelong fascination with this Ming classic. After 1950, Roy returned to the U.S. with his brother and continued to study Chinese under the tutelage of sinologist and historian Derk Bodde (1909–2003). Roy later gained admission to Harvard University, where he majored in History and Far Eastern languages.

Before completing his undergraduate studies at Harvard, Roy was drafted into the U.S. Army, completing two years of military service in Japan and Taiwan. While in Tokyo, Roy obtained a copy of *Jin Ping Mei* with Zhang Zhupo's commentary, and brought it back to the U. S., where it has been well kept to this day. Upon returning home in 1956, Roy continued his studies at Harvard until 1965 when he completed his doctoral research on the early years of the Chinese writer, historian, archaeologist, and social activist Kuo Mo-jo 郭沫若 (1892–1978). Harvard University Press later published his dissertation, titled *Kuo Mo-jo: The Early Years*. Subsequently, he taught Chinese literature at Princeton, where he introduced *Jin Ping Mei* in his classes using Miall's translation due to his students' proficiency in Chinese at the time. Two years later, he joined the University of Chicago, remaining there until his retirement in 1999. From 1967, Roy started teaching Chinese language and literature, conducting extensive research on the novel *Jin Ping Mei* and inspiring generations of students to study premodern Chinese literature (Abowd 2016). Roy drew parallels between *Jin Ping Mei* and comparably ambitious Western works, suggesting that it "is an enormous, complex and sophisticated novel, surprisingly modern in its design" and that "there is no earlier work of prose fiction of equal sophistication in world literature with the possible exception of *Don Quixote*" (Roy 1993, xvii). He created tens of thousands of index cards to document the sources of every line of poetry, idioms, proverbs, stock epithets, and other borrowed material in *Jin Ping Mei*, forming the foundation for the extensive endnotes in his later translation. Some scholars, however, suggest that Roy's intimidating expertise in these endnotes sometimes hinders rather than helps anyone but the most learned professional sinologists (Radford 2012, 253). Other scholars maintain that Roy's annotations would "make seasoned readers of monographs smile in quiet disbelief," asserting that he has elevated the art of the textual glossing to a new level (Spence 1994). While these extensive annotations, coupled with the distinctive typographic design, lend *Plum* the semblance of an academic monograph, they simultaneously serve as a unique manifestation of Roy's personal interest, cultural authority, erudition, ethical attitude, and individual approach to his role as a researcher-translator. Furthermore, they shed light on Roy's endeavors to position himself as an authority with a more profound understanding of Chinese literature, culture, and history compared to previous translators of the same novel.

Inspired by his colleague Anthony C. Yu (1938–2015), who translated the Ming novel *Xiyou ji*, Roy planned to retranslate *Jin Ping Mei* in 1982 after twenty years of research. In 1983, Roy decided to produce a full, unexpurgated, and annotated English translation of *Jin Ping Mei*. He contracted with Princeton University Press and completed the project in 2012, mainly because he took early retirement and could work full-time on it. Roy's decision to present a new translation was based mainly on the following reasons: firstly, he believed that the Wanli recension of the novel was superior to the Chongzhen edition and no previous English renderings were based on the former; secondly, there were too many deletions and omissions in previous English, French, and German translations, which detracted from the novel's rhetorical style and structural features; thirdly, the novel's polyphonic nature derived from literary borrowings needed to be represented in translation (Roy 1993, xlvii; also quoted in the translator's archival documents). Roy declared that, until World War Two, most translations by native-English translators of Chinese and Japanese novels were made to sound much like Western literature (for example, cutting out unfamiliar rhetorical features) to prevent the translated texts from appearing too alien or esoteric to English-language readers; he insisted that "the great works of Chinese and Japanese deserve to be taken seriously, just as we treat our own literary masterpieces" (Makos 1993; Roy 2013).

Distinguishing his translation from earlier versions, Roy's goal was to preserve as many features of the original as possible. He aimed for his translation method to allow "English readers to appreciate not only the story told by a master story-teller but also at least something of the complex experimental rhetorical techniques by which he strove to accomplish his purpose" (as quoted in the translator's archival documents). This demonstrated his concern for cultural distinction, as Pierre Bourdieu (2013, 226) describes it, in contrast to cultural proselytism, characterized by expanding the audience to win a market. Unlike previous renderings, which left out much of the original and presented the juicier, risqué passages in, for instance, Latin, Roy adopted a scholarly attitude towards his translation project and preserved everything of the original in the target text, highlighting the foreign or exotic flavor of the text deeply rooted in the cultural milieu of dynastic China. Roy followed the example of Hawkes and Minford, who co-translated *Honglou meng* during the 1970s, in attempting to render the complete text into English, including puns and wordplay. However, Roy's translation style differs tremendously from that of the Hawkes/Minford translation because the latter seeks to enter the "realm of transformation" through transcreation and creative fidelity (Wong 2014; Fan 2022). Roy's translational intent was clearly stated in an elaborate introduction to the first volume of his translation, that is, to translate everything in the earlier, most complete Wanli edition of *Jin Ping Mei* (Roy 1993, xlviii). This was by no means an easy task, given that the body of this recension includes hybrid texts drawn from a wide spectrum of literary genres and other sources aside from the prose narrative per se (Luo 2012, 178). However, Roy de facto translated more than everything that is in the original, even though it produces an odd, unnatural effect on the English ear. He used typographical means to indent almost every line of idioms, proverbs, and aphorisms in the text, as will be shown later in this study. This method, while not inherent in the original text, could disrupt the narrative's flow and the vigor and vivacity of fictional dialogue (Hardie 1994, 42; Børdahl 2022, 196). Despite its advantage in reproducing the original text's cultural worldview as faithfully as possible, ordinary readers are likely to feel frustrated due to their own cultural presuppositions or horizon of expectations. Additionally, Roy incorporated woodblock illustrations from the original, provided a useful full cast of characters, and added endnotes, a bibliography, and an index to his translation, resulting in a hefty volume of peritexts. All of these, naturally, mirrored the translator's meticulous scholarship on *Jin Ping Mei* and its literary context, unveiling his foreignizing ethos that defined his translation philosophy. However, Roy's decision and his mode of translating, as Campbell (2008) suggests, might lead to unexpected results, as such kind of "thick" translation could contribute to the loss of some of the essential features (for example, humor, colloquial color, readability, plainness, and accessibility) of the original text. It will become clear in this study that Roy's translation strategies, centered on metaphrase or literalism, were partially influenced by the specific circumstances of his project and its publication, including the institutional context. The inclusion of voluminous endnotes and short essays (namely, drawing analogies between *Jin Ping Mei* and Charles Dickens's *Bleak House*), while flattering the assumed knowledge of the intended reader, played a crucial role in shaping the specific strategies employed to translate aspects of the novel. Collectively, as shown by the type of paratextual framing, these elements contributed to constructing a fresh image for *Jin Ping Mei* and established an overarching context of reception for the projected readership.

Granted, Roy translated *Jin Ping Mei* within a specific institutional context. To some extent, Roy's translation practice could be considered institutional translation. This term refers to translation activities that occur within specific institutions and are intended to benefit those institutions (Baker and Saldanha 2020, 256). He continued to translate this magnum opus while working as a teacher and researcher at the University of Chicago. The entire project was carried out in a pedagogical or research context, as he also taught and wrote academic papers on *Jin Ping Mei* while carrying out his translation project. Before undertaking the translation project, Roy had already translated much of Kuo Mo-jo's work, as evidenced by his monograph *Kuo Mo-jo: The Early Years*. His translation philosophy, principles, or prose style were nearly established during his work on Kuo Mo-jo's texts or texts about Kuo Mo-jo while being a Kuo Mo-jo scholar. Put another way, Roy had already developed a prose style that was more or less the same for writing *Plum*, if not for everything he wrote. Roy's translation of Zhang Zhupo's *Jin Ping Mei du fa* (How to Read *Jin Ping Mei*) (1990) also showed a style similar to *Plum*. Roy's established background as a researcher of Kuo Mo-jo and Jin Ping Mei when he commenced translating the latter implies a distinct style that might invade his translation. Moreover, it suggests a substantial foundation to advocate for any agenda he had regarding his vision of the translation. In practice, Roy's translation principles bear resemblance to those of Vladimir Nabokov (1899–1977), whose notably literal translation of Alexander Pushkin's (1799–1837) *Evgenij Onegin* (1833) reflected a profound commitment to preserving the intricate nuances of Pushkin's text, showcasing his deep appreciation for the art and poetics of Pushkin. Regarding the use of extensive notes in translation, Nabokov expressed, "I want translations with copious footnotes, footnotes reaching up like skyscrapers to the top of this or that page so as to leave only the gleam of one textual line between commentary and eternity" (Loison-Charles 2022, 98). Evidently, Roy's approach to retranslating *Jin Ping Mei* finds an analogous precedent in Nabokov's renowned translation of *Eugene Onegin*, published in 1964. Nonetheless, Roy only briefly references Nabokov in the acknowledgments for *Plum*, without delving into the specifics of Nabokov's approach to translation. As subsequent chapters will reveal, Roy advocates for a type of interlinear translation in capturing the various dimensions of *Jin Ping Mei*. This approach goes beyond the well-known *belles infidèles* (beautiful renderings that are unfaithful to the original) and is instead marked by a form of literalism or "metaphrase" in John Dryden's (1631–1700) sense (Munday 2001, 25), involving a word-by-word and line-by-line transfer. While this method may result in an inelegant text, it provides the most comprehensive access to the original for those interested in delving into the intricacies of late Ming culture and history. Roy didn't publish much before writing and publishing *Plum*. As suggested above, Roy provided a lengthy, informative introduction to the translation of *Jin Ping Mei*, which also reflects a prose style very similar to that of the translated text. Scholar Katherine Carlitz was an advisee of Professor Roy's and was in pretty close touch with Roy during the time Roy was working on the translation of *Jin Ping Mei*.

Carlitz reminds us that Roy also tended to be a bit formal in his own speaking style in his daily life, and this may have also influenced his translation (personal communication, December 4, 2021). Another influential factor should be his proficiency in Chinese, having been born in China and spending his childhood there. This background provided him with a thorough understanding of the material, given his ability to speak and write proficient Chinese. After reading several translated passages in *Kuo Mo-jo: The Early Years*, it has been found that the prose in Roy's translation of *Kuo Mo-jo* is very similar to the prose in *Plum*. Overall, the translating language in both *Kuo Mo-jo* and *Plum* bears similarities in terms of diction and syntactical choices. It is safe to assume that, as stated earlier, Roy's translation appears to target a specialist audience, specifically students of classical Chinese literature and literary historians or researchers in the field of Chinese Studies during the late twentieth and early twenty-first centuries in North America.

Roy's work on *Jin Ping Mei* also relates to a critical trend that emerged in the late twentieth century (Luo 2012, 180). The study of Ming dynasty literature, including fiction, poetry, drama, and classical prose, flourished in the 1970s and 1980s and continued to thrive in North America from the 1990s through the first decade of the millennium (Carlitz 2011). In the 1970s and 1980s, vernacular texts of the Ming dynasty were rediscovered and treated by critics as serious products of Ming literati culture (Plaks 1987, 3–54; Hsia 1988, 139). The depiction of quotidian minutiae in Ming vernacular works such as *Jin Ping Mei*, along with their extraordinary breadth, epitomized the Ming literati's erudition and sophistication and contributed to their narrative aesthetics. As Carlitz (2011, 5) puts it, the methodological approach to studying Ming literature in North America was historical in establishing genres and canons, and (post)structural in analyzing content in the 1970s and 1980s, and the research focus shifted to the areas of gender, sexuality, and subjectivity in Ming and even Qing literary texts after the early 1990s. The research focus on Ming vernacular literature during this long, productive period is reflected in the selection of texts for translation (Carlitz 2011). Prime examples include Cyril Birch's translation of the Ming plays *Mudan ting* 牡丹亭 (Peony Pavilion) and *Jiaohong ji* 嬌紅記 (Mistress and Maid), Shuhui Yang and Yunqin Yang's translations of the vernacular tales *San yan* 三言 (Sanyan Stories) and *Erh pai* 二拍 (Slapping the Table in Amazement), Patrick Hanan's translations of *Pingyao zhuan* 平妖傳 (Quelling the Demons' Revolt) and Ming vernacular love stories, to name only a few. Therefore, one can argue that Roy's translation of *Jin Ping Mei* was intimately connected to the intellectual vogue for and scholarly interest in Ming dynasty literature prevailing in North American academia. The critical trend likely influenced Roy's perception of *Jin Ping Mei*, shaping how he structured his translation of the novel (Luo 2012, 180).

There was, of course, a larger context for Roy's translation. There are some geopolitical considerations that demand our attention here. Since World War Two, sinology or Chinese studies have developed rapidly in North America. In the 1950s, ambitious scholars, including John King Fairbank (1907–91), Knight Biggerstaff (1906–2001), and C. Martin Wilbur (1907–97) played a crucial role in promoting Chinese studies in the United States. After decades of study in China, they also contributed to the development of a distinctive style for North American sinology, ushering it into a new era (Chen 2007, 4). Chinese studies had thus become an independent discipline, focusing on the literature, culture, and history of modern and contemporary China, as well as pre-modern China. In the 1970s, China witnessed dramatic changes in the political, economic, cultural, and diplomatic spheres. Notably, the establishment of Sino-U.S. diplomatic relations, marked by President Richard Nixon's (1913–94) official visit to China in 1972, and the subsequent implementation of the reform and opening-up policy stimulated increased interest in China Studies in North America. In 1958, the National Defense Education Act was enacted in the United States to encourage American universities to establish foreign language teaching centers to produce experts in area studies (Zhang 2022, 121). According to statistics, from the late 1950s to the 1970s, the U.S. government allocated more than 15 million dollars for research on China; in addition, public and private funds invested in Chinese studies totaled about 70 million dollars, which greatly promoted the development of sinology in the U.S. during this period (Zhang 2022, 122). From the 1960s to the 1970s, the number of college students studying Chinese in the United States tripled, thanks to the U.S. government's provision of funds for study materials, research grants, and study-abroad programs (Ruan et al. 2016, 49). For instance, in Roy's translation project, he received substantial support from various grants provided by the U.S. government. Notably, these included a Grant for Research on Chinese Civilization from the American Council of Learned Societies in 1976 and 1977, as well as a grant from the Translation Program of the National Endowment for the Humanities in 1983 and 1986 (Roy 1993, xiv). According to Roy, the project could not have been completed without the assistance of these and other grants.

By the 1970s, numerous Chinese studies research institutions and centers had emerged, including departments of East Asian Languages and Cultures or departments of Asian Languages, attracting a multitude of students and scholars such as Andrew Plaks in Princeton, Cyril Birch in Berkeley, C. T. Hsia (1921–2013) in Columbia (Zhang 2022, 123). For example, the East Asian Research Center at Harvard University, spearheaded by John King Fairbank, played an important role in advancing Chinese studies in the U.S. However, East Asian area studies, including Sinology and Japanology, established in leading U.S. universities after World War Two, carried larger geopolitical implications and served strategic purposes, such as functioning as domestic cultural support for American diplomatic relations with China and Japan; they were inseparable from political agendas (Fowler 1992; Saur 1998, 8–12; Venuti 1998, 72; Chan 2013, 20). An important goal of these studies' research centers was to collect and systematically study information about those areas to serve the political, military, and diplomatic needs of the U.S. government (ibid.). In the field of Chinese studies, translation has played a crucial role in advancing research, and most of the Chinese texts studied are variedly translated by academic translators and their editors into English (ibid.). Undoubtedly, the Chinese literary cannon projected in the U.S. evolved with the changing political circumstances since the 1970s. As a result of the increased emphasis on East Asia in the United States in the post-war period and the growing interest in Asian studies, Princeton University Press, along with other academic publishers, launched a project to publish translated Asian classics and to establish a library of Asian classics. Princeton University Press's decision to contract with Roy to publish the translation of *Jin Ping Mei* in the 1980s was not unrelated to the broader geopolitical factors in the promotion of Chinese studies in North America. Roy's translation was published by Princeton University Press as part of the Princeton Library of Asian Classics translation series, which has provided students and scholars with valuable materials on the history and culture of East Asia. Indeed, the translation of various kinds of Chinese literature in North America really boomed after World War Two and the founding of the PRC. The Western world was fascinated by the way China was pulling itself together under Mao and gradually becoming a major world power (Carlitz, personal communication, December 4, 2021). Part of that was a fascination with Chinese literature.

It is noticeable that since World War Two, there has been a trend among sinologist-cum-translators of Chinese classical literature in the West, if not solely the U.S., to bolster their translations with ample notes and other scholarly aids. As C. T. Hsia puts it, more recent translators seem to recognize that their work could not attract the general reading public, who may not have been impressed to read classical literature. The intended audience for these translations is the translators' fellow specialists and research students interested in the field (Hsia 1988, 139; Roy 2012, as quoted in Qi 2016, 216). William H. Nienhauser contends that it is helpful to "provide an annotative context for all translations intended for the modern scholarly reader" (as quoted in Eoyang and Lin 1995, 23). While Roy's translation may seem tailored for a scholarly audience, it also attempts to appeal to general readers who, as the blurb of the translation states, are looking for "a compelling narrative replete with convincing portrayals of the darker side of human nature." According to Campbell (2008) and Vibeke Børdahl (2022), Roy's translation grants access to the material and popular literary world of late Ming China, serving as a valuable resource for students and teachers in the West interested in this fascinating and rapidly transforming period of late imperial Chinese history.

When the first volume of Roy's translation was published in 1993, it was met with mixed reviews, as mentioned earlier. As Jeff Makos (1993) has noted, Roy's translation stands as a significant contribution to the cultural history of China itself. Charles Horner goes on to declare that the Roy translation "does more than showcase the literary merits of an old Chinese book; it also sketches the moral topography of another culture" (Horner 1994, 71). Roy's accomplishment, as Horner puts it, would rank with that of James Legge (1815–97), H. A. Giles, and Waley among the great presenters in English of the Chinese canon. Scholar and translator Yang Shuhui goes further, identifying Roy as the greatest scholar-translator in the field of Chinese classical fiction (Yang 2008, 214). Indeed, the Roy translation has garnered increasing attention from specialist readers who, as Putin has it, can "derive great enjoyment from the lively evocations of domesticity, murder, intrigue and corruption in an upwardly mobile family in the Ming dynasty" (1995, 156). Nonetheless, it remains to be seen how many general readers would be attracted to the massive translation. This is primarily because the general readership indeed plays a crucial role in determining and amplifying the collective impact on the reception of a given work of literature. This consideration is especially pertinent given that Egerton's translation, *Lotus*, has been reprinted numerous times, with the most recent reprint released in a single volume in 2023, while Roy's *Plum* has not received any reprints as of today. Following in the footsteps of Anthony Yu and Moss Roberts, who released streamlined versions of their acclaimed translations of *Xiyou ji* and *Sanguo yanyi*, respectively, Roy's publisher plans to release a condensed edition by excluding, for example, the index and heavy endnotes (Qi 2016, 214; Schuessler 2013). Such a streamlined version might serve as a gateway for more specialist readers, especially those unwilling or unable to access the larger edition straight-away.

Ever since the appearance of Roy's translation, the title *The Plum in the Golden Vase* has been incorporated into several influential histories of Chinese literature, including *A Concise History of Chinese Literature* (2011), *The Cambridge History of Chinese Literature* (2010), and *Chinese Literature: A Very Short Introduction* (2012), among others. Roy's translation has sparked critical interest among translation studies scholars, which has partially shaped the subject of analysis discussed in the book.

1.4 Research Aims and Scope

As the title of this book indicates, the focus of this book is on the translation of *Jin Ping Mei* by two English-language translators. Specifically, it undertakes a critical comparison between Egerton's translation, *Lotus*, and Roy's latest retranslation, *Plum*. The selection is based on three main criteria. Firstly, both translations, *Lotus* by Egerton and *Plum* by Roy, are full-length and readily available for data collection. Secondly, the translations were published in different historical contexts within the Anglophone world, and the translators, with diverse societal and cultural backgrounds, are likely to employ distinct textual strategies. The third criterion involves the translators' different aesthetic attitudes towards the source text and their unique translational philosophies.

It goes without saying that any study of a complex, hybrid, and sophisticated literary classic such as *Jin Ping Mei* cannot be exhaustive. This study specifically delves into the analysis and discussion of the translators' choices and strategies in dealing with several significant dimensions of the novel. Drawing upon a carefully selected set of textemes, which are instances of certain prominent themes in the source text, the present study aims to discuss the translation of (1) the various representations of late Ming culture; (2) the multi-layered narrative voice; (3) gender matters or representations of women; and (4) (homo)sexual-related narratives. It necessarily grapples with both linguistic and extralinguistic cultural, social, aesthetic, and historical dimensions of the novel. By taking into account multiple dimensions of or interpretive perspectives of the novel, it helps to avoid one-sidedness and partial vision, and to overcome narrow interpretations when analyzing and discussing the novel within English translations. The subjects of analysis are chosen for their diverse themes and functional relevance, embodying textemes that contribute to the intrinsic thematic and aesthetic characteristics of the novel. As said above, these subjects represent the salient features of the novel. The manner and extent to which they are transposed into the target texts can profoundly influence the target reader's perception and interpretation of the novel on various levels. Importantly, they are essential for tracing and discerning translational shifts, especially those that bring about both major and subtle changes to the text. Moreover, there has been limited and unsystematic exploration of how these meaningful elements, especially culturemes, narratological resources, gender matters, and homosexual subjects, have been treated by the translators to achieve the intended effects in the receptor culture.

Previous studies have not given sufficient attention to examining in-depth the translators' choices in relation to the target literary culture when the translations were produced. This book intends to bridge this research gap. So, aside from providing a descriptive comparative analysis at the textual level, the study also seeks to explore in-depth whether and how situational and sociohistorical contingencies may have shaped the translators' translatorial behavior. The rationale behind this approach lies in the understanding that everything – people, cultures, events, social practices, and the like, – is essentially determined by a certain set of historical conditions. Translation is no exception; it never occurs in a vacuum but is always embedded in cultural, political frameworks, and in history (Bassnett and Lefevere 1998, 5; Bassnett and Trivedi 1999, 6). While translators, as intimate readers of the source text, may have their own distinctive points of view or positioning and perform their craft according to their translational poetics, their subjective attitudes towards the source text are necessarily influenced by public and institutional perceptions, taste, values, and other external factors grounded in their surroundings (Lambert 1992, 19). Therefore, it is imperative for translators to actively respond to or engage with the societal, cultural, political, and literary currents in their surroundings. This active engagement ensures that their translations seamlessly integrate into the receptive environment, becoming an integral part of the target literary culture.

1.5 Research Hypothesis

The general hypothesis for this study posits that while each translator displays autonomy or subjectivity based on their individual dispositions and motives, revealing their own translational poetics, their subjectivity is nevertheless necessarily influenced either by the sociocultural constraints in the receiving situation or by the expectations of the target audience.[21] These influences ultimately give rise to divergent representations of the original text in the target culture. Specifically, the Egerton translation actively engages with its immediate social conditions, intending to align with target aesthetic or poetic norms and literary currents and to ensure reader enjoyment and engagement. In contrast, the Roy translation strives to achieve perfect conformity with the Chinese original, with a tendency to celebrate academic or pedagogical features and serve as an adequate rendering that emphasizes the historico-cultural value of the original composed in the late Ming.[22]

1.6 Research Questions

To test this general hypothesis, the study aims to address the overarching question of how and to what extent some of the salient features of *Jin Ping Mei* are handled by English-language translators and what likely factors influence their translational decisions. To answer this research question, the study has formulated the following four sub-questions:

(1) How does each translator manage the novel's rich representations of late Ming culture in their English translations, and what likely factors motivate their choices?
(2) How does each translator navigate the multilayered narrative voices of both the characters and the narrator in the novel, and what factors might determine their choices during translation?
(3) To what extent are the gender-related narratives in the novel, such as misogynistic narratives, sexist discourse, or gender stereotypes about female characters, reframed and reconfigured in each translation, and why?
(4) How is the novel's representation of sexuality and erotic sensations treated in the two translations, and what are the reasons and potential results for these treatments?

The answers to these questions can illuminate patterns and commonalities in the translators' textual behavior, suggesting specific causes, whether intrinsic, extrinsic or both, that shape their decision-making in handling the range of textemes during the translation process.[23] These insights contribute to our understanding of the translators' role as textual-social mediators in different historical and socio-political settings and, ultimately, help validate or falsify the working hypothesis outlined above.

1.7 Methodological Approach

Given the wide-ranging scope of the study, encompassing literary, linguistic, sociocultural, political, and intellectual concerns, my approach is inevitably an interdisciplinary one. I subscribe to Mona Baker's belief that translation studies research can and should be multidisciplinary or interdisciplinary (Baker 1996, 10). Baker emphasizes that "translation studies can and should draw on a variety of discourses and disciplines that each will have much to offer in some areas and be seriously limited in others (linguistics being no exception)." I also share Edoardo Cristafulli's (2002) observation that translation studies research should be eclectic and consider both descriptive empirical and critical interpretative methods. The methodological framework is based on the paradigm of Descriptive Translation Studies (DTS).

DTS moves translation studies from prescribing what translation should be to describing and explaining actual translational behavior in a real cultural context. It addresses questions such as "who translates what, when, how, for whom, in what context, with what effect, and why?" (Hermans 2007, 88). In *Descriptive Translation Studies and Beyond*, Gideon Toury asserts that it is only "through studies into actual behavior that hypotheses can be put to a real test" (1995, 16). To promote descriptivism in translation criticism, Toury suggests research methods involving the analysis of a substantial corpus of purposefully selected material to observe the translator's (and other agents involved in the act of translation) textual behavior and to provide "exhaustive **descriptions** and viable **explanations** with justifiable **predictions**" (ibid., 302, original emphasis). Clearly, the rationale that Toury has endorsed for DTS involves separate parts: a descriptive part, and an explanatory part. Because DTS is characterized by "carefully performed studies into well-defined corpuses, or sets of problems" (Toury 1995, 1), it has been labeled as "empirical" (Hermans 1999, 7). Moreover, Toury views all translations as "facts of target cultures" and perceives the act of translating as governed or determined by forces or influences (for example, norms and constraints) of the host culture or as a cause for introducing changes to the target system (1995, 28). Thus, the DTS model is identified as descriptive-explanatory and target-context-oriented, which "takes [translation] as it is and tries to determine the various factors that may account for its particular nature" (Hermans 1999, 13). Within this model, translations can be perceived as records of past translation choices, elucidating the relationship among the translator, the translated text, and the context, as well as functions performed by the target text and linguistic and cultural asymmetries (Tymoczko 2007, 40). Such analyses often draw upon literary theory, linguistics, critical textual analysis, and other disciplines (ibid., 41). Thus, researchers with multidisciplinary awareness attempt to analyze textual strategies in the translated texts and then seek to account for the forces shaping them in the host culture (Rosa 2010, 98).

According to Toury (1995, 11), DTS can be understood as a model for the comparative analysis of source and target texts. Operating within the DTS framework, this study describes and compares two English translations of *Jin Ping Mei* occurring at different historical moments. It not only involves close textual analysis but also relates the translations to the sociocultural context in which they were produced. Toury (1995, 74) also distinguished three types of description and comparison in translation studies. The first is to compare the multiple translations of a single source text into one language, with the translations appearing in different historical periods, and produced by different translators. The second is to compare different phases of the appearance of a single translation vis-à-vis its source text; The third is to compare translations into different languages (ibid.). The present study involves the first two types of comparison: it compares two translations of *Jin Ping Mei* into English with each other and both of them to the Chinese source text.

Moreover, this study follows Toury's three-stage method by describing Egerton's and Roy's translations of *Jin Ping Mei* at both textual and extratextual levels. The first stage involves identifying and describing texts that the target culture considers to be translations; the second consists of a comparative analysis of source and target texts, mapping target text segments onto source text segments; and the third involves identifying patterns or tendencies evinced by translational shifts and relating them to contextual constraints or motivations and to the intended function of the target texts (Toury 1995, 37). The focus here is on the last two stages of this three-stage method. Following this framework, the study pursues the analysis of both "process" and "product." The analysis of "process" focuses on the translators' strategies and solution-types in responding to the challenges of the source text. Subsequently, the analysis of "product" involves examining the translators' immediate social and cultural milieu that shape their translational decisions.

In selecting the source text for analysis, this study seeks to access both editions – Chongzhen (*xiuxiang*) and Wanli (*cihua*) – utilized by the two translators. However, for citation purposes, the study primarily employs the *cihua* edition (namely, the facsimile edition released by Daian in 1963). The study aims to quote textual passages or examples for analysis from this facsimile edition, as it encompasses nearly all the content of the Chongzhen edition. Notably, Roy's translation was based on the facsimile edition, as indicated in Table 1.1 Table 1.1 shows that the Chongzhen edition, published in Singapore, is designated as the reference text for several reasons. Firstly, Egerton's translation was based on this edition. Secondly, the facsimile edition lacks specific, clear page numbers. Further, the Chongzhen edition preserves all primitive information, including two hundred illustrations, without any textual expurgation or subsequent emendation. However, traditional Chinese characters in this edition have been converted to simplified Chinese characters for ease of access in Singapore. Importantly, the textual examples selected for analysis in the subsequent chapters are present in both the Chongzhen

Table 1.1 List of Source and Target Texts

Book Information	Source Text	Target Texts	
		Earlier Translation	*Latest Retranslation*
Title	1. *Xinke xiuxiang piping Jin Ping Mei;* 2. *Jin Ping Mei cihua* (facsimile edition)	*The Golden Lotus*	*The Plum in the Golden Vase* (5 vols)
Author/ Translator	Xiao Xiao Sheng	Clement Egerton	David Tod Roy
Date of Publication	1. 2003, reprinted in 2006, 2009, 2016; 2. released in 1963	1939 (4 vols); reprinted in 1953, 1955, 1972, 2011 (2 vols), and 2023 (single volume)	1993 (vol. 1); 2001 (vol. 2); 2006 (vol. 3); 2011 (vol. 4); 2013 (vol. 5)
Publisher	1. South Ocean Publishing House, Singapore; 2. The facsimile edition was released by Daian Co. Ltd., Japan.	George Routledge & Sons Ltd. Tuttle Publishing	Princeton University Press

and *cihua* recensions. Any inconsistent textual passages, deemed minor and irrelevant, are excluded to avoid confusion, given the established fact that this inconsistency is solely attributed to the two translators' use of different recensions, rather than any other factors. Textual examples are collected following the principle of purposive sampling (Saldanha and O'Brien 2014; Toury 1995). This involves selecting textual samples based on certain parameters (for example, cultural, narratological, gender, sexual, and the like.) to form sets of corpus material for close analysis. This sampling technique ensures diversity and variety of textual samples, mitigating bias and enhancing the validity of findings. Additionally, any differences in translation arising from the distinct recensions of the Chinese original will be explained and endnoted. Table 1.1 provides a comprehensive list of the source and target texts used in this study, including their respective dates of publication and publishing houses.

Regarding the target texts, Egerton's translation has undergone multiple reprints. The 1939 edition is chosen as the reference for this study since it represents the initial publication in London without any amendment seen in reprinted versions. Roy's translation, unlike Egerton's, has not undergone any reprints, leaving no alternative choices. Notably, both Egerton's and Roy's translations use the Wade-Giles system for character names. However, a significant difference arises in the translation of female characters' names in Egerton's (1939) version. For example, Pan Jinlian is rendered as Golden Lotus, Li Ping'er as Lady of the Vase, Song Huilian 宋慧蓮 as Wistaria, Chunmei as Plum Blossom, Sun Xue'e as Beauty of the Snow, and so forth.[24] This aspect will be further explored in Chapter 4

This study also relies on meta-translational materials to support its arguments, including paratexts, translators' archival materials, and personal communications. Borrowing the concept of paratexts from Gérard Genette (1997), translational paratexts encompass elements such as prefaces, interviews, correspondences, introductions, afterword, blurbs, and translator's notes attached to the published translations. In the case of Egerton's translation, relevant archival material can be accessed at the University of Reading, Special Collections (Routledge & Kegan Paul Archive). This collection comprises several documents relating to Egerton's translation of *Jin Ping Mei*. Archival documents relating to Roy's translation of *Jin Ping Mei* are housed in the Special Collections of the University of Chicago Library. This collection includes Roy's biographical information, interviews, media reports, correspondences, publication lists, index cards, and contracts with his publisher. By tapping into these diverse sources, the study can acquire valuable testimony, obtain a more direct understanding of the translator's methods, and gain crucial insights into both historical circumstances and the intricacies of the translation process (Munday 2014, 66; Qi 2018; Gerber and Qi 2020). For personal communications, I engaged in email exchanges with Katherine Carlitz and David Rolston concerning Roy's translation. Both scholars show familiarity with Roy's translation project. Their insights provided valuable information on various aspects of Roy's project. Permission to reference archival documents related to Egerton's and Roy's translations was obtained from the University of Reading, Special Collections, and the University of Chicago, Special Collections.

1.8 Significance of the Study

To the best of my knowledge, this study represents the first to integrate cultural representation, narratological elements, women and gender portrayal, and (homo) sexual discourse of *Jin Ping Mei* into a discussion of the problematics of literary translation in the Chinese-English context. Refraining from value judgments and based on systematic description and in-depth analysis of texts or textual passages in relation to societal, geographical, cultural, and historical contexts,[25] the present study holds significance in several ways. Firstly, it advances new insights into how the translation of *Jin Ping Mei* into English is intricately connected to the specific cultural, ideological, geopolitical, and historical context of the target language. Secondly, it sheds light on the pivotal role played by English-language translators of Chinese literature in shaping Chinese literary traditions, constructing Chinese culture, and contributing to *Jin Ping Mei* reaching a broader, more diverse audience, including both general readers and specialists within the receptor context. Thirdly, it highlights the changing interpretations, perceptions, and reception environment of *Jin Ping Mei* within the target English literary and cultural context. Fourthly, it illustrates how different translation methods employed by English-language translators can influence the reception of Chinese literary works in the English-reading context. Fifthly, it underscores that the act of translation is a continual journey of interpretation and reinterpretation. Language, culture, and context are dynamic, and hence there is no truly complete or completely faithful translation. Each translation is a snapshot in time, capturing a particular interpretation, yet it remains susceptible to new insights, evolving perspectives, and changing linguistic landscapes. Lastly, it deepens our current understandings of the functions fulfilled by different translations of *Jin Ping Mei* at different historical moments within the Anglophone context.

1.9 Chapter Outline

The book is organized in the following way. Chapter 1 serves as the introduction, providing an overview of the novel *Jin Ping Mei* and its two English-language translators, along with their translations that appeared in different historical periods. It also outlines the theoretical framework guiding this study and the research methodology utilized. Starting from Chapter 2, the focus shifts to describing and comparing the translators' textual behavior, utilizing an empirical study of various categories of textemes in the source text and their English renderings, alongside relevant extratextual contextual explanations. These chapters encompass the analysis of textual and metatranslational information, including relevant extratextual contextual factors.

Specifically, Chapter 2 undertakes a detailed analysis of how translators navigate the intricate tapestry of cultural elements from the late Ming period. It examines the ways in which these culturemes are conveyed and transformed in the target language to capture the essence of late Ming culture. Furthermore, the chapter explores the multifaceted factors that influence translators' decisions in representing late Ming culture. These factors may include considerations such as the target audience's familiarity with ancient Chinese culture, the level of historical detail retained in the translation, and ideological imperatives. Understanding these influences provides valuable insights into the dynamics of cross-cultural translation and the tension between faithfulness to the source text and accessibility to the target audience. By examining the intricate decisions made by translators and the factors that shape these decisions, the chapter offers a nuanced understanding of the challenges and complexities involved in representing late Ming culture within translational and transnational contexts.

In Chapter 3, the analytical focus shifts to the narratological dimensions of the novel. The chapter gives a thorough analysis of the voices of central characters and the narrator. The aim is to describe how the multiple or polyphonic voices, specifically the lively and animated language in fictional dialogues and the narrator's formulaic remarks, are treated in the target texts. This involves a close analysis of linguistic choices, stylistic elements, narrative tone, and the overall strategies employed by translators to convey the liveliness and distinctiveness of the original voices. The analysis seeks to unravel whether the treatment of polyphonic voices influences the target reader's perception of the story and characterization, exploring the potential impacts of translational decisions on the overall narrative flow and reader engagement. The chapter also identifies factors that contribute to any alterations in the rendering of polyphonic voices. These factors may include linguistic challenges, cultural nuances, poetic norms, reader expectation, commercial considerations, and the translator's specific purposes. Understanding these influences is crucial for understanding how the original vibrancy and nuances of the voices are maintained, adapted, silenced, or potentially transformed in the translated versions.

Moving on to Chapter 4, the study takes a focused look on the motifs and themes within the novel, focusing on their representation in English translations. It explores the choices made by translators in rendering gender-specific motifs and examines how these decisions contribute to the overall framing of narratives related to gender dynamics. The chapter investigates linguistic choices, cultural adaptations, and the interpretative lenses through which translators approach gendered themes. This investigation includes exploring various forms of gendered narratives, including instances of sexist language and gender stereotypes associated with female characters. By shedding light on these aspects, the chapter seeks to unravel how translators grapple with and potentially challenge gender biases inherent in the source text. This analysis allows for a deeper understanding of the impact of translational decisions on the portrayal of female characters and the preservation or transformation of gender stereotypes in the target language. Additionally, the chapter tries to examine the important factors influencing translators' decisions. This includes considerations such as the target cultural norms, gender ideology, the audience's reading tastes, and the translator's own interpretative stance. Understanding the complexities involved in these decisions contributes to a more comprehensive analysis of the translational process and its implications for the literary representation of gendered narratives within transnational contexts.

Chapter 5 focuses on the intricate realm of sexual-related narratives, placing a specific emphasis on the nuanced portrayal of sexuality and erotic sensations in translation. The chapter investigates how these intimate and amorous narratives undergo transformation when transposed into the target language. It meticulously examines the choices made by translators in reconfiguring these narratives, shedding light on the potential impacts of such treatment on the overall tone and resonance of the translated texts and, by extension, on the readers' perception and engagement with them. Additionally, it seeks to unveil the layers of meaning inherent in these amorous narratives and to assess how the cultural nuances and societal attitudes toward (homo)sexuality and eroticism are preserved, adapted, or eliminated in the translated versions. In doing so, the chapter contributes to a deeper understanding of the challenges and complexities inherent in renarrating intimate desires within different linguistic, cultural, and historical contexts.

Finally, the concluding chapter serves to reflect on the main findings of this study by connecting them to the research questions formulated earlier. It illustrates the primary differences between the translators in handling various salient features of *Jin Ping Mei* and proposes translation as a hermeneutic act – a never-ending task shaped by different historical contexts. The concluding chapter also establishes links between the findings and the study's aims, recapitulating its contribution to literary translation studies in the Chinese-English context. Additionally, it provides a methodological evaluation and suggestions for future research.

Notes

1 The four masterworks were all vernacular texts of massive length and published anonymously in Ming China, including Luo Guanzhong's 羅貫中 (1330–1400) *Sanguo yanyi* 三國演義 (Romance of the Three Kingdoms), Shi Nai'an's 施耐庵 (1296–1370) *Shuihu zhun* 水滸傳 (The Marshes of Mount Liang), Wu Cheng'en's 吳承恩 (1500–82) *Xiyou ji* 西遊記 (Journey to the West), and *Jin Ping Mei*. The themes of rebellion, revolt, moral decadence, and war in these popular novels revealed a departure from the official, orthodox neo-Confucian cultural ideology, showcasing subversive tendencies or potential of vernacular texts during that time. These texts, mainly written in the premodern vernacular by literati, had great appeal to urban population in Ming China. They gained classic status in the twentieth century and played a crucial role in modernizing Chinese language (see Rudolph and Szonyi 2018). Moreover, they have inspired many novelists in modern China in terms of their aesthetics and philosophical ideas. Each of these novels has several different translations available in the English-speaking world. In the 1840s, the *Universal-Lexikon* listed these four masterworks as the most important novels for Westerners, particularly German intellectuals, to acquaint themselves with Chinese culture (see Lehner 2011).
2 Xinxinzi, Nongzhuke, and Niangong are pseudonyms and their genuine identity remains a mystery.
3 Despite that several things were removed from this Chongzhen edition, the notorious depictions of sex were not removed during the time.
4 *Jin Ping Mei* was subjected to censorship in the Qing period, along with other controversial texts. For more details, see Winston L.Y. Yang and Curtis P. Adkins, *Critical Essays on Chinese Fiction* (Hong Kong: The Chinese University Press, 2002), 202-203.

5 The so-called merchant-cum-official is also known as the *shishang* 仕商, referring to a new elite class whose wealth was based on business dealings and whose culture was based in the urban centers of late imperial China. See Yu Ying-shih, *The Religious Ethic and Mercantile Spirit in Early Modern China* (New York: Columbia University Press, 2021), 124–146.

6 *Xu Jin Ping Mei* was written by Ding Yaokang 丁耀亢 (1599–1669) in 1660, about fifteen years after the Manchus took over Peking. *Xingshi yinyuan zhuan* was authored by Xizhousheng 西周生, a pseudonym, in the early Qing; the genuine identity of the author remains unknown. *Honglou meng* was written by Cao Xueqin 曹雪芹 (1715–63) in the Qing dynasty; it is generally regarded as the greatest work of fiction in China.

7 There are several adaptations of the novel *Jin Ping Mei* circulating in the English-speaking world, but they are not discussed here in this work. For details on these adaptations, see Qi Lintao, *Jin Ping Mei English Translations* (London: Routledge, 2018).

8 The term "sinologist" is often ambiguous, carrying an orientalist ethos and lacking a clear definition. In this study, sinologists refer to scholars in China Studies without Chinese origin or Confucian influences in their education and cultural traditions, especially in Western Europe, North America, and other major Anglophone countries, including Australia and New Zealand. The root "sino" (Chinese) and terms such as "sinology" (the study of China) are derived from the Latin term "sinae" for Chinese; see D. E. Mungello's *The Great Encounter of China and the West, 1500–1800*, 4th edition (Lanham: Rowman and Littlefield, 2013), 14.

9 In the first decades of the twentieth century, Shanyn Fiske contends, Britain saw many Modernist writers and intellectuals (for example, Christopher Isherwood (1904–86), W. H. Auden (1907–73), Somerset Maugham (1874–1965) either traveling to China or engaging in correspondences with Chinese writers, artists, and scholars. Chinese influences played an important part in challenging traditional Western art and literary forms (2011, 276). For more details about British writers' interest in and appropriation of Asian culture for artistic innovation, see Louise Blakeney Williams's *Modernism and the Ideology of History* (Cambridge: Cambridge University Press, 2002), Chapter Six.

10 By referring to the translator's archival documents, it is found that Egerton finished his translation in 1930 but it was not published until 1939. That would mean that Egerton might have refined his work several times before final publication. For instance, as Egerton (1939) claims in Translator's Note, German sinologist Walter Simon (1893–1981) helped him clear up doubtful points during translation; A. S. B. Glover and L. M. Chefdeville had read the proofs and checked the Chinese names throughout.

11 In the first decades of the twentieth century, Britain's growing interest in China generated a large demand for Chinese courses in higher institutions. Apart from Lao She, other Chinese intellectuals such as Chiang Yee 蔣彝 (1903–77) and Shih-I Hsiung 熊式一 (1902–91) also taught at the School at different points during the 1920s and 1930s. See Diana Yeh's *The Happy Hsiungs: China and the Struggle for Modernity* (HK: Hong Kong University Press, 2014), and Da Zheng's *Chiang Yee: The Silent Traveler from the East: A Cultural Biography* (Piscataway: Rutgers University Press, 2010).

12 David Hawkes was one of the greatest translators of classical Chinese literature. He studied Classics at Oxford University in the 1940s and went to Beijing, China, in 1948. From 1959 to 1971, he was a Professor of Chinese at Oxford and a Research Fellow of All Souls College, Oxford. His translation of of *Honglou meng* was completed in the years after he resigned from his position at Oxford and has been regarded as his greatest achievement. John Minford is also one of the greatest translators of Chinese literature and philosophical classics. He studied Chinese at Oxford and at Australian

National University and has taught in New Zealand, Hong Kong, and mainland China. He also translated numerous works from the Chinese, including *I Ching* (2014), *Tao Te Ching* (2018), *The Art of War* (2008), *Strange Tales from a Chinese Studio* (2006), and *The Story of the Stone*.

13 William John Francis Jenner was a sinologist and translator, whose translation of Pu Yi's autobiography was adapted by the famous Italian film director, Bernardo Bertolucci (1942–2018) into the film, *The Last Emperor*, which won the Academy Award in 1987. Jenner also translated *Xiyou ji* into English in the 1980s and his translation, *Journey to the West*, was published by Foreign Languages Press in Beijing in 1986. His translation is characterized by plainness, fluency, readability, and a non-academic tendency, focusing on the vivid story and entertainment value for English-language readers.

14 "Lao Shê." *Encyclopedia of World Biography Online*, Gale, 1998. Gale in *Context: World History*, link.gale.com/apps/doc/K1631003786/WHIC?u=vuw&sid= bookmark-WHIC&xid=7556d6fb. Accessed 26 June 2022.

    On August 23, 1966, Lao She and twenty-eight others were escorted by the Red Guards to a Confucian temple in Beijing, where they were forced to kneel and were humiliated and beaten for several hours in front of a bonfire of Peking Opera costumes and stage props. The following night, Lao She drowned himself in Taiping Lake in the Xicheng district of Beijing. For more details on Lao She's sufferings, see George Kao's *Two Writers and the Cultural Revolution* (Hong Kong: The Chinese University Press, 1980), 5–14; see also Wang Youqin and Stacy Mosher's *Victims of the Cultural Revolution: Testimonies of China's Tragedy* (London: Oneworld Academic, 2023), 226–231.

15 The concept of readability, as referred to in this study, pertains to the relation between a given text and the cognitive load of a reader in comprehending it.

16 Both the Chongzhen edition and the Wanli edition of *Jin Ping Mei* referred to in this study are complete, unexpurgated recensions containing controversial passages of sex and erotism. The two translations under study were based on these complete editions of the novel.

17 According to Anne Witchard, chinoiserie is a French term, coined to "describe an aesthetic mode that originates from the seventeenth century, a time when few Europeans had actually visited China but when a profound fascination with every aspect of Chinese culture resulted in a fantastical idealized landscape"; Chinoiserie became a renewed intellectual enthusiasm for a mythic China and was a foundational element of British modernism in the early twentieth century; see Anne Witchard, *British Modernism and Chinoiserie*, (Edinburgh: Edinburgh University Press, 2015), 2–12.

18 The term Yellow Peril, allegedly invented by Kaiser Wilhelm II (1859-1941), refers to the perception of a potential threat posed to white populations by "yellow hordes", who walked westward to overwhelm Europe; fear of the Yellow Peril spread across the world after 1900; see Gregor Benton and Edmund T. Gomez, *The Chinese in Britain, 1800-Present: Economy, Transnationalism, Identity* (London: Palgrave Macmillan, 2008), 293.

19 Dr Fu Manchu was the creation of the thriller writer Sax Rohmer (1883-1959), who never went to China but drew inspiration from a superficial acquaintance with the Limehouse Chinatown in London's West End (ibid.).

20 The biographical information of David Roy was referred to from his archives, which are stored in the Special Collection of the University of Chicago Library. Specifically, documents from the David Roy Collection (Box 26) provided valuable insights into the

translation of *Jin Ping Mei*, with some of these archival materials consulted and used in this study.

21 Here subjectivity indicates that individual translators have their own thoughts and actions while translating. This subjectivity is subject to various constraints imposed by the immediate social and cultural environment in which the translator lives; see Jean Boase-Beier and Michael Holman, *The Practices of Literary Translation: Constraints and Creativity* (London: Routledge, 2014), Chapter One.

22 It is my contention that it is highly necessary to consider the translators' personal and ideological dimensions (e.g., their biography, distinctive personalities, the declared intents on translation, and the purported or desirable effects on the target reader).

23 A translated work that enters the book market has been manipulated not just by the author/translator himself but also by those who participate in co-translating, editing, proofreading, publishing, and distributing that work (Bassnett and Trivedi 1999; Tahir Gurcaǧlar 2002). By examining the two translators' archival materials, this study could affirm that the two English translations of *Jin Ping Mei* are the translators' own works. Unless there is robust evidence showing translative strategies were not made by the translators themselves, translational choices and strategies identified are attributed to the translators themselves. Put differently, this study treats the translator as metonymic of all the agents involved in a translation project.

24 In this study, I employ Pinyin, the contemporary transliteration system for Chinese characters. This system differs from the Wade-Giles system used by the two translators, as exemplified by Ximeng Qing/Hsi-men Ch'ing. I reproduce the old transliteration only when quoting texts from their translations.

25 To completely refrain from value judgments seems not possible in humanities research. As Cristafulli posits, no descriptive framework in translation studies is immune from interpretative bias since "empirical facts of the analysis do not exist independently of the researcher's viewpoint"; see Theo Hermans, *Crosscultural Transgressions* (Manchester: St. Jerome, 2002), 33–35. In this study, certain interpretative bias should be inevitable.

References

Abowd, Mary. 2016. "David Tod Roy, translator of Chinese Literary Classic, 1933–2016." *Chicago News*, June 8.

Bai, Limin. 2013. "Robert Morrison and his China: A Dialogue (1824): A Missionary Memento." *International journal for the Study of the Christian Church* 13 (3): 192–207.

Bai, Weiguo 白維國. 2015. *Jin Ping Mei fengsu tan* 金瓶梅風俗談 (Social Customs in *Jin Ping Mei*). Shanghai: The Commercial Press.

Baker, Mona. 1996. "Linguistics and Cultural Studies: Complementary or Competing Paradigms in Translation Studies." In *Ubersetzungswissenshaft: Probleme und Methoden*, edited by Angelika Lauer, 9–19. Tubingen: Gunter Narr.

Baker, Mona, and Gabriela Saldanha. 2020. *Routledge Encyclopedia of Translation Studies*. London: Routledge.

Bancroft, Christian. 2020. *Queering Modernist Translation: The Poetics of Race, Gender, and Queerness*. London: Routledge.

Barthes, Roland. 1977. *Image-Music-Text*. London: Fontana Press.

Bassnett, Susan, and André Lefevere, eds. 1998. *Constructing Cultures: Essays on Literary Translation*. Clevedon: Multilingual Matters.

Bassnett, Susan, and Harish Trivedi, eds. 1999. *Post-Colonial Translation: Theory and Practice*. London: Routledge.

Beach, Christopher. 1992. *ABC of Influence: Ezra Pound and the Remaking of American Poetic Tradition*. Berkeley: University of California Press.

Benjamin, Walter. (1923) 2021. "The Task of the Translator." In *The Translation Studies Reader*, edited by Lawrence Venuti, 89–97. London and New York: Routledge.

Benton, Gregor, and Edmund T. Gomez. 2008. *The Chinese in Britain, 1800-Present: Economy, Transnationalism, Identity*. London: Palgrave Macmillan.

Berman, Antoine. 1984. *The Experience of the Foreign: Culture and Translation in Romantic Germany*. Albany: State University of New York Press.

Berry, Margaret. 1988. *The Chinese Classic Novels: An Annotated Bibliography of Chiefly English-Language Studies*. New York and London: Garland Publishing, Inc.

Bickers, Robert A., and Jonathan J. Howlett. 2016. *Britain and China, 1840–1970: Empire, Finance and War*. New York: Routledge.

Birch, Cyril. 1974. "The Golden Lotus, translated by Colonel Clement Egerton." *The New York Review of Books*, January 24.

Birsanu, Roxana. 2011. "T. S. Eliot and the Modernist Approach to Translation." *Scientia Traductionis* 9: 179–190.

Boase-Beier, Jean, and Michael Holman. 2014. *The Practices of Literary Translation: Constraints and Creativity*. London: Routledge.

Børdahl, Vibeke. 2022. "The Translation into Danish of Jin Ping Mei cihua-Jin Ping Mei ivers og prosa: Personal Recollections and Reflections." In *Encountering China's Past Translation and Dissemination of Classical Chinese Literature*, edited by Qi Lintao and Shani Tobias, 185–206. Singapore: Springer.

Borges, Jorge Luis. 1999. *Borges en Sur 1931–1980*. Buenos Aires: Emece' Editores.

Bourdieu, Pierre. 2013. *Distinction: A Social Critique of the Judgment of Taste*. Abingdon: Routledge.

Bubb, Alexander. 2023. *Asian Classics on the Victorian Bookshelf: Flights of Translation*. Oxford: Oxford University Press.

Bush, Christopher. 2013. "Modernism, Orientalism, and East Asia." In *A Handbook of Modernism Studies*, edited by Jean-Michel Rabate, 193–208. Chichester: John Wiley & Sons Ltd.

Campbell, Duncan M. 2005. "Chinoiserie in Thorndon." In *East by South: China in the Australasian Imagination*, edited by Charles Ferrall, Paul Millar, and Keren Smith, 173–182. Wellington: Victoria University Press.

Campbell, Duncan M. 2008. "David Tod Roy, trans., *The Plum in the Golden Vase or Chin P'ing Mei: Volume Three: The Aphrodisiac*." *New Zealand Journal of Asian Studies* 10 (1): 161–164.

Cao, Xiaoqin. 2020. "Virginia Woolf's Chinese Narrative and the Chinese Vogue in Victorian and Modern Britain." *International Journal of Critical Cultural Studies* 18 (1): 1–9.

Carlitz, Katherine. 2011. "State of the Field: The Study of Ming Literature in North America, 1995–2011." *Ming Studies* 63: 5–8.

Chan, Leo Tak Hung. 2013. "Hidden Translation as Academic Practice: Translating Xiaoshuo (Small talk) and American Sinology." *Korea Journal of Chinese Language and Literature* 3: 303–330.

Chang, Chung An. 2020. " Revisiting Qian Zhongshu's *Huajing* and its English Translations and Interpretations." *Compilation and Translation Review* 13 (2): 117–164.

Chang, Kang-i Sun, and Stephen Owen. 2010. *The Cambridge History of Chinese Literature*. Cambridge: Cambridge University Press.

Chang, Su-lee. 1940. "Review of Chin P'ing Mei tr. By Bernard Miall." *Asiatic Review* 36: 616–618.

Chen, Runcheng. 2007. "Deng Siyu (Teng Ssu-yu) and the Development of American Sinology After World War II." *Chinese Studies in History* 41 (1): 3–40.

Cheng, Shuoyi. 1998. "Daniel Defoe, China's Severe Critic." In *The Vision of China in the English Literature of the Seventeenth and Eighteenth Centuries*, edited by Andrian Hsia, 215–248. Hong Kong: The Chinese University Press.

Chien, Ying-Ying. 1987. "The Feminine Struggle for Power: A Comparative Study of Representative Novels East and West." PhD Diss., University of Illinois at Urbana-Champaign.

Clarke, John James. 1997. *Oriental Enlightenment: The Encounter between Asian and Western Thought*. London and New York: Routledge.

Cohen, John Michael. 1970. "Dr. Waley's Translations." In *Madly Singing in the Mountains: An Appreciation and Anthology of Arthur Waley*, edited by Ivan Morris, 29–36. London: George Allen and Unwin Ltd.

Collier, H. Bruce. 1944. "Djin Ping Meh by Artur Kibat and Otto Kibat: King Ping Meh by Franz Kuhn: Chin P'ing Mei, the Adventurous History of Hsi Men and His Six Wives by Bernard Miall and Franz Kuhn: The Golden Lotus by Clement Egerton." *Isis* 35 (4): 344–346.

Cristafulli, Edoardo. 2002. "The Quest for an Eclectic Methodology of Translation Description." In *Crosscultural Transgressions: Research Models in Translation Studies II (Historical and Ideological Issues)*, edited by Theo Hermans, 26–42. Manchester: St. Jerome.

Davis, Walter W. 1983. "China, the Confucian Ideal, and the European Age of Enlightenment." *Journal of the History of Ideas* 44 (4): 523–548.

Dawson, Raymond. 1964. *The Legacy of China*. Oxford: Clarendon Press.

de Gruchy, John Walter. 2003. *Orienting Arthur Waley: Japonism, Orientalism, and the Creation of Japanese Literature in English*. Honolulu: University of Hawai'i Press.

Drury, Annmarie. 2015. *Translation as Transformation in Victorian Poetry*. Cambridge: Cambridge University Press.

Eagleton, Terry. 1996. *Literary Theory: An Introduction*. Oxford and Malden: Blackwell Publishing.

Egerton, Clement. (1909) 2012. *A Handbook of Church Music*. London: Forgotten Books.

Egerton, Clement. 1914. *The Future of Education*. London: G. Bell and Sons, Ltd.

Egerton, Clement. 1939. *African Majesty: A Record of Refuge at the Court of the King of Bangantse in the French Cameroons*. New York: Scribners.

Egerton, Clement. 1939. *The Golden Lotus*. 4 vols. London: George Routledge and Sons, Ltd.

Emmerich, Karen. 2017. *Literary Translation and the Making of Originals*. New York and London: Bloomsbury Academic.

Endicott, Stephen Lyon. 1975. *Diplomacy and Enterprise: British China Policy, 1933–1937*. Manchester: Manchester University Press.

Eoyang, Eugene Chen, and Lin Yaofu. 1995. *Translating Chinese Literature*. Bloomington and Indianapolis: Indiana University Press.

Fan, Shengyu. 2022. *The Translator's Mirror for the Romantic: Cao Xueqin's Dream and David Hawkes' Stone*. London: Routledge.

Fiske, Shanyn. 2011. "Orientalism Reconsidered: China and the Chinese in Nineteenth-Century Literature and Victorian Studies." *Literature Compass* 8 (4): 214–226.

Fitzgerald, Penelope. 1982. "Sonata for Second Fiddle." *London Review of Books*, October 7.

Foucault, Michel. 1977. *Language, Counter-Memory, Practice.* Ithaca: Cornell University Press.

Fowler, Edward. 1992. "Rendering Words, Traversing Cultures: On the Art and Politics of Translating Modern Japanese Fiction." *Journal of Japanese studies* 18 (1): 1–44.

France, Peter, ed. 2000. *The Oxford Guide to Literature in English Translation.* Oxford: Oxford University Press.

Gadamer, Hans- Georg. 2003. *Truth and Method.* New York and London: Continuum.

Genette, Gérard. 1997. *Paratexts: Thresholds of Interpretation.* Cambridge: Cambridge University Press.

George, Theodore. 2022. "Gadamer on the Politics of Translation." In *The Gadamerian Mind*, edited by Theodore George and Gert-Jan van der Heiden, 155–164. London: Routledge.

Gerber, Leah, and Lintao Qi. 2020. *A Century of Chinese Literature in Translation (1919– 2019).* London: Routledge.

Giles, Herbert Allen. 1901. *A History of Chinese Literature.* New York and London: D. Appleton Century Company.

Giles, Lionel. 1940. "The Golden Lotus. A translation, from the Chinese original, of the novel, Chin P'ing Mei. By Clement Egerton. 9× 6, 4 vols. London: G. Routledge, 1939. Vol I, pp. xvii+ 387; Vol. II, pp. v+ 376; Vol. III, pp. v+ 385; Vol. IV, pp. v+ 375. £ 4 4s. the set. Chin P'ing Mei. The adventurous history of Hsi Men and his six wives. (Translated by Bernard Miall from the abridged German version by Franz Kuhn.) With an introduction by Arthur Waley. 9× 6, pp. xxii+ 852. London: John Lane, The Bodley Head, 1939. 25s." *Journal of the Royal Asiatic Society* 72 (4): 368–371.

Ginsburgh, Victor, Shlomo Weber, and Sheila Weyers. 2011. "The Economics of Literary Translation: Some Theory and Evidence." *Poetics* 39: 228–246.

Gopnik, Adam. 2015. "Why an Imperfect Version of Proust Is a Classic in English." *The New Yorker*, March 30.

Gragnolati, Maneule. 2017. "Without Hierarchy: Diffraction, Performance, and Re-writing as Kippbild in Dante's Vita nova." In *Renaissance Rewritings*, edited by Helmut Pfeiffer, Irene Fantappiè, and Tobias Roth, 9–24. Berlin: Walter de Gruyter GmbH.

Grandy, Christine. 2016. *Heroes and Happy Endings: Class, Gender, and Nation in Popular Film and Fiction in Interwar Britain.* Manchester: Manchester University Press.

Gu, Ming Dong. 2004. "Brocade of Human Desires: The Poetics of Weaving in the Jin Ping Mei and Traditional Commentaries." *The Journal of Asian Studies* 63 (2): 333–356.

Gu, Ming Dong. 2006. *Chinese Theories of Fiction.* Albany: SUNY Press.

Gunn Jr., Edward Mansfield. 2009. "Lao She." In *Encyclopedia of Modern China*, edited by David Pong, 433–435. Detroit, MI: Charles Scribner's Sons.

Hanan, Patrick. 1961. "A Landmark of the Chinese Novel." *University of Toronto Quarterly* 30 (3): 325–335.

Hanan, Patrick. 1962. "The Text of the Jin Ping Mei." *Asia Major* 9 (1): 1–57.

Hanan, Patrick. 1963. "Sources of the Jin Ping Mei." *Asia Major* 10 (1): 23–67.

Hardie, Alison. 1994. "Dirty Ming Soap Opera." *Far Eastern Economic Review* 42: 1-2.

Hawkes, David. 1964. "Chinese Poetry and The English Reader." In *The Legacy of China*, edited by Raymond Dawson, 90–115. London: Oxford University Press.

Hawkes, David. 1970. "From the Chinese." In *Madly Singing in the Mountains: An Appreciation and Anthology of Arthur Waley*, edited by Ivan Morris, 45–51. London: George Allen and Unwin Ltd.

Hawkes, David. 2000. *The Story of the Stone: A Translator's Notebooks.* Hong Kong: Center for Literature and Translation, Lingnan University.

Hayot, Eric. 1999. "Critical Dreams: Orientalism, Modernism, and the Meaning of Pound's China." *Twentieth Century Literature* 45 (4): 511–533.

Hayot, Eric. 2012. *Chinese Dreams: Pound, Brecht, Tel Quel.* Ann Arbor: The University of Michigan Press.

Hayot, Eric, Haun Saussy, and Steven G. Yao. 2008. *Sinographies: Writing China.* Minneapolis: University of Minnesota Press.

Hegel, Robert E. 1998. *Reading Illustrated Fiction in Late Imperial China.* Stanford: Stanford University Press.

Hegel, Robert. E. 2011. "Introduction to The Golden Lotus." In *The Golden Lotus*, translated by Clement Egerton, 5–21. North Clarendon: Tuttle Publishing.

Henig, Suzanne. 1974. "The Bloomsbury Group and Non-Western Literature." *Journal of South Asian Literature* 10 (1): 73–82.

Hermans, Theo. 1999. *Translation in Systems: Descriptive and System-Oriented Approaches Explained.* Manchester: St. Jerome.

Hermans, Theo. 2002. *Crosscultural Transgressions.* Manchester: St. Jerome.

Hermans, Theo. 2007. "Literary Translation." In *A Companion to Translation Studies*, edited by Piotr Kuhiwczak, and Karin Littau, 77–91. Clevedon: Multilingual Matters.

Hightower, James Robert. 1953. "Chinese Literature in the Context of World Literature." *Comparative Literature* 5 (2): 117–124.

Hill, Michael Gibbs. 2013. *Lin Shu, Inc. Translation and the Making of Modern Chinese Culture.* New York: Oxford University Press.

Horner, Charles. 1994. "The Bad Earth-The Plum in the Golden Vase, or Chin P'ing Mei." *Commentary* 98 (4): 71.

Huber, Rosario. 2015. "Sinology on the Edge: Borges's Reviews of Chinese Literature (1937–1942)." *Variaciones Borges* 39: 81–101.

Hsia, Adrian. 1998. *The Vision of China in the English Literature of the Seventeenth and Eighteenth Centuries.* Hong Kong: Chinese University Press.

Hsia, Chih-tsing. 1968. *The Classic Chinese Novel: A Critical Introduction.* New York: Columbia University Press.

Hu, King. 1978. "Lao She in England." *Renditions* 10: 46–52.

Hu, Siao-Chin. 2004. "In the Name of Correctness: Ding Yaokang's Xu Jin Ping Mei as a Reading of Jin Ping Mei." In *Snakes' Legs: Sequels, Continuations, Rewritings, and Chinese Fiction*, edited by Martin W. Huang, 75–97. Honolulu: University of Hawai'i Press.

Huang, Martin W. 2001. *Desire and Fictional Narrative in Late Imperial China.* Cambridge, MA: Harvard University Press.

Huo Songlin 霍松林. 1988. *Zhongguo gudian xiaoshuo liuda mingzhu jianshang cidian* 中國古典小說六大名著鑒賞辭典 (Anatomy of Six Chinese Classical Novels). Xi'an: Huayue wenyi chubanshe.

Jaivin, Linda. 2021. *The Shortest History of China.* Carlton: Black Inc.

James, Robert. 2013. *Popular Culture and Working-class Taste in Britain, 1930-39: A Round of Cheap Diversions?* Manchester: Manchester University Press.

Johns, Francis A. 1968. *A Bibliography of Arthur Waley.* New Brunswick, NJ: Rutgers University Press.

Johns, Francis A. 1983. "Manifestations of Arthur Waley: Some Bibliographical and Other Notes." *British Library Journal* 9 (2): 171–184.

Kao, George. 1980. *Two Writers and the Cultural Revolution: Lao She and Chen Jo-hsi.* Hong Kong: The Chinese University Press.

Kenner, Hugh. 1971. *The Pound Era.* Berkeley: University of California Press.

Kitson, Peter J. 2013. *Forging Romantic China: Sino-British Cultural Exchanges 1760–1840*. Cambridge: Cambridge University Press.

Knechtges, David R. 1975. "The Golden Lotus by Clement Egerton." *Journal of the American Oriental Society* 95 (2): 359.

Kristal, Efraín. 2002. *Invisible Work: Borges and Translation*. Nashville: Vanderbilt University Press.

Kristal, Efraín. 2023. "Jorge Luis Borges's Theory and Practice of Translation." In *The Routledge Handbook of Latin American Literary Translation*, edited by Delfina Cabrera, and Denise Kripper, 177–192. London and New York: Routledge.

Lai, Ming. 1964. *A History of Chinese Literature*. London: Cassell.

Lambert, Jose. 1992. "The Cultural Component Reconsidered." In *Translation Studies: An Interdiscipline*, edited by Mary Snell-Hornby, Franz Pöchhacker, and Klaus Kaindl,17–26. Amsterdam: John Benjamins.

Larsen, Svend Erik. 2017. *Literature and the Experience of Globalization*. London: Bloomsbury Academic.

Lathbury, Roger. 2008. "Pound, Ezra." In *Encyclopedia of American Literature: 1607 to the Present*, edited by Marshall Boswell, and Carl Rollyson, 897–901. New York: Infobase Publishing.

Laurence, Patricia. 2013. *Lily Briscoe's Chinese Eyes: Bloomsbury, Modernism, and China*. Columbia: University of South Carolina Press.

Lefevere, André. 1999. "Composing the Other." In *Postcolonial Translation: Theory and Practice*, edited by Susan Bassnett, and Harish Trivedi, 75–94. London: Routledge.

Lefevere, André. 2000. "Mother Courage's Cucumbers: Text, System and Refraction in a Theory of Translation." In *The Translation Studies Reader*, edited by Lawrence Venuti, 468–488. London: Routledge.

Lehner, Georg. 2011. *China in European Encyclopaedias, 1700–1850*. Leiden: Brill.

Li, Kay. 2016. *Bernard Shaw's Bridges to Chinese Culture*. Switzerland: Springer Nature.

Lin, Hsiu-ling. 2001. "Reconciling Bloomsbury's Aesthetics of Formalism with the Politics of Anti-Imperialism: Roger Fry's and Clive Bell's Interpretations of Chinese Art." *Concentric: Studies in English Literature and Linguistics* 27 (1): 149–190.

Liu, Wu-chi.1966. *An Introduction of Chinese Literature*. Bloomington: Indiana University Press.

Liu, Xin. 2023. *Anglo-Chinese Encounters Before the Opium War*. London: Routledge.

Loison-Charles, Julie. 2022. *Vladimir Nabokov as an Author-Translator: Writing and Translating between Russian, English and French*. London: Bloomsbury Academic.

Lu, Tina. 2008. *Accidental Incest, Filial Cannibalism, and Other Peculiar Encounters in Late Imperial Chinese Literature*. Cambridge, MA: Harvard University Press.

Lu, Xun. (1923) 1959. *A Brief History of Chinese Fiction*. Translated by Yang Hsien-Yi, and Gladys Yang. Beijing: Foreign Languages Press.

Lung, Rachel. 2004. "The Oral Translator's 'Visibility': The Chinese Translation of *David Copperfield* by Lin Shu and Wei Yi." *TTR* 17 (2): 161–184.

Luo, Junjie. 2012. "The Plum in the Golden Vase or, Chin P'ing Mei, Volume 4: The Climax by David Roy." *Chinese Literature: Essays, Articles, Reviews* 34: 178–183.

Mair, Victor H. 2001. *The Columbia History of Chinese Literature*. New York: Columbia University Press.

Makos, Jeff. 1993. Roy Translates Controversial Chinese Classic. *The University of Chicago Chronicle* 13 (8): 1–4. http://chronicle.uchicago.edu/931209/roy.shtml

Mayers, William Frederick. 1867. "Chinese Works of Fiction. IV. Romantic Novels." *Notes and Queries on China and Japan* 1 (10): 137–139.

Mayers, William Frederick. 1867. "Chinese Works of Fiction. VI. Romantic Novels (concluded)." *Notes and Queries on China and Japan* 1 (12): 165–169.

Morris, Ivan, ed. 1970. *Madly Singing in the Mountains: An Appreciation and Anthology of Arthur Waley*. London: George Allen and Unwin Ltd.

Munday, Jeremy. 2001. *Introducing Translation Studies: Theories and Applications*. London: Routledge.

Munday, Jeremy. 2014. "Using Primary Sources to Produce a Microhistory of Translation and Translators: Theoretical and Methodological Concerns." *The Translator* 20 (1): 64–80.

Mungello, David E. 2013. *The Great Encounter of China and the West, 1500–1800*. Lanham and New York: Rowman and Littlefield.

Ning, Zongyi, and Lu Derong. 1984. *The Art of Chinese Classical Novels*. Tianjin: Nankai University Press.

Nylan, Michael. 2013. "Arthur Waley and Li Zehou: Two Aesthetes Translating." *Art in Translation* 5 (2):165–182.

Plaks, Andrew H. 1987. *The Four Masterworks of the Ming Novel: Ssu Ta Ch'i-Shu*. Princeton, N.J: Princeton University Press.

Plomer, William. 1939. "The Golden Lotus. Translated by Clement Egerton. Four Vols." *The Spectator*, August 11.

Pong, David, and Danke K. Li. 2009. *Encyclopedia of Modern China*. Detroit, Mich: Charles Scribner's Sons.

Porter, David. 2010. *The Chinese Taste in Eighteenth-Century England*. Cambridge: Cambridge University Press.

Prado-Fonts, Carles. 2014. "The Anxiety of Fiction: Reexamining Lao She's Early Novels." *Modern Chinese Literature and Culture* 26 (2): 177–215.

Purdy, Daniel Leonhard. 2021. *Chinese Sympathies*. Ithaca and London: Cornell University Press.

Putin, Jennifer. 1995. "The Plum in the Golden Vase or, Chin P'ing Mei Vol. I. The gathering. Translated by David Tod Roy. (Princeton Library of Asian Translations.) pp. civ. 610, 40 illus. Princeton, NJ, Princeton University Press, 1993. US $39.95." *Journal of the Royal Asiatic Society* 5 (1): 156–157.

Qi, Lintao. 2016. "The Plum in the Golden Vase or, Chin P'ing Mei, Volume 5: The Dissolution by David Tod Roy." *Chinese Literature: Essays, Articles, Reviews* 38: 214–218.

Qi, Lintao. 2018. *Jin Ping Mei English Translations: Texts, Paratexts, and Contexts*. London: Routledge.

Qian, Zhaoming. 1993. "Ezra Pound's Encounter with Wang Wei: Toward the 'Ideogrammic Method' of The Cantos." *Twentieth Century Literature* 39 (3): 266–282.

Qian, Zhaoming. 1995. *Orientalism and Modernism: The Legacy of China in Pound and Williams*. Durham: Duke University Press.

Qian, Zhaoming. 2000. "Pound and Chinese Art in the 'British Museum Era'." In *Ezra Pound and Poetic Influence*, edited by Helen M. Dennis, 100–112. Amsterdam: Rodopi.

Qian, Zhaoming. 2003. *Ezra Pound and China*. Ann Arbor: The University of Michigan Press.

Qian, Zhaoming. 2003. *The Modernist Response to Chinese Art: Pound, Moore, Stevens*. Charlottesville: University of Virginia Press.

Qian, Zhaoming. 2017. *East-West Exchange and Late Modernism: Williams, Moore, Pound*. Charlottesville and London: University of Virginia Press.

Qian, Zhongshu. 1940. "China in the English Literature of the Seventeenth Century." *Quarterly Bulletin of Chinese Bibliography* 1: 351–384.

Qian, Zhongshu. 1941. "China in the English Literature of the Eighteenth Century (II)" *Quarterly Bulletin of Chinese Bibliography* 2: 113–152.

Qian, Zhongshu. 1981. *Lin Shu's Translation*. Beijing: The Commercial Press.

Qian, Zhongshu, and Duncan Campbell. 2014. *Patchwork: Seven Essays on Art and Literature*. Amsterdam: Brill.

Radford, Andrew. 2012. "The Plum in the Golden Vase or Chin P'ing Mei, Volume 4: The Climax. Translate by David Tod Roy." *Translation and Literature* 21 (2): 251–255.

Riggs, Thomas. 2013. "The Cantos." In *The Literature of Propaganda*. Gale. https://go.openathens.net/redirector/wgtn.ac.nz?url=https%3A%2F%2Fsearch.credoreference.com%2Fcontent%2Fentry%2Fgalelp%2Fthe_cantos%2F0%3FinstitutionId%3D5378

Rizzo, Christopher. 2011. "Pound, Ezra." In *The Encyclopedia of Literary and Cultural Theory*, edited by Michael Ryan, 396–398. New York: John Wiley & Sons, Inc.

Rojas, Carlos, and Andrea Bachner, eds. 2016. *The Oxford Handbook of Modern Chinese Literatures*. New York: Oxford University Press.

Rolston, David L. 1997. *Traditional Chinese Fiction and Fiction Commentary: Reading and Writing Between the Lines*. Stanford: Stanford University Press.

Roy, David T. 1993. *The Plum in the Golden Vase or, Chin P'ing Mei* (vol. 1). Princeton, NJ: Princeton University Press.

Roy, David T. 1998. "The Use of Songs as a Means of Self-Expression and Self-Characterization in the Chin P'ing Mei." *Chinese Literature: Essays, Articles, Reviews* 20: 101–126.

Roy, David T. 2013. "A Lifetime Fascination." *TABLEAU*, August.

Ruan, Jiening, Zhang Jie, and Cynthia B. Leung. 2016. *Chinese Language Education in the United States*. Singapore: Springer.

Rudolph, Jennifer, and Michael Szonyi, eds. 2018. *The China Questions: Critical Insights into a Rising Power*. Cambridge, Mass: Harvard University Press.

Saldanha, Gabriela, and Sharon O'Brien. 2014. *Research Methodologies in Translation Studies*. London: Routledge.

Saur, Pamela S. 1998. "The Place of Asian Literature in Translation in American Universities." *CLA Journal* 41 (3): 349–364.

Schafer, Edward H. 1971. "Reviewed Work(s): Madly Singing in the Mountains. An Anthology of Arthur Waley." *Pacific Affairs* 44 (1):117–118.

Schuessler, Jennifer. 2013. "An Old Chinese Novel Is Racy Reading Still." *New York Times*, November 19.

Scott, Mary Elizabeth. 1989. "Azure from Indigo: Honglou Meng's Debt to Jin Ping Mei." PhD Diss., Princeton University.

Shang, Wei. 2005. "The Making of the Everyday World: Jin Ping Mei Cihua and Encyclopedias for Daily Use." In *Dynastic Crisis and Cultural Innovation*, edited by Wang David Der-wei, and Shang Wei, 63–92. Cambridge, MA: Harvard University Press.

Shen Defu 沈德符. 1958. *Wanli yehuo bian* 萬曆野獲編 (Historical Materials on Ming Wanli Reign Period). Beijing: Zhonghua shuju.

Shinobu, Ono. 1963. "Chin P'ing Mei: A Critical Study." *Acta Asiatica* 5: 76–89.

Simon, Walter. 1967. "Obituary: Arthur Waley." *Bulletin of the School of Oriental and African Studies* 30 (1): 268–271.

Special Collections, Library of the University of Chicago, The David Tod Roy Archive.

Special Collections, University of Reading, Routledge & Kegan Paul Archive.

Spence, Jonathan D. 1984. *The Memory Palace of Matteo Ricci*. New York: Viking Penguin.

Spence, Jonathan D. 1992. *Chinese Roundabout: Essays in History and Culture*. New York: Norton.

Spence, Jonathan D. 1994. "Remembrance of Ming's Past." *The New York Review of Books*, June 23.

Steiner, George, ed. 1966. *The Penguin Book of Modern Verse Translation*. Harmondsworth: Penguin.

Steiner, George.1975. *After Babel: Aspects of Language and Translation*. London: Oxford University Press.

Tahir Gurcağlar, Şehnaz. 2002. "What Texts Don't Tell: The Use of Paratexts in Translation Research." In *Crosscultural Transgressions: Research Models in Translation Studies II (Historical and Ideological Issues)*, edited by Theo Hermans, 44–60. Manchester: St Jerome.

Teele, Roy E. 1969. "A Bibliography of Arthur Waley by Francis A. Johns." *Books Abroad* 43 (3): 367–368.

Thorpe, Ashley. 2016. *Performing China on the London Stage: Chinese Opera and Global Power, 1759–2008*. London: Palgrave Macmillan.

Tian, Xiaofei. 2002. "A Preliminary Comparison of the Two Recensions of 'Jinpingmei'." *Harvard Journal of Asiatic Studies* 62 (2): 347–388.

Toury, Gideon. 1995. *Descriptive Translation Studies and Beyond*. Amsterdam: John Benjamins.

Tymoczko, Maria. 2007. *Enlarging Translation, Empowering Translators*. Manchester: St Jerome.

Venuti, Lawrence. 1998. *The Scandals of Translation: Towards an Ethics of Difference*. London and New York: Routledge.

Vohra, Ranbir. 1974. *Lao She and the Chinese Revolution*. Cambridge, MA. Harvard University Press.

Waisman, Sergio. 2005. *Borges and Translation: The Irreverence of the Periphery*. Lewisburg: Bucknell University Press.

Waley, Alison. 1982. *A Half of Two Lives*. London: Weidenfeld.

Wang Rumei 王汝梅. 2014. *Jiedu Jin Ping Mei* 解讀金瓶梅 (Interpreting *Jin Ping Mei*). Changchun: Shidai wenyi chubanshe.

Wang Rumei 王汝梅. 2015. *Jin Ping Mei banben shi* 金瓶梅版本史 (A Survey of *Jin Ping Mei*'s Recensions). Jinan: Qilu shushe.

Wang, Youqin, and Stacy Mosher. 2023. *Victims of the Cultural Revolution: Testimonies of China's Tragedy*. London: Oneworld Academic.

Williams, Louise Blakeney. 2002. *Modernism and the Ideology of History*. Cambridge: Cambridge University Press.

Wilson, Alexandra. 2019. *Opera in the Jazz Age: Cultural Politics in 1920s Britain*. Oxford: Oxford University Press.

Witchard, Anne. 2012. *Lao She in London*. Hong Kong: Hong Kong University Press.

Witchard, Anne. 2015. *British Modernism and Chinoiserie*. Edinburgh: Edinburgh University Press.

Wong, Laurence K. P. 2014. *Dreaming across Languages and Cultures: A Study of the Literary Translations of the Hong Lou Meng*. Newcastle: Cambridge Scholars Publishing.

Woodsworth, Judith. 2017. *Telling the Story of Translation: Writers Who Translate*. London and New York: Bloomsbury Academic.

Woodsworth, Judith. 2018. "Writers as Translators." In *Routledge Handbook of Literary Translation*, edited by Kelly Washbourne, and Ben van Wyke, 369–381. London: Routledge.

Woolf, Virginia. 2002. *The Common Reader*. Boston: Mariner Books.

Wu Gan 吳敢. 2009. *Zhang Zhupo yu Jin Ping Mei yanjiu* 張竹坡與金瓶梅研究 (Zhang Zhupo and *Jin Ping Mei* Studies). Beijing: Wenwu chubanshe.

Wu, Yenna. 1986. "Marriage Destinies to Awaken the World: A Literary Study of 'Xingshi Yiyuan Zhuan'." PhD Diss., Harvard University.

Xiao, Shuangjin. 2022. "Paratextual Framing for Translating and Disseminating the Ming Novel *Jin Ping Mei* in the Anglophone World." *International Journal of Translation and Interpretation Studies* 2 (2): 59–73.

Xiao Xiao Sheng of Lanling 蘭陵笑笑生. 1963. *Jin Ping Mei cihua* (facsimile edition) 金瓶梅詞話. Fukuoka: Daian Co., Ltd.

Xiao Xiao Sheng of Lanling 蘭陵笑笑生. 2003. *Xinke xiuxiang piping Jin Ping Mei* 新刻繡像批評金瓶梅. Singapore: South Ocean Publishing.

Xie, Ming. 2021. *Ezra Pound and the Appropriation of Chinese Poetry: Cathay, Translation, and Imagism*. New York: Routledge.

Xie, Yaqiong. 2018. "G. L. Dickinson and China: Behind the Mask of John Chinaman." *ELT* 61 (4): 496–519.

Yang, Shuhui. 2008. "The Plum in the Golden Vase or, Chin P'ing Mei, Volume Three: The Aphrodisiac by David Tod Roy." *Chinese Literature: Essays, Articles, Reviews* 30: 212–218.

Yang, Winston L. Y., Peter Li, and Nathan K. Mao. 1978. *Classical Chinese Fiction: A Guide to its Study and Appreciation*. Boston: G. K. Hall Publishers.

Yang, Winston L.Y., and Curtis P. Adkins. 2002. Critical Essays on Chinese Fiction. Hong Kong: The Chinese University Press.

Yao, Steven G. 2010. *Foreign Accents: Chinese American Verse from Exclusion to Postethnicity*. New York: Oxford University Press.

Yao, Steven G. 2013. "Translation Studies and Modernism." In *A Handbook of Modernism Studies*, edited by Jean-Michel Rabate, 209–224. Chichester: John Wiley & Sons Ltd.

Ye, Gongping. 2019. "Pearl Buck's Three Chinese Collaborators." Wenhuibao, January 18.

Ye, Yang. 2000. "Jin Ping Mei 16th Century." In *Encyclopedia of Literary Translation into English, Volume 1*, edited by Olive Classe, 732–734. London and Chicago: Fitzroy Dearborn Publishers.

Yeh, Diana. 2014. *The Happy Hsiungs: Performing China and the Struggle for Modernity*. Hong Kong: Hong Kong University Press.

Yeh, Diana. 2015. "Staging China, Excising the Chinese: Lady Precious Stream and the Darker Side of Chinoiserie." In *British Modernism and Chinoiserie* , edited by Anne Witchard, 177–199. Edinburgh: Edinburgh University Press.

Yeh, Michelle. 2016. "Inventing China: The American Tradition of Translating Chinese Poetry." In *Reading the Past Across Space and Time: Receptions and World Literature*, edited by Brenda Deen Schildgen, and Ralph Hexter, 285–296. New York: Palgrave Macmillan.

Yu, Ying-shih. 2021. *The Religious Ethic and Mercantile Spirit in Early Modern China*. Translated by Yim- tze Kwong. New York: Columbia University Press.

Zeitlin, Judith. 2007. "Xiaoshuo." In *The Novel, Volume 1: History, Geography, and Culture*, edited by Franco Moretti, 249–261. Princeton, NJ: Princeton University Press.

Zeng Qingyu 曾慶雨 and Xu Jianping 許建平. 2000. *Jin Ping Mei zhong de nuren* 金瓶梅中的女人 (Women in *Jin Ping Mei*). Kunming: Yunnan University Press.

Zhan, Chunhua. 2018. "Hermann Hesse's Concept of World Literature and His Critique on Chinese Literature." *Neohelicon* 45 (1): 281–300.

Zhang Guixing 張桂興. 2010. *Lao She lunji* 老舍論集 (Collected Essays on Lao She). Beijing: Renmin chubanshe.

Zhang, Chunjie. 2008. "From Sinophilia to Sinophobia: China, History, and Recognition." *Colloquia Germanica* 41 (2): 97–110.

Zhang, Longxi. 1988. "The Myth of the Other: China in the Eyes of the West." *Critical Inquiry* 15 (1): 108–131.

Zhang, Longxi. 1998. *Mighty Opposites: From Dichotomies to Differences in the Comparative Study of China*. Stanford: Stanford University Press.

Zhang, Longxi. 2023. *A History of Chinese Literature*. New York: Routledge.

Zhang Man 張曼 2016. *Lao She wenxue fanyi yanjiu* 老舍文學翻譯研究 (Lao She's Literary Translation Practice). Shanghai: Shanghai Jiaotong University Press.

Zhang, Xiping. 2022. *A Study on the Influence of Ancient Chinese Cultural Classics Abroad in the Twentieth Century*. Singapore: Springer.

Zheng, Da. 2010. *Chiang Yee: The Silent Traveler from the East: A Cultural Biography*. Piscataway: Rutgers University Press.

Zheng Zhengduo 鄭振鐸. 2005. *Xidi shuhua* 西諦書話 (Selected Essays of Zheng Xidi). Shanghai: Sanlian Bookstore.

Zhou Juntao 周鈞韜. 2010. Jin Ping Mei yanjiu wenji 金瓶梅研究文集 (Collected Essays on Jin Ping Mei). Changchun: Jilin renmin chubanshe.

Zhou Zhongming 周中明 and Wu Jiarong 吳家榮. 2012. *Xiaoshuo shihua*/小說史話 (A Brief History of the Novel in China). Beijing: Social Sciences Academy Press.

Zhu Yixuan 朱一玄. 2002. *Jin Ping Mei ziliao huibian* 金瓶梅資料彙編 (Collected Materials on *Jin Ping Mei*). Tianjin: Nankai University Press.

2 Late Ming (Un)veiled

Cultural Representations within Translational and Transnational Contexts

2.1 Introduction

One of the most fascinating aspects of *Jin Ping Mei* is that it offers unique scope for getting acquainted with late Ming culture and history. Infused with rich philosophical, humanistic, and cultural values, *Jin Ping Mei* has evoked polemical reactions and become the subject of rigorous scholarship. Widely regarded as an encyclopedia of late Ming society, it is celebrated for its subtle and realistic delineation of social and cultural detail (Shang 2005, 63). The quotidian minutiae delineated in the novel are culturally verisimilitudinous and historically contingent, contributing to the novel's prodigious appeal that endures to this day. The English translations of *Jin Ping Mei* provide an illuminating case for exploring how "Western cultures translated non-Western cultures into Western categories" (Lefevere 1999, 77). A fruitful avenue for investigation lies in examining how the representation of late Ming culture, namely the encyclopedic culturemes in *Jin Ping Mei*, is treated in English translations.

Culturemes in literary prose are textual units, of any length, that allude to historical and cultural phenomena and facts with few or no equivalents in other languages (Rura 2015, 258). Rooted in the cultural and historical milieu where a text emerges, these elements embody the values and essence of a civilization. In *Jin Ping Mei*, culturemes span a wide range of areas, including appellations, slang, cuisine, antiques, rituals, customs, medicine, religions, and more. While they are axiomatic and self-explanatory for source readers, they may appear disconcertingly unfamiliar and undecipherable to those from a completely different cultural background. This is primarily because, according to the Sapir/Whorf hypothesis, different cultural communities have different ways of representing, structuring, and interpreting social reality (Qvale 2003, 207). Translating involves more than just transferring between two languages. It is, fundamentally, a transfer from one culture to another (Snell-Hornby 1995, 40). The treatment of culturemes in narrative prose translation goes beyond facilitating communication between the text and the reader; it significantly influences the reader's identification with the story and characters. Since translators are cultural "mediators between two parties for whom mutual communication might otherwise be problematic" (Hatim and Mason 1990, 223), it would be productive to investigate how the novel's cultural representations

DOI: 10.4324/9781003472674-2

evolve when transposed to another cultural territory through translation. To date, the English translations by Egerton and Roy have received limited attention from translation studies scholars regarding the translation of the wide variety of culturemes in *Jin Ping Mei*. The present chapter attempts a systematic examination of this important area to contribute to a comprehensive and nuanced understanding of how culturemes are treated in the two translations and the multiple causality behind the treatment.

The chapter undertakes a descriptive and comparative analysis of the two translations of *Jin Ping Mei*, focusing on the treatment of culturemes. The rationale for this endeavor lies in the novel's encyclopedic knowledge of various aspects of late Ming culture, presenting a potential source of translational challenges. The overarching question guiding this exploration is: How does the rich tapestry of culturemes in *Jin Ping Mei* fare in the two translations, and what are the main factors shaping the resultant translations. To answer this question, the chapter examines how important culturemes are treated in the target texts, identifies key procedures and strategies employed by the translators, and evaluate the extent to which each translator adopts domesticating or foreignizing approaches and the causality behind their choices? Engaging with these questions, the chapter draws on theoretical insights and analytical tools derived from translation studies (for example, Venuti's concepts of domestication and foreignization) and cultural studies. The aim is to offer a panoramic view of the intricate operations involved in translating *Jin Ping Mei*'s representation of Ming culture for English-speaking readers at different historical moments.

In what follows, the chapter first elaborates on relevant theoretical concepts and outlines the analytical procedures employed, serving as a foundation for the subsequent discussion. It then presents a fine-grained comparative analysis of micro-level translational choices regarding the treatment of various culturemes in the two translations. This is followed by an additional quantitative statistical analysis. Subsequently, a detailed discussion of the research results follows, emphasizing the crucial factors shaping the translators' choices. Finally, the chapter presents some concluding remarks.

2.2 Theoretical Concepts and Analytical Methods Defined

This section begins by defining and categorizing culturemes and then sets out the analytical procedures to be used in subsequent analysis carried out in Section three.

2.2.1 Defining and Categorizing Culturemes

A discussion of translation inevitably involves addressing the issue of culture, as translation is essentially a communicative act between different cultural systems. Translating from one culture to another not only fulfills the needs of a target culture but also introduces new ideas, concepts, and facts to recipients, expanding their cultural horizons (Komissarov 1991, 46; Toury 1995, 28). The concept of culture is inherently abstract and has been variously defined by scholars from different fields.

W. H. Goodenough argues that "... culture consists of whatever it is one has to know or believe in order to operate in a manner acceptable to its members, and do so in any role that they accept for any one of themselves" (Wilss 1996, 87). Similarly, Peter Newmark describes culture as "the way of life and its manifestations that are peculiar to a community that uses a particular language as its means of expression" (1988, 94). According to Hans J. Vermeer, a culture encompasses "the entire setting of norms and conventions an individual as a member of his society must know in order to be 'like everybody' – or to be able to be different from everybody" (Nord 1997, 32). However, J. R. McQuilkin's definition is more relevant: "Culture refers to the total way of life of particular groups of people. It includes everything that a group of people think, say, do, and make – their customs, language, material artefacts and shared systems of attitudes and feelings" (1980, 113). McQuilkin's wide-ranging conceptualization provides a useful starting point for discussing the interlingual transfer of culturemes in *Jin Ping Mei*.

Over the last three decades, ongoing debates in translation studies have centered on the transfer of cultural references. Scholars, such as Andrew Chesterman and Emma Wagner (2002, 18), note that translation theory has predominantly focused on the translation of classical literary texts. This focus stems from the perception that translating such texts is deemed "Culturally Important" due to their traditionally high status. Classical literary texts are rich with culture-bound concepts intricately woven into the source culture. These elements bear the strong imprint of national and regional identity, forming an integral part of the literary repertoire (Schwartz, 2007). They reflect the values and dynamics of a specific culture, manifesting differences between languages and cultures. Consequently, the translation of these texts necessitates cross-cultural mediation and negotiation throughout the process.

In the realm of translation studies, various terms are used to denote cultural references, including "culture-specific items," "culturemes," "realia," "culture-specific references," and "extralinguistic cultural references" (Aixelà 1996; Nord 1997; Davies 2003; Ranzato 2015; Pedersen 2007). This study, however, adopts the term "culturemes" as an umbrella term to avoid terminological confusion. Definitions of culturemes exhibit some variation, but they share common ground. J. F. Aixelà (1996, 57) posits that culturemes can pose translatorial challenges due to their nonexistence or differing values in the receiving culture. Aixelà defines culturemes as "those textually actualized items whose function and connotations in a source text involve a translation problem in their transference to a target text" (1996, 58). For Vermeer, a cultureme is "a social phenomenon of a culture X that is regarded as relevant by the members of this culture and, when compared with a corresponding social phenomenon in a culture Y, is found to be specific to culture X" (Nord 1997, 32). Similarly, David Katan defines culturemes as "formalized, socially, and juridically embedded phenomena that exist in a particular form or function in only one of the two cultures compared" (2009, 79). Jean-Pierre Mailhac (1996, 134) considers a cultureme, due to its distance from the target culture, as a cultural entity characterized by a high degree of opacity for the target reader, constituting a problem. Harald Martin Olk (2013, 346) identifies culturemes as names of objects or concepts in the original text that lack lexical equivalents, denotations, and connotations available in the translating culture. In literary texts, Lidia Rura (2015, 258) describes culturemes as textual units of any length alluding to historical and cultural phenomena and facts with few or no equivalents in other languages.

In this study, however, culturemes are defined uniquely to account for their diversity, complexity, and particularity inherent in the novel under scrutiny. Specifically, culturemes are understood as terms or expressions indicating objects, concepts, events, and themes unique to the lifestyle, culture, or social development of the Ming dynasty. They manifest a distinct regional, historical, or even stylistic essence, which remains unclear or totally unknown to most English-language audiences. Appreciating them requires a significant cognitive effort due to their sharp differences from familiar concepts. The translation of culturemes poses a challenge for translators, given the stark contrast in form and function of these elements between the cultures being compared (Katan 1999). Unsurprisingly, the handling of culturemes in translation has been acknowledged as one of the most challenging "cultural bumps" (Leppihalme 1997).

As a rule, culturemes can be categorized in different ways, and several translation studies scholars have developed taxonomies to distinguish various types. For example, Eugene Albert Nida (1964, 91) proposes five categories of culturemes that may lead to translational dilemmas: ecological culture, material culture, social culture, religious culture, and linguistic culture. Peter Newmark (1988, 96) similarly identifies five types of culturemes, including ecological culture, material culture, social culture, institutional culture, and gestures and habits. Hongwei Chen (1999) divides culturemes into three main groups: material culture, institutional culture, and mental culture. Certain overlapping or interweaving areas can be observed in these typologies. More recently, another interesting framework is offered by Stephan-Alexander Ditze (2006, 52), who groups cultural images in literary works into non-personal, transpersonal, and personal dimensions. An apparent disadvantage of Ditze's framework is that the three dimensions cannot be clearly defined. Thus, Nida's taxonomic framework is considered most relevant to this study, providing a clear guideline for categorizing the various culturemes present in *Jin Ping Mei*.

2.2.2 Corpus Design and Analytical Procedures

This subsection delineates the analytical methods utilized in this chapter. To address the proposed questions, a qualitative textual analysis is conducted. Due to space limitations, it is unfeasible to take account of all culturemes in *Jin Ping Mei*, given the novel's magnum opus status with one-hundred chapters. Therefore, the corpus under analysis includes only the most representative examples, randomly selected from the original text, based on the previously provided definition of culturemes. These selected instances are sufficient for observing translators' patterns in deploying specific translation procedures and strategies. These selected excerpts are meticulously compared against their English counterparts, with particular attention to translational shifts and their potential results. For ease of analysis, all selected samples, or "coupled pairs," in Toury's (1995, 70) terminology, are categorized according to the typology proposed by Nida (1964, 91). However, this typology is modified and adapted to suit the specificity of this study. The adapted framework (refer to Table 2.1) is deemed more relevant, as it can incorporate virtually all major types of culturemes present in *Jin Ping Mei*, allowing for a comprehensive translational analysis.

After singling out and categorizing culturemes, the next step involves classifying the specific procedures and strategies to describe translative solutions. However, these procedures and strategies, as proposed in previous studies (Díaz-Cintas and Remael 2007, 202; Aixelà 1996, 60), are adapted to suit the specificity of this study. The modified typology is illustrated in Table 2.2. Notably, the procedures are arranged along a continuum based on the paradigm of foreignization and domestication. Venuti (2017, xiii) suggests that these two approaches are not in dichotomy or binary opposition but exist along a continuum, determining the overall impact or tendency of a translation. This paradigm serves as a crucial theoretical underpinning for this chapter. It is worth noticing that Venuti associates domestication and foreignization with ethical and political agendas. However, this chapter does not aim to delve deeply into those

Table 2.1 Categorization of Culturemes in Jin Ping Mei

linguistic culturemes:	terms of address, appellations, colloquialisms, etc.
material culturemes:	food, drink, clothes, goods, instruments, etc.
social culturemes:	customs, festivals, rituals, organizations, etc.
medical culturemes:	traditional medicine, medical treatment, etc.
religious culturemes:	religious beliefs, values, names of deities, etc.
ecological culturemes:	landscape, flora and fauna, geography, etc.

Table 2.2 Typology of Procedures and Strategies for Rendering Culturemes (CRs) in *Jin Ping Mei*

Domestication (TT oriented)	Omission	CRs are ignored or deleted in the target text
	Substitution	CRs are replaced with target cultural items easier to be understood
	Paraphrase	using familiar terms to explain the original CRs
	Generalization	simplifying those complex CRs; using hypernym
	Literal translation	translating CRs verbatim or in a word-for-word way
	Explicitation	over-literal transfer; giving the full meaning of CRs;
Foreignization (ST oriented)	Calque	using notes
		inventing new lexical terms based on the source writing system
	Transliteration	Using the source pinyin system to represent CRs in the target text

aspects; instead, both foreignization and domestication are considered as translational strategies employed by translators. Specifically, domestication is viewed as aligning with Friedrich Schleiermacher's (1768–1834) methods of leaving the reader in peace, as much as possible, and moving the original author and text towards the reader. On the other hand, foreignization is deemed as aligning with Schleiermacher's approach of leaving the writer alone, as much as possible, and moving the target reader towards the original writer and text (Munday 2001, 146). In this study, domestication involves omission, substitution, paraphrasing, and generalization procedures, while foreignization entails literary translation, explicitation, calque, and transliteration (see Table 2.2).

The above classification of translation procedures and strategies presented in Table 2.2 aligns with the corpus of the present chapter. This alignment will be exemplified in the ensuing textual analysis and subsequent quantitative analysis.

2.3 Analysis of Culturemes in Translation

Building upon the analytical procedures established in the previous section, this section presents a qualitative textual analysis. To facilitate discussion, culturemes are marked in bold, with the source text abbreviated as ST and the target text as TT. Furthermore, TT1 indicates Egerton's version, while TT2 refers to Roy's translation. It's important to note that these abbreviations will be consistently used in the subsequent chapters. More than twenty sets of examples are systematically analyzed and discussed, each sequentially numbered. This ensures data diversity and variety for obtaining valid findings. The discussion begins with the category of linguistic culturemes.

2.3.1 Linguistic Culturemes

This subsection places special emphasis on linguistic culture, encompassing terms of address such as honorifics, self-abasing terms, and kinship terms, along with colloquialisms. Linguistic communities vary in how they structure reality, and the translation of linguistic culturemes calls for the application of different coping strategies due to the huge differences between Chinese and English. The following examples serve to illustrate the treatment of these elements in English renderings.

2.3.1.1 Appellations

Jin Ping Mei contains various forms of address used by characters on different occasions. These terms of address are culture-specific and historically determined, seldom appearing in modern Chinese. If translated unchanged, they are likely to interrupt the flow of comprehension. The treatment of these pedantic, old-fashioned appellations in translation may also influence the target reader's perception of the story and characters. Below, we discuss several illustrative instances.

Table 2.3 Honorifics and Self-abasing Terms

ST	TT1	TT2
第六個房下。甚是不好的重。如之奈何。[2] (Xiao 2003, chap. 61, 564)	"My sixth **wife**," he said, "is very ill. What can I do about it?" (Egerton 1939, vol. 3, 116)	"My sixth **consort** has become seriously ill. What am I to do about it?" (Roy 2011, vol. 4, 32)
倒是老拙。常出來看病。 (Xiao 2003, chap. 61, 565)	**I myself** have to go and see those patients… (Egerton 1939, vol. 3, 117)	**It is my aged self** who most often has to go out to examine the sick." (Roy 2011, vol. 4, 34)

Table 2.4 Honorifics and Self-abasing Terms

ST	TT1	TT2
西門慶謝道。學生生一豚犬。不足為賀。 (Xiao 2003, chap. 31, 280)	Hsi-men Ch'ing thanked them. "This ignorant fellow has but **a little dog**. The occasion is not worthy of such honor, … (Egerton 1939, vol. 2, 56)	Hsi-men Ch'ing expressed his gratitude, saying, "The fact that your pupil has been able to sire **a shoat or a whelp**: Is not worthy of congratulation. (Roy 2001, vol. 2, 239)

In Table 2.3, expressions such as "房下," and "老拙" in the ST are honorifics and self-abasing terms commonly used in premodern Chinese society. They are seldom used in modern Chinese writings. Faced with this reality, Charles Kwong claims that an appropriate strategy would be "to abide by the original's basic semantic meaning, keeping reductive or distorting interpretation of the text to a minimum, and letting the translated language generate its artistic chemistry" (Kwong 2011, 200). The term "房下" is used to address someone's wife and concubine while dealing with others (Bai 1991, 155). TT1 is clear for the reader, but TT2 has the word "consort" (designating the ruling monarch's wife or husband) for "房下," which might confuse the reader. Moreover, the literal rendition of "老拙" as "my aged self" in TT2 may appear unnatural and obscure to the reader. Due to cultural differences between Chinese and English, these obsolete appellations cannot find counterparts in the target language. The same is true of the next example.

In Table 2.4, the term "豚犬" denotes a young pig and dog. Here, it is used as a self-abasing term to refer to someone's own son. In premodern China, people used special appellations to address sons and daughters on formal occasions. In

Table 2.5 Honorifics and Self-abasing Terms

ST	TT1	TT2
親家。明日好歹下降寒舍。那裡久坐坐。(Xiao 2003, chap. 41, 366) 西門慶道。乾娘。你且來。(Xiao 2003, chap. 2, 27)	**"My dear relative,"** she said to Madam Ch'iao, "you must come to our poor house tomorrow." (Egerton 1939, vol. 2, 195) "Please come here, **Stepmother,"** Hsi-men said. ... (Egerton 1939, vol. 1, 44)	**Kinswoman,** tomorrow whatever you do, deign to drop in on our humble abode and visit with us for a while. (Roy 2006, vol. 3, 10) **"Godmother,"** said His-men Ch'ing, "come here. ... (Roy 1993, vol. 1, 55)

the ST, Ximen addresses his own son as "豚犬" while dealing with court officials. Comprehension of the implications of this term requires familiarity with premodern Chinese culture. TT1 has "a little dog" for "豚犬," which is fluent and readable for general readers. TT2 is simply a word-for-word transfer, using two archaic words, "a shoat" and "a whelp," to convey the denotative meaning of "豚犬." Moreover, the word "whelp" is a derogatory term, showing contempt for a youth or child in English. Hence, the difference between two cultures makes this mode of address difficult to transfer and literal transfer may sometimes be inaccessible to a common reader.

According to Eva Hung (1993), a common practice in Chinese culture is the use of kinship terms to address people outside the family. In Table 2.5, the term "親家" is one of the most culturally specific honorifics used to address the son-in-law's or daughter-in-law's parents in Chinese society. There is no English counterpart for the term because, oftentimes, names are used to address relatives in the English-speaking community. The term appears frequently considering the story of *Jin Ping Mei* is set in a polygamous household. In TT2, "親家" is translated verbatim as "Kinswoman," suggesting someone's female relative. It is generalized as "My dear relative" in TT1, which is intelligible and conforms to the target norms. The term "乾娘" is an honorific for senior women in premodern Chinese society; it is a polite form of address in this exchange (He 1990, 497). The woman Ximen Qing addresses is not his family member but a neighbor who is senior to Ximen. In TT1, "乾娘" is paraphrased as "Stepmother," a very familiar term, though not exactly accurate, for the target reader. Yet it is literally rendered as "Godmother" in TT2, which reveals the character relationship described in the novel, as "Godmother" refers to a woman who acts as an advisor or mentor to someone. In *Jin Ping Mei*, this godmother indeed offers many "suggestions" to Ximen.

In *Jin Ping Mei*, some pejorative epithets are used to convey ironic or satiric effect in the narrative. These terms are so culture-specific that they pose significant challenges for translation. In Table 2.6, the term "扒灰" suggests an illicit love

Table 2.6 Pejorative Terms

ST	TT1	TT2
認的他有名叫做陶扒八灰。 (Xiao 2003, chap. 33, 296)	… he had been given **a rude nickname** in consequence. (Egerton 1939, vol. 2, 83)	…recognized the oldster to be the notorious **Crudcrawler Tao**, … (Roy 2001, vol. 2, 279)

Table 2.7 Appellations and Labels for Females

ST	TT1	TT2
你家第五的秋胡戲。你娶他來家。多少時了。是女招的是後婚兒來。西門慶道。也是回頭人兒。 (Xiao 2003, chap. 23, 204)	"Was your **Fifth Lady** married before she came here?" she heard Wistaria say. "Yes," Hsi-men replied, "she is one of the **changeable kind**." (Egerton 1939, vol. 1, 325)	"How long is it since you married that fifth '**object of Ch'iu Hu's roving eye**' of yours? Was she a **virgin** when you married her, or had she been married before?" "She'd been **married before**," said His-men Ch'ing. (Roy 2001, vol. 2, 53)

affair between a man and his daughter-in-law in premodern Chinese society (Bai 1991, 383).

The appellation "陶扒八灰" in the ST signifies a person named Tao, who has an affair with his daughter-in-law. It is paraphrased as "a rude nickname" in TT1 for the sake of accessibility. In TT2, however, a coinage "Crudcrawler Tao," is introduced to express the original meaning, but it also produces a defamiliarizing effect for the reader. Further, an endnote is added to aid the reader's apprehension (Roy 2001, 545).

In *Jin Ping Mei*, one may encounter several special appellations or labels used to refer to different types of women. These are obsolete, out-of-the-way phrases and locutions, which pose significant challenges for interlingual transfer. As McQuilkin points out, "determining the meaning intended by another person is not always easy, and least of all when the original was given in another language and cultural setting" (1980, 113). Table 2.7 presents some typical examples.

In Table 2.7, the dialogue is colloquial and humorous. In the ST, "秋胡戲" is a historical allusion referring to a person named Qiu Hu who left home for long. On his way back home, he met a beautiful woman and flirted with her, only to realize that the woman was actually his wife (He 1990, 225). The term also suggests someone's wife; "回頭人" refers to remarried women; "女招" indicates an unmarried virgin (Wang 1988, 132; 36). All these references were colloquial of the Ming era, carrying sarcasm and pejorativeness that reflect the speaker's attitude in the exchange. In TT2, "秋胡戲" is transliterated as the "object of Ch'iu Hu's roving eye"; "女招" is replaced with "virgin"; and "回頭人" is paraphrased as "married before." Apparently, TT2 is constrained by excessive reverence for the ST to the extent that it exhibits an exotic touch. In comparison, TT1 provides a smooth and reductive version from which the two culturemes "秋胡戲" and "女招" are expurgated all together. The term "回頭人" is also paraphrased as "changeable kind." While a reductive version like TT1 may not be entirely faithful to the original, it refashions the past, capturing the ancient spirit of the original for present readers with high readability.

2.3.1.2 Slang and Colloquialisms

Jin Ping Mei is replete with slang and colloquialisms that were prevalent in the novelist's day. However, these linguistic elements may not be familiar to present-day readers, especially those from non-Sinophone culture. Cultural barriers exist if they are translated into English. The target audience may not be able to grasp the narrative if these linguistic elements are not treated appropriately in translation. Common sayings are typically anchored in a cultural tradition characterized by special morphological, syntactical, and lexical traits. As Christiane Nord (1997, 61) points out, structural differences in the lexical, syntactic, and suprasegmental features of different languages may pose crucial problems in translation. The following examples illustrate how translators address these challenges.

Table 2.8 contains popular sayings alluding to historical figures. The four-character expression "班馬之上" in the ST implies that someone's talent eclipses that of Ban Gu (or Pan Ku) 班固 (A.D. 32–92) and Sima Qian (or Ssu-ma Ch'ien) 司馬遷 (circa. 135 B.C.), both renowned historians and litterateurs in China's

Table 2.8 Slang and Colloquialisms

ST	TT1	TT2
他胷中才學。果然班馬之上。就是他人品。也孔孟之流。 (Xiao 2003, chap. 56, 507)	… but he is a learned man and will **stand comparison with P'an and Ssu-ma**. He is **a follower of Confucius**. (Egerton 1939, vol. 3, 34)	The talent and learning he has acquired actually make him **superior to Pan Ku or Ssu-ma Ch'ien**, while, as for his personal integrity, he is **in a class with Confucius and Mencius**. (Roy 2006, vol. 3, 387)
又有幾個服侍的小廝。也一個個都是標緻。龍陽的 (Xiao 2003, chap. 56, 509)	There were a host of beautiful maids there and several **good-looking boys**. (Egerton 1939, vol. 3, 36)	Moreover, there were also a number of page boys, each and every one of which was a **good-looking catamite**. (Roy 2006, vol. 3, 392)

Han dynasty (202 B.C.–A.D. 220). The elegant phrase "孔孟之流" involves two philosophers in ancient China: Confucius and Mencius. As for the English texts, TT1 restructures the original by trimming redundant material, resulting in a precise and natural translation for the benefit of the target reader. In contrast, TT2 preserves all cultural images, including even the stylistic features, building a bridge for English-language readers to access Chinese historical figures.

The reference "標緻龍陽" points to the Lord of Longyang 龍陽君, whose birth and death remains a mystery in history. This historical figure is first mentioned in the book *Zhanguo Ce* 戰國策 (Ode to Warring States). The Lord of Longyang held a prominent position in the State of Wei and was a homosexual partner of the King of Wei during China's Warring States period (770–B.C.476). His name became a byword for male homosexuals in imperial China and was linked to the "obsession for the cut sleeve" (Vitiello 2000, 229). To enhance intelligibility, TT1 attempts a

Table 2.9 Slang and Colloquialisms

ST	TT1	TT2
老婆道。嗔道恁恁久慣老成。 (Xiao 2003, chap. 23, 204)	"But how charming she is," Wistaria said, … (Egerton 1939, vol. 1, 325)	"No wonder she's such **a practiced old hand**," the woman said. … (Roy 2001, vol. 2, 54)
鄭愛香道因把貓兒的虎口內。火燒了兩醮。和他丁八著好一向了。這日只散走哩。 (Xiao 2003, chap. 32, 284)	"Yes," Zheng Perfume said, "and set fire to the tiger's mouth, and then the turtle broke with her." (Egerton 1939, vol. 2, 63)	"Because, in the course of his devotions, he burnt incense in two places on her tiger's mouth," said Cheng Ai-hsiang, "their affair has been '**a-nail-eighted**' for some time. Right now they're running loose." (Roy 2001, vol. 2, 249)
應伯爵一見戲道。怎的三個零布在那里來。 (Xiao 2003, chap. 32, 284)	Po-chüeh, as soon as he saw them, said, jokingly: "Where have you **three odd things** come from? … (Egerton 1939, vol. 2, 63)	No sooner did Ying Po-chueh spot them than he started to joke, saying, "Where did these **three sweethearts** of yours come from? … (Roy 2001, vol. 2, 250)
暗暗三兩成羣。背地講論。看他背地與什麼人有首尾。 (Xiao 2003, chap. 33, 296)	In twos and threes they discussed the situation, and made up their minds to find out who was the **favored suitor**. (Egerton 1939, vol. 2, 83)	Gathering together in twos and threes, they surreptitiously discussed her conduct and determined to find out if she were engaged in **hanky-panky** with anyone behind her husband's back. (Roy 2001, vol. 2, 277)

paraphrase of the ST, abandoning the source cultural image. On the other hand, TT2 aims to evoke cultural associations attached to the original by resorting to the term "catamite," defined in *Collins English Dictionary* (online edition) as a boy or youth used for sexual purposes by a man in ancient Greece and Rome. This choice allows the target reader access to the sexual suggestiveness associated with the historical figure. Table 2.9 illustrates how several slang terms are handled by the translators.

The colloquialism "久慣老成" in the ST describes a person who is sophisticated and experienced in accomplishing certain things (Bai 1991, 281). It is omitted from TT1 but translated verbatim as "a practiced old hand," in TT2, revealing the connotative sense but being less intelligible. The slang term "丁八" implies a clandestine love affair between a man and a woman (ibid., 127). It is omitted in TT1 and rendered as "a-nail-eighted," a coinage in TT2, creating an exotic flavor. An endnote is provided for "a-nail-eighted," which is homophonic to "annihilated" (Roy 2001, 538). However, it remains challenging for the reader to capture the meaning of "a-nail-eighted." The colloquial word "零布" implies useless or unimportant things in Chinese, but here it is used to convey a jocular tone in the ST (ibid., 328; Sun 2005, 337). It is paraphrased as "three odd things" in TT1, intelligible to the reader as "odd things" can mean unimportant things in English. Yet, the "three sweethearts" in TT2 gives a different meaning but fits the context. The term "首尾" implies a dubious relationship or an illicit affair in the context (Wang 1988, 278; Bai 1991, 487). TT1 paraphrases it as "the favored suitor," which is certainly more intelligible to the reader than "hanky-panky" in TT2, which is a literal transfer and not easy for the reader to grasp the term.

2.3.2 Material Culturemes

Jin Ping Mei is a novel of manners, with much of the action taking place in a domestic setting, namely the male protagonist's household. The novel's primary focus lies in delineating the protagonists' daily life and activities from various perspectives. The male protagonist, Ximen Qing, is a wealthy merchant and official who leads an extravagant life with his wife and mistresses. In the novel, various material objects are delineated, contributing to the story's authenticity and realism. These material elements not only reflect the culture and values of the novelist's time but are also closely interrelated with the fictional themes. The following examples illustrate how material culture is entertained in English renderings.

2.3.2.1 Food and Drink

The culture of food and drink has played a vital role in the development of Chinese civilization, and the language of culinary culture has been an important theme in China's premodern literary productions (Yue and Tang 2013). Textual representations help elucidate the unique appeal of food and its outstanding cultural significance in Chinese society. As Newmark puts it, "food is, for many, the most sensitive and important expression of national culture" (1988, 97). The narratives of food and wine in *Jin Ping Mei* are vital for plot advancement and characterization, making it a necessary subject for translation. However, conveying the aesthetic characteristics of food names poses challenges due to the difference between cultures.

In Table 2.10, the item "炊餅" is a traditional Chinese food that remains popular in China today. Originally known as "蒸餅" or steamed cakes, it originated in China's Song dynasty (960–1121); due to its homophonic resemblance to the Zhengzong 真宗 Emperor (968–1022) of Song, the food name was changed to "炊餅" (He 1990, 853). In *Jin Ping Mei*, it serves as an important aesthetic marker, recalling the character Wu Da, who makes a living by selling "炊餅" in the story. Most mainland Chinese people can associate "炊餅" with Wu Da. In TT1, "炊餅" is substituted with the familiar term "cakes," fostering the reader's understanding. In TT2, the food name is explicitated as "steamed wheat cakes," conveying the specificity of the foodstuff. As for the foodstuff "元宵," it refers to a special type of food enjoyed by the Chinese at the Lantern Festival, possessing significant cultural value. TT1 simplifies it as "pastries," a popular food among English-reading audiences. TT2 opts for explicitation and renders "元宵" as "Lantern Festival dumplings," manifesting cultural specificity and an exotic flavor for the target reader. Regarding the culturemes "雄黃酒" and "粽," both are popular food and alcoholic drinks enjoyed by the Chinese at the Dragon Boat Festival for

Table 2.10 Food and Drink

ST	TT1	TT2
假如你每日賣十扇籠炊餅。你從明日為始。 (Xiao 2003, chap. 2, 23)	You have been in the habit of selling ten trays of **cakes**, but in future … (Egerton 1939, vol. 1, 39)	If you normally sell ten trays of **steamed wheat cakes** in a day, starting tomorrow… (Roy 1993, vol. 1, 45)
唱畢。吃了元宵。韓道國先往家去了。 (Xiao 2003, chap. 42, 376)	When the song was ended, they ate the **pastries**. Han Tao-kuo was the first to go home. (Egerton 1939, vol. 2, 213)	When the singing was over, they ate the **Lantern Festival dumplings**, and then Han Tao-kuo was the first to go home. (Roy 2006, vol. 3, 35)
和孫二娘陳經濟吃雄黃酒。解粽歡娛。 (Xiao 2003, chap. 97, 955)	She and the Second Lady and Ching-chi drank together to celebrate the festival. (Egerton 1939, vol. 4, 325)	Together with Sun Erh-niang and Ch'en Ching-chi, the three of them enjoyed drinking **realgar-flavored wine** and eating festival *tsung-tzu*… (Roy 2013, vol. 5, 337)
兩盞粳米粥。 (Xiao 2003, chap. 62, 570)	There were two bowls of porridge and … (Egerton 1939, vol. 3, 125)	…two cups of congee made from the **nonglutinous rice**, … (Roy 2011, vol. 4, 48)

detoxification and celebration (He 1990, 896). They are left out in TT1, resulting in a reductive but readable text. TT2 attempts an unmodified (literal) rendition, with terms such as "realgar-flavored wine" and "tsung-tzu" displaying a strong exotic flavor. Moreover, "tsung-tzu" is further annotated as "triangular masses of rice wrapped in leaves that are traditionally consumed on this occasion" to bring the reader closer to the source culture (Roy 1993, 522). As for the final cultureme "粳米," it has been a staple food for the Chinese since time immemorial but is not popular in the target culture. TT2 provides an explicitation, rendering it as "nonglutinous rice." To avoid unnecessary exoticism or radical inaccessibility for the reader, TT1 advocates readability by excising the source cultureme.

2.3.2.2 Objects and Instruments

Beyond the realm of food, the novel portrays certain facts and objects characteristic of life and culture in premodern Chinese society. These elements, often unfamiliar or unknown to other cultural systems, require flexible solutions in terms of intercultural transfer. Below are examples that illustrate the translators' choices and strategies.

In Table 2.11, the boldfaced concepts represent objects and artefacts specific to the source culture. The item "南京拔步床" was a type of luxury furniture with

Table 2.11 Objects and Instruments

ST	TT1	TT2
南京拔步床。也有兩張。金鐲銀釧不消說。 (Xiao 2003, chap. 7, 58)	She has a couple of **Nanking beds** ... Her **jewelry** is beyond counting ... (Egerton 1939, vol. 1, 95)	She owns two **Nanking beds, with retractable steps** ... and **gold and silver bracelets and bangles**, it goes without saying. (Roy 1993, vol. 1, 126)
西門慶便坐在炕沿上 (Xiao 2003, chap. 62, 573)	Hsi-men Ch'ing sat down beside the **bed** ... (Egerton 1939, vol. 3, 129)	Hsi-men Ch'ing then sat down on the edge of the **k'ang** ... (Roy 2011, vol. 4, 53)
西門慶飲酒中間。看見婦人壁上。掛著一面琵琶。 (Xiao 2003, chap. 6, 56)	While Hsi-men was drinking, he saw a **lute** hanging on the wall ... (Egerton 1939, vol. 1, 92)	As he was drinking His-men Ch'ing noticed that there was a **p'i-p'a**, or **balloon guitar**, hanging on the wall ... (Roy 1993, vol. 1, 122)
那長老宣揚已畢。就教行者拏過文房四寶。 (Xiao 2003, chap. 57, 511)	He bade one of them to bring him **ink and a brush**. ... (Egerton 1939, vol. 3, 39)	When the abbot had finished his announcement, he told an acolyte to bring him the **four treasures of the writer's studio** ... (Roy 2006, vol. 3, 400)

delicate design and multiple functions, quite popular in Ming and Qing China (*Guoyu Cidian*, online edition[1]). It was affordable only by officials and wealthy merchants and appears several times in the story of *Jin Ping Mei* (Wang 1988, 206). In TT1, the item is generalized as "Nanjing beds," maintaining simplicity and fluency. In contrast, TT2 introduces the function or specific attribute of this particular bed through explicitation. The same approach applies to the item "金鐲銀釧." It is simplified as "jewelry" in TT1, creating a concise and intelligible text. In TT2, the word-for-word rendition "gold and silver bracelets and bangles" makes the text informative but may be considered verbose for some readers. The object "炕" is a type of bed made from bricks or earth with a hole under it to make fire for warmth, popular in Northern China where cold weather lasts for a long time every year (He 1990, 730). TT1 simplifies it as "bed," which is less difficult to understand than "k'ang" in TT2, a calqued term for the target readers. The item "琵琶" is a traditional Chinese musical instrument somewhat resembling a guitar but producing a distinct sound. TT1 substitutes it with the adaptive "lute," a familiar instrument for English-speaking audiences. In TT2, "琵琶" is transliterated as "p'i-p'a," an imported loanword adding an exotic tone to the text. The same approach is used for the reference "文房四寶," which is simplified in TT1 for concision and readability. TT2, on the other hand, employs a literal translation tactic, resulting in a less intelligible text for general readers without necessary source cultural knowledge.

2.3.3 Social Culturemes

Social culture encompasses a wide array of culturemes, including customs, folk activities, games, organizations, rituals, and more. In *Jin Ping Mei*, numerous references to social culture are embedded within a distinctly Chinese context, posing a challenge for English-reading audiences. The translation of these culturemes, often involving festivals, games, rituals, and other elements, is a complex task due to their unfamiliarity in an English-speaking context.

2.3.3.1 Festivals

The novel mentions several traditional festivals, posing challenges for interlingual translation. Table 2.12 below illustrates some instances.

In China, the festival "端陽佳節" is held in memory of Qu Yuan 屈原 (340–278 B.C.), a great poet and scholar, on the fifth day of the fifth lunar month. Notably, both the Gregorian calendar and the lunar calendar are in use in Chinese society, but traditional Chinese festivals are based on the latter. "端陽佳節" holds significant importance for the Chinese and is commonly known as the Dragon Boat Festival in English, a term derived from a calque/loanword. TT2 adds the date of the festival to enhance familiarity for English-language readers. As for the reference "重陽," it is a quintessentially Chinese festival observed on the ninth day of the ninth lunar month. The number "nine" in Chinese culture represents a *yang* number according to *Yi Jing* 易經 (The Book of I Ch'ing). Since this day contains two nines, it is also known as the Double Yang festival. TT2 unpacks the nuances

Table 2.12 Traditional Festivals

ST	TT1	TT2
一日將近端陽佳節。 (Xiao 2003, chap. 6, 54)	It was the **Festival of the Dragon Boat**. (Egerton 1939, vol. 1, 89)	One day the **Dragon Boat Festival, on the fifth day of the fifth month,** rolled around. (Roy 1993, vol. 1, 117)
光陰迅速。又早九月重陽令節。 (Xiao 2003, chap. 13, 111)	The days passed quickly. It was **the Feast of the Ancestral Tombs.** (Egerton 1939, vol. 1, 181)	Light and darkness alternate swiftly. Before long the **Double Yang festival, on the ninth day of the ninth month** rolled around. (Roy 1993, vol. 1, 259)
清明日 (Xiao 2003, chap. 48, 422)	**the Festival of the Dead** (Egerton 1939, vol. 2, 282)	**Ch'ing-ming Festival** (Roy 2006, vol. 3, 153)

of the festival and manifests the cultural difference by coining a new term, emphasizing the underlying cultural specificity. By contrast, TT1 paraphrases "重陽" as the "Feast of the Ancestral Tombs," making it more accessible to English-language readers. This alternative simplifies the understanding of the festival mentioned in the narrative. Similar treatment is given to other Chinese festivals, such as "清明日." In Chinese society, "清明日" is a festival when people offer sacrifices to ancestors and sweep ancestral tombs. TT1 paraphrases it as the "Festival of the Dead," offering transparency and accessibility to the target reader compared to TT2, which transliterates it as "Ch'ing-ming festival," potentially creating an alienating effect for Anglophones.

2.3.3.2 Games, Rituals, and Customs

It is crucial to note that *Jin Ping Mei* contains exhaustive descriptions of the characters' daily activities, including gaming, singing, praying, and the like. These culturemes represent traditional customs and rituals prevalent in late Ming China. While some of these traditions may have a long history in China, they might not have survived in contemporary Chinese society, becoming integral parts of the cultural heritage for the Chinese ethnicity. Finding equivalents for these categories presents a perpetual challenge, making creative transposition the preferred approach. In the following, several examples are discussed.

In Table 2.13, "吃鞋盃耍子" refers to a leisure game played by scholar-officials in imperial China, involving placing a cup in a foot-binding woman's tiny shoes for amusement. Such a cup is also known as the "golden lotus cup," carrying sexual connotations (Wang 1988, 425). In *Jin Ping Mei*, the male and female protagonists enjoy playing this game. TT1 opts to abandon this cultureme for the sake of clarity, as it does not significantly impact the plot. However, TT2 values the

Table 2.13 Games

ST	TT1	TT2
放一小盃酒在內。吃鞋盃耍子。 (Xiao 2003, chap. 6, 57)	… poured a cup of wine into it, and drank. (Egerton 1939, vol. 1, 93)	… put a little cup of wine in it, and then **drank a "shoe cup"** for the fun of it. (Roy 1993, vol. 1, 123)
良久。都出來院子內投壺頑耍。 (Xiao 2003, chap.19, 166)	After a while they all went to the courtyard to **play "arrows through the Jar."** (Egerton 1939, vol. 1, 270)	After a while, they went into the courtyard together and amused themselves by **playing at "pitch-pot."** (Roy 1993, vol. 1, 393)

game, keeping it relatively intact by coining a new term, "shoe cup," which might be unfamiliar or unintelligible to general readers. Another traditional game, "投壺," was quite popular in premodern China and often played at official banquets to enliven the atmosphere. It was first recorded in the Book of Rites, a Confucian classic (ibid., 171). Initially enjoyed by social elites, it eventually spread to lower classes, requiring players to throw sticks or arrows from a certain distance into a large, sometimes ornate, canister. In TT1, "投壺" is paraphrased as "play Arrows through the Jar," offering ready accessibility to the average reader, as arrows and jar are familiar objects in the receptor culture. TT2 introduces the item "pitch-pot" to describe the game, supported by additional information in an endnote to aid the reader in comprehending this popular game within a distant cultural context.

In Table 2.14, the boldfaced references in the ST are distinctive to traditional Chinese culture. For instance, "弄璋之喜" implies the joy of Ximen Qing's wife giving birth to a son for the family. The item "璋" represents a type of ritual instrument in ancient China, symbolizing brilliance and lofty character (Wang 1988, 159). TT1 paraphrases this cultureme as "toy scepter," a familiar term for the target reader as a scepter symbolizes authority and power in the target culture. In comparison, TT2 is more explicit in representing the original meaning. In Chinese society, "招贅" suggests that a girl from a wealthy family selects or invites a suitable man to be her husband (Bai 1991, 669). In British culture, there is no such custom, so TT1 simply paraphrases it as "married," which is easy for the reader to comprehend. TT2 has "brought … across her threshold in wedlock" for "招贅," resulting in a text that is somewhat obscure and less intelligible than TT1. The same is true of the cultureme

"滿月," which refers to a formal birthday party held for a month-old baby in Chinese society (He 1990, 297). TT2 provides a literal rendition with "full month celebration," which may sound unnatural and unfamiliar to general readers. In contrast, TT1 is more readable and accessible by paraphrasing "滿月" as "a month old." The cultureme "插定" refers to a marriage custom in premodern Chinese society where a man uses a hairpin to insert into a girl's hair to establish marital

Table 2.14 Rituals and Customs

ST	TT1	TT2
怎的是弄璋之喜。 (Xiao 2003, chap. 31, 280)	"Why do you mention a **"toy scepter"**?" (Egerton 1939, vol. 2, 56)	"What is all this about: **The joy of giving his son a jade scepter to play with**?" (Roy 2001, vol. 2, 239)
卻說李瓶兒。招贅了蔣竹山。約兩月光景。 (Xiao 2003, chap. 19, 163)	It was now two months since the Lady of the Vase had **married** the doctor. (Egerton 1939, vol. 1, 265)	To resume our story, two months or so had now passed since Li P'ing-erh **brought** Chiang Chu-shan **across her threshold in wedlock**. (Roy 1993, vol. 1, 385)
哥兒滿月。抱出來不曾 (Xiao 2003, chap. 31, 278)	"Has your young son been out yet, now that he is **a month old**?" (Egerton 1939, vol. 2, 53)	"At the **fullmonth celebration** yesterday, was your son brought out and shown to the company?" (Roy 2001, vol. 2, 231)
曾受了那人家插定不曾。 (Xiao 2003, chap. 7, 62)	"My mistress would like to know whether you have accepted **the man's proposal**," (Egerton 1939, vol. 1, 102)	"I've been sent to ask whether you've accepted that person's **betrothal gifts** or not," (Roy 2001, vol. 2, 137)
家家門插艾葉。處處戶掛靈符。 (Xiao 2003, chap. 16, 140)	[omitted]	In each household **artemisia leaves** adorn the gate, In every dwelling **efficacious charms** deck the door. (Roy 1993, vol. 1, 329)

relationship; it also represents betrothal gifts (Bai 1991, 52). TT2 preserves the expression "betrothal gifts," which is close to the ST, while TT1 paraphrases "插定" as "the man's proposal," idiomatic and natural for English-language audiences. References like "插艾葉" and "掛靈符" were customs prevailing in premodern Chinese society. "艾葉" is a plant used to purify the air in the house, and "靈符" suggests yellow paper with deities painted on it, used to dispel evil spirits (He 1990, 292). TT1 excises both culturemes, whereas TT2 preserves them, resulting in a text that may strike the reader as alien and exotic.

2.3.3.3 Bureaucratic System

Jin Ping Mei serves as a rich source for those interested in exploring the bureaucratic system in late imperial China. While official posts are undoubtedly familiar to the source reader, they pose challenges for readers from different cultural

Table 2.15 Official Post

ST	TT1	TT2
蔡太師與我這四門親家楊提督。都是當朝天子面前。說得話的人。 (Xiao 2003, chap. 14, 118)	I believe the Governor of Kaifengfu is a ward of the **Imperial Tutor** Cai. Both Cai and my relative, **Marshal** Yang, have a certain influence with **his Majesty**. (Egerton 1939, vol. 1, 192)	**Grand Preceptor** Ts'ai, along with my kinsman by marriage at four removes, **the commander in chief of the Imperial Guard**, Yang Chien, are both people who have the ear of **the reigning emperor** himself. (Roy 2001, vol. 2, 278)

backgrounds. The following examples illustrate various solutions to this translation problem.

In Table 2.15, the boldfaced references "太師," "提督," and "天子" represent important official posts in late imperial China. The title "太師" refers to one of the eminent court dignitaries known as the *sanshi* 三師 (Three Preceptors) (Hucker 1985, 481). The term "提督" signifies senior military officials (He 1990, 394–400; see also Hucker 1985, 496). The cultureme "天子" designates the emperor in dynastic China. In TT1, an Anglicized or domesticating strategy is employed, rendering these culteremes as "the Imperial Tutor," "Marshal," and "his Majesty," respectively, assimilating them to the target-cultural conventions. This approach allows ordinary readers to easily identify with the characters and their social status described in the story. On the other hand, TT2 adopts a wordier, source-oriented strategy, creating associations between the bureaucratic terms and their distinctive cultural contexts.

2.3.3.4 Imperial Examination System

Jin Ping Mei introduces the civil service examination system in late imperial China. Anything related to this system can be challenging for ordinary readers unfamiliar with the source culture and history. To address this challenge, appropriate strategies are needed to make translations communicative and intelligible enough for the target audience. The following example illustrates solutions to this problem.

In Table 2.16, the culatureme "頭甲" encompasses the top three places in the palace examination, the highest level of the imperial civil examinations in late imperial China. The examination system includes various levels such as *tongshi* 童試 (county and prefectural licensing exams), *suishi* 歲試 (biennial local exams), *keshi* 科試 (triennial qualifying exams), *xiangshi* 鄉試 (triennial provincial exams), *huishi* 會試 (triennial metropolitan exams) (Elman 2000 659). The top three places, collectively known as *jinshi* 進士 or chin-shih, consist of *zhuangyuan* 狀元 (optimus), *bangyan* 榜眼 (secundus), and *tanhua* 探花 (tertius) (ibid.).

Table 2.16 Examination System

ST	TT1	TT2
當初安忱。取中頭甲。 (Xiao 2003, chap. 36, 326)	An Shen had passed the examination **in the highest place** ... (Egerton 1939, vol. 1, 131)	Originally An Ch'en had been placed **at the head of the list in the chin-shih examinations** ... (Roy 2001, vol. 2, 349)

In TT1, the term "頭甲" is simplified as "in the highest place," erasing cultural markers from the text to enhance accessibility for the target reader. In TT2, the term is explicitated with additional explanation, fully revealing the cultural connotations of "頭甲," though introducing alien terms such as "chin-shih" that might be challenging for ordinary readers.

2.3.4 Medical Culturemes

Jin Ping Mei contains detailed descriptions of sickness, medicine, and medical treatment, which are closely intertwined with the plot and characterization. These passages reveal the novelist's creativity in devising plot mechanisms. As postulated by Christopher Cullen, the author of *Jin Ping Mei* was apparently quite familiar with contemporary medical practices and had a certain enthusiasm for introducing technical medical knowledge to late Ming readers, who would presumably have no difficulty understanding it, as there is little difference between the medical knowledge of readers of medical texts and that of readers of novels (Cullen 1993, 120). By describing the characters' experience of illness and the medical treatment they undergo, the author of *Jin Ping Mei* introduces rich medical expressions unique to traditional Chinese culture. These medical culturemes are characterized by their antiquity, the concision of the classical language, and the specificity of ancient Chinese thought, posing a challenge for cross-cultural transfer. The following examples should suffice to illustrate this problem.

In Table 2.17, expressions such as "脫陽," "陰虛," "太極邪火," "膏肓," and "陰陽交爭" in the ST are important medical culturemes specific to traditional Chinese medicine, with no direct equivalents in English. Specifically, "脫陽" suggests the syndrome induced by excessive sexual escapades or intercourse; "陰虛" here indicates syndromes caused by the overconsumption of body fluids; "太極" refers to human organs such as the heart and kidney; "欲海" signals carnal or sensual desire; "膏肓" suggests the most hidden part of the body, medically untestable or treatable; the phrase "病在膏肓" means incurable diseases, and "陰陽交爭" suggests a type of disease caused by yin-yang disequilibrium in the body (*Guoyu Cidian*, online edition; He 1990, 929–931). In traditional Chinese philosophy, the concept of yin-yang describes opposite but interconnected forces (Feuchtwang 2016, 146). It can be used to explain weather changes, the structure of the human body, the origin of diseases, the formation of all things in the universe,

Table 2.17 Medical Culturemes

ST	TT1	TT2
乃是脫陽之症。須是補其陰虛。方纔好得。 (Xiao 2003, chap. 79, 798)	It is clearly a case of **sexual exhaustion**. I will give you something to supply the missing element. (Egerton 1939, vol. 4, 91)	This lack of equilibrium in your system is **symptomatic of a loss of yang energy**. Your **yin vacuity** must be replenished before you can recover. (Roy 2011, vol. 4, 646)
是太極邪火。聚於慾海。病在膏肓。難以治療。 (Xiao 2003, chap. 79, 801)	… **a furious fever** has taken hold upon the instrument of your **passion**. I fear I can do nothing for you, your case is hopeless … (Egerton 1939, vol. 4, 95)	The **pathogenic fire** of your **generative organ**, Is choking the conduit leading to your heart. The disease has penetrated your **vital organs**, And is no longer possible to treat medically. … (Roy 2011, vol. 4, 652)
陰陽交爭。乍寒乍熱。 (Xiao 2003, chap. 17, 148)	The **masculine and feminine** principles are at war within you … you sometimes feel hot and sometimes cold. (Egerton 1939, vol. 1, 242)	**Yin and yang** contend with one another, Producing alternate fevers and chills … (Roy 1993, vol. 1, 350)

and even the laws of the universe (see *Guoyu Cidian*; Feuchtwang 2016, 146). These terms are so culture-specific that their translation into English calls for flexible strategies to make the target text communicative and intelligible. Evidently, medical culturemes are either omitted or paraphrased in TT1, where the original text's meaning is re-expressed in a clear, logic fashion, resulting in an easily accessible text with few cultural associations. In contrast, TT2 translates medical culturemes literally, without omitting any source terms. While TT2 becomes lengthy and informative, it runs the risk of creating unnecessary obscurity or complexity. General readers need to expend extra cognitive effort to decipher medical narratives. The treatment of medical culturemes emerges as a major difference between the two translations under examination.

2.3.5 Religious Culturemes

In Chinese society, three important religions, namely Confucianism, Taoism, and Buddhism, have powerful impacts on language and culture, although Confucianism is considered by many as a philosophical school rather than a religion. As essential parts of Chinese culture, the three religions influence Chinese people's social life, ideology, and values. Religious culturemes are pervasive in traditional Chinese fiction, carrying important hallmarks of Chinese culture. As far as *Jin Ping Mei* is concerned, the book incorporates many religious references to Buddhism and Taoism, which are entwined with the narrative structure to the point of constituting an essential part of the plot. In Anglophone culture, Christianity is the predominant religion and exerts a powerful influence on various aspects of native English speakers' lives and ways of thinking. Religious differences between China and the Western world play a vital role in cross-cultural encounters. Some translation problems may arise regarding the treatment of religious concepts in the novel. The following are several examples illustrating whether and how religious culture is represented in the two translations.

In Table 2.18, religious references pertain to Buddhism and Taoism. The term "阿彌陀佛" refers to one of the most important Buddhas in Mahāyāna. In the Encyclopedia of Buddhism, Amitābha is interpreted as "one of the so-called celestials or mythic buddhas who inhabit their own buddha-field and intervene as a saving force in our world" (Buswell 2005, 14). Residing in a purified world, Amitābha welcomes the dead and leads them to rebirth in his pure buddha-field. Amitābha has been widely known by generations of Chinese ever since Mahāyāna Buddhism was introduced to China. In English texts, "阿彌陀佛" is generalized as "Buddha" in TT1 but specified as "Amitabha Buddha" in

Table 2.18 Religious Culturemes

ST	TT1	TT2
阿彌陀佛。這是西門老爹門首。麼。 (Xiao 2003, chap. 57, 512)	Outside the gate, he called loudly upon **Buddha** and asked: "Is this the noble Hsi-men's house? (Egerton 1939, vol. 3, 41)	**Amitabha Buddha**! Is this the gate to the residence of His Honor His-men Ch'ing? (Roy 2006, vol. 3, 402)
咱聞那佛祖西天。也止不過要黃金舖地。 (Xiao 2003, chap. 57, 515)	Besides, they tell me that gold is not despised, even in **Paradise**, ... (Egerton 1939, vol. 3, 44)	I've heard it said of the **Jetavana Park, in the western realm of the Buddhist patriarch** himself, ... (Roy 2006, vol. 3, 411)
恠不的那賊淫婦。死了墮阿鼻地獄。 (Xiao 2003, chap.18, 252)	When that thievish whore died, she went to **the lowest depths of Hell**. (Egerton 1939, vol. 2, 10)	No wonder that lousy whore went straight to **the Avici Hell** when she died. (Roy 2001, vol. 2, 164)
請了六個僧。在家做水陸。超度武大。 (Xiao 2003, chap. 8, 72)	Hsi-men Qing ... and ask six monks to come and sing a dirge for Wu Ta ... (Egerton 1939, vol. 1, 119)	His-men Ch'ing ... to engage the services of six Buddhist monks, who were to come to the house and **perform a "land and water" mass** for the benefit of Wu the Elder ... (Roy 1993, vol.1, 164)

TT2. The referential meaning is made explicit in TT2 by preserving the full name of the Buddha. The reference "佛祖西天" is specific to Buddhism, indicating Amit ā bha's western pure land (He 1990, 359).

In TT1, religious expressions are anglicized, replaced with terms more familiar to the target audience. In contrast, TT2 transfers them verbatim, ensuring the full conveyance of religious content to the reader. Similarly, "阿鼻地獄" is a well-known Buddhist term, representing the "deepest, largest, and most tortuous of the eight great, or eight hot, hells" (Buswell et al. 2013, 188). In TT1, it is simplified as a familiar term easily comprehensible for the target readers. In TT2, it is specified as "Avici Hell," invoking local color. The reference "做水陸" represents a Buddhist ritual popular in premodern Chinese society involving the singing of dirges or showing reverence for the dead (Sun 2005, 195). By leaving out this cultureme, TT1 becomes more readable and intelligible than TT2, which features a word-for-word transfer and might burden or puzzle non-specialist readers unfamiliar with Buddhist culture.

In Table 2.19, the religious terms "道士" and "老君" are classical Taoist categories specific to Chinese mythology. In the ST, "道士" refers to a person who believes in Taoism and eventually becomes a Taoist priest, while "老君" refers to

Table 2.19 Religious Culturemes

ST	TT1	TT2
李瓶兒道今已是寄名做了道士。 (Xiao 2003, chap. 46, 411)	"My child has been **enrolled at the Taoist Temple**," Li Ping'er said. (Egerton 1939, vol. 2, 264)	"He has already **had a religious name bestowed upon him** as a Taoist priest," said Li P'ing-erh. (Roy 2006, vol. 3, 127)
我有一枝藥。乃老君練就。 (Xiao 2003, chap. 49, 440)	I have one medicine made by **Lao Chün**, … (Egerton 1939, vol. 2, 309)	I have in my possession a remedy that was: perfected by **the Lord Lao-tzu** himself, … (Roy 2006, vol. 3, 199)
潘道士觀看。卻是地府勾批。 (Xiao 2003, chap. 62, 579)	The priest looked at it. It was the final judgment of **Hades**. (Egerton 1939, vol. 3, 138)	When Taoist Master P'an examined it, he saw that it was an arrest warrant issued by the **court of the underworld**, which bore three official seals. (Roy 2011, vol. 4, 66)
潘道士道。定數難逃。不能搭救了。 (Xiao 2003, chap. 62, 579)	"It is the **will of Heaven**," said the priest. "There is nothing I can do." (Egerton 1939, vol. 3, 139)	"One's **allotted years** are hard to evade." said Taoist Master P'an. "It will be difficult to save her." (Roy 2011, vol. 4, 67)

one of the three most revered deities in Taoism (*Guoyu Cidian*, online edition). As a Taoist notion, the cultureme "寄名" suggests that, for a young child to grow healthy and live a secure, happy life, the parents send him/her to a Taoist temple for a dharma name. This name symbolically entrusts the child to the temple to ensure safety or to avoid disasters (He 1990, 332; Wang 1988, 356). In TT1, it is generalized as "enrolled," while in TT2, it is explicitated as "had a religious name bestowed upon him." Due to the trend of *sanjiao heyi* 三教合一 (the syncretism of the three doctrines or "the unity of the Three Teachings" of Confucian ethics, the Daoist system of merits, and the Buddhist concept of reincarnation) in late imperial China, the terms "地府" and "定數" are often considered Taoist entities, although they also have connections to Buddhism. In Taoism, "地府" indicates the underworld, while "定數" suggests a person's destiny determined by *tian* 天, or Heaven (Sun 2005, 235; He 1990, 370; Brook 1993, 13; Bai 2018, 42). Here, Heaven does not imply a personal creator God but refers to an unknown force or power whose constant action can maintain nature's balance and, at times, bring about changes (Bai 2018, 42). These religious culturemes are familiar to the source readers, but they may be unfamiliar to an English-speaking audience without relevant cultural background knowledge. In TT1, the term "道士" is omitted, but the cultureme "老君" is transliterated as "Lao Chün," a literal transfer. TT2 favors a flexible approach, combining literal transfer plus paraphrasing. The treatment of the terms "地府" and "定數" also differs. TT1 replaces the Taoist term "地府" with "Hades," an ancient god of the underworld in Greek mythology, familiar to the average Anglophone audience. Similarly, "定數" is paraphrased as "will of Heaven" in TT1, making it more accessible than TT2, which renders it directly as "allotted years." It seems that pragmatic strategies are employed by the translators to render complex religious culturemes. This aligns with James Holmes (1988, 48) postulation that translators can make pragmatic choices by considering flexible approaches to achieve intended effects. Thus, it is not surprising to identify different tendencies within a given translated text in terms of the translation strategies deployed.

2.3.6 Ecological Culturemes

The final category of culturemes in *Jin Ping Mei* concerns nature and geography. Within the text, natural scenes, weather, historical locations, flora, and fauna are vividly portrayed. While they may have less relevance to the plot or characterization, they play a crucial role in determining a specific cultural setting and add a certain amount of local color. Moreover, they contribute to certain images of Chinese culture, given the tradition of "exhausting meaning through images" in Chinese literature (Cao 2010, 31). In translation, these elements constitute a major locus of cultural representation and manipulation. Ecological references also present challenges due to multiple levels of metaphorical associations in different cultures. Chinese literary texts often imbue depictions of nature, plants, animals, and place names with rhetorical qualities and symbolic value. Translators may face

Table 2.20 Flora

ST	TT1	TT2
又有那耐寒君子 竹。欺雪大夫松。 (Xiao 2003, chap. 19, 160)	They looked at the **bamboos that bore the cold like supermen**, and the proud **pine trees boldly contemptuous of the snow**. (Egerton 1939, vol. 1, 261)	That "**cold-enduring gentleman**," the **bamboo**, and that "**snow-despising grandee**," the **pine**. (Roy 1993, vol. 1, 379)

cross-cultural problems in deciding translatorial choices that best benefit the target readers. The following examples may illustrate this point.

In Table 2.20, bamboo and pine trees are two types of plants that symbolize tenacity and stamina in the Chinese cultural tradition. In the ST, bamboo is likened to a gentleman, while pine trees are compared to scholar-officials. The aesthetic appreciation of symmetry is highly valued in Chinese culture, evident in various artistic forms such as literature, architecture, and sculpture. The example in Table 2.19 illustrates this cultural aspect. However, such an aesthetic tradition does not exist in the target culture. TT1, therefore, opts for a paraphrastic translation, prioritizing fluency and readability at the expense of aesthetic form. It still effectively conveys to its readers a scene that is visually evocative similar to the original. In contrast, TT2 chooses a word-for-word transfer to preserve the aesthetic or stylistic feature of the original, resulting in an alien or defamiliarizing effect for the target readers. As Nicky Harman (2006, 18) suggests, the more distant the two languages, the less likely it is that following the ST would guide the translator to produce a natural-sounding target text. Thus, TT2 may appear unnatural and awkward to lay or ordinary readers due to its replication of the stylistic form of the ST.

Table 2.21 involves geographical allusions presented as historical place names. In the case of "西域天竺國," most Chinese readers would recall the Ming novel *Xiyouji*, or *Journey to the West*, a predecessor of *Jin Ping Mei*. The historical toponym "天竺" can be traced back to China's Tang dynasty (618–709) when Xuanzang (602–64) went on a pilgrimage for Buddhist scriptures in the western regions, roughly signaling today's India. Conspicuously, in TT1, "西域天竺國" is generalized as "India," which is familiar and recognizable to the target readers. In contrast, TT2 explicitates it as "the land of India in the Western Regions," fully reproducing the intended meaning of the source text.

The place name "中國" suggests the Middle Kingdom or Central Plains, carrying symbolic value that implies *Zhongyuan* "中原", an alternative for imperial China. This geographical referent has evolved into a significant cultural imagery, evoking the depth of Chinese history. While easily understood by Chinese and Western readers familiar with Chinese history, the nuances of the term may be challenging for non-specialist readers to grasp. In TT1, the cultureme "中國" is simplified as "China," catering to the reader's preferences. TT2 attempts to capture the historical

Table 2.21 Geographical Terms

ST	TT1	TT2
乃西域天竺國。 (Xiao 2003, chap. 49, 438)	I come from a foreign land, from the deep pine forests of **India**, … (Egerton 1939, vol. 21, 306)	I am a foreign monk from **the land of India in the Western Regions**, … (Roy 2006, vol. 3, 195)
原來那寺里有個道長老。原是西印度國出身。因慕中國清華 (Xiao 2003, chap. 57, 511)	Then there came a monk from India who was impressed with the greatness of **China**. (Egerton 1939, vol. 3, 39)	He was originally a native of western India who so admired the splendour of **the Middle Kingdom** … (Roy 2006, vol. 3, 398)
江淮河濟添新水。 (Xiao 2003, chap. 6, 56)	New water races down **the four rivers** … (Egerton 1939, vol. 1, 92)	**The waters of the Yangtze, Yellow, Huai, and Chi Rivers** are newly augmented; (Roy 2001, vol. 2, 138)

and cultural nuances of the cultureme but may be challenging for non-specialist readers to fully understand the subtleties.

The final ecological reference, "江淮河濟," refers to four great rivers in mainland China: the Yangtze River, the Huai River, the Yellow River, and the Ji River. In TT1, for the sake of conciseness and fluency, this reference is simplified or generalized as "the four rivers," with the names of the rivers elliptical. By contrast, TT2 faithfully represents the same reference, explicitly stating the names of the four rivers for the target reader.

2.4 Additional Quantitative Analysis

The qualitative textual analysis conducted in the preceding section gives the impression that Egerton's translation (TT1) is generally target-text-oriented, while Roy's (TT2) keeps closer to the source culture. Egerton's version mainly adopts procedures such as paraphrase, generalization, and omission, whereas Roy's uses literal translation, calquing, transliteration, and explicitation. This section aims to complement the qualitative textual analysis with quantitative approaches to offer a full picture of the difference in dealing with culturemes between the two translations. Quantitative analysis can help validate qualitative studies by widening the analytical scope. Thus, a statistical analysis is carried out to determine the frequencies of the translation procedures and strategies employed by Egerton and Roy.

Considering the large number of culturemes in *Jin Ping Mei*, it would be challenging to consider all of them in this chapter. Based on the typology of cultureme outlined earlier, a total of 312 representative instances are selected to form the corpus for statistical analysis. While the corpus may not allow us to obtain generalizable results, it should suffice to observe the general tendency followed by each translator in handling culturemes. The procedures and strategies are

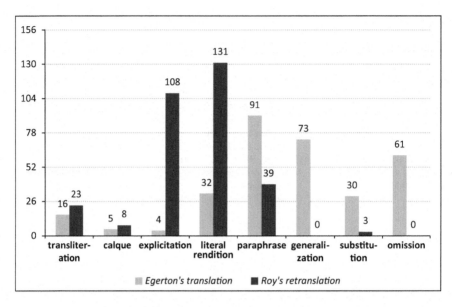

Figure 2.1 Distribution of Procedures and Strategies Used by Egerton and Roy

subsumed under the principles of foreignization and domestication, as mentioned above. The frequency of each procedure is calculated to illustrate the general tendencies of the two translators. As noted earlier, foreignization involves calquing, literal translation, transliteration, and explicitation, while domestication includes omission, substitution, generalization, and paraphrase. Figure 2.1 displays the frequency of procedures and tactics used in Egerton's translation and Roy's retranslation.

Egerton's translation features a great number of instances of generalization, paraphrasing, and omission, amounting to around 225 instances. This contrasts with Roy's translation, which features over 200 instances of literal rendition and explicitation, about half the total number in the corpus. Paraphrasing is less frequent in Roy's translation, adding up to less than 40 instances, while omission is used very sparingly. This quantitative result aligns with the qualitative textual analysis carried out in the preceding section, where Egerton's solution-types were found to be more flexible and diversified than Roy's in rendering the wide variety of culturemes in *Jin Ping Mei*. This demonstrates that Egerton's renderings appear fluent, readable, and easily comprehensible on the part of the target readers. While Roy's renderings have a strong foreignizing or exotic effect, it does not suggest that Roy totally gives up domestication tactics. In fact, both translators have recourse to foreignizing and domesticating approaches when translating culturemes, as reflected in the percentages presented in the following.

Table 2.22 Percentages of Procedures and Strategies Adopted by Egerton and by Roy

	transli-teration	calque	explici-tation	literal rendition	para-phrase	generali-zation	substi-tution	omi-ssion
Egerton's translation	5.12	1.60	1.28	10.25	29.16	23.39	9.61	19.55
Roy's retranslation	7.37	2.56	34.61	41.98	12.5	0	0.96	0

Table 2.23 Tendencies towards Domestication and Foreignization in the Two Translations

	foreignization		domestication	
	total	percentage	total	percentage
Egerton's translation	57	18.26	255	81.73
Roy's retranslation	270	86.53	42	13.46

With regard to the percentages of procedures and strategies employed by Egerton and Roy, Table 2.22 and Table 2.23 show that Roy uses the foreignizing strategy around 270 times, with a percentage as high as 86.53%, and makes few concessions to the domesticating strategy, with a percentage as low as 13.46%.

By comparison, paraphrasing (29.16 %) represents the most frequently used procedure in Egerton's translation, while generalization (23.39 %) and omission (19.55 %) are also common. Thus, the statistics reveal two different tendencies established in the process of rendering culturemes in *Jin Ping Mei*. Egerton's translation leans toward domestication, whereas Roy's translation exhibits a marked foreignizing tendency. These tendencies have implications for understanding the translators' cultural attitudes towards the original work and their positioning in presenting translations to the assumed readership. They also prompt us to further examine the potential factors that contribute to the results, which will be discussed in the next section. The statistical data also indicates that neither of the translators has recourse to exclusively domesticating or exclusively foreignizing strategies in rendering culturemes. Rather, their translational strategies fall along the continuum of domestication and foreignization with different frequencies. This tallies with Venuti's observation that foreignization and domestication are not binary opposites but should be perceived as a question of degree in rendering a given source text (Venuti 1998, 13). The next section will explain the significance of the findings and discuss the relevant factors contributing to the different tendencies for the two translators.

2.5 Discussion

In light of the descriptive analysis in the preceding section and based on the main findings, this section sets out to discuss the contributing factors shaping the differences between the two translations. As analyzed above, Egerton's version employs more domesticating tactics to render the six types (namely, linguistic, material, societal, medical, religious, and ecological) of culturemes in *Jin Ping Mei*. This approach considers the target reader's tastes and aesthetic expectations by reducing the novel's cultural anchorage, elevating its significance from the culturally specific to a more general level, and creating easy accessibility for readers who might find culturemes strange, alien, or incomprehensible. This strategy leaves ample room for a pleasurable reading experience unrestricted by culture-specific content. On the other hand, Roy's version employs more foreignizing tactics. His renderings pursue cultural facsimile, bringing the rich culturemes of the original to the target readers to the greatest possible extent. This approach challenges English-speaking audiences with unexpected cultural imagery and unfamiliar lexical choices. The identified differences in tendencies between the two translations can be attributed to several factors. Overall, three significant considerations may have come into play in shaping the tendencies. The following discussion will elaborate on these.

The first consideration is the different cultural and historical context in which the two translations emerged. Translations, being artefacts of the host culture, are inevitably shaped by the specific cultural milieu in which the translator operates, rather than in a vacuum, and thence "any attempt to offer exhaustive descriptions and viable explanations would necessitate a proper contextualization" (Toury 1995, 24–29; Bassnett 2007, 13). Since translation is a communicative activity embedded in a given sociocultural context, the translator's priorities, agendas, and strategies must be examined within this context. Rodica Dimitriu (2015, 5) postulates *context* as a key parameter for "complex analyses of the translator's activities and decisions" in modern translation studies. As mentioned in the previous chapter, Egerton's translation was produced in Britain during the early twentieth century, a time when Chinese literature and culture were still somewhat unfamiliar or unknown to most West European readers. English-language readers faced the challenge of comprehending numerous unfamiliar culturemes in a sixteenth-century novel translated from Chinese. Although China and its ideals, aesthetic, and art had been much admired in Britain and Western Europe by the mid-nineteenth century, the discourse on China shifted dramatically by the century's end. Chinese culture was no longer highly regarded; instead, things Chinese were criticized as negative and inferior compared to European progress and expansiveness in industry, commerce and intellectual thought (Kern 2009, 174; Peak 2015, 431). Historian Leopold von Ranke (1795–1886), for instance, famously regarded the Chinese as the "eternal standstill" people (Kern 2009, 176). Interest in things Chinese in Britain faded from the late nineteenth century. The two Opium Wars (1839–1842 and 1858–1860) played a pivotal role in reshaping British perceptions of the Chinese, leading to a decline in esteem for China and its people due to the humiliating defeats in these Wars (Barringer and Flynn 1998, 28). By the time of the Boxer Rising in 1900, sinophobia and the Yellow Peril were in full swing in Western Europe, and the Chinese continued to be stereotyped as a curious people (Benton and Gomez 2008, 294). This sentiment was reflected in popular novels and films like those of Sax Rohmer, which embraced the Yellow Peril trope and gained widespread popularity in the early twentieth century. As Robert Bickers states, "the more that was known first-hand about China, the less positively it was reported and deemed" during the time (Peak 2015, 432). China remained marginal to the British perception of the world order in the first decades of the twentieth century. For instance, when a Chinese literary or cultural text appeared in a translation into English, it had to leap a credibility gap in the British public, reflecting the prevailing sinophobia (Liu et al. 2012, 18). It was only after the First World War that sinophobia diminished a lot due to the rise of business interest in China and the growing antifascism sentiment in Britain (Yeh 2008, 301). The British antifascism sentiment prompted sympathy for the Chinese when Japan invaded Manchuria in the early 1930s, leading to a positive shift in British views of the Chinese (Ma and Guan 2017, 568).

During the 1920s, Britain experienced a fascination with chinoiseries, marking a renewed intellectual enthusiasm for a mythic China (Witchard 2015, 12). This period saw the onset of "China fever" in Britain, driven by new economic, cultural, and political interests in China (Yeh 2008, 301). Chinese commodities, fashion, furniture, and art found a warm reception in Britain during this time. Notably, the Bloomsbury Group's profound interest in oriental culture played a significant role in popularizing East Asian literature in Britain. Writers, scholars, and poets alike showed keen interest in Chinese literature and culture, translating a variety of Chinese poems and fictional works in the early twentieth century (Fiske 2011, 216). The imagist poet Pound, as previously mentioned, translated numerous Chinese classical poems for contemporary readers. His work, *Cathay*, published in London in 1915, created a sensation, inspiring many others to read and translate Chinese poetry (Yeh 2016, 288). The famous poet T. S. Eliot even declared that Pound was "the inventor of Chinese poetry for our time" (Eliot 1928, xvii). In addition to Pound, Waley presented China as "an aesthetic Utopia," translating numerous Chinese classic poems into English, gaining widespread attention in the first decades of the twentieth century (Witchard 2012, 37). As discussed earlier, Waley's *Chinese Poems* (1916) received acclaim from contemporaries such as Yeats, Pound, Eliot, and Bertrand Russell (1872–1970) (Chan and Pollard 1995, 423). Waley's *A Hundred and Seventy Chinese Poems* was even regarded as "one of the most memorable books of recent years" (Johns 1982, 18). Some of the poems translated from Chinese have been anthologized more than once and enjoyed as English literature in their own right.

However, most of these translations were by no means faithful to the Chinese originals. Instead, they were largely abridgements, adaptations, and re-creations, in Gadamer's (2003) words. In both Pound's *Cathay* and Waley's *Chinese Poems*, for instance, visible traces of adaptation, transmutation, and invention, or skillful "improvement" were apparent. The translators took great liberties to manipulate or recast the Chinese texts to meet the horizon of expectations of the target readers or to appropriate them for literary modernism purposes (Witchard 2015, 12). This pattern extended to translations of Chinese prose fiction and drama during that time. An example is Pearl S. Buck's *All Men are Brothers*, a translation of the Ming novel *Shuihu zhuan*, published in London in 1933. Buck adapted and abridged to suit the tastes of contemporary Western audiences. She omitted numerous elements such as poems and the narrator's formulaic expressions which she believed interrupted the narrative flow. Buck stated that her translation aimed to provide contemporary readers who knew little or no Chinese with the illusion that they were reading an English original (Zhang 2022, 133). Buck's writing not only fostered favorable attitudes among Westerners toward the Chinese but also kindled an interest in Chinese culture. Translations of Chinese plays translated into English, such as Shih-I Hsiung's *Lady Precious Stream* (1934), serve as remarkable examples, reflecting the British chinoiserie tradition of imagining and appropriating Chinese culture during the interwar period (Tian 2017, 171). Hsiung, a Chinese diaspora writer in London, achieved commercial success by Anglicizing Peking Opera and adapting it to conform to or valorize the chinoiserie tradition in Britain. According to Diana Yeh, there was indeed "an emerging fashion for an exotic China in the UK" during the 1920s and '30s, with traditional Chinese elements being what a British audience desired to perceive, appropriate, or imagine (Yeh 2014, 35). The play, *Lady Precious Stream*, a translation of *Wang Baochuan* 王寶釧, was a prime example of this trend.

As Yeh explains, despite the "emerging fashion for an exotic China" in Britain in the 1920s, China was still imagined as remote and less appealing than India and Japan in culture and the arts (Yeh 2014, 50). The dominant ideology in the target culture during the first decades of the twentieth century viewed China and its culture as quite alien, elusive, and lacking mass appeal (Liu et al. 2012, 18). Moreover, a geopolitical imbalance characterized cross-national literary exchanges during that time. In Britain, a lingering sense of nationalism regarded the languages of all colonial nations or former colonial powers as less appealing than English. The incipient "jingoist insularity" among Britons worked against acknowledgment of the merits of other literatures, which might be as good or even greater in some instances (Henig 1974, 73). Asian literature, such as Chinese and Japanese works, was only selectively translated by Western intellectuals and often negotiated and compromised to fit the cultural values of the Western world. Meanwhile, intellectuals in China viewed learning from the West (namely, West-European countries) as the only choice to modernize China. Countless English texts were translated into Chinese to enlighten the Chinese public. The unequal dynamics between China and the West never fundamentally changed, and the relationship remained one of dependency and manipulation (Zhang 2022, 255). Chinese culture had lost its significance, and few vestiges of global influence remained (ibid.). It should come as no surprise that translators such as Waley favored adaptation and abridging techniques when translating Chinese and Japanese literary texts to acquire their desired knowledge about the East. As illustrated by Waley's translation of the Japanese masterpiece *Genji monogatari* (or *The Tale of Genji*) between 1925 and 1933, he drew upon the language of medieval period to make the story relevant and intelligible to a Western audience; this involved cutting out passages or even chapters that Waley considered boring or obscure, substituting them with something agreeable in contemporary English (Johnson 2020, 3). As Lefevere (1992, 48) aptly puts it, "ideology and poetics particularly shape the translator's strategy in solving problems raised by elements in the Universe of Discourse of the original and the linguistic expressions of that original." According to Kern, the translation of Chinese texts into English was also "governed by an ethnocentric, orientalist outlook, so that Chinese texts often appear to have been appropriated or even 'colonized' by their translators for their purposes or overall agenda" (2009, 172). Egerton undertook his translation during this historical period, and he could not be exempt from the influence of the dominant ideology in his society. Given the then receptive environment for Chinese literature and culture in Britain, it is no surprise that Egerton opted for more domesticating strategies. His goal was to reduce, filter, or dilute the culturemes of *Jin Ping Mei* in his translation to make his work more agreeable, natural, familiar, conventional, and appealing to a wide, popular readership unfamiliar with foreign culturemes and settings.

Furthermore, domestication, as J. M. Cohen (1962, 35) posits, was upheld by translators in Britain during the 1920s and '30s. This inclination was influenced by the prevailing science teaching of the early twentieth century, which emphasized matter over manner. Translators tended to abandon the imitation of form, with simplicity, plainness, and readability deemed the acceptable form. Hilaire Belloc went so far as declaring that any hint of foreignness in translation was flawed, asserting that a translation "should read like a first-class native thing" (1931, 13). T. S. Eliot, the famous modernist poet of the time, averred that a good translator should never imitate the original but "give the original through himself and find himself through the original" (Pound 1968, 13). A notable example is Constance Garnett's (1861–1946) translations of Russian literature, wherein she smoothed out the stylistic peculiarities of Fyodor Dostoevsky's (1821–1881) works to domesticate or tame them, making them more palatable to British readers by presenting a familiar taste or style and avoiding the perception of being incomprehensibly alien and foreign (Ryan and Ross 2018, 265). Another related instance is Bernard Shaw's translation of Siegfried Trebitsch's (1868–1956) play, *Frau Gittas Sühne*, in 1926. This translation represents an extreme form of domestication since Shaw simply rewrote the play for his contemporary audience. As Shaw declared, readers would not tolerate the dreary ending of Trebitsch's play, so he transformed the tragedy into a comedy, which proved to be a huge success (Woodsworth 2018, 373). During the first decades of the twentieth century, as noted in Chapter 1, many British modernist writers engaged in translating classical texts from other languages and cultures to serve their own literary purposes or to revitalize the culture of their time (Yao 2002, as quoted in Hickman 2019, 3). For these writers, translation was viewed as "a creative force in which specific translation strategies might serve a variety of cultural and social functions" (Venuti 2000, 11). Translation strategies such as liberal transfer, adaptation, intervention, appropriation, remodeling, and re-creation were necessarily employed by these writers in their translation process (Hickman 2019, 3). Strikingly, traditional "fidelity" and the conveyance of literal meanings of a source text were deemed only secondary or unnecessary (ibid., 4). Moreover, the so-called scholarly command of the language of the original text was conceived of as unnecessary or even "a barrier to authentic translation" (ibid.). According to Miranda Hickman (2019, 4), modernist writers emphasized the temporality of translation and approached it with an obvious sense of "irreverence," as they aimed to reimagine and reinvigorate classic texts for a new era or to respond to the needs and questions of the early twentieth century. Viewed in this light, the intellectual environment could necessarily affect Egerton's value orientations while translating the classic novel *Jin Ping Mei*, especially in the treatment of culturemes. By value orientations, they indicate "preferences for certain outcomes over others" (Brake and Walker 1995, 29). This tallies with Gadamer's (2003, 386) observation on translation, indicating that to highlight a specific aspect of the original that holds significance for us, we must inevitably downplay or completely omit other features. The adaptive or domesticating orientation for Egerton's translation, in handling culturemes, aimed to avoid confronting the targeted readers with much of the unfamiliar and unfathomable cultural heterogeneity of the work. The translation strategies employed by Egerton were similar, if not identical, to those utilized by his predecessors and contemporaries, such as H. A. Giles, Pound, Buck, Bethge, and Waley, as mentioned in Chapter 1. As far back as the 1880s, H. A. Giles, for instance, in his well-known work, *Gems of Chinese Literature*, noted that translators dealing with less familiar languages, such as Chinese and Arabic, typically prioritized the requirements and expectations of English readers (Drury 2015, 233). This can be evidenced in the translation endeavors of Bengali poet, novelist, and playwright Rabindranath Tagore (1861–1941), who translated his own poetry into English from 1912 to 1921. Tagore chose to adapt his poetry for English readers, tailoring it to accommodate the staid, even stale Edwardian verse forms. In doing so, Tagore's poetry became well read in the classics of English literature (Hokenson and Munson 2007, 168). Evidently, the reader-centered strategies contributed to bringing reading pleasure to English-language readers, enhancing their reading experience, and fostering comprehension and communication. In brief, Egerton's reader-friendly tendency in handling complex culturemes is primarily shaped by sociohistorical factors.

By comparison, Roy undertook his translation project in the 1980s. His translation was not unrelated to the rapid development of Chinese studies in North America during the late twentieth century. By the 1980s, sinology as an academic discipline had been firmly established in the U.S., and hundreds of research institutions focusing on Chinese studies were established under the auspices of the U.S. government (Zhang 2022, 123). Chinese studies, as noted earlier, have become popular in North American institutions from the 1980s, offering various avenues, (for example, via translation) of understanding China and its history (ibid.). Moreover, the establishment of China-U.S. diplomatic relations in 1979 and the implementation of China's reform and opening-up in the 1980s have brought China to the forefront of Western consciousness. Western scholars' regular communication with their Chinese counterparts and increased access to China's historical archives for research significantly improved (Rudolph and Szonyi 2018, 303). Since the 1990s,

China's economic achievements and full integration into the global economy have further enhanced its soft power on several levels. Soft power, as Joseph S. Nye Jr. (2004, 11) posits, is the ability of a country to persuade others to do what it wants through projecting and maintaining a positive national image. Nye reminds us that the primary sites of soft power entail "culture, values and foreign policies," with culture remaining the most important (ibid.). The Western interest in China's rise, whether as an economic powerhouse or a political threat in this globalized world, has also prompted a growing interest in Chinese culture and literature (Yeh 2010, 117). Given the increasing recognition and importance of Chinese literature in the "world republic of letters" (Casanova 2004), a growing number of translations of Chinese literary works have been produced in North America since the 1990s. Most of these translations are done by professional and scholarly translators, each appealing to different segments of English-reading audiences.

Significantly, many translators are experts in Chinese studies, engaging not only in academic research on China but also in translating Chinese literature and historiography. This mirrors a cultural trend within the sinological circle in North America. Prime examples of this trend include William H. Nienhauser's *The Grand Scribes Records* (1994), Victor H. Mair's edited *Columbia Anthology of Traditional Chinese Literature* (1994), and Stephen Owen's edited *Anthology of Chinese Literature* (1996), among others. As noted by Jon Kowallis (1996, 153), "the importance of expert translation in the whole enterprise of getting the West to take Chinese literature seriously seems, finally, on the verge of being recognized." With sinology gaining popularity in Western Europe and North America, the Western public has become more reactive and receptive to Chinese literature and culture, which no longer appear as remote. This trend began to surface in the 1970s when non-Western literature, including Asian classical works, was printed and distributed by leading publishers in North America (Henig 1974, 73). According to Michelle Yeh, translated literature struggles to achieve significant sales in the North American book market, representing only a small and specialized niche. Despite this, there is a discernible interest in translations of Chinese literary works within educational settings, particularly classrooms. The use of translated texts has proven successful in the United States, evidenced by a growing enrolment in Chinese language courses at the college level nationwide. Moreover, a growing number of high schools offer Chinese as an elective (Yeh 2010, 118). Yeh asserts that for American students preparing for a future in which China plays a significant role, translated Chinese literature provides a practical means to understand China's history and culture. She contends that literature not only documents history but is, in essence, a reflection of history itself (ibid.). Notably, over fifty percent of students enrolled in Chinese courses belong to the elite class and envision themselves as future leaders of the United States in roles such as diplomats, businessmen, and statesmen engaged in dealings with China (Wang 2022, 163). Wang Ban emphasizes the pragmatic implications of Chinese pedagogy within the geopolitical context, especially considering the perception of China as a rival, object, and target for the United States (2022, 164). According to Wang, these implications can never be underestimated. Chinese culture, Wang argues, "is a means, not an end," and "Chinese studies was and is the academic arm of the State Department, an enterprise of strategic importance and interstate rivalry, and academic research is no different from strategic think tanks" (ibid.). With more than two decades of experience teaching Chinese literature in translation in the United States, Yeh explains that translated Chinese literature holds a crucial place in U.S. higher education (Yeh 2010, 119). The promotion of teaching translated Chinese literature is bolstered by educational initiatives such as the Asian Studies Development Program in the U.S., which effectively introduces teachers to Chinese culture and various other Asian traditions (ibid.).

Furthermore, in the late twentieth century, a critical trend emerged in North American sinology that treated Ming vernacular texts as products of Ming literati culture (Luo 2012, 180; Plaks 1987, 3–54; Hsia 1988, 139). Andrew Plaks, for instance, asserts that several outstanding novels of Ming China are almost comparable to the greatest examples of the European novel (1987, 52). Evidently, the literary value of these classic novels was acknowledged, making them accessible to English-reading audiences through acclaimed translations. There was also a trend for sinologist-cum-translators of Chinese classical literature to enrich their translations with ample notes and other scholarly aids (Hsia 1988, 139). This practice aims to create a more informed intellectual or cultural context, reflecting the sophistication and profundity of the Chinese originals for the targeted readership. Such a practice is by no means limited to translations of traditional Chinese texts in the Anglophone world. Penguin Classics translations of modern Chinese literary works in Britain also demonstrate this tendency (Qian 2017, 295–316). These translations of traditional Chinese works are mainly intended for specialist readers and students interested in Chinese language and literature. As one of the sinologists in the U.S., Roy not only focused on Chinese history but also actively engaged in teaching and translating Chinese literary works. It is highly likely that the critical trends within the domain of premodern Chinese literature scholarship in North America influenced Roy's perception and criticism of *Jin Ping Mei*, shaping his approach to translating the novel. Little wonder that Roy's version tends to employ more foreignizing strategies in translating the abundant culturemes found in *Jin Ping Mei*. As revealed by the in-depth analysis in this chapter, Roy's translation takes the approach of leaving no culturemes untranslated and even provides notes for many culturemes. In effect, Roy's translation of culturemes, following Venuti's (1995, 20) tenets, is meant to "register the linguistic and cultural difference of the foreign text" and to provide target readers a window onto the late Ming society and culture.

Another significant factor to consider is the translators' diverse cultural backgrounds and their translational motives. Egerton, a writer and freelance translator, had already authored several books on music, education, and anthropology before undertaking the translation of *Jin Ping Mei*. His decision to translate this Chinese classic was motivated by his personal interest, driven by the popularity of things Chinese or chinoiserie in Britain during his day. Egerton's primary goal was to share his pleasure of reading the novel with contemporary readers, as indicated in his own words (Egerton 1939, ii). His translation was published by George Routledge and Sons, Ltd., a commercial publishing house in London, targeting readers who were not extensively familiar with Chinese literature and culture. To achieve the objective of sharing his own reading pleasure with the intended audience, Egerton needed to ensure that his readers could understand, accept, and enjoy his work. Additionally, meeting contemporary readers' needs was exceedingly important for commercial publishers during this time, as Britain witnessed a rapid development of popular culture in the interwar years. Popular mass culture, including films, novels, periodicals, and newspapers, thrived and held considerable appeal for the British public (Grandy 2016, 3). Reading and libraries became integral parts of everyday lived culture, with popular fiction, such as love and romance, detective, and thriller genres, finding a broad and enthusiastic audience across different social classes (James 2013, 27; Sterry 2017, 6). To attract a broader reading public, authors were encouraged to produce novels that could be quickly and easily absorbed and appreciated by readers without requiring extended reading sessions (James 2013, 27). Book publishers and film producers were largely market-intended and privileged the preferences of the mass audience (Grandy 2016, 7). According to Robert James (2010, 6), book publishers took great pains to tailor their products for their target audiences and to present material in a way that would bring pleasure to the mass readership; books failing to appeal to their target audiences were unlikely to succeed; that is why readers' tastes and their cultural competences were prioritized. In this context, reading had to be a source of joy or pleasure in the first place, even as it remained a voyage of discovery (ibid.). To accommodate a wider reading public and align with their tastes and reading habits, Egerton, from the outset, envisioned his readers, the audience for whom he believed he was translating. Accordingly, he resorted to more domesticating strategies to handle the various types of culturemes in *Jin Ping Mei*, emphasizing readability and intelligibility to align his work with the cultural preferences of his immediate social context. As Nord (1997, 92) states, the translator interprets the original work not only considering the original author's intention but also in terms of its compatibility with the receiving situation. In Egerton's case, the target situation significantly influenced his choices.

By contrast, as a researcher-translator, Roy chose to retranslate *Jin Ping Mei* primarily due to his deep affection for this masterpiece and his many years of research on it. Having been born and educated in China, Roy's cultural background and life experiences differed significantly from Egerton's, shaping Roy's unique perception and interpretation of the novel. Generally, the translator often acts as the initial reader of a given source work. The reader's (in this case, the translator) understanding of a literary text is often influenced by theirpreconceptions and life experiences, as individuals tend to apply their pre-existing knowledge or pre-understanding to fuse their horizon with the text's horizon, forming a new horizon, namely their unique understanding of the text (Holub 1984, 59; Eagleton 1996, 65; Gadamer 2003, 267). This also relates to the subjective and diverse nature of interpretation, which implies that different translators may bring unique perspectives and biases, influencing the way they render a text. Moreover, these perspectives and biases are always historically conditioned, further influencing their decision-making during translation. Roy initiated his retranslation project by contracting with Princeton University Press in the 1980s. The publication by an academic press also points to the scholarly nature of his translation. Both Roy and his patron place emphasis on the completeness of the original text. The peritext accompanying the published volumes underscored their shared goal: to provide readers with a genuinely complete version of *Jin Ping Mei*, revealing its true value not only within Chinese literature but also as a contribution to world literature or "Weltliteratur," to use Goethe's term (Damrosch, 2018). Roy's translation philosophy, encapsulated in his commitment to "translate everything" in *Jin Ping Mei* for his projected readers (Roy 1993, xlvii), explains his inclination towards foreignizing strategies. These strategies aimed at retaining all culturemes, including the provision of endnotes for many culturemes, without allowing himself much creativity and great liberties (namely, striking a compromise or a balance between fidelity to the ST and the relevance of the TT) because of the *skopos* predetermined from the outset.

The final consideration involves the aesthetic disparities between literary traditions, given that Chinese and English belong to entirely different language families – Sino-Tibetan and Indo-European, respectively. The substantial gaps in artistic expression between these languages can significantly impact the process of translation, influencing the translator's logical judgement and aesthetic expression (Wong and Shen 1999, 88). Even at the close of the nineteenth century, Chinese language and culture were perceived as challenging and quite remote to most British individuals (Liu et al. 2012, 18). Chinese literature, especially classic novels, differs significantly from its English counterparts in aesthetic tradition. A translator deeply immersed in their native culture is inevitably shaped by the aesthetic traditions inherent to that culture (Wong and Shen 1999, 91). In the case of a translator who is also a writer, such as Egerton in this study, their aesthetic preferences and writing styles are likely to be knowingly or unwittingly influenced by their own cultural aesthetic. Taking linguistic and ecological culturemes as examples, Egerton utilizes flexible tactics to downplay the alien nature of the original, aligning with the aesthetic expectation of the target readers. By contrast, Roy's translation exhibits a high frequency of literal transfer, often amplifying the original text. Roman Jakobson (1959, 234) argued for translatability by stating that "all cognitive experience and its classification is conveyable in any existing language. Whenever there is deficiency, terminology may be qualified or amplified by loan-words or loan-translations, neologisms or semantic shifts, and finally, by circumlocutions." Jakobson aims to justify translatability but neglects the resulting effect produced by such a translation. Roy's fidelity to both content and form, especially in rendering culturemes described in four-character phrases and parallel clauses in *Jin Ping Mei*, might elicit a negative aesthetic reaction among English-speaking audiences with aesthetic habits differing from those of Chinese readers. Clearly, Egerton's approach tends to prioritize meaning over form, resulting in a translation that is natural, fluent, and enjoyable to read. These observations underscore the crucial role of aesthetic variations as a determining factor affecting the transfer of culturemes in *Jin Ping Mei*.

2.6 Concluding Remarks

In conclusion, this chapter has systematically explored the intricate tapestry of late Ming culture as portrayed in *Jin Ping Mei*. Through meticulous analysis, it has brought to light a noteworthy pattern of increased preservation of foreign elements or cultural heterogeneity within the Chinese original text. This tendency becomes even more conspicuous when comparing Roy's retranslation with an earlier rendition by Egerton. This finding aligns with the ideas put forward by Paul Bensimon and Antoine Berman, who demonstrate that initial translations often lean towards familiar aspects of the receptor culture, whereas subsequent retranslations strive to recapture the original work's linguistic intricacies and cultural nuances (Bensimon 1990, iv; Berman 1990, 1). Yet, on the other hand, this striving to recapture the original's linguistic subtleties and cultural nuances may not necessarily bring about positive or desired effects in the receiving literary and cultural context. To a certain extent, it could instead result in a compromise of the spirit and tone of the original, as well as the smoothness, readability, and convenient understanding of the translated content on the part of the target-language readership. Consequently, whether this endeavor to recapture could create any significant added value to the retranslated work and maintain relevance in the target context of current cultural and social dynamics is worth further consideration. Furthermore, the chapter has illustrated the significant influence of sociohistorical, cultural, and aesthetic factors in determining the translational approaches adopted by these translators when dealing with the complex culturally specific elements embedded in *Jin Ping Mei*. The detailed examination has revealed that translators adeptly utilize both domesticating and foreignizing strategies in handling culturemes. However, a thorough and systematic analysis exposes distinct tendencies in each translator. Egerton, for instance, tends to leave his contemporary readers in peace as much as possible, moving the source text closer to them. On the other hand, Roy emphasizes outright faithfulness to the original content and the intention to preserve cultural subtleties, particularly for an academic audience. The next chapter will provide a meticulous examination of how narratological resources in *Jin Ping Mei* are handled within the two translations. It aims to deepen the understanding of the unique inclinations demonstrated by each translator in navigating the narratological dimensions embedded within *Jin Ping Mei*. It is hoped that a more profound comprehension of the translators' choices and their impact on the narrative structure will be revealed, further enriching the understanding of the dynamics of this seminal work in Chinese literature when translated in a major European language.

Notes

1 The *Guoyu Cidian* is a Taiwan based online dictionary, which can be accessed through the link: https://dict.revised.moe.edu.tw/

2 In this study, Chinese passages are quoted mainly from the facsimile edition, namely the Wanli or *cihua* edition. In the facsimile edition, there are no punctuation marks except for the period used for sentence division. Furthermore, the texts were printed from top

to bottom and from right to left. For the reader's convenience, all selected passages from the facsimile edition are adapted to the "modern" form, that is, they are presented in horizontal style and edited them from left to right. All other things remain unchanged.

References

Aixela, Javier Franco. 1996. "Culture-Specific Items in Translation." In *Translation, Power, Subversion*, edited by Alvarez Rodriguez, Roman, and M. Carmen Africa Vidal, 52–78. Clevedon: Multilingual Matters.

Bai Weiguo 白維國. 1991. *Jin Ping Mei cidian* 金瓶梅詞典 (Jin Ping Mei Dictionary). Beijing: Zhonghua shuju chubanshe.

Barringer, Tim, and Tom Flynn. 1998. *Colonialism and the Object: Empire, Material Culture and the Museum*. London: Routledge.

Bassnett, Susan. 2007. "Translation and Culture." In *A Companion to Translation Studies*, edited by Piotr Kuhiwczak, and Karin Littau, 13–23. Clevedon: Multilingual Matters.

Belloc, Hilaire. 1931. *On translation*. Oxford: Clarendon Press.

Bensimon, Paul. 1990. "Presentation." *Palimpsestes* 4: iv–xiii.

Benton, Gregor, and Edmund Terence Gomez. 2008. *The Chinese in Britain, 1800-Present: Economy, Transnationalism, Identity*. London: Palgrave Macmillan.

Berman, Antoine. 1990. "Laretraduction comme espace de traduction." *Palimpsestes* 4: 1–8.

Brake, Terrence, and Danielle Medina Walker. 1995. *Doing Business Internationally: The Guide to Cross-Cultural Success*. Burr Ridge: Irwin.

Brook, Timothy. 1993. "Rethinking Syncretism: The Unity of the Three Teachings and their Joint Worship in Late-Imperial China." *Journal of Chinese Religions* 21 (1): 13–44.

Buswell, Robert E. 2005. *Encyclopedia of Buddhism*. New York: Macmillan.

Buswell, Robert E., and Donald S. Lopez. 2013. *The Princeton Dictionary of Buddhism*. Princeton, NJ: Princeton University Press.

Cao, Shunqing. 2010. *Chinese and Western Comparative Poetics*. Beijing: Renmin University of China Press.

Casanova, Pascale. 2004. *The World Republic of Letters*. Translated by M.B. DeBevoise. Cambridge, MA: Harvard University Press.

Chan, Sin-Wai, and David E. Pollard. 1995. *An Encyclopaedia of Translation*. Hong Kong: The Chinese University Press.

Chen, Hongwei.1999. "Cultural Differences and Translation." *Meta: journal des traducteurs* 44 (1): 121–132.

Chesterman, Andrew, and Emma Wagner. 2002. *Can Theory Help Translation. A Dialogue Between the Ivory Tower and the Wordface*. Manchester: St. Jerome.

Cohen, John Michael. 1962. *English Translators and Translations*. London: F. Mildner and Sons.

Cullen, Christopher. 1993. "Patients and Healers in Late Imperial China: Evidence from the Jin Ping Mei." *History of Science* xxxi: 99–150.

Damrosch, David. 2018. *What Is World Literature?* Princeton, NJ: Princeton University Press.

Davies, Eirlys E. 2003. "A Goblin or a Dirty Nose? The Treatment of Culture-Specific References in Translations of the Harry Potter Books." *The Translator 9* (1): 65–100.

Díaz-Cintas, Jorge., and Aline Remael. 2007. *Audiovisual Translation: Subtitling*. Manchester: St. Jerome.

Dimitriu, Rodica. 2015."The Many Contexts of Translation (Studies)." *Linguaculture* 1: 5–23.

Ditze, Stephan-Alexander. 2006. *America and the Americans in Postwar British Fiction: An Imagological Study of Selected Novels*. Heidelberg: Universitaetsverlag Winter.

Drury, Annmarie. 2015. *Translation as Transformation in Victorian Poetry*. Cambridge: Cambridge University Press.

Eagleton, Terry. 1996. *Literary Theory: An Introduction*. Oxford and Malden: Blackwell Publishing.

Egerton, Clement. 1939. *The Golden Lotus*. 4 vols. London: George Routledge and Sons, Ltd.

Eliot, Thomas Stearns. 1928. "Introduction." In *Selected Poems of Ezra Pound*, xvii. London: Faber and Gwyer.

Elman, Benjamin A. 2000. *A Cultural History of Civil Examinations in Late Imperial China*. Berkeley: University of California Press.

Feuchtwang, Stephan. 2016. "Chinese Religions." In *Religions in the Modern World: Traditions and Transformations*, edited by Linda Woodhead, Christopher Partridge, and Hiroko Kawanami, 144–171. London: Routledge.

Fiske, Shanyn. 2011. "Orientalism Reconsidered: China and the Chinese in Nineteenth-Century Literature and Victorian Studies." *Literature Compass* 8/4: 214–226.

Gadamer, Hans-Georg. 2003. *Truth and Method*. Second revised edition, translated and revised by Joel Weinsheimer, and Donald G. Marshall. New York and London: Continuum.

Grandy, Christine. 2016. *Heroes and Happy Endings: Class, Gender, and Nation in Popular Film and Fiction in Interwar Britain*. Manchester: Manchester University Press.

Harman, Nicky. 2006. "Foreign Culture, Foreign Style." *Perspectives: Studies in Translatology* 14 (1): 13–31.

Hatim, Basil, and Ian Mason. 1990. *Discourse and the Translator*. London: Routledge.

He Manzi 何滿子. 1990. *Jin Ping Mei jianshang cidian* 金瓶梅鑒賞詞典 (A Dictionary for Jin Ping Mei). Shanghai: Shanghai guji chubanshe.

Henig, Suzanne. 1974. "The Bloomsbury Group and Non-Western Literature." *Journal of South Asian Literature* 10 (1): 73–82.

Hickman, Miranda. 2019. "Introduction." In *The Classics in Modernist Translation*, edited by Miranda Hickman, and Lynn Kozak, 1–7. London: Bloomsbury Publishing.

Holmes, James S. 1988. *Translated!: Papers on Literary Translation and Translation Studies*. Leiden: Brill.

Holub, Robert C. 1984. *Reception Theory: A Critical Introduction*. London and New York: Methuen.

Hokenson, Jan Walsh, and Marcella Munson. 2007. *The Bilingual Text: History and Theory of Literary Self-Translation*. Manchester: St. Jerome Publishing.

Hsia, Chih-tsing. 1988. "Classical Chinese Literature: Its Reception Today as a Product of Traditional Culture." *Chinese Literature: Essays, Articles, Reviews* 10 (1/2): 133–152.

Hucker, Charles O. 1985. *A Dictionary of Official Titles in Imperial China*. Stanford: Stanford University Press.

Hung, Eva. 1993. "All in the family? Translating Names and Honorifics in Chinese Fiction." *Perspectives: Studies in Translatology* 1 (1): 69–78.

Jakobson, Roman. 1959. "On Linguistic Aspects of Translation." In *On Translation*, edited by Reuben A. Brower, 232–239. Cambridge, MA: Harvard University Press.

James, Robert. 2013. *Popular Culture and Working-class Taste in Britain, 1930–39: A Round of Cheap Diversions?* Manchester: Manchester University Press.

John, Francis A. 1982. "Arthur Waley and Amy Lowell: A Note." *The Journal of the Rutgers University Libraries* 44 (1): 17–22.

Johnson, Ryan. 2020. *Transnationalism and Translation in Modern Chinese, English, French and Japanese Literatures*. London: Anthem Press.

Katan, David. 1999. *Translating Cultures: An Introduction for Translators, Interpreters and Mediators*. Manchester: St. Jerome.

Katan, David. 2009. "Translation as Intercultural Communication." In *Routledge Companion to Translation Studies*, edited by Jeremy Munday 74–92. London: Routledge.

Kern, Robert. 2009. *Orientalism, Modernism, and the American Poem*. Cambridge: Cambridge University Press.

Komissarov, Vilen N. 1991. "Language and Culture in Translation: Competitors or Collaborators?" *TTR* 4 (1): 33–47.

Kowallis, Jon E. 1996. "Interpreting Lu Xun." *Chinese Literature: Essays, Articles, Reviews* 18: 153–164.

Kwong, Charles. 2011. "Problems in Translating Culture: The Translated Titles of Fusheng Liuji." *TTR* 24 (2): 177–206.

Lefevere, André. 1992. *Translating Literature: Practice and Theory in a Comparative Literature Context*. London: Routledge.

Lefevere, André. 1999. "Composing the Other." In *Postcolonial Translation: Theory and Practice*, edited by Susan Bassnett, and Harish Trivedi, 75–94. London: Routledge.

Leppihalme, Ritva. 1997. *Culture Bumps: An Empirical Approach to the Translation of Allusions*. Clevedon: Multilingual Matters.

Liu, Tao Tao, Laurence K. P. Wong, and Chan Sin-wai. 2012. *Style, Wit and Word-play: Essays in Translation Studies in Memory of David Hawkes*. Newcastle: Cambridge Scholars Publishing.

Luo, Junjie. 2012. "The Plum in the Golden Vase or, Chin P'ing Mei, Volume 4: The Climax by David Roy." *Chinese Literature: Essays, Articles, Reviews* 34: 178–183.

Ma, Huijuan, and Guan Xingzhong. 2017. "On the Transcultural Rewriting of the Chinese Play Wang Baochuan." *Perspectives* 25 (4): 556–570.

Mailhac, Jean-Pierre. 1996. "The Formulation of Translation Strategies for Cultural References." In *Language, Culture and Communication in Contemporary Europe*, edited by Charlotte Hoffmann, 132–151. Clevedon: Multilingual Matters.

McQuilkin, Robertson J. 1980. "Limits of Cultural Interpretation." *Journal of the Evangelical Theological Society* 23 (2): 113–124.

Munday, Jeremy. 2001. *Introducing Translation Studies: Theories and Applications*. London: Routledge.

Newmark, Peter. 1988. *A Textbook of Translation*. New York: Prentice Hall.

Nida, Eugene Albert. 1964. *Toward a Science of Translating: With Special Reference to Principles and Procedures Involved in Bible Translating*. Leiden and Boston: Brill.

Nord, Christiane. 1997. *Translating as a Purposeful Activity: Functionalist Approaches Explained*. Manchester: St. Jerome.

Nye, Joseph S., Jr. 2004. *Soft Power: The Means to Success in World Politics*. New York: Public Affairs.

Olk, Harald Martin. 2013. "Cultural References in Translation: A Framework for Quantitative Translation Analysis." *Perspectives: Studies in Translatology* 21 (3): 344–357.

Peak, Anna. 2015. "The Chinese Language in the 'Saturday Review': A Case Study in Sinophobia's Scholarly Roots." *Victorian Literature and Culture* 43 (2): 431–444.

Pedersen, Jan. 2007. "Cultural Interchangeability: The Effects of Substituting Cultural References in Subtitling." *Perspectives: Studies in Translatology* 15 (1): 30–48.

Plaks, Andrew H. 1987. *The Four Masterworks of the Ming Novel: Ssu Ta Ch'i-Shu*. Princeton, N.J: Princeton University Press.

Pound, Ezra. 1968. *Ezra Pound: Selected Poems*. London: Faber & Faber.

Qian, Menghan. 2017. "Penguin Classics and the Canonization of Chinese Literature in English Translation." *Translation and Literature* 26 (3): 295–316.

Qvale, Per. 2003. *From St. Jerome to Hypertext: Translation in Theory and Practice*. London: Routledge.

Ranzato, Irene. 2015. *Translating Culture Specific References on Television: The Case of Dubbing*. London: Routledge.

Roy, David T. 1993. *The Plum in the Golden Vase or, Chin P'ing Mei* (vol. 1). Princeton, NJ: Princeton University Press.

Roy, David T. 2001. *The Plum in the Golden Vase or, Chin P'ing Mei* (vol. 2). Princeton, NJ: Princeton University Press.

Roy, David T. 2006. *The Plum in the Golden Vase or, Chin P'ing Mei* (vol. 3). Princeton, NJ: Princeton University Press.

Roy, David T. 2011. *The Plum in the Golden Vase or, Chin P'ing Mei* (vol. 4). Princeton, NJ: Princeton University Press.

Roy, David T. 2013. *The Plum in the Golden Vase or, Chin P'ing Mei* (vol. 5). Princeton, NJ: Princeton University Press.

Rudolph, Jennifer, and Michael Szonyi. 2018. *The China Questions*. Cambridge, MA: Harvard University Press.

Rura, Lidia. 2015. "Translating Cultural Content in Poetry: Cultural References in the English and Dutch Translations of the Russian Poet Alexander Galich." In *Translation, Transnationalism, World Literature*, edited by Francesca Benocci, and Marco Sonzogni, 255–274. Italia: Edizioni Joker.

Ryan, Derek, and Stephen Ross. 2018. *The Handbook to the Bloomsbury Group*. London: Bloomsbury Academic.

Schwartz, Shalom H. 2007. "Universalism Values and the Inclusiveness of Our Moral Universe." *Journal of Cross-Cultural Psychology* 38 (6): 711–728.

Shang, Wei. 2005. "The Making of the Everyday World: Jin Ping Mei Cihua and Encyclopedias for Daily Use." In *Dynastic Crisis and Cultural Innovation*, edited by Wang David Der-wei, and Shang Wei, 63–92. Cambridge, MA: Harvard University Press.

Snell-Hornby, Maria. (1988) 1995. *Translation Studies: An Integrated Approach*. Amsterdam: John Benjamins Publishing.

Sterry, Emma. 2017. *The Single Woman, Modernity, and Literary Culture*. London: Palgrave Macmillan.

Sun Xun 孫遜. 2005. *Jin Ping Mei jianshang cidian* 金瓶梅鑒賞辭典 (Jin Ping Mei Appreciation Dictionary). Shanghai: Hanyu da cidian chubanshe.

Tian, Mian. 2017. "Lady Precious Stream: A Chinese Chinoiserie Anglicized on the Modern British Stage." *Comparative Drama* 51 (2): 158–186.

Toury, Gideon. 1995. *Descriptive Translation Studies and Beyond*. Amsterdam: John Benjamins.

Venuti, Lawrence. 1995. *The Translator's Invisibility: A History of Translation*. London: Routledge.

Venuti, Lawrence. 1998. *The Scandals of Translation: Towards an Ethics of Difference*. London: Routledge.

Venuti, Lawrence. 2000. *The Translation Studies Reader*. New York: Routledge.

Venuti, Lawrence. 2017. *The Translator's Invisibility: A History of Translation*. London: Routledge.

Vitiello, Giovanni. 2000. "The Forgotten Tears of the Lord of Longyang: Late Ming Stories of Male Prostitution and Connoisseurship." In *Linked Faiths: Essays on Chinese Religions and Traditional Culture in Honour of Kristofer Schippers,* edited by Jan de Meyer, and Peter M. Engelfriet, 227–247. Boston: Brill.

Wang, Liqi 王利器. 1988. *Jin Ping Mei cidian* 金瓶梅詞典 (A Dictionary on Jin Ping Mei). Changchun: Jilin Wenshi chubanshe.

Wang, Ban. 2022. *China in the World: Culture, Politics and World Vision.* Durham and London: Duke University Press.

Wilss, Wolfram. 1996. *Knowledge and Skills in Translator Behavior.* Amsterdam: John Benjamins.

Witchard, Anne. 2012. *Lao She in London.* HK: Hong Kong University Press.

Witchard, Anne. 2015. *British Modernism and Chinoiserie.* Edinburgh: Edinburgh University Press.

Wong, Dongfeng, and Shen Dan. 1999. "Factors Influencing the Process of Translating." *Meta* 44 (1): 78–100.

Woodsworth, Judith. 2018. "Writers as Translators." In *Routledge Handbook of Literary Translation,* edited by Kelly Washbourne and Ben van Wyke, 369–381. London: Routledge.

Xiao Xiao Sheng of Lanling 蘭陵笑笑生. 2003. *Xinke xiuxiang piping Jin Ping Mei* 新刻 繡像批評金瓶梅. Singapore: South Ocean Publishing.

Yao, Steven G. 2002. *Translation and the Languages of Modernism: Gender, Politics, and Language.* New York: Palgrave Macmillan.

Yeh, Diana. 2008. "Contested Belongings: The Politics and Poetics of Making a Home in Britain." In *China fictions/English language*, edited by Robert A. Lee, 299–325. Boston: Brill.

Yeh, Diana. 2014. *The Happy Hsiungs: Performing China and the Struggle for Modernity.* HK: Hong Kong University Press.

Yeh, Michelle. 2010. "Literature in Identity Formation: Reading Chinese Literature in Translation." In *Literature in Translation: Teaching Issues and Reading Practices*, edited by Carol Maier, and Francoise Massardier-Kenney, 117–135. Kent, OH: The Kent State University Press.

Yeh, Michelle. 2016. "Inventing China: The American Tradition of Translating Chinese Poetry." In *Reading the Past Across Space and Time: Receptions and World Literature*, edited by Brenda Deen Schildgen, and Ralph Hexter, 285–296. New York: Springer Nature.

Yue, Isaac, and Siufu Tang. 2013. *Scribes of Gastronomy: Representations of Food and Drink in Imperial Chinese Literature.* Hong Kong: Hong Kong University Press.

Zhang, Xiping. 2022. *A Study on the Influence of Ancient Chinese Cultural Classics Abroad in the Twentieth Century.* Singapore: Springer.

3 In Search of a Varied Voice

Remodeling Narratological Elements Through Translation

3.1 Introduction

In fictional prose, language often manifests in the form of different voices, including the narrator's or the implied author's, and those of different characters (Alvstad 2013, 208). These voices contribute significantly to our understanding of a novel's thematic meaning and aesthetic value. The narrator's voice encompasses distinctive storytelling traits, the depiction of fictional events, and narratorial commentary. On the other hand, characters' voices are enacted through speech and thought presentation, involving direct and free (in)direct speech or thought (Leech and Short 1981, 381). While character speech in prose fiction can by no means be equated with real-life speech but rather created by novelists as fictive orality (Fludernik 2009, 64), it can be portrayed through register variables and various linguistic devices like literary dialect, slang, and punning diction. These elements serve to depict scenes and characters for specific literary purposes. The multitude of narrative voices provides crucial cues guiding the reader's interpretation of the story and aiding them in entering the fictional world (Hoffmann 2017, 159). In literary translation, as noted by Charlotte Bosseaux (2018, 130), any alteration in the way characters or narrators express themselves could result in a change in the *feel* of the narrative text or the fictional universe represented within that text.

To date, scant attention has been devoted to the interlingual transfer of the plurality of voices in *Jin Ping Mei*. This chapter attempts, albeit modestly, to address this lacuna in the literature, aiming to enrich existing studies on *Jin Ping Mei* and literary translation studies at large. To this end, I will conduct a systematic analysis of the narrative voice, encompassing both the narrator's and characters' voices in the novel. I will consider their literary significance and examine how they are represented in interlingual translation. The main aim of this chapter is not to evaluate the quality of the translations but rather to identify and present important voices in the ST and examine how, and to what extent, they are reconstructed or transformed in the English versions (namely, the target texts, TTs). The analysis aligns with descriptive translation studies, as stated in Chapter 1, and relates to the broader analysis of vernacular fiction in the Ming period. Specifically, the chapter addresses the question of how the main characters' voices and that of the narrator are portrayed in English renderings, and it delves into the contributing factors shaping

DOI: 10.4324/9781003472674-3

the translators' decisions. I will illustrate this inquiry with examples extracted from both the source and target texts. By answering this question, the chapter aims to shed light on the narrative features of *Jin Ping Mei*, the complexities involved in transposing these features to a different literary context across time and space, and the potential impact of specific translational choices on these features as well as on the overall *feel* of the novel.

The rest of the chapter is structured in the following way. It first offers a brief introduction to voices in *Jin Ping Mei*, serving as a starting point for subsequent discussion. It then provides a comparative analysis of the treatment of characters' and the narrator's voices in two English translations, drawing on examples from the source and target texts. This analysis assesses the impact of translational shifts and considers the extratextual forces and reasons underlying the translators' strategies. Subsequently, the chapter presents a detailed discussion on translational results. The final section concludes the chapter.

3.2 Mapping Voice in *Jin Ping Mei*

Traditionally, narrative texts feature multiple voices, which can be mediated by a narrator or presented as character monologues and dialogues. In narratological terms, *Jin Ping Mei* is narrated by an external "heterodiegetic narrator" who knows virtually everything about the story and characters but is not a participant in the story world (Genette 1988, 84). Apart from the self-effacing omniscient narrator, the novel also depicts various characters from all walks of life, whose voices contribute to their characterization. The voice studied in this chapter includes characters' voices and the narrator's voice. In the following, I will elaborate on each of these categories.

3.2.1 Character Voice

As already noted, as a milestone in the development of Chinese fiction or *xiaoshuo*, *Jin Ping Mei* distances itself from its predecessors, focusing on the detailed depiction of ordinary people and their everyday lives in urban settings. The novel belongs to the realistic tradition with a naturalistic tendency, prioritizing verisimilitude as the novelist's primary goal. This is exemplified by the textualization of living speech types in the narrative to achieve "the closest imitation of reality" (Page 1988, 3). The plot of *Jin Ping Mei* is grounded in a particular social setting, featuring characters from different strata of society who frequently employ various forms of non-standard speech, such as colloquialisms, slang, aural puns, bawdy words, and sociolects, anchored in the late Ming sociolinguistic milieu. The goal is to strike a chord in the heart of the general reading public of the novelist's day. As a result, the narrative takes on a heteroglossic character, showcasing a multitude of speech patterns. The term heteroglossia, developed by Mikhail Bakhtin (1895–1975), indicates the stratification of language or an assortment of differentiated language varieties in narrative fiction. This covers the diverse speech patterns and registers used by distinct social classes, professions, and individuals in the fictional universe (Bakhtin 1981, 290). Regarding the language of a novel, Bakhtin writes that "the language of the novel is the system of its "languages." [...] The novel can be defined as a diversity of social speech types (sometimes even diversity of languages) and diversity of individual voices, artistically organized" (Bakhtin 1981, 262). Most crucially, Bakhtin emphasizes the pragmatic and ideological implications behind the linguistic stratification in the novel, maintaining that "all languages of heteroglossia, whatever the principle underlying them and making each unique, are specific points of view on the world, forms for conceptualizing the world in words, specific world views, each characterized by its own objects, meanings and values" (Bakhtin 1981, 292).

Jin Ping Mei's voice structure is characterized by heteroglossia in the Bakhtinian sense. The novel contains multiple speech types or language registers – contemporary vernacular, literary language, archaic classicism, the language of the illiterate, marketplace speech, and the like. This diversity allows the voices of fictional characters to sound natural, authentic, and elicit empathy from the reader. In *The Chinese Vernacular Story*, Patrick Hanan maintains that the diversified language used in the Ming novel indicates an intention to reach a wider reading audience (1981, 5–11). This is partly because traditional Chinese fiction is considered to have evolved from street talk and popular gossip, holding a lower literary status than poetry (Gu 2006, 313). The narrative language spans from the most vulgar voice of the lower class to the most elegant voice of the elite. In the fictive dialogue of *Jin Ping Mei*, characters' voices adopt different tones and styles: casual and pompous, formal and bantering, plain and down to earth, sarcastic and emotionally charged, and so forth. This diversity of usage contextualizes the narrative socially and culturally, enhances the portrayal of characters, and bridges the psychological gap between the characters and the reader.

Jin Ping Mei's author demonstrates proficiency in making characters idiosyncratic, not only in physical appearance but also in the way they talk. In his commentary on *Jin Ping Mei*, Zhang Zhupo emphasizes the novelist's subtle and nuanced representation of speech, stating that each individual character is delineated not just by what they say, but also by how they say it (Wu 2009, 183). Indeed, almost every principal character speaks in ways that manifest their individual personalities and values. These individualized styles of fictional speech deserve special attention, inasmuch as this type of discourse exhibits linguistic features related to both users (who speaks) and uses (what and how he or she speaks) (Bell 1991, 186).

Notably, the distinctive voices of characters in *Jin Ping Mei* are dynamic and engage with each other in a dialogic manner. They can imply social consciousness, create a somatic effect on the reader, and provoke amusement or enjoyment. Additionally, these voices add communicative meaning and sociocultural value to the narrative, drawing the reader into the sociocultural and interpersonal dynamics of the relationships depicted. As Alexandra Assis Rosa puts it, communicative meaning signals information on "time, space (physical or social), and a speaker's individuality, while sociocultural value suggests degrees of power, social status, and prestige associated with different characters in a given community" (Rosa 2012; Rosa 2015, 210). Through their speech, the reader can gain insight into the identity, the strengths, and weaknesses of a character, the nuances of social relationships between characters, and the attitudes of the narrator/implied author (Hanan 1981, 14). More importantly, as noted by Roger Fowler (1977, 103), in novels, a character's manner of speech is closely tied to their characterization, as discerned in dialogic exchanges. In short, the centrality of these functions justifies an in-depth analysis of characters' voices in translation. This analysis aims to establish whether and how their speech presentation is recreated in a different language environment, with poetics and communicative richness resembling that of the original.

The challenge of translating *Jin Ping Mei* is compounded by character discourse associated with (in)formal registers and other non-standard varieties, including vulgarisms, swearwords, and bawdy language. Register variation and non-standard speech varieties carry crucial information about the characters and the story. Their treatment in translation significantly influences the target reader's conception of characters' identities, status, and personal qualities, and the textual world of the novel (Locher and Jucker 2017, 272). Rosa asserts that "translating formal features correlated with information on the speaker, situation, and prestige, further filtered by a poetics of fiction and used to indirectly offer contextual information about a character, however, does pose problems" (2015, 213). All told, the diversity of character speech and its functions in *Jin Ping Mei* illustrates the intricate challenges of narrative voice in interlingual translation.

3.2.2 The Narrator/Storyteller's Voice

With regard to the narrator/storyteller's voice, this chapter specifically focuses on the narrator's meta-narrative remarks, which encompass his recurrent use of fixed or formulaic phrases and expressions for mediation. As previously mentioned, *Jin Ping Mei*'s narrator tells and comments on the story from a position outside of the reported events, effectively engaging the audience with both the story and himself. The narrator exhibits a high degree of textual control evident in the main body of the work. He not only "sees, hears, and reports on every detail in the story," but he also "takes the reader into his confidence and imbues him with his own feelings and attitudes; whenever appropriate he makes his own comments and asides" (Liu 1966, 234). This characteristic stems from the fact that, as a typical Ming novel, *Jin Ping Mei* is characterized by a narrative style known as the mimesis of oral story-telling. As articulated by Ge Liangyan (2001, 194), writers of vernacular novels in the Ming dynasty tended to imitate oral storytellers in framing or structuring the text. Storytellers, individuals skilled in narrating stories to a large audience in public places, were part of the Chinese oral storytelling tradition, involving verbal art performances based on scripts, which had a millennial history (Børdahl 2003, 66). Ming vernacular fiction directly inherited and evolved from this storytelling tradition (Huang 2018, 14). In *Out of the Margins*, Ge describes the novelists' simulation of the oral storytelling tradition as "linguistic empathy," as seen in the case of *Shuihu zhuan* and *Sanguo yanyi*. Ge further explains that

> For later writers of vernacular fiction, 'linguistic empathy' means, first of all, identification with the linguistic stance of a storyteller on a metadiegetic narrative

level. Even when no character speaks in the story or when a character's speech is narrated instead of quoted, the writer still seems to be transferring himself into someone else's voice – namely, the voice of a storyteller, real or imagined. The entire narrative is therefore assumed to be the recording of an oral delivery. (Ge 2001, 193)

(Ge 2001, 193)

Jin Ping Mei is closely tied to this oral tradition, with the storyteller's voice permeating the narrative (Plaks 1980, 9). The storyteller, who narrates the story from a third-person point of view, uses various rhetorical techniques that qualify the ways he addresses the audience. This chapter does not delve into a detailed analysis of the storytelling manner in *Jin Ping Mei*, as it falls outside the purview of this study. Rather, it intends to examine one specific aspect: the distinctive phraseological markers used by the narrator. These linguistic signals encompass a plethora of stock phrases and formulaic expressions, such as *huashuo* 話說, *qieshuo* 且說, *huaxiu xufan* 話休絮繁, and *danjian* 但見. Referred to as the narrator's "meta-narrative remarks" (Børdahl 2016, 36), these fixed expressions are a salient feature of the Ming vernacular fiction genre (Børdahl 2003, 72). They signal narratorial mediation and intervention in the story, creating a "distancing effect" (Birch 1974, 304). Of particular interest for this study is that these meta-narrative remarks draw attention to the narrator's voice. As Hanan maintains, such formal features or meta-narrative markers in vernacular fiction belong to the narrative devices of formal realism due to their close mimesis of reality, echoing the public storyteller addressing listening audiences in public settings (Birch 1974, 307). The novelist uses these strategies to control the narrative space, adjust perspectives among the narrating self, the narrated world, and the reader, and reveal the narrator himself.

Such narrative conventions in Chinese fiction have been perceived as shortcomings when compared to Western fiction. Some scholars argue that these conventions, once functional devices in oral storytelling, should not be retained in written genres. According to this perspective, they are considered unnecessary literary clichés that undermine the illusion of veracity created by naturalistic plot details (Bishop 1956, 241). However, Ming Dong Gu (2006, 313) asserts that these formal idiosyncrasies are not limitations but rather aspects of fictional artistry in the Chinese tradition. In a similar vein, Hanan identifies these formal features as essential for Chinese vernacular tales, arguing that English translations of Chinese vernacular texts often "fall flat" primarily because translators have not successfully rendered these formal qualities (Birch 1974, 306).

According to Børdahl, meta-narrative markers in *Jin Ping Mei* can be grouped into three major categories: markers of narrative beginning, transition, progression, and conclusion; pre-verse markers (indicating the shift from verse to prose and vice versa); and markers of narrative commentary and simulated dialogue with the narratee (Børdahl 2016, 36). Table 3.1 provides lists of the narrator's stylistic means found in *Jin Ping Mei*, adapted from Børdahl's (2016) typology. The lists showcase some representative examples from the novel.

These lexical markers can help us identify the narrator's voice and locate the narrator in the story world. Børdahl (2010, 87) explains that such formulaic

Table 3.1 The Narrator's Voice or Meta-narrative Markers (adapted from Børdahl's [2016] typology)

---

(1) Markers of narrative beginning, transition, progression, and conclusion

---

話說/再說/單說/且說/卻說	*huashuo/zaishuo/danshuo/qieshuo/queshuo*
不必細/盡說	*bu bi xi/jin shuo*
俱不必說	*ju bu bi shuo*
不說/不提	*bu shuo/bu ti*
且表/卻表	*qie biao/que biao*
表過不提	*biao guo bu ti*
話休絮煩	*hua xiu xu fan*
當晚無話	*dang wan wu hua*
不在話下	*bu zai hua xia*
話分兩頭	*hua fen liang tou*
說時遲那時快	*shuo shichi, na shi kuai*
有話卻長/無話即短	*you hua que chang, wu hua ji duan*
且聽下回分解	*qie ting xia hui fen jie*
……	…

---

(2) Pre-verse markers

但/怎見	*dan/zen jian*
正/怎/真個是	*zheng/zen/zhenge shi*
單道/表	*dan dao/biao*
詩曰/有詩為證	*shiyue/youshi weizheng*
詞曰/有詞為證	*ci yue/youci weizheng*
有分教	*you fenjiao*
有詩單表	*youshi danbiao*
……	…

---

(3) Markers of the narrator's comment and his simulated dialogue with the narratee

---

看官聽說	*kan guan ting shuo*
說話的	*shuo hua de*
你道/你說	*ni dao/ni shuo*
……	…

---

expressions are essential for meta-narrative functions, such as marking shifts of narrative mode, time, and focus. According to Hanan (2005, 10), one purpose of these phraseological units is to *sectionalize* the text, as the traditional writing does not allow for paragraphing or using punctuation marks in premodern Chinese writings. Other purposes include interaction with the narratee, simulating dialogue with the audience, revaluation, asserting ideology, and personal revealing (Hanan 2005, 10). Given these functions, this chapter seeks to scrutinize what happens to the narrator's voice, including character voice, in translation. It is my contention that the extent to which the voice structure of the source text undergoes transformation during translation depends on how the translator perceives, interprets, and re-encodes it within specific literary and cultural context. According to Giuliana Schiavi (1996), a source text's voice structure necessarily changes in translation due to the translator's discursive manipulation. Similarly, Kristiina Taivalkoski-Shilov (2015) demonstrates that the translator tends to simplify the source text's voice structure when rendering polyphonic novels. In her research into the voice of Friday, a character in Daniel Defoe's (1660–1731) *Robinson Crusoe*, in six Finnish retranslations, Taivalkoski-Shilov shows that Friday's voice is significantly altered in the translated versions to fit specific translational purposes. Moreover, a more recent work by Charlotte Bosseaux (2018) examines three main characters' voices in Christopher Brookmyre's novel *Quite Ugly One Morning* and their treatment in French translation. The results indicate that characters' speech idiosyncrasies are simplified, flattened or smoothed over in the French context, causing the novel's characterization to suffer tremendously in translation tailored to a new audience. In *Voices in Translation*, Gunilla Anderman (2007, 7) emphasizes the importance of translators recognizing characters' origin, position, and verbal idiosyncrasies. Anderman argues that reproducing these individualized voices in translation can captivate the interest of the target audience. Building on these premises, I will argue that the transformation of the voice structure in *Jin Ping Mei* is both necessary and inevitable. This transformation can arise from various extratextual factors, including commercial considerations, ideological influences, reader expectations, different fictional poetics, and unequal power dynamics between languages and cultures. The next two sections will provide a systemic and comprehensive examination of how the varied voices, including tone, language, and the unique way of conveying thoughts and emotions, fare in Egerton's and Roy's versions of *Jin Ping Mei*, including exploring the contributing factors shaping the resulting outcomes.

3.3 Analysis of Character Voice in Translation

This section provides a discussion of the voices of characters in *Jin Ping Mei* and their treatment in English translations. The primary corpus for analysis comprises verbal exchanges from fictive dialogues, including monologic voices. Due to space constraints, the discussion centers on the voices of two central characters: the male protagonist, Ximen Qing, and his female counterpart, Pan Jinlian, who is the lead heroine. The speech segments of the protagonists are extracted from various chapters of the novel. Their voices are characterized by a mixture of linguo-stylistic devices, including archaic classicism, aphorisms, idioms, puns, and double entendre, regional dialects, slang, foul language, and the like. Their idiolectal discourse reflects different aspects of orality, revealing their sociocultural origins and highly developed personalities. Still, the individualized voices of the two characters shape their fictional characterization and manifest the style of dramatic dialogue of the novel. These voices are meticulously crafted to evoke specific connotations, such as humor, satire, and banter, in the reader's mind, thereby shaping and influencing their overall perception of the novel. As is known, the portrayal of *Jin Ping Mei*'s characters as multi-dimensional or with multi-style speakers attests to the polyvalence of the novelist's prose. As Bronwen Thomas puts it, fictional characters' speech and mannerisms offer "the reader direct, unmediated access to their emotions, desires, habits, and predilections" (2012, 57). Norman Page maintains that character speech functions as a distinctive "linguistic fingerprint"

(1988, 97), which can exert a specific effect on the reader. Therefore, it becomes a rewarding task to examine the voices of *Jin Ping Mei*'s two protagonists and their transposition into the English-language context. The ensuing analysis aims to pinpoint the speech idiosyncrasies of the two protagonists, illustrating how their voices resonate in English and exploring the potential impact of the translators' textual strategies on the target readers' perception of character and plot.

3.3.1 Politeness Markers

Politeness markers are prominent in the male protagonist's speech throughout the novel. The protagonist often uses honorifics and self-deprecating terms when interacting with other characters in the story. Let us consider the following example:

(1)

ST: 西門慶道。小人不敢動問娘子青春多少。婦人應道。奴家虛度二
       十五歲
       (Xiao 2003, chap. 3, 38)

       西門慶一面捧著他香腮。說道我怎肯忘了姐姐。
       (Xiao 2003, chap. 6, 56)

TTs:

TT1	*TT2*
"May **I** ask **your** age?" Hsi-men said. "I'm twenty-five," Golden Lotus said, bowing her head again. (Egerton 1939, vol. 1, 62)	"**I** hardly dare ask," said Hsi-men Ch'ing, "how old you are, **young lady**?" "I'm twenty-four, the woman responded. (Roy 1993, vol. 1, 79)
"How can I forget **you**?" Hsi-men cried, as he stroked her soft cheeks. (Egerton 1939, vol. 1, 93)	Hsi-men Ch'ing pinched her cheeks and said, "How could I ever forget you, **darling**?" (Roy 1993, vol. 1, 123)

In the ST, the male protagonist's speech is distinguished by honorifics and self-abasing terms. His speech is gentle and elegant, featuring politeness markers such as "小人," "娘子," and "姐姐," to refer to himself and to show respect to the inter-locutor. The exchange illustrates the protagonist's sociability and skill in endearing himself to women through affective words and genteel behavior. The term "小人" is rendered as "I" in both English texts mainly due to the absence of a direct equivalent in English. In TT1, the honorifics "娘子" and "姐姐" are paraphrased as "you," offering a natural and familiar tone for the target readers. On the other hand, TT2 uses "young lady" for "娘子" and "darling" for "姐姐," reproducing the tenor characterizing the male protagonist's speech in the exchange. Tenor, one of the three variables of register, links language usage to different social contexts, reflecting the relationship between discourse participants and their power, status, and social roles (Halliday 1978, 64; Hasan and Halliday 1985, 12). TT2 is contextually appropriate as it documents both what the character says and how he says it, revealing the relationship between the participants in the exchange.

3.3.2 Using Wenyan or Literary Chinese

In *Jin Ping Mei*, the male protagonist's speech register changes according to context. On some occasions, his speech takes on an exceptionally formal tenor. He skillfully employs *wenyan*, or literary Chinese, when interacting with individuals of higher social standing. As Don Snow (2010, 124) explains, literary Chinese served as the high language variety in premodern China, with *baihua*, or vernacular Chinese, considered a low variety. Literary Chinese was predominantly used for literary, scholarly, and official purposes. The following example illustrates this dynamic:

(2)

ST: 安進士道。今日相別何年再得。奉接尊顏。西門慶道。學生蝸居。屈尊。多有藝慢。幸惟情恕。本當遠送。奈官守在身。先此告過。
(Xiao 2003, chap. 36, 329)

TTs:

TT1	TT2
"I hope to behold the glory of your dignity again," An said. "Indeed," Hsi-men said, "I only hope your honor has not been tarnished by this stay in my snail's nest. I beg your indulgence for all that has been done amiss. I would come to see you on your way, but, unfortunately, my duty calls me and I can only say good-bye." (Egerton 1939, vol. 2, 137)	"Though we must part today," said Metropolitan Graduate An, "I trust thaton some future occasion we will have the opportunity to reciprocate by receiving your distinguished countenance." "Though you have condescended to visit your pupil's snail-like abode," said Hsi-men Ch'ing, "I fear you have experienced but too shabby a reception. I hope that you will be considerate enough to overlook it. I really ought to see you off for some distance were it not for the responsibilities of my office. I must therefore bid you a premature farewell." (Roy 2001, vol. 2, 359)

In this highly ritualized conversation among the male protagonist and his peers in officialdom, the tenor is exceedingly formal. The protagonist's speech exudes elegance, bordering on pedantic. This formality sharply contrasts with the offensive, rustic, and earthy diction he employs in domestic settings with other characters, a category that will be discussed later. The formal and standard register utilized in the above exchange highlights the social distance and power dynamics between the protagonist and his interlocutor. It is crucial to note that the author of *Jin Ping Mei* presents the protagonist's speech as dynamic rather than static, indirectly manifesting his multiple identities and mobile social status in the fictional universe. Both translated texts achieve a degree of interpersonal equivalence in recreating the protagonist's refined speech. As Juliane House (1997) suggests, interpersonal equivalence ensures that the target reader gains the same or at least a similar idea of the interpersonal relationship between the interlocutors as the source readers. The protagonist's formal and refined manner of speaking is reflected in the English texts, achieving interpersonal equivalence in this exchange. However, a notable difference arises in TT1, where the protagonist's dialogue appears more succinct, possessing a smooth, almost conversational flow. In this sense, TT1 captures the essence of the protagonist's formality without unnecessary verbosity. The decision to render the dialogue in a more concise manner not only aligns with the protagonist's formal tenor but also imparts a sense of naturalness, making it read more like spoken language.

3.3.3 Monologue

The author of *Jin Ping Mei* occasionally employs characters voicing their inner thoughts as a narrative device to dramatize hidden feelings, intense passion, and to paint more vivid portraits. For instance, the female protagonist is portrayed as a versatile figure skilled in playing various musical instruments. When left alone by her husband, she turns to playing pipa, a Chinese lute, to vent anger or express subtle complaints and deep depression due to her husband's unjust treatment. Her monologues, presented in the form of songs sung in private moments, allow her motivations and personal viewpoints to be revealed for the reader. In the following example, the heroine's monologue takes the form of a song, aptly disclosing her delicate thoughts and state of mind.

(3)

ST:　於是獨自彈奏著琵琶。唱一個綿搭絮為證。
　　　誰想你另有了裙釵氣的奴似醉如痴。斜傍定幃屏。故意兒猜。不
　　　　明白。怎生丟開。傳書寄柬。你又
　　　不來。你若負了奴的恩情。人不為仇天降災。
　　　(Xiao 2003, chap. 8, 69)

TTs:

TT1	*TT2*
And as she played, she sang. (Egerton 1939, vol. 1, 113)	Who would have thought you'd have found another sweetheart? It makes me so mad I'm: "Half drunk and half crazy." Leaning against the standing screen, I try to figure it out; I don't understand it, how could you abandon me this way? Though I: "Send letters and post notes," you still refuse to come. If you are really betraying, my affections, If no one else gets to you first, Heaven will destroy you. (Roy 1993, vol. 1, 156)

The heroine's monologue in this instance can evoke a prismatic imagination in perceptive readers. It is both imaginative and carries symbolic meaning, representing women's subordination to their husbands in traditional polygamous households. In *Jin Ping Mei*, women play significant roles in the male protagonist's life, leading to jealousy and competition among them to win his favor. Despite the protagonist being a libertine or a spoiled sex maniac who is not easily pleased, his women, especially the heroine Pan Jinlian cannot resist him. In this monologue, the combination of a naïve and tender expression with such a depressing content leaves a strong impression on the reader.

The translators have different interpretations regarding the aesthetic and characterizing function of the monologue. The heroine's distinctive monologic voice, which sets her apart from other female characters in the story, is omitted from TT1 but is maintained and highlighted in TT2. Consequently, TT2 provides a more revealing insight into the heroine's inner feelings, frustration, and feminine delicacy, enhancing the narrative effect for the target readers. On the other hand, TT1 benefits from a smoother narrative flow due to the absence of the quoted song but fails to grant the reader access to the heroine's inner thoughts and attitudes toward her husband. This pattern continues in the next example.

(4)

ST:　他不念咱。咱想念他。想著門兒。私下簾兒。悄呀。空教奴被兒裡叫著他那名兒罵。你怎戀煙花。不來我家。
　　　(Xiao 2003, chap. 8, 66)

TTs

TT1	*TT2*
[omitted]	... As for him, He doesn't think of me; As for me, I think longingly of him. Quietly taking down the bamboo blind, Leaving the door to creak, All I can do is lie underneath my quilt, cursing his name. How can you care so much for "misty willows," That you won't come to my place anymore? ... (Roy 1993, vol. 1, 150)

Likewise, the nuanced aspects of the heroine's personality are vividly portrayed through her monologue. Left alone by her husband for an extended period, she begins to doubt her ability to regain his husband's love in the polygamous household. The heroine's voice conveys her passion and hidden feelings, especially her sense of insecurity, longing for her husband's favor, and resentment about his prolonged neglect. TT2 adeptly captures these nuanced meanings. In contrast, TT1 omits the heroine's monologue, somewhat influencing the reader's perception of her characterization, though it doesn't significantly impact the plot. As explained by Egerton himself, he acknowledges that certain content such as numerous *ci*-poems and songs presented in the form of poetry may not qualify as good poems even when translated into English (Egerton 1939, vii). It is likely that Egerton viewed these poems more as embellishments to the plot rather than integral elements. This pattern can be further observed in Chapter 4.

3.3.4 Aphorism

The heroine frequently employs aphorisms in her daily conversations. These aphorisms are pithy in structure and rustic in tone, expressing general truths or astute observations. Within fictive dialogue, they serve as speech presentation resources used to characterize the female character. Here are two prime examples:

(5)

ST: 你不聽只顧求他。問姐姐。常信人調丟了瓢。你做差了。你抱怨那個。
       (Xiao 2003, chap.18, 158)

TTs:

TT1	TT2

You wouldn't listen to me; you went and asked what the Great Lady thought about it. I tell you: **those who must always take the opinion of somebody else will never get what they want.** You went the wrong way about things, and nobody is to blame but yourself."
(Egerton 1939, vol. 1, 258)
	But you didn't pay any attention to me and insisted on getting Elder Sister's permission. As the saying goes:
	    To defer when you differ,
	    Is to give up the dipper.
	It was your mistake. You've got no one to blame but yourself."
	(Roy 1993, vol. 1, 373)

The aphorism "信人調丟了瓢" in the ST renders the exchange vivid and amusing, displaying the heroine's eloquence and sharp tongue while interacting with her husband. The expression "信人調丟了瓢" means those who blindly trust others leading to a great loss in the end (He 1990, 532; see *Guoyu Cidian* online edition). TT1 avoids literalist accuracy or translationese in favor of paraphrasing, resulting in an idiomatic and smooth target text. On the other hand, TT2 creates an ad hoc idiom: "To defer when you differ, is to give up the dipper," characterized by assonance and alliteration, but which might pose challenges for readers in understanding the connotative meaning.

(6)

ST: 金蓮拉頭兒道。我是不卜他。常言筭的著命。筭不着行。
       (Xiao 2003, chap. 46, 411)

TTs:

TT1	TT2

"I don't want my fortune told," said Golden Lotus. "There is a proverb: '**Fortunes may be foretold, but not our conduct.**'
(Egerton 1939, vol. 2, 265)
	"Fortune-telling is not for me," said Chin-lien, with a shake of her head. "As the saying goes:
	    You may calculate a person's fate,
	    But you can't predict his conduct.
	(Roy 2006, vol. 3, 127)

In (6), the Chinese expression "筭的著命。筭不著行" is explained as follows: one should not take the fortune telling too seriously, as a person's fate can be predicted, but their conduct cannot be accurately foretold (He 1990, 556).

Both translated texts have successfully reproduced the semantic meaning of the source aphorism. Egerton's rendition, "Fortunes may be foretold, but not our conduct," carries the tone of austere clarity and exhibits high idiomaticity. Aside from conveying the dynamism and spontaneity of the protagonist's speech, Roy's version emphasizes the formal features of the original.

3.3.5 *Slang and Local Dialect*

The heroine is also portrayed as having the talent to beguile with words. The examples below illustrate her proficient use of slang and local dialects, reflecting not only her verbal talent but also her strong personality and her envy of her rival in love.

(7)

ST: 婦人道我兒。你但行動瞞不過當方土地。
(Xiao 2003, chap. 27, 240–242)

金蓮道。一個是大老婆。一個是小老婆。明日兩個對養。
(Xiao 2003, chap. 30, 268)

TTs:

TT1	TT2
"My boy," Golden Lotus said, "you may try as hard as you like, but you will **never succeed in deceiving the God** who watches over Hearth and Home. (Egerton 1939, vol. 1, 382) "Oh," Golden Lotus said, "**one is great and one is small**. They seem to have a competition in this baby getting ... (Egerton 1939, vol. 2, 38)	"My child," the woman said: "No matter what you do, you **cannot deceive the local tutelary god**." (Roy 2001, vol.2, 141) "**One of them is the legitimate wife**," said Chin-lien, "and **the other is merely a concubine**. But it seems that, in the future, so long as it's a childbearing competition they're engaged in, ... (Roy 2001, vol. 2, 208)

In (7), the Chinese sentences are plebeian and colloquial, brimming with humorous hues. The spicy and earthy expressions such as "當方土地," "大老婆," and "小老婆" make the heroine's spontaneous oral speech vivid and cordial, also reflecting her inner feelings – envy of her husband's other concubines. TT1 is styled as simple and laconic, giving the impression of an oral discourse, while TT2 has the characteristics of a written discourse due to interlinear translation. To illustrate, TT2 gives "the local tutelary god" for "當方土地" and specifies "大老婆"

and "小老婆" as "the legitimate wife" and "a concubine." While the vividness and conversational flow of the heroine's speech are compromised, TT2 closely adheres to the original in both content and formalistic structure. The same pattern persists in the next example:

(8)

ST: 金蓮道南京沈萬三。北京枯柳樹。人的名兒。樹的影兒。怎麼不
       饒的
       (Xiao 2003, chap. 72, 684)

TTs:

TT1	TT2

"It's common gossip," Golden Lotus said. **"Everybody knows it …"**
(Egerton 1939, vol. 3, 306)
	Chin-lien said:
	    "Just as Nanking has its Shen Wan-san,
	    Peking has its withered willows;
	    Just as a man has his reputation,
	    A tree has its shadow.
	    …"
	(Roy 2011, vol. 4, 348)

In (8), the heroine's speech is marked with dialectal expressions such as "南京沈萬三。北京枯柳樹" and "人的名兒。樹的影兒," suggesting that one cannot deny a known or established fact, just as one cannot ignore the fame of Shen Wansan (1330–1379), the richest man in early Ming, and the shadow of the withered willows in Beijing city (He 1990, 563; Sun 2005, 338). The use of dialectal words creates an accelerated reading rhythm and vividly recreates everyday conversation. TT2 preserves the original dialectal expression through literal transfer, albeit at the cost of diminishing the dynamism of oral conversations and rendering it less accessible to ordinary readers unfamiliar with the source culture. In comparison, TT1's brevity and simplification still makes sense and recreates the spontaneity of the heroine's voice, making the English dialogue natural and more easily comprehensible.

3.3.6 Four-Character Idioms

The heroine also has a predilection for using four-character idioms on several occasions, which is another important feature of her idiolectal speech. The following examples will suffice:

(9)

ST: 婦人道。你好小胆子兒。明知道和來旺兒媳婦子七個八個。你還
      調戲他。
      (Xiao 2003, chap. 28, 250)

TTs:

TT1	*TT2*
"Oh, aren't you brave? Though you knew quite well he was **carrying on with** Laiwang's wife, that didn't prevent you from finishing his work for him. (Egerton 1939, vol. 2, 7)	… she said, "You've got quite a nerve, don't you?" the woman said. "You knew perfectly well that Father was: **Playing at sevens and eights,** with Lai-wang's wife, but you flirted with her anyway. …" (Roy 2001, vol. 2, 159)

In (9), the idiom "七個八個" suggests inappropriate relations between man and woman (Wang 1988, 401). It is also interpreted as love affair (Bai 1991, 401). In this exchange, the idiomatic phrase does not explicitly mention sex but clearly implies it. Here, the heroine's use of the slang is a face-saving strategy (not mentioning the affair directly) while interacting with her interlocutor. TT1's "carrying on with" felicitously explains the source idiom, making the English text both economical and accessible to the average reader. Yet, TT2's word-for-word transfer, "Playing at sevens and eights," creates a misleading effect and might be challenging for general readers to comprehend. Let us turn to the next example:

(10)

ST: 金蓮道。我的兒。老娘猜不著你。那黃貓黑尾的心兒。
      (Xiao 2003, chap. 67, 631)

TTs:

TT1	*TT2*
"My son," Golden Lotus said, "I can see through you as clearly as I can see **a cat with a black tail**." (Egerton 1939, vol. 3, 223)	"My son," responded Chin-lien, "do you really think this old mother of yours is oblivious to the fact that: **You may be a brown cat, but you've got a black tail**?" (Roy 2011, vol. 4, 202)

In (10), the idiom "黃貓黑尾" is explained as referring to a hypocritical person whose words and deeds are often incongruent (He 1990, 512; Bai 1991, 233; see *Guoyu Cidian*). The heroine ironically and metaphorically uses it to satirize Ximen Qing, whose words and deeds often contradict. TT1 has "I can see through you as clearly as I can see a cat with a black tail," effectively conveying both the intended meaning and the vivaciousness of the heroine's voice to the reader. In contrast, TT2's literal transfer conceals the connotative sense of the heroine's speech, providing the reader the opportunity to discern the meaning and the ironic tone of the heroine's speech. The next example is similar:

(11)

ST:　金蓮道。一遭二遭我不信你。既要這奴才淫婦兩個瞞神諕鬼。弄
　　　刺子兒。我打聽出來。休怪了我。卻和你每答話。
　　　(Xiao 2003, chap. 22, 196)

TTs:

TT1	TT2
Golden Lotus declared she did not believe a word he said, and Hsi-men Ch'ing went off, laughing. (Egerton 1939, vol. 1, 314)	"Once? Twice? I don't believe you," said Chin-lien. "But if you think you can continue to carry on your tricks with that slave of a whore while: 　　**Deceiving spirits and** 　　**stupefying demons,** you've got another thing coming. If I ever find out about it, then forgive you me, but I'll have something to say to the two of you." (Roy 2001, vol. 2, 36)

In (11), the idiom "瞞神諕鬼" suggests someone who does evil things without letting anyone else know (Bai 1991, 344). It is simply ignored in TT1, serving the purpose of a smooth and fluid narrative. However, TT2's word-for-word transfer, "Deceiving spirits and stupefying demons" for "瞞神諕鬼," provides access to the Chinese idiom, despite this approach making the narrative dialogue sound obscure, lacking the vivacity or colloquial effect appropriate for the represented oral speech situation.

3.3.7 *Puns and double entendre*

Puns and double entendre are important sources of humor in *Jin Ping Mei*. They invite the reader to go beyond referential meanings to deeper or illocutionary meanings for deciphering character discourse. The characters' playing on words often adds humor to dialogic interactions, while also manifesting a likable side to their characterization. The humor it creates cannot be fully translated without loss, given the cultural and linguistic differences. Let us look at some illustrative examples:

(12)

ST: 西門慶笑。我問你這梅湯。你却說做媒。差了多少。王婆道。老
       身只聽得大官人問這媒做得好。
       (Xiao 2003, chap. 2, 27)

TTs:

TT1	*TT2*
"I was talking about **damsons**, not **damsels**," said Hsi-men. "You are getting a little mixed up." "It was **damsels** you are thinking about, nonetheless," the old lady retorted. (Egerton 1939, vol. 1, 46)	"It was **damsons** I asked about," said Hsi-men Ching, laughing in turn, "but you're talking about **damsels**. There's quite a difference between the two. "All I heard, sir, was something about fixing **damsels**," said Dame Wang, "so I thought you were talking about the way I fix them up." (Roy 1993, vol. 1, 55)

The play on words in (12) centers on the characters "梅" and "媒," which are homophones in Chinese. The word "梅" in the dialogue refers to a type of fruit and is homophonic to "媒," which means matchmaking. The play on these two words injects humor into the conversation. The English renderings of the ST wordplay evoke a similar pleasurable and playful response. In particular, the English words "damsons" and "damsels" are almost homophonic, recreating the punning effect. There is a high degree of interpretive resemblance between the source and target texts. Like the male protagonist's speech patterns, wordplay is also characteristic for the heroine's, as is the case with the following example:

(13)

ST: 西門慶道。怪奴才。八十歲媽媽沒牙。有那些唇說的。
       (Xiao 2003, chap. 38, 346)

TTs:

TT1	*TT2*
"You marvelous little slave!" Hsi-men said, "you are like an eighty-year-old woman who has lost her teeth but can still **make shift to chatter without them**. (Egerton 1939, vol. 2, 164)	"You crazy slave!" said Hsi-men Ch'ing. "An eighty-year-old crone may lack teeth, **But she's still got plenty of lip**. (Roy 2001, vol. 2, 401)

In (13), the wordplay is based on the homophony between the Chinese expressions "唇說" and "陳說" (He 1990, 570). The pun suggests someone who should not talk too much. "唇說" is also homophonic to "蠢說," suggesting that one should stop talking nonsense (Bai 1991, 716). Clearly, TT1's paraphrastic rendering, "make shift to chatter without them," effectively conveys the connotative sense of the ST wordplay, creating a highly intelligible text. On the other hand, TT2 has "she's still got plenty of lip," follows the ST closely at the formal level and ordinary readers are left to infer what the character says based on the narrative context.

(14)

ST: 金蓮道。俺的小肉兒。賣蘿蔔的跟著鹽担子走。好個閒嘈心的小肉兒。

   (Xiao 2003, chap. 20, 172)

TTs:

TT1	*TT2*
"The young rascal," Golden Lotus cried. "… She is a meddlesome young hussy." (Egerton 1939, vol. 1, 278)	"That little piece of mine is the limit," said Chin-lien. "… That little piece of mine is like: **The radish peddler who tags along after the salt vendor: forever horning in where she doesn't belong**." (Roy 1993, vol. 1, 403)

In (14), the punning effect is attained through the sentence "賣蘿蔔的跟著鹽擔子走。好個閒嘈心的小肉兒." The wordplay in the ST centers on "閒嘈心," which is homophonic to "閒操心" (He 1990, 536; Bai 1991, 726). The heroine's play on words implies that her maidservant is meddlesome and nosy. Regarding wordplay translation, Katharina Reiss (2000, 169) claims that "in translation, puns and other kinds of play with language will have to be ignored to a great extent so as to keep the content invariant." By abandoning the complex wordplay, TT1 becomes succinct and economical, possessing a smooth, almost conversational flow. TT2 replicates the elaborate structure of the ST wordplay, at the expense of capturing the essence of the heroine's playful speech. While TT1's literal transfer skillfully conveys the substance of the original, it compromises the vivacity and punning effect of the heroine's speech.

(15)

ST: 金蓮道。賊小肉兒。不知怎的聽見。幹恁個勾當兒。雲端裡老
        鼠。天生的耗。
        (Xiao 2003, chap. 20, 172)

TTs:

TT1	*TT2*
"Look at those young rascals," Golden Lotus cried. "Why are they doing this? They are like rats flying in the skies … (Egerton 1939, vol. 1, 279)	"You lousy little piece!" said Chin-lien. "I don't know why it is, but whenever you get wind of a job like this, you seem to think it's: **Like a rat stationed in the clouds:** **The 'furry pest' Heaven has** **to offer.** (Roy 1993, vol. 1, 404)

The play on words in (15) is based on the allegorical saying "雲端裡老鼠。天生的耗." It is true that the double meanings of puns in the source language are always the combined effect of phonological and semantic characteristics. The character "耗" in the ST is homophonic to "好," connoting that someone is born to be fond of doing evil things (He 1990, 536, also see *Guoyu Cidian*). However, "耗" is also considered homophonic to "號," indicating someone who is born to be that kind of people fond of doing evil things (Bai 1991, 738). While the wordplay is omitted from TT1, it gains by effectively conveying its intended meaning. TT2's word-for-word transfer captures the substance of the original, yet it detracts from the impression of oral discourse, sacrificing the sly humor and spontaneity of the heroine's vivid speech.

3.3.8 Swearwords and Expletives

In narrative prose, offensive language serves a characterizing function and plays pragmatic and comedic roles (Espunya and Pintarić 2018, 353). According to Karyan Stapleton (2010, 291), swearing and foul language perform interpersonal functions, such as expressing emotion (for example, anger, envy, or joy) and establishing humor and verbal emphasis. Thus, foul language cannot be divorced from the context in which it is used or from the idiolect of the speaker, including their social, cultural, and geographical background (Morillas 2012, 321). Within *Jin Ping Mei*, various forms of foul language can be found in characters' verbal exchanges. Verbal frankness is a defining aspect of characterization in the novel, with both male and female protagonists portrayed as using strong or offensive language on several occasions. As a rule, an offensive, indecent register is often employed for interjections, expressing the emotional force of the characters' beliefs and attitudes towards certain events or people. The following examples illustrate this point:

(16)

ST: 西門慶聽了。跌腳笑道。莫不是人叫他三寸丁。谷樹皮的武大郎麼。

(Xiao 2003, chap. 2, 27)

TTs:

TT1	*TT2*
When Hsi-men Ch'ing heard this, he nearly jumped out of his chair. "You can't mean that Wu Da whom people call **Tom Thumb or Old Scraggy Bark**." (Egerton 1939, vol. 1, 45)	When Hsi-men Ch'ing heard this he stamped his feet and laughed. "You don't mean to say he's the Wu the Elder, whom everyone calls the **Three-inch Mulberry-bark Manikin**, do you?" (Roy 1993, vol. 1, 54)

In (16), the reference "三寸丁。谷樹皮" is intended for describing a person's height and physical appearance. The expletive is explained as follows: "三寸" signifies someone being very short; "丁" suggests "a little" in Chinese; "谷樹皮" implies a person's skin that is coarse, rough, and dark (He 1990, 495). So, the swearing entails humor and sarcasm, aimed at describing an ugly, weak, and short person with little machismo (Wang 1988, 448; see *Guoyu Cidian*). In this example, the idiomatic profanity is intended by the male protagonist to jest at the character Wu Da. In TT1, the ST swearing interpreted as "Tom Thumb or Old Scraggy Bark," which is familiar and intelligible to the target readers because Tom Thumb is a household character in English folklore, no bigger than his father's thumb. However, due to cultural difference, expletives are context-dependent and sometimes cannot be rendered literally into the target language to avoid semantic ambiguity or unnaturalness (Andersson and Trudgill 2007, 195). For instance, TT2's "Three-inch Mulberry-bark Manikin" creates a less familiar or natural text through interlinear transfer, with a structure unlikely to be encountered in vivid oral speech. As Fernández Dobao (2006, 240) postulates, what matters is the emotional charge of swearwords, as it evinces the speaker's emotion and attitude in certain circumstances. In this sense, the emotional or illocutionary force of the male protagonist's utterance is more evident in TT1. Similar considerations apply in the following:

(17)

ST: 聽信你兄弟。說空生有卵鳥嘴。也不怕別人笑恥。
       (Xiao 2003, chap. 2, 25)

TTs:

TT1	*TT2*
You are just like the **new born babe** who has to do what his brother tells him. Aren't you ashamed to have everybody laughing at you?" (Egerton 1939, vol. 1, 41)	You'll do anything your brother says. **A lot of good your own cock and balls do you!** Aren't you ashamed to make such a laughingstock of yourself?" (Roy 1993, vol. 1, 47)

Here in (17), the tone of the heroine's speech is offensive and aggressive. The pejorative reference "卵鳥嘴" reflects her truculence and overbearing attitude toward her husband Wu Da. Semantically, the term "卵鳥嘴" hints at a person's docility and meekness and carries sexual suggestiveness (Wang 1988, 276; He 1990, 494). This old-fashioned swearword has no functional equivalent in English and requires a flexible approach to match English uses and habits. With "You ignorant nincompoop" standing in for "不識時濁物," TT2 is as colloquial as Egerton's "You horrible creature," effectively capturing aspects of orality. Regarding the expletive "卵鳥嘴," TT1 paraphrases it as "You are just like the new born babe," which is easily understandable for the average reader. However, TT2 has "A lot of good your own cock and balls do you," a mechanical, literal transfer of the expletive "卵鳥嘴," showcasing the vulgar side but sacrificing speakability in terms of the oral dimension of the exchange. As noted above, expletives are context-dependent and cannot be rendered verbatim. In this sense, TT1 communicates more naturally to the target readers than TT2, ensuring the narrative flows effortlessly.

(18)

ST: 婦人道。我不好罵出來的。甚麼瓶姨鳥姨
       (Xiao 2003, chap. 18, 158)

TTs:

TT1	TT2
"I can't tell you what I think of you," Golden Lotus said. "And what do I care for **that woman**?" (Egerton 1939, vol. 1, 257)	"I'd only be wasting my breath on you!" said the woman. "**My sister P'ing-erh! Sister my prick!** (Roy 1993, vol. 1, 372)

In (18), the expressive force in the heroine's use of the expletive "瓶姨鳥姨" guides the reader's perception of her inner world, revealing her psychological tension and hostility toward her husband's mistress. TT1 omits the swearword, dampening the indecent colloquial color of the original. Hence, the heroine's speech is toned down to become polite and less transgressive, rather than surprising the reader with her momentary linguistic daring in the ST. In contrast, TT2 does not balk at any offensiveness and successfully recreates the emphatic tone of the heroine's voice through the use of emphatic intensifiers such as "Sister my prick" and "that whore."

3.3.9 Bawdy Language and Obscenities

Apart from swearwords, bawdy language and obscenities also find their way into the protagonists' speech to portray their emotions and forms of behavior or to characterize them in a negative light. The following examples highlight instances of bawdy discourse in dialogic exchanges and how they are treated in the translations.

(19)

ST: 被西門慶聽見。走向前把他兩隻小金蓮。扛將起來。戲道我把這小淫婦。不看世界面上。就合死了。
(Xiao 2003, chap. 27, 242)

TTs:

TT1	TT2
Hsi-men Ch'ing seized her tiny feet. "You little villain," he cried, "if I weren't afraid of somebody seeing us, **I'd make you die of delight**." (Egerton 1939, vol. 1, 382)	When Hsi-men Ch'ing heard this, he stepped forward and, hoisting her two tiny golden lotuses into the air, threatened mischievously, "You little whore! **If I didn't care for the opinion of the world, I'd fuck you to death**." (Roy 2001, vol. 2, 141)

In (19), the exchanges exhibit an amusing yet coarse tone. The interaction is highly informal, featuring explicit "sex talk." The protagonist engages with his women using colloquial language that is consistently rustic and ribald. Bawdy expressions like "合死" are unsavory and sexually stimulating, eliciting a range of somatic responses from titillation to embarrassment. These bawdy expressions reflect the vulgar, philistine aspect of the male protagonist's character. Yet in TT1, they are skirted around by opting for neutral, innocuous terms. The protagonist's erotic speech is euphemized or elevated to a higher register, devoid of any explicit bawdy color. On the contrary, TT2 retains all the bawdy elements, effectively conveying the dysphemistic impact of the ST. Expressions like "fuck you to death" recreate a tickling or tingling sensation in the protagonist's voice. The word "fuck" is the most interesting and colorful word in the English language today (Andersson and Trudgill 1990, 60). In TT2, the original old-fashioned risqué vocabulary is modernized, rendering the language as contemporary as possible. Like the male protagonist, the heroine's speech is at times marked by bawdiness or ribaldry, conveying emotional information such as anger or frustration and revealing her crudeness or moral weakness. The following example illustrates this:

(20)

ST: 俺每是雌剩鬌髤合的。你還說你不偏心哩。
       (Xiao 2003, chap. 51, 457)

TTs:

TT1	*TT2*
She stared at Hsi-men Ch'ing and said: "...**I can serve the meanest of your purposes.** Then you pretend to be fair to me. ..." (Egerton 1939, vol. 2, 336)	Casting an amorous glance at Hsi-men Ch'ing, she said, "... **Am I only fit to be fucked by what's left of that spent prick of yours**? And you claim not to be practicing favoritism! ..." (Roy 2006, vol. 3, 236)

In (20), the heroine's voice is charged with a sexual tone, embodying the unpleasant side of her character. The bawdy expression "雌剩鬌髤合的" is simultaneously coarse and obscene, showcasing the heroine's feelings such as envy or anger towards her object of desire. In TT1, the bawdy language is significantly softened, adapting the original to the point of neutralizing or excising those bawdy elements. The heroine's speech is modified and sanitized, devoid of the bawdiness present in the original. Conversely, TT2 effectively conveys the heroine's speech and mannerisms, retaining gross and erotic expressions such as "fuck" and "prick." The graphic, rustic nature of the heroine's voice creates an echo effect that elicits a somatic response in the reader.

3.4 Analysis of the Narrator/Storyteller's Voice in Translation

As discussed earlier, a striking feature of the Ming vernacular novel is that the narrator's voice resembles oral performance. In *Jin Ping Mei*, for instance, the omniscient narrator tells the story, knows the events and characters, and interpolates comments from a position outside the narrated events. The narrator's distinctive voice is manifested through various linguistic and linguo-stylistic forms and devices, including markers of narrative beginning, transition, progression, and conclusion, pre-verse markers (the shift from verse to prose and vice versa), and markers of narrative commentary and imitated dialogue with the imaginary audience (Børdahl 2016, 36). In this section, I will examine the representation of the narrator's voice in the English translations. The discussion will specifically center on the translation of passages drawn from several chapters of the novel. It aims to demonstrate that nearly all of the meta-narrative remarks are eliminated from the Egerton translation, and this pattern remains consistent throughout. In contrast, all the meta-narrative markers are fully retained in Roy's version.

3.4.1 Markers of Narrative Beginning, Transition, Progression, and Conclusion

In *Jin Ping Mei*, the heterodiegetic narrator's voice is characterized by a set of linguistic devices signaling narrative transition and progression. These numerous linguistic markers have a fixed formulaic form and, in combination, create a dialogic impression. According to Børdahl (2016, 39), the variety of linguo-stylistic forms, such as "卻表," "單表," "單道," and "話休饒舌," manifest the narrator's oral performance, providing oral entertainment to the reader. In interlingual translation, these lexical and phraseological units present serious translational problems as they might be overlooked, dismissed, or significantly altered. Let us consider several examples:

(1)

ST: 話說五月二十日。帥府周守偹生日。
      (Xiao 2003, chap. 17, 143)
      卻說西門慶。當晚在前邊。廂房睡了一夜。
      (Xiao 2003, chap. 18, 155)

TT1:
The twentieth day of the fifth month was Major Chou's birthday.
(Egerton 1939, vol. 1, 232)

Hsi-men Ch'ing spent the night in his study.
(Egerton 1939, vol. 1, 254)

TT2:

The story goes that the twentieth day of the fifth month was the birthday of
  Commandant Chou Hsiu of the Regional Military Command.
(Roy 1993, vol. 1, 337)

To resume our story, that evening Hsi-men Ch'ing spent the night in the
  anteroom on the west side of the front courtyard.
(Roy 1993, vol. 1, 366)

In (1), the lexical items "話說" and "卻說" serve as signals for narrative beginning, keeping the reader engaged with the story and directing their attention to
the reported events. However, these lexical items are eliminated in TT1 but fully
maintained in TT2, which uses similar stock phrases: "The story goes that ..." and
"To resume our story" to echo the oral storytelling tradition that define the original. TT1 seems to avoid semantic overloading and, as a result, appears quite lucid
and laconic, while TT2's phrasing may seem redundant but maintains the morphological and syntactic features of the source narrator's voice.

(2)

ST: 這裡西門慶在家。納悶不題。且說李瓶兒等了。一日兩日。不見
      動靜。
      (Xiao 2003, chap. 17, 147)

      單表西門慶至晚進入金蓮房內來。
      (Xiao 2003, chap. 12, 103)

      此事表過不題。且說當日西門慶。率同妻妾。闔家歡喜。在芙蓉
      亭上飲酒。至晚方散。
      (Xiao 2003, chap. 7, 86)

TT1:

Hsi-men Ch'ing remained sadly at home. The Lady of the Vase waited for him,
  one day, two days, but he did not come.
(Egerton 1939, vol. 1, 240)

Cassia had to go away, greatly abashed. That evening Hsi-men Ch'ing went to
  see Golden Lotus.
(Egerton 1939, vol. 1, 167)

Hsi-men Ch'ing and his ladies made merry in the Hibiscus Arbor. They drank
  till it was late, and then went to their own apartments.
(Egerton 1939, vol. 1, 142)

TT2:

Hsi-men Ch'ing remained at home in a state of deep depression, **but we will say no more about it. To resume our story**, Li P'ing-erh waited first one day and then another, but nothing happened.
(Roy 1993, vol. 1, 347)

We will say no more for the moment about how Li Kuei-chieh went home, **but return to the story of** Hsi-men Ch'ing. That evening he appeared in Chin-lien quarters ...
(Roy 1993, vol. 1, 241)

Now that this matter has been explained, we will say no more about it. To resume our story, that day Hsi-men Ch'ing and his wife and concubines enjoyed a feast in the Hibiscus Pavilion for the: Jollification of the entire family. The party did not break up until evening.
(Roy 1993, vol. 1, 201)

In (2), unlike "話說" and "卻說," which mark narrative beginning, the phraseological units "這……不題" and "此事表過不題" mark the conclusion of previous narrative, while "且說" and "單表" signal narrative transition, directing the reader's attention to the next events reported by the narrator. In TT1, these narrator's stock phrases are deleted altogether, making the translated narrative natural and fluent, with the story advancing quickly. In TT2, however, we come across elements such as "but we will say no more about it," "To resume our story," "We will say no more for the moment about ... ," "but return to the story of ... ," and "Now that this matter has been explained ..." By preserving these formulaic phrases in the translation, TT2 renders the narrator more visible, allowing the target reader to perceive his voice in a more straightforward way. However, TT2 also becomes more complex and obscure, and these translated meta-narrative remarks might be disruptive and unacceptable to readers who prefer a very natural, fluent, and pleasurable reading of romantic novels. Something similar can be observed in the following:

(3)

ST: 西門慶道。我知道。明日到他房中去。當晚無話。
(Xiao 2003, chap. 12, 102)

絕早五更。顧腳夫起程。上東京去了。不在話下。
(Xiao 2003, chap. 17, 147)

初時徃人家看病只是走。後來買了一疋驢兒騎著。在街上徃來搖擺。不在話下。
(Xiao 2003, chap. 17, 150)

西門慶自此沒三五日不來。俱不必細說。
(Xiao 2003, chap. 16, 140)

TT1:
"I will go and see her tomorrow," Hsi-men promised.
(Egerton 1939, vol. 1, 167)

Next morning, before it was night, they rose, hired drivers, and started for the
    Easter Capital.
(Egerton 1939, vol. 1, 239)

Before this he had always gone on foot to visit his patients. Now he bought a
    donkey and rode up and down the street.
(Egerton 1939, vol. 1, 246)

Thenceforth Hsi-men Ch'ing went every few days to visit the Lady of the Vase.
(Egerton 1939, vol. 1, 226)

TT2:
"I know," said Hsi-men Ch'ing. "I'll go to her quarters tomorrow." **Of the
    events of that evening there is no more to tell.**
(Roy 1993, vol. 1, 240)

Early in the fifth watch they hired drivers and set out on their way to the Eastern
    Capital. **But no more of this**.
(Roy 1993, vol. 1, 347)

Originally, when he made calls on his patients, he had had to go on foot. But
    now he was able to buy a donkey to ride. He cut quite a figure as he came and
    went in the streets. **But no more of this**.
(Roy 1993, vol. 1, 355)

From this time on, Hsi-men Ch'ing came to see her every three to five days,
    without fail, **but there is no need to describe this in detail**.
(Roy 1993, vol. 1, 329)

As in the previous example, here in (3), formulaic expressions appear in different
forms but fulfil a similar function: signaling narrative conclusion and foreshadowing
new events to be reported. These markers, as explained earlier, commonly occur
in oral storytelling and are appropriated by the author of *Jin Ping Mei* to make
the narrative titillating and appealing to contemporary readers. The overall tenor
of TT1 is pithy and laconic, and his narrator expresses only essential facts in an
economical manner; the Chinese narrator's linguo-stylistic devices "當晚無話,"
"不在話下," and "俱不必細説" are not retained, which increases narrative
smoothness and rhythm. Rather than effacing these phrases, TT2 retains all meta-
narrative remarks to give its readers full access to the narrator's intervention and
the stylistic nuances of the original. This tendency is also manifested in the next
example:

(4)

ST:　話分兩頭。不說蔣竹山。在李瓶兒家招贅。單表來保來旺二人上
　　　東京打點。
　　　(Xiao 2003, chap. 18, 151)

　　　話休饒舌。一日會了經紀。
　　　(Xiao 2003, chap. 16, 138)

TT1:
Lai Pao and Lai Wang set out to the Eastern Capital to try to put matters
　right there.
(Egerton 1939, vol. 1, 247)

Hsi-men Ch'ing went to see the valuers …
(Egerton 1939, vol. 1, 223)

TT2:

**At this point the story divides into two. We will say no more, for the
　moment**, about Chiang Chu-shan's marriage into Li P'ing-erh's household,
　but return to the story of Lai-pao and Lai-wang's trip to the Eastern Capital
　to fix things up on Hsi-men Ch'ing's behalf.
(Roy 1993, vol. 1, 356)

To make a long story short, one day Hsi-men Ch'ing met with the appropriate
　brokers …
(Roy 1993, vol. 1, 325)

The example (4) demonstrates that the narrator knows how to keep the reader
engaged. The skillful use of the formulaic phrases "話分兩頭" and "話休饒舌"
serve as navigational tools, illustrating the narrator's intention to guide the reader's
attention. For the sake of achieving a sense of naturalness and maintaining a smooth
narrative rhythm, TT1 expurgates all the meta-narrative markers. As a result, the
narrator's voice, with its stylistic coloring, is muted and downplayed. However,
this choice helps to make the reported events become concise, fluid, and compact
in the translation. By streamlining the text, TT1 becomes more aligned with conventional English narrative expectations. In TT2, we find features similar to the
ST: "At this point the story divides into two" and "To make a long story short."
These elements allow the narrator's voice to stand out, making it recognizable for
readers familiar with this oral storytelling mode. The downside is that the target
text becomes intricate and loquacious. The decision to preserve all these markers,
while beneficial for maintaining authenticity, can result in a text that deviates from

Table 3.2 The Treatment of Markers of Narrative Beginning, Transition, Progression and Conclusion in TTs

Occurrence in ST	Egerton's translation	Roy's translation
話說 話休饒舌 單……不提 卻表 卻說 這裡……按下不提 單表 話休絮煩 有話即長，無話即短 且說 只說 且看下回分解 不在話下 單道 話分兩頭 當夜無話 不必細說 此事表過不提 不由分說 不說	omitted altogether	all are faithfully rendered, with similar lexical pattern and syntax

the generic expectations among general readers in the receiving culture. To give a fuller picture of how markers of narrative transition and progression in *Jin Ping Mei* are treated in English translations, Table 3.2 collates such details.

3.4.2 Pre-Verse Markers

Lingua-stylistic devices marking narrative transition and progression are just one component of the narrator's expressive repertoire. Pre-verse markers also figure prominently in his array of stylistic devices. These markers consist of stock phrases used by the narrator whenever he introduces a poem or a lyric-song to describe or comment on events and characters. An essential function of pre-verse markers is to draw a line between prose and poetry and between narrative and commentary. Let us consider the following examples:

(5)

ST: 正是
       紫陌春光好 紅樓醉管弦
       人生能有幾 不樂是徒然
       有《西江月》為證
       (Xiao 2003, chap. 10, 86)

TT1:
[Omitted]

TT2:
Truly:
On the purple roads spring is at its height;
In the red bowers the music is intoxicating.
How long a span of life are we allotted?
Not to enjoy it is to live in vain.
(Roy 1993, vol. 1, 203)

There is a lyric to the tune "Moon on the West River" **that testifies to this**: ...
(Roy1993, vol. 1, 203)

In (5), the pre-verse marker "正是" separates prose from poetry, and "有《西江月》為證" introduces a lyric-song or *ci*-poem. Following these stock phrases, the reader is invited to appreciate the verse before the prose narrative continues. These poems and lyric-songs often belong to the narrator's commentary on what has already been narrated. Both the stock phrases and the verse content are eliminated from TT1, which benefits readers seeking a more straightforward reading experience without too many disruptive details. In TT2, all pre-verse markers, including poems, are preserved with the same sense and stylistic coloring as the original. Expressions like "Truly" and "There is a lyric to the tune ..." contribute to the narrative depth but might pose challenges for non-specialist readers, making it demanding to navigate through dense prose. The same is true of the next case:

(6)

ST: 正是今宵勝把銀缸照。秖恐相逢是夢中。有詞為證。
       (Xiao 2003, chap. 20, 172)

TT1:
[Omitted]

TT2:
Truly:
This evening let the silver lamp burn brightly as it will;
They're still afraid this tryst of theirs is nothing but a dream.
There is a lyric to the tune "Partridge Sky" **that testifies to this**: ...
(Roy 1993, vol. 1, 406)

In (6), a similar pattern can be observed in the treatment of pre-verse markers. Evidently, the entire Chinese passage is once again left out in TT1 but fully preserved in TT2. This different pattern in translational choices embodies the

Table 3.3 The Treatment of Pre-Verse Markers in ST and TTs

Occurrences in ST	Egerton's translation	Roy's translation
詩曰 正是 但見 有詩為證 詞曰 有詞為證	omitted	all are faithfully maintained

nuanced decisions made by each translator, reflecting their individual interpretative lenses and stylistic preferences. There are other pre-verse markers in the novel, and a similar pattern can be observed in the two English versions. Due to space limitations, they are not discussed here. Although these additional instances are not discussed here, their alignment with the observed pattern suggests a deliberate and systematic decision-making process by the translators. Table 3.3 provides a comprehensive overview of how pre-verse markers are handled in *Jin Ping Mei* within the translations of both Egerton and Roy.

3.4.3 Markers of Narrative Commentary and Simulated Dialogue with the Audience

The markers of narrative commentary and dialogue with the reader are fewer in number and less varied compared with the two categories of meta-narrative remarks already discussed. The following examples illustrate the difference between the two translators in dealing with this type of narrative intervention.

(7)

ST: 看官聽說。但凡世上婦人。有你十八分精細。被小意兒過。縱十
　　個九個。着了道兒。
　　(Xiao 2003, chap. 3, 35)

　　看官聽說。巫蠱魘昧之事。自古有之。
　　(Xiao 2003, chap. 13, 116)

TT1:
It would seem that in all the world there is not a single woman, no matter
　　how intelligent she may be, who cannot be led astray by some trivial act of
　　kindness. Nine women out of ten are caught this way.
(Egerton 1939, vol. 1, 58)

Readers, the wonders of witchcraft have been known to us since the most
　　remote periods of antiquity.
(Egerton 1939, vol. 1, 189)

TT2:

Gentle reader take note: Nine out of ten of the women of this world, no matter how smart they are, prove susceptible to flattery.
(Roy 1993, vol. 1, 72)

Gentle reader take note: Black magic and sorcery have existed since ancient times.
(Roy 1993, vol. 1, 272)

In (7), the recurrent use of the formulaic expression "看官聽說" serves as a narrative device when the narrator engages in commentary, particularly concerning certain characters, especially female characters. This stock phrase gives the impression that the narrator is talking directly to the reader, conveying an atmosphere where the narrator assumes the role of a storyteller offering moral caveats or didactic insights. Moreover, the term "看官," which can mean "gentlemen" or "honorable readers", plays a pivotal role in addressing the audience in a respectful manner and positioning the narrator/storyteller in a humble stance. According to Zunshine, the use of "看官" serves to "humble the narrator to the position of a servant who has the tough job of pleasing or amusing a person [the audience] of privilege" (Zunshine 2020, 233). It seems that this intentional humility in addressing the audience reflects a nuanced understanding of the power dynamics inherent in storytelling, where the narrator/storyteller or even the novelist seeks to attract and entertain a much wider esteemed audience. In the English texts, the formulaic phrase in the first Chinese passage is removed from TT1, which nevertheless retains the narrator's comment. However, the same phrase in the second Chinese passage is preserved and rendered as "Readers." This strategic decision showcases the translator's flexibility, opting to emphasize certain features of the original while consciously renouncing others. In doing so, TT1 preserves the essence of the narrator's commentary without replicating the specific linguistic formula employed in the original. However, TT2 uniformly renders both instances with the expression "Gentle reader take note," which captures the original's didactic quality but also ensures a seamless transposition of the narrative style to the target language, allowing the reader to engage with the text in a manner that is the same as the ST.

(8)

ST: 要知後項事情。且聽下回分解。
       (Xiao 2003, chap. 2, 30)

TT1:
[Omitted]

Table 3.4 The Treatment of Markers of Narrative Commentary and Simulated Dialogue with the Audience in ST and TTs

Occurrences in ST	Egerton's translation	Roy's translation
看官聽說 你道 原來 看官試想 且聽下回分解	occasionally retained omitted	all are adequately transferred

TT2:

**If you want to know the outcome of these events,
Pray consult the story related in the following chapter**.
(Roy 1993, vol. 1, 61)

In (8), the formulaic expression represents a typical stylistic characteristic inherent in Ming vernacular texts. This formula only appears at the end of each chapter, except the final chapter. The recurrent use of the stock phrase "且聽下回分解," together with "原來" and "你道," evokes a strong resonance with the oral storytelling tradition. This distinctive linguistic feature adds a layer of cultural depth to the narrative, anchoring it within the rich tradition of spoken tales. In TT1, the dialogic phrase "且聽下回分解" is deleted. In fact, this formulaic expression seldom occurs in the source text on which Egerton's translation is based, except in chapter one. In TT2, the narrator's dialogue with the audience is consistently maintained. The phrase "且聽下回分解" recurs methodically at the end of each chapter in the source text of Roy's translation. Roy's choice emphasizes a commitment to retaining the oral storytelling flavour inherent in the Chinese original. Table 3.4 illustrates the approaches employed by the two translators in handling markers of narrative commentary and simulated dialogue with the audience in *Jin Ping Mei*.

3.5 Discussion

This chapter has examined the voices of the narrator and characters in *Jin Ping Mei* and their treatment in the English translations. The stylistic features of the narrator's voice evoke a spoken or vernacular context that harkens back to an oral storytelling tradition. Both the characters' and the narrator's voices are characterized by a panoply of rhetorical devices typical of spoken language during the late Ming period. As integral parts of the text-world of *Jin Ping Mei*, both character discourse and the narrator's meta-narrative discourse appear archaic even to present-day source language readers. These heteroglossic features are destined to undergo transformation when crossing cultural borders in the hands of translators. The detailed translational analysis of the voices of the central characters and narrator yields several observations about the translators' choices and strategies.

On the one hand, Egerton tends to strike a balance between faithfulness to the source text and loyalty to his intended readers. Given that *Jin Ping Mei* is notably distant to his contemporary readers in language, narrative style, and historical background, Egerton acknowledges the wide temporal gap between the original text and his translation. His treatment of the narrative voice aims to preserve the voice-structure of the original while ensuring the readability of the target text. Egerton's translation highlights the modern-day relevance of the target text by employing contemporary language. The translation is evidently tailored to his contemporary readers and is therefore characterized as domesticated or reader-centered. Reader-centered translation respects the tastes and palates of readers who have limited knowledge of the source language, showing less concern about the stylistic features of the source text (Gu 2014, 91). According to Ernst-August Gutt (2000), what readers can understand depends on their pre-existing schemas, or relevant background knowledge, and text-processing abilities. As the foregoing analysis reveals, the translational strategy employed by Egerton in handling the narrative voice prioritizes the preferences and expectations of his contemporary readers who are predominantly unfamiliar with Chinese literature and culture. This strategy is multifaceted. Firstly, he significantly simplifies the protagonists' speech content and reduces their speech varieties, bringing the text closer to his contemporary reader. Additionally, he softens and sanitizes vulgarisms, expletives, and bawdy diction used by the characters, presenting them as more euphemistic or at least less transgressive, thereby improving their moral status in the story. Moreover, characters' local dialects, proverbial sayings, and wordplay are either eliminated or rendered sense-for-sense. While this undoubtedly renders the characters' voices less distinctive and blander, it enhances readability and intelligibility for the target readers. Most strikingly, Egerton simplifies the narrator's voice significantly. The narrator's meta-narrative remarks are mostly streamlined or excised in the translation. By flattening or smoothing out the generic features that mark *Jin Ping Mei* as a Ming vernacular novel, the Egerton translation significantly reduces textual complexity, allowing the story to progress smoothly without the recurrent intrusion of the narrator. The reduction of linguo-stylistic peculiarities makes the translation highly readable and accessible to the average English-language reader of the time, creating an "illusion of transparency" (Venuti 1995, 1). The multi-level changes to the narrative voice align with Egerton's views on *Jin Ping Mei*, which he considers to be written in a sort of telegraphese, conveying the essential with the utmost economy in the use of stylistic devices (Egerton 1939, ii). It is thus hardly surprising that both the characters' and the narrator's discourse in Egerton's translation appears simple, laconic, natural, and easily accessible, exhibiting a sort of expressive economy or telegraphic style reminiscent of twentieth-century American writer Ernest Hemingway (1899–1961), whose novels, such as *A Farewell to Arms* published in 1929, are characterized by simple, terse, and forceful language without much embellishment or picturesque quality. As noted in Chapter 1, Hemingway was significantly influenced by Pound in prose style during the 1920s and '30s. In short, then, characters' idiolects or their distinctive linguistic fingerprints are simplified and naturalized in Egerton's translation. The result is a less varied text with the original polyphonic aesthetics flattened, altering the novel's characterization as well as the overall feel of the novel at large. However, this approach gains by seamlessly integrating the translated narrative into the linguistic nuances and cultural sensibilities of the translator's contemporary audience, ensuring a more engaging and accessible reading experience. The emphasis on simplicity, limpidity, and expressivity implies a linguistic finesse that goes beyond mere word-for-word translation, allowing the reader to capture the essence and smooth flow of the narrative. Through careful consideration of contemporary language conventions and cultural schema of his readership, Egerton's translation becomes a dynamic and relevant piece for contemporary audience, transcending the barriers of temporal and linguistic differences.

Egerton's reader-centered approach, often described as domestication, especially his simplification of the narrative voice of the source text, can be connected to the unique literary and cultural milieu of his time. As discussed in Chapter 1, he produced his translation in Britain during the interwar period, a moment of significance in British literary and political history (Colt and Rossen 1992, 1). Similar to late Ming China, which was regularly fêted as a "Golden Age" of popular fiction, Britain in the interwar years also witnessed significant experimentation with various literary forms, particularly in the development of the novel, with the emergence of modernist works (Gindin 1992, 3). During this period, many British writers explored the flexibility of the novel and its adaptability to popular fictional genres. Sub-genres such as romance, comedy, the detective novel, the historical novel, the speculative novel, and thriller gained much popularity, especially among women and working-class writers, who maintained a strong genre-consciousness (ibid.). These emerging writers advocated for the democratization of literature, initiating a major cultural transformation (Hubble et al. 2021, 2). The appearance of multiple popular genres and the diversification of popular taste signified a significant departure from early modernism's perceived elitism and difficulty, giving rise to a mass culture characterized by accessibility and reader-friendliness (Hopkins 2007, 4). This shift represented a turn towards a more democratic aesthetic and conception of readership, aligning with the universal literacy that shaped the reading habits of Britons (MacKay 2019, 32).

Also significant is that during the interwar period, public activities were less common in Britain, and expenditure was limited due to the economic recession, indirectly increasing the demand for reading (Maddison 2019, 85). Paradoxically, the reduced availability of reading material caused by paper rationing did not decrease but intensified reading demand (McAleer 1992, 46). The explosive demand for reading material meant that literary hierarchies, such as high-, middle-, or low-brow, became less important than commercial concerns for publishers. Books, especially cheap, light, and easily accessible ones, became a more affordable and adaptable form of leisure entertainment. As indicated by Joseph McAleer, books even became the daily necessities, and indispensable for the life of Britons

(McAleer 1992, 43). Statistics show that book sales amounted to 7.2 million in 1928, soaring to 26.8 million in 1939 (Glover 2005, 305). Popular fiction, exemplified by Agatha Christie's detective tales, garnered significant popularity and became fetishized by the general reading public. According to Clive Bloom, popular fiction does not pay much attention to style, opting instead to make language transparent to tell a story and employing simple, uncomplicated literary techniques to convey stable meanings reflecting fundamental truths (Bloom 2021, 21). Plots, themes, readability, intelligibility, and accessibility took precedence over a book's aesthetic value or innovative style. Many sub-genres, such as the thriller, were characterized by popularity, fantasy, inauthenticity, unsophistication, and the ability to fully engage the reader (Hopkins 2007, 120). For instance, several of Graham Greene's (1904–91) bestselling novels in the 1920s and '30s were influenced by popular sub-genres, with the style and the form marked by superficial inauthenticity. As literary critic Robert Liddell (1908–92) has it, readers who enjoy "concentrating on the people and the happenings are not refreshed but annoyed to have to focus on a cluster of irrelevant details" (1947, 120). This implies that instead of feeling invigorated by the narrative's progression, readers may find their enjoyment disrupted when forced to divert their attention to a superfluous cluster of irrelevant details. These unnecessary details, rather than enhancing the reading experience, act as stumbling blocks, impeding the flow of the narrative and detracting from the core essence of the characters and their experiences. Positioned within mass culture and benefiting from technological innovations in publishing, popular fiction aligned well with the reading habits of broader social classes, especially the lower middle class and working class. Against this backdrop, Egerton's *middlebrow strategies* (translational tactics employed) can be seen as aligning with the literary and cultural democratization of his time. His reduction of the source text's sophistication and simplification or neutralization of its intricate narrative style, especially the complex and archaic narrative voice (such as the various archaic collocations and stock, formulaic phrases analyzed above), enabled his translation, shaped as a popular novel, to cater to the reading habits and tastes of the wider reading public.

A related point is that during the interwar period, literary taste and value were redefined, giving rise to a new notion for defining the literary novel: middlebrow (a post-World War I invention) in contrast to highbrow or lowbrow (Maddison 2019, 81). Middlebrow writers did not align with high modernism or lowbrow culture but aimed to strike a balance between them. In her 1932 essay "Middlebrow," Virginia Woolf (1882–1941) derided middlebrow writers as those who "amble on both sides in quest for no single object, such as art or life, but mix both in pursuit of money, power, and fame" (Ewins 2015, 251). The term middlebrow is vague, and the boundary between popular and middlebrow was often blurred, as bestsellers shareed features associated with all three levels (Ewins 2015, 251). In *Fiction and the Reading Public*, Queenie Dorothy Leavis (1906–81) demonstrates that middlebrow works appealed especially to the middle-class, a primary target for commercial publication (Leavis 1932, 45). The rise in commercial publication in the first decades of the twentieth century fostered the proliferation of middlebrow novels aimed at a wider readership, especially middle-class women. Novels for female readers, as Isobel Maddison (2019) suggests, were generally classified as middle-brow, often featuring feminine themes such as family, manners, food, romance, gender, and the like. The domestic novel or family saga gained popularity during this period, particularly after John Galsworthy (1867–1933) won the Nobel Prize for Literature in 1932. Galsworthy's series of novels, including *The Forsyte Saga*, served as inspiration for many family or domestic novels throughout the 1930s. The middlebrow fashion may explain why Egerton chose the name of the lead heroine of the novel as the book title, *The Golden Lotus*, for his translation of *Jin Ping Mei*, as mentioned previously. His intention was likely to appeal to a broad (female) readership, a topic that will be further discussed in the next chapter. In a word, Egerton's treatment of the narrative voice of *Jin Ping Mei* not only strives for linguistic appropriateness but also emphasizes the importance of ensuring that the translated text resonates with the sensibilities of contemporary readership. This not only facilitates a more profound understanding of the narrative content but also enhances the overall accessibility and enjoyment for contemporary readers, making the translated narrative a meaningful and culturally relevant contribution to the target literary landscape.

On the other hand, Roy follows a different path in the treatment of the narrative voice in his *highbrow* style translation of *Jin Ping Mei*. As the above analysis demonstrates, Roy favors a source-text-oriented approach, a strategy that aligns with his role as a researcher-translator. His translation introduces few changes to the narrative voice, at the level of either content or form. Instead, it highlights the historicity of the text by representing every single detail of non-modern text-world content. It can thus be termed a text-centered translation, a strategy pursued by several sinologists aiming to replicate the Chinese original as closely as possible (Gu 2014, 91). The so-called sinological translations that adopt a similar approach include Anthony C. Yu's version of *Journey to the West* and Jeffrey Kinkley's translation of Shen Congwen's (1902–88) *Biancheng* 邊城 (Border Town). Kinkley argues that a scholar has a duty to educate and contribute new knowledge (Xu 2018, 6), an attitude that undoubtedly shapes a researcher-translator's translational philosophy and practice. Roy's status as a sinologist aligns with his prioritization of strict accuracy and outright faithfulness to the original in his *re*translation of *Jin Ping Mei*. In transferring the narrative voice, as well as the various culturemes discussed in Chapter 2, Roy's solution is at once less autonomous and less flexible than Egerton's. In his handling of character speech, for instance, Roy adheres scrupulously to the source text, preserving all sorts of speech mannerisms to the extent that the orality, readability, and intelligibility of the translated dialogue are sometimes reduced to verbosity and unnecessary complexity. This detracts from the original style characterized by colloquiality, vividity, and simplicity. He often employs special syntax and idiosyncratic stylistic means, such as indentation, to convey his interpretation of the source author's style and to reproduce an effect of historical distance for his intended readership. This practice establishes his translation as a representation of the text-world of the Ming novel. In his treatment of the narrator's voice, Roy maintains the original author's storytelling style and keeps the narrator's various meta-narrative markers intact, thus foregrounding the oral storytelling tradition represented by the narrator of *Jin Ping Mei*. This approach proves essential to maintaining the narrative's integrity. As Hanan points out, the presence of the authorial rhetoric is natural and necessary in Chinese vernacular fiction, and recognition and perception of this formal realism, specifically, the various stock or formulaic phrases, should be vital in reading the tale (Birch 1974, 306). As a researcher-translator, Roy certainly stresses the peculiar qualities of the source text and succeeds in reproducing them in the target text. His treatment of narrative voice provides non-specialist readers, if not his projected audience, with "an alien reading experience" (Venuti 1995, 20). The alien, defamiliarizing touch brought out by his full reproduction of the source text's heteroglossia aligns with his observation on *Jin Ping Mei*:

> [T]he text of the *Chin P'ing Mei* is characterized by an amazingly dense net-work of internal, as well as external, allusions, verbal repetitions, resonances, cross-references, and patterns of incremental repetition or replication. [...] Since I believe that these repetitious elements are not fortuitous, but part of the author's conscious artistry, I have striven, to the extent possible, to render all such passages in exactly the same way whenever they occur or recur. Occasionally this may produce a slight awkwardness in the English, but I hope that the reader will put up with this flaw in order to better appreciate one of the salient features of the text. (Roy 1993, xlviii)

Unlike Egerton, who prioritizing adapting the source text's narrative voice for con-temporary readers, Roy tends to stress the antiquity or historicity of the source text's composition by signaling its temporal and cultural distance to the reader. Moreover, he opts to serve his intended readers, mostly the specialists in the field of traditional Chinese literature, by fully reproducing the narrative voice of the source text. As he rightly posits,

> My one abiding principle is to translate everything – even puns. [The novel] was written [...] by a great artist with his own lifeblood. I have therefore assumed that whatever I find in it is there for a purpose and must be dealt with somehow or other. I cannot pretend always to have done that so successfully, but if I can convey to the reader even a fraction of the pleasure this Chinese novel has given me, I shall not have lived in vain. (Roy 1993, xlviii)

By maintaining an unwavering commitment to the source text, Roy's translation becomes a testament to the intricate details and cultural nuances embedded in the novel. Through this meticulous approach, Roy provides readers with an oppor-tunity to immerse themselves in the historical and cultural context of the Chinese original, allowing it to serve as a valuable resource for those seeking a nuanced understanding of the oral storytelling tradition exemplified by *Jin Ping Mei*. Hence, it is safe to assume that Roy's treatment of narrative features of *Jin Ping Mei* is largely governed by his distinctive translation philosophy. Not being a translator by profession frees him to some extent from the norms of translatorial behavior.

His scholarly, or rather academic-oriented, translational principle makes his trans-lation a highbrow work and gives the Ming novel a different "afterlife," in Walter Benjamin's (2000, 16) words, than that given by Egerton, enabling the novel to be available to English-language readers as an object of linguistic, narratological, anthropological, and historical enquiry.

3.6 Concluding Remarks

This chapter has examined the narratological dimensions of *Jin Ping Mei* in trans-lation. It has provided a clear understanding of the intricate ways in which both characters' and the narrator's voices undergo transformations at the hands of the two translators. The alterations made by both translators to narrative content and style result in shifts in established narrative conventions and the novel's charac-terization. Particularly noticeable is Egerton's translation, which, while failing to fully capture the essence of the oral storytelling tradition and the novel's narrative features, significantly contributes to simplicity, naturalness, readability, and acces-sibility, thereby enhancing the reading enjoyment. These qualities align with the literary and cultural norms of early twentieth-century Britain, catering to the tastes and preferences of the general reading public at that time. In contrast, Roy's emphasis on an all-dimensional representation of the novel's heteroglossia firmly anchors his work firmly in the historical, literary, and cultural context in which the novel appeared. This approach adds ethnographical and pedagogical value to his translation, enabling potential readers to grasp the literary and historical sig-nificance of the novel. The juxtaposition of Egerton's approach, driven by con-temporary norms, and Roy's commitment to historical authenticity showcases the divergent strategies employed by translators in navigating the intricate terrain of cultural and literary adaptation. In brief, this chapter has offered a nuanced ana-lysis of the narratological dimensions of *Jin Ping Mei*, providing insights into the complexities of translating polyphonic voices in the novel. By exploring the treatment of lively dialogues and narrator remarks, the chapter contributes to a deeper understanding of how translational choices can impact the narrative experi-ence, tone, character portrayal, and overall reader perception of the story. The next chapter will shift focus to a discussion of how gender matters are handled by the two translators, shedding light on their nuanced approaches to gender dynamics and the impact on the overall interpretation and perception of the translated work in the receiving culture.

References

Alvstad, Cecilia. 2013. "Voices in Translation." In *Handbook of Translation Studies*, edited by Yves Gambier, and Luc Van Doorslaer, 207–210. Amsterdam: John Benjamins.

Anderman, Gunilla. 2007. *Voices in Translations*. Clevedon: Multilingual Matters.

Andersson, Lars-Gunnar, and Peter Trudgill.1990. *Bad Language*. Oxford: Basil Blackwell.

Andersson, Lars-Gunnar, and Peter Trudgill. 2007. "Swearing." In *A Cultural Approach to Interpersonal Communication*, edited by Leila Monaghan, and Jane Goodman, 195–199. Oxford: Blackwell.

Bai Weiguo 白維國. 1991. *Jin Ping Mei cidian* 金瓶梅詞典 (Jin Ping Mei Dictionary). Beijing: Zhonghua shuju chubanshe.

Bakhtin, Mikhail M. 1981. *Dialogic Imagination: Four Essays*. Austin: University of Texas Press.

Bell, Roger T. 1991. *Translation and Translating*. London: Longman.

Benjamin, Walter. 2000. "The Task of the Translator." In *The Translation Studies Reader*, edited by Lawrence Venuti, 15–22. London: Routledge Benjamins.

Birch, Cyril.1974. *Studies in Chinese Literary Genres*. Oakland: University of California Press.

Bishop, John L. 1956. "Some Limitations of Chinese Fiction." *The Far Eastern Quarterly* 15 (2): 239–247.

Bloom, Clive. 2021. *Bestsellers: Popular Fiction Since 1900*. Cham: Springer.

Børdahl, Vibeke. 2003. "The Storyteller's Manner in Chinese Storytelling." *Asian Folklore Studies* 62 (1): 65–112.

Børdahl, Vibeke. 2010. "Storytelling, Stock Phrases and Genre Conventions: The Case of *Wu Song Fights the Tiger*." In *The Interplay of the Oral and the Written in Chinese Popular Literature*, edited by Vibeke Bordahl, and Margaret B. Wan, 83–156. Copenhagen: NIAS Press.

Børdahl, Vibeke. 2016. "Tentative thoughts on the 'Storyteller's Manner' in *Jin Ping Mei cihua*." In *Modrý Jasmín*, edited by Jiřina Vaclová, Ivana Perútková, and Mgr. Jana Kreiselová, 33–47. Olomouc: Univerzita Palackého v Olomouci.

Bosseaux, Charlotte. 2018. "Translating Voices in Crime Fiction: The Case of the French Translation of Brookmyre's Quite Ugly One Morning." In *The Palgrave Handbook of Literary Translation*, edited by Jean Boase-Beier, Lina Fisher, and Hiroko Furukawa, 125–144. London: Palgrave Macmillan.

Colt, Rosemary M, and Janice Rossen. 1992. *Writers of the Old School: British Novelists of the 1930s*. London: Palgrave Macmillan.

Dobao, Fernández. 2006. "Linguistic and Cultural Aspects of the Translation of Swearing: The Spanish Version of Pulp Fiction." *Babel* 52 (3): 222–242.

Egerton, Clement. 1939. *The Golden Lotus*. 4 vols. London: George Routledge and Sons, Ltd.

Espunya, Anna, and Anita Pavić Pintarić. 2018. "Language Style in the Negotiation of Class Identity in Translated Contemporary Spanish Fiction: Vázquez Montalbán's Los mares del surin English and Croatian." *Babel* 64 (3): 348–369.

Ewins, Kristin. 2015. "'Revolutionizing A Mode of Life': Leftist Middlebrow Fiction by Women in the 1930s." *ELH* 82 (1): 251–279.

Fludernik, Monika. 2009. *An Introduction to Narratology*. London: Routledge.

Fowler, Roger. 1977. *Linguistics and the Novel*. London: Methuen.

Ge, Liangyan. 2001. *Out of the Margins*. Honolulu: University of Hawai'i Press.

Genette, Gérard. 1988. *Narrative Discourse Revisited*. Ithaca, NY: Cornell University Press.

Gindin, James. 1992. *British Fiction in the 1930s: The Dispiriting Decade*. London: Palgrave Macmillan.

Glover, David. 2005. "Speed, Violence, Women, America: Popular Fictions." In *The Cambridge History of Twentieth-Century English Literature*, edited by Laura Marcus, and Peter Nicholls, 304–317. Cambridge: Cambridge University Press.

Gu, Ming Dong. 2006. "Theory of Fiction: A Non-Western Narrative Tradition." *Narrative* 14 (3): 311–338.

Gu, Ming Dong, ed. 2014. *Translating China for Western Readers: Reflective, Critical and Practical Essays*. Albany: SUNY Press.

Gutt, Ernst-August. 2000. *Translation and Relevance*. Manchester: St. Jerome.

Halliday, Michael Alexander Kirkwood. 1978. *Language as Social Semiotic: The Social Interpretation of Language and Meaning*. London: Edward Arnold.

Hanan, Patrick. 1981. *The Chinese Vernacular Story*. Cambridge, MA: Harvard University Press.

Hanan, Patrick. 2005. "The Narrator's Voice Before the 'Fiction Revolution'." In *Dynastic Crisis and Cultural Innovation: From the Late Ming to the Late Qing and Beyond*, edited by David Der-wei Wang, and Shang Wei, 420–447. Cambridge, MA: Harvard University Asia Center.

He Manzi 何滿子. 1990. *Jin Ping Mei jianshang cidian* 金瓶梅鑒賞詞典 (A Dictionary for Jin Ping Mei). Shanghai: Shanghai guji chubanshe.

Hoffmann, Christian R. 2017. "Narrative Perspectives on Voice in Fiction." In *Pragmatics of Fiction*, edited by Miriam A. Locher, and Andreas H. Jucker, 159–196. Berlin: Walter De Gruyter.

Hopkins, Chris. 2007. *English Fiction in the 1930s: Language, Genre, History*. London: Bloomsbury Publishing.

Huang, Yonglin. 2018. *Narrative of Chinese and Western Popular Fiction*. Singapore: Springer.

Hubble, Nick, Luke Seaber and Elinor Taylor. 2021. *The 1930s: A Decade of Modern British Fiction*. London: Bloomsbury Academic.

Leavis, Queenie Dorothy. 1932. *Fiction and the Reading Public*. London: Chatto and Windus.

Leech, Geoffrey N., and Mick Short. (1981) 2007. *Style in Fiction: A Linguistic Introduction to English Fictional Prose*. London and New York: Longman.

Liddell, Robert. 1947. *A Treatise on the Novel*. London: Cape.

Liu, Wu-chi. 1966. *An Introduction to Chinese Literature*. Bloomington: Indiana University Press.

Locher, Miriam A., and Andreas H. Jucker, eds. 2017. *Pragmatics of Fiction*. Berlin/ Boston: De Gruyter Mouton.

MacKay, Mrina. 2019. "The Literary Novel." In *The Cambridge Companion to British Literature of the 1930s*, edited by James Smith, 32–46. Cambridge: Cambridge University Press.

Maddison, Isobel. 2019. "The Middlebrow and Popular." In *The Cambridge Companion to British Literature of the 1930s*, edited by James Smith, 81–96. Cambridge: Cambridge University Press.

McAleer, Joseph. 1992. *Popular Reading and Publishing in Britain 1914–1950*. Oxford: Oxford University Press.

Morillas, Esther. 2012. "Four-letter Words and More: Regarding Vulgar Language and Translation." In *Iberian Studies on Translation and Interpreting*, edited by Isabel García-Izquierdo, and Esther Monzó, 317–335. Bern and New York: Peter Lang.

Page, Norman. 1988. *Speech in the English Novel*. London: Longman.

Plaks, Andrew H. 1980. "Shui-hu Chuan and the Sixteenth-Century Novel Form: An Interpretive Reappraisal." *Chinese Literature: Essays, Articles, Reviews* 2 (1): 3–53.

Reiss, Katharina. 2000. *Translation Criticism: The Potentials and Limitations*. Manchester: St. Jerome.

Rosa, Alexandra Assis. 2012. "Translating Place: Linguistic Variation in Translation." *Word and Text: A Journal of Literary Studies and Linguistics* 2 (2): 75–97.

Rosa, Alexandra Assis. 2015. "Translating Orality, Recreating Otherness." *Translation Studies* 8 (2): 209–225.

Roy, David T. 1993. *The Plum in the Golden Vase or, Chin P'ing Mei* (vol. 1). Princeton, NJ: Princeton University Press.

Roy, David T. 2001. *The Plum in the Golden Vase or, Chin P'ing Mei* (vol. 2). Princeton, NJ: Princeton University Press.

Roy, David T. 2006. *The Plum in the Golden Vase or, Chin P'ing Mei* (vol. 3). Princeton, NJ: Princeton University Press.

Roy, David T. 2011. *The Plum in the Golden Vase or, Chin P'ing Mei* (vol. 4). Princeton, NJ: Princeton University Press.

Schiavi, Giuliana. 1996. "There is Always a Teller in a Tale." *Target* 8 (1): 1–21.

Stapleton, Karyn. 2010. "Swearing." In *Interpersonal Pragmatics*, edited by Miriam A. Locher, and Sage L. Graham, 289–306. Berlin and New York: De Gruyter Mouton.

Sun Xun 孫遜. 2005. *Jin Ping Mei jianshang cidian* 金瓶梅鑒賞辭典 (Jin Ping Mei Appreciation Dictionary). Shanghai: Hanyu da cidian chubanshe.

Taivalkoski-Shilov, Kristiina. 2015. "Friday in Finnish: A Character's and (Re)translators' Voices in Six Finnish Retranslations of Daniel Defoe's Robinson Crusoe." *Target* 27 (1): 58–74.

Thomas, Bronwen. 2012. *Fictional Dialogue: Speech and Conversation in the Modern and Postmodern Novel*. Lincoln: University of Nebraska Press.

Venuti, Lawrence. 1995. *The Translator's Invisibility: A History of Translation*. London: Routledge.

Wang Liqi 王利器. 1988. *Jin Ping Mei cidian* 金瓶梅詞典 (A Dictionary on Jin Ping Mei). Changchun: Jilin Wenshi chubanshe.

Wu Gan 吳敢. 2009. *Zhang Zhupo yu Jin Ping Mei yanjiu* 張竹坡與金瓶梅研究 (Zhang Zhupo and *Jin Ping Mei* Studies). Beijing: Wenwu chubanshe.

Xiao Xiao Sheng of Lanling 蘭陵笑笑生. 2003. Xinke xiuxiang piping Jin Ping Mei 新刻繡像批評金瓶梅. Singapore: South Ocean Publishing.

Xu, Minhui. 2018. "The Voice of a Scholar-Translator: Interview with Prof. Jeffrey C. Kinkley." *Translation Review* 102 (1): 1–13.

Zunshine, Lisa. 2020. "Who Is He to Speak of My Sorrow?" *Poetics Today* 41 (2): 223–241.

4 Navigating Gender Dynamics
The Representation of Women in Translation

4.1 Introduction

Acclaimed as a landmark work in Chinese fiction, *Jin Ping Mei* has left a lasting impact on several other Chinese vernacular novels, notably influencing *Honglou meng*, particularly through its exploration of domestic themes and female characterization. Therefore, *Jin Ping Mei* holds significance not only for literary critics but also for anyone interested in Chinese culture and social history. Despite its standing as the first significant domestic novel delineating the lives of Chinese women, the aspect of gender and femininity has been under-researched, to say nothing of the translation of these gendered elements into a different language like English. This chapter sets out to investigate the gender-specific aspects of *Jin Ping Mei*, with a specific focus on how they are handled in the translations by Egerton and Roy.

Similar to its predecessor *Shuihu zhuan*, *Jin Ping Mei* exudes a pronounced misogynist tone characterized by male elitism and the perpetuation of various stereotypes about women (McMahon 2003, 506). Its depictions of wanton women, prostitutes, and courtesans have gained notoriety in Chinese literary history. The female protagonist, Pan Jinlian, is portrayed as a prominent figure embodying promiscuity and unchastity, becoming an elaboration of stereotypical female characters commonly found in Ming moral tales (Fore 1993, 64). Conducting a comparative analysis of two English translations alongside the Chinese original text aims to illuminate whether the translators have altered and reconfigured the novel's diverse forms of gendered narrative to either obscure or reinforce the prevailing stereotypes about women in the patriarchal society depicted in the source work. This examination also seeks to elucidate the sociocultural ramifications of mediating and re-negotiating gender stereotypes during the translation process. Ultimately, it can offer insights into the distinctive perspectives of the two translators regarding gender stereotypes and femininity embedded in this Chinese domestic novel.

The remainder of this chapter is divided into five main sections. Firstly, it presents a brief overview of gender and translation, serving as a starting point for the ensuing analysis. Following that, it scrutinizes the gendered dimensions of *Jin Ping Mei* in detail, offering a brief exploration of the literary and sociocultural context that gave rise to the novel. The chapter places particular emphasis

DOI: 10.4324/9781003472674-4

on the interplay between the literary mise-en-scène of gender stereotypes and the prevailing neo-Confucianist ideology during the late Ming period. Moving forward, it conducts an exhaustive examination of gender-specific elements within *Jin Ping Mei*, with a focus on how Egerton's and Roy's English translations handle these elements to discern potential alterations in the stereotypical images of femininity. Subsequently, the chapter highlights the implications of varying gender stereotypes in elucidating the distinct strategies employed by the translators. Finally, some concluding remarks are provided.

4.2 Mapping Gender Matters in Literary Translation

Gender-related concerns have become well-explored terrain in the realm of translation studies. In the early 1990s, discussions regarding the handling of gender matters in translation surfaced among both feminist critics and translation scholars. Paralleling the cultural turn in translation studies, feminist theorists noted the correlation between the status of translation and that of women in society (Wang et al. 2019). Translation was usually considered inferior and subservient to the original work. As H. A. Giles has it, translations may be likened to "moonlight and water," while the originals are compared to "sunlight and wine" (Drury 2015, 28). This metaphoric thinking understands translations as having a less privileged position than their originals. Translation is at times even condemned as an act of betrayal. This parallels the similarly inferior position attributed to women in both patriarchal society and literature (Godard 1990; Simon 1996; von Flotow 1997). This observation forms the foundation of feminist translation theory, which seeks to recognize and criticize the complex set of ideas that consign both women and translation to a marginalized position within the social and literary hierarchy (Simon 1996, 1). Initially, the strong ideological agendas of feminist theorists limited their focus to the translation of experimental feminist texts and works by women (von Flotow 2011; Wang et al. 2019). These theorists sought to elevate women's status by making their identity and role in sociocultural practices more visible. Translation became an effective means for them to highlight their presence and authority in literature (Wang et al. 2019). For instance, feminist theorist and translator Barbara Godard (1990, 91) asserts that the feminist translator, acknowledging her unique critical perspective and finding pleasure in persistent rereading and rewriting, proudly showcases the indicators of her intentional intervention in the text.

However, feminist and non-feminist scholars alike have critiqued the limiting political agendas of these early theorists (von Flotow 1997, 77; Bengoechea 2014). Several scholars have broadened their concerns by looking at gender-related issues in translation from various new angles. Sherry Simon highlights the contribution of cultural studies to translation and illustrates that "cultural studies brings to translation an understanding of the complexities of gender and culture. It allows us to situate linguistic transfer within the multiple 'post' realities of today: poststructuralism, postcolonialism and postmodernism" (Simon 1996, 136). In a similar vein, Luise von Flotow opines that "gender awareness in translation practice poses questions about the links between social stereotypes and linguistic forms, about the politics of language and cultural differences, about the ethics of translation, and […] it highlights the importance of the cultural context in which translation is done" (von Flotow 1997, 14). Evidently, the boundaries of translation and gender have broadened considerably, unveiling new research avenues and expanding our understanding of these interconnected domains.

Current topics relating to gender and translation cover many areas including, among other things, gender in audio-visual translation (de Marco 2012), gay identity transfer (Harvey 1998), masculinity in translation (Breen 2011), gender and ideology in medical textbooks (Leonard 2017), women's identity construction in printed magazines (Arcos 2017), the translation of gender stereotypes in global telefiction and prose fiction (de Heredia 2016; Wang et al. 2019) and the female protagonists' masculine gender presentation in translation (Campbell 2019). All such studies have expanded earlier narrow perspectives by inquiring into a variety of issues pertaining to -gender, sexual identity, and power within translation. Furthermore, corpus linguistics, cultural studies, postcolonial studies, queer studies, and sociology have also brought new vigor and vitality to the study of translation and gender (Wang et al. 2019). Tuuli Lähdesmäki (2010, 5) states that the cross-fertilization nature of these new approaches demonstrates the plurality and complexity of investigating the construction of gender and sexual identities across languages and cultures. Therefore, gender issues constitute a critical locus for investigating the dynamics of translation, history, and culture.

Adding to this field, the present chapter aims to examine sexist language and gender stereotypes articulated in *Jin Ping Mei*, a novel deeply grounded in traditional Chinese neo-Confucian culture. More significantly, it seeks to investigate how the stereotypical and atypical gender roles evoked in the novel are mediated, negotiated, and reconstituted in the English translations by Egerton and Roy. The aim of the chapter is threefold. First, it looks at the relationship between gender stereotypes and linguistic forms in the source text. Second, it delves into the translators' strategies in dealing with gender-related elements. Finally, it examines potential instances of intervention and manipulation that might have influenced the translators' negotiation and reconstruction of gender stereotypes.

4.3 Gender Stereotypes and Their Manifestations in *Jin Ping Mei*

The gender stereotypes and their manifestations in *Jin Ping Mei* have historical roots in the sociocultural landscape of the Song dynasty, with significant influences continuing into the Ming period. During the Ming dynasty, Cheng-Zhu *lixue* 理學, known as neo-Confucianism and advocated by scholars such as Cheng Yi 程頤 (1033-1107), Cheng Hao 程顥 (1033-85), and Zhu Xi 朱熹 (1130-1200), as well as others from the Song dynasty, still exerted great influence over social norms and values of the time (Birge 2003; Cua 2003, 364). Neo-Confucianism, as a prevailing ideology, dismisses human desires and centers instead on *tianli* 天理 or the "principle of nature" (Cua 2003, 636). This philosophical framework aimed to construct new paradigms of social morality and manners, deeply influencing the prevailing gender dynamics. The ethos of neo-Confucianism tended to downplay individual desires, reinforcing a societal structure that rigidly adhered to prescribed roles and expectations based on gender (ibid.). The diminishing of human desires and the prioritization of abstract principles reinforced traditional gender norms, further entrenching the notion of women as subservient and men as the custodians of societal order. For instance, the neo-Confucianist school advocated fundamental principles for governing society and regulating human behavior: the king rules the subject, the father rules the son, and the husband rules the wife; additionally, neo-Confucianism promotes the isolation of women, the practice of foot-binding, and the emphasis of widow chastity (Ebrey 2003, 11). Cheng Yi's famous statement is that starvation to death is a minor concern compared to the significant matter of preserving a woman's chastity. This belief is often attributed to contribute to much of the misery of women in late imperial China (ibid.). Neo-Confucianism highlights the idea of female inferiority and absolute submission to maintain patriarchal society in late imperial China. The three-obedience, four-virtue principle was prioritized in Confucian ethics for women (Szonyi 2017, 168). Specifically, the three-obedience principle refers to obedience to the father before marriage, to the husband after marriage, and to the sons after the death of the husband. The four-virtue principle points to faithfulness, physical charm, proper speech and manners, and hard work (Croll 1978, 13). Additionally, women were required to perform domestic duties and master essential skills in fine arts, music, and calligraphy. Keith McMahon elaborates on the feminine ideal: "the civilized and respectable woman keeps to her inner chambers; she has bound feet; she is discouraged from practical education; if a widow, she ought to stay chaste and never (re)marry" (1987, 220). In brief, neo-Confucianism offers a perspective on the universe and societal structure that justified the traditional Chinese system of patrilineal and patriarchal family organization (Ebrey 2003, 12). Influenced by the philosophy of neo-Confucianism, women were highly regulated and constrained by social mores and the Confucianist ethical system in late imperial China. They were relegated to a very low position to maintain the normal functioning of a male-dominated patriarchal society. Given that language plays a crucial role in social positioning, Chinese features a repertoire of proverbial sayings codifying discrimination against women, stressing male control over them, and relegating them to a lower status (Lee 2015, 563). Examples include "a daughter after marriage is like water poured out," "sons are a gold wall while daughters are a clay wall," and "there will be no peace in a family when a daughter-in-law gets in." As Suzanne Romaine points out, "any and all representations, whether of women, men or any other group, are embedded first in language, and then in politics, culture, economics, history, and so on" (1999, 3). The proverbs mentioned above entrench the subordinate status of women in traditional Chinese society dominated by the Confucian social order.

Jin Ping Mei reflects the cultural milieu of the Ming period, becoming a rich tapestry where various historical undercurrents play out. It is a novel of social manners and social realism, authentically delineating various aspects, including gender dynamics, of late Ming society influenced by neo-Confucian ideology. As noted previously, *Jin Ping Mei* is notorious for the misogynous undertones permeating its narrative. The misogynistic logic of the novel has been discussed by several scholars (Chien 1988; Ding 2002). The novel incessantly presents encounters between men and women, between women and women, and between women and obscene objects believed to be weapons for gaining power and status. Women are largely sexualized in the story, and for the most part, their behaviors index the norms of late Ming society, although certain women behave in unusual ways that transgress prevailing norms. There are chaste women, wanton women, prostitutes, and adulteresses. *Jin Ping Mei* is a novel where the themes of lust and desire permeate the bulk of the narrative.

The characterization of the female protagonist illustrates that women in traditional Chinese society are devoid of any right to control their own fate. Instead, they are forced to be subservient to the patriarchal hierarchy. Take, for example, the female protagonist Pan Jinlian in *Jin Ping Mei*: she has bound feet or three-inch golden lotus, has been sold several times by her poor family to wealthy households, and has been abused, punished, and tortured by her husband for unfaithfulness, even though the latter is a libertine.

As mentioned in previous chapters, *Jin Ping Mei* is mimetic in both quotidian minutiae and characterization. According to C. T. Hsia (1968), the novel naturally and realistically presents different types of life-like men and women in a materialistic society. Additionally, Hanan stresses that the female characters in *Jin Ping Mei* are depicted with "a satisfying, astonishing degree of complexity" (1961, 325). This is neatly expressed in the power struggles of female characters in a polygamous household. Among the principal female characters, most are depicted negatively as behaving in a socially unacceptable manner that contradicts neo-Confucianist propriety. The heroine Pan Jinlian, for instance, is portrayed as a *yinfu*, or nymphomaniac, many times throughout the novel, and she is also likened to animals, such as a snake and a fox. Like the beautiful heroine, women are typically identified as *les belles infidèles*, incapable of following the three-obedience, four-virtue principle, and they are often belittled. It may well be that the author of *Jin Ping Mei* wished to underscore the importance of maintaining the Confucian moral order by portraying women negatively and attributing their tragic destinies to transgressive acts.

Gender inequality and stereotypes about women in *Jin Ping Mei* reflect the reality of late Ming society. As Dorothy Ko has it, the negative images of women portrayed in Ming-Qing novels could be understood as the projections of male writers "who saw the gender hierarchy and familial order eroding" (1995, 103). This is presumably because male authors quite unconsciously projected the values of their own time into their writing, such as unquestioned male superiority, the propriety of social order, and the rightness of the Confucian autocratic state (Hegel 1998, 70). In the story, the Ximen household serves as a microcosm of patriarchal society. Female characters, depicted as unfaithful, wicked, and reckless, are mainly driven by a desire for sex and status, with Pan Jinlian being the most representative. This portrayal clashes with neo-Confucianist orthodox values aimed at controlling and suppressing human desires. Pan Jinlian is portrayed as flawed due to her various transgressions, including committing adultery, murdering two husbands, and refusing to observe rituals for them or to mend her ways. Such a lack of morality, as the narrative unfolds, could wreak havoc on a traditional Chinese family and undermine the patriarchal order. Perhaps for this reason, unfaithful women indifferent to traditional morality in *Jin Ping Mei* all suffer retribution in the end. In short, the story of *Jin Ping Mei* seemingly serves as a mirror for the reader, warning that the unbridled pursuit of sexual and social fulfilment is unacceptable and will be punished by social norms and the moral order. But then again, there is also the titillation for the implied reader who is invited to enjoy the characters' antics and transgressions. Evidently, there is tension between condemnation and titillation, prohibition, and the desire for transgression. Therefore, the moralistic implications in the narrative appear to be fundamentally hypocritical.

In passages describing female characters, the narrative discourse appears to be driven by contradictory impulses. There exist, for instance, contradictions between the narrator's portrayal of female characters, especially the description of physical appearance, and his condemnation of their actions. To all appearances, the narrator's intention is to convey both sexual attraction and repulsion. In other words, the ostensible purpose of the text is to condemn the immoral or transgressive practice of women, yet it concomitantly offers readers potentially fascinating and arousing material. The demarcation line between titillation and condemnation is often blurred in the narrative discourse. At the same time, it is crucial not to make simplistic assumptions about the author's intentions. We should allow for the possibility that the author's attitude toward the narrator is parodistic. The narrator's moralistic condemnation of his female characters' expressions of their own sexuality is severe enough to suggest that it might be tinged with irony. Reading between the lines, we might interpret such passages as celebrations of individualism and self-expression, values opposed to the narrator's orthodox neo-Confucian ideology. As noted by Moss Roberts, "radical social criticism in [late imperial] China is expressed more through the popular [vernacular] literature and less through philosophy and history as in the west" (1978, 66). The narrator's critique and condemnation seem to reveal a titillating impulse to offer an alibi for the (male) reader's enjoyment of gendered portrayals in the narrative.

Several scholars have conducted feminist readings of *Jin Ping Mei*. For example, Ying-Ying Chien (1988) discusses sexuality and power in the novel, focusing on the re-evaluation of the heroine, Pan Jinlian, through the lens of femininity. Ding Naifei (2002) analyzes depictions of obscenity and sexual language in the novel, centering on the lasciviousness of the female characters. Ding argues for the late-Ming misogyny inherent in the narrative, approaching the novel as a gendered narrative palatable to late Ming male audiences. Ding's emphasis on the novel's fundamentally misogynist nature aligns with Zhang Zhupo's commentary. She also argues that the portrayal of sex in *Jin Ping Mei* is indispensable for evincing gender politics, as the female characters depend on sex to survive in a male-dominated world. In her study on the practice of gift exchange among women in the novel, Sarah Dauncey (2003) demonstrates that the fictional world of *Jin Ping Mei* reflects socially significant practices such as dowry preparation and the everyday exchange of gifts to develop friendships and relationships among women. He Jianjun (2007) examines a scene in the twenty-first chapter of *Jin Ping Mei* through a discussion of a female character performing the ritual of burning incense at night. He demonstrates the sophisticated construction of the novel and the density of its authorial control. More recently, Shu-min Wee (2009) has studied feminine sexuality in *Jin Ping Mei*, arguing that the heroine's insatiable physical and material desire is responsible for many deaths in the novel.

The aforementioned studies have significantly enriched our understanding of the importance of gender matters present in *Jin Ping Mei*. Although there have been studies on the cross-cultural transfer of gender aspects of other Ming-Qing novels, such as *Shuihu zhuan* and *Honglou meng* (Yang and Zhu 2017; Wang et al. 2019), the translation of gendered narratives in *Jin Ping Mei* across languages and cultures has not been studied to date. Drawing inspiration from previous research mentioned above, this study seeks to fill the gap in the literature by examining how gendered narratives described in *Jin Ping Mei* are handled in English translations. More specifically, the study employs a "micro-analysis of individual translations, the focus of which is on the minute details of language that (may) reflect the gendered aspects of a text, or seek to conceal them" (von Flotow 2011, 124). The chapter asks how and to what extent the different gender portrayals are treated and represented in the two English versions, and why. To provide answers, a descriptive and comparative analysis of the Chinese text vis-à-vis its two English translations will be conducted.

4.4 Analysis of Gendered Narratives in Translation

This section provides an in-depth analysis of gender stereotypes depicted in *Jin Ping Mei* and their interlingual transfer. Key passages are selected from the Chinese original, and the analysis considers how lexical and syntactic choices by the translators influence the reframing or reconstruction of gender stereotypes in the target texts. The two English translations were produced over half a century apart, and this temporal gap might be reflected in distinctions regarding the translators' re-interpretations of gendered discourse within the novel. Particularly, ideas concerning femininity and women's position in society differ when comparing Egerton's translation with Roy's retranslation. This discrepancy can be linked to the target social context and its changes over the intervening decades. Egerton's treatment of gendered discourse constructed in the source work might refract the feminist thoughts of his own time, such as softening misogyny. This section is divided into five sub-sections, each discussing one of the following areas: naming and addressing, usage of verse, visual cues, and narrative categories and foregrounding.

4.4.1 Naming and Addressing

In this subsection, I look at the naming and addressing of female characters. Jonathan Culpeper postulates that "a writer can exploit the meaning potential of names in constructing a character" (2014, 230). Rimmon-Kenan (2002, 84) notes that naming and addressing are the simplest and most effective way of portraying characters in narrative fiction. This is mainly because the attitude of the narrator or implied author toward a particular character can be neatly evinced through naming.

In *Jin Ping Mei*, we observe that the omniscient narrator seldom addresses female characters by their true names. Instead, female figures are often addressed as "歪淫婦," "表子," or "淫婦," which are idiomatic phrases reflecting gender-related stereotypes grounded in the patriarchal order. Notably, the term "淫婦" appears hundreds of times throughout the novel, suggesting that women are consistently discredited and devalued in the world of *Jin Ping Mei*. Charles Ettner recognizes that Chinese terms used in addressing or referring to one's wife or husband vividly denote the social positions and relative values traditional Chinese society assigned to males and females, respectively (Hellinger and Motschenbacher 2015, 42). The examples that follow illustrate how naming and addressing are used to portray female characters.

In Table 4.1, female characters are addressed as "表子," "歪淫婦," "賊淫婦," and "老豬狗" in the narrative, which are blatantly derogatory, revealing a sexist outlook or a disparaging attitude toward female characters. Broadly speaking, such language epitomizes the implied author's intent to establish certain social and ethical norms (Booth 1983). As mentioned earlier, these norms are intricately linked to neo-Confucianist values and ideology, as belittling and demeaning terms of address in the Chinese language are primarily directed at females (Ettner 2015, 42). Hellinger and Motschenbacher (2015, 3) assert that using pejorative or abusive language to address someone may provoke anger, aversion, and a sense of inferiority, while using polite terms of address signifies respect or the maintenance of one's identity. As Table 4.1 indicates, the terms of address are so offensive and stigmatized that they impart a strong patriarchal tone to the narrative. The stereotypical images of women suggested by the narrator's and male characters' pejorative appellations almost certainly influence the reader's perception of the gender images constructed by the implied author. However, when the source text is rendered into another language, these stereotypical representations can be reproduced or undergo transformation.

Table 4.1 The Chinese Text (Hereafter ST)

---

(1) 孫寡嘴道。我是老實說。哥如今新敘的這個表子。不是裡面的。是外面的表子。
   (Xiao 2003, chap. 15, 130)
(2) 信那沒廉恥的歪淫婦。浪著嫁了漢子。來家拿人煞氣。
   (Xiao 2003, chap. 18, 155)
(3) 便道淫婦自說你伶俐不知你心怎麼生着我試看一看
   (Xiao 2003, chap. 87, 866)
(4) 不想被西門慶聽見了。複回來。又打了幾拳。罵道。賊奴才淫婦。
   (Xiao 2003, chap. 11, 91)
(5) 这西門慶聽了此言。心中大怒。罵道賊淫婦。還不過去。人這裡說話。也插嘴插舌的。
   (Xiao 2003, chap. 41, 367)
(6) 武松道老豬狗我都知道了你賴那個。先剐了這個淫婦。後殺你這老豬狗。
   (Xiao 2003, chap. 87, 865)

Table 4.2 TT1

---

(1) "Let me explain," Sun Kua-tsui said. "His **new girl** does not live in any bawdy house. **She** is independent."
(Egerton 1939, vol. 1, 212)

(2) "So, just because that **shameless hussy** chooses another man, he must come home and take it out on us!"
(Egerton 1939, vol. 1, 252)

(3) "**You whore**," he cried, "you make yourself out to be a very clever woman. I would like to know what sort of heart you have, and I will see."
(Egerton 1939, vol. 4, 193)

(4) Hsi-men Ch'ing heard everything she said. He went back, and struck her several blows with his fist. "**You thievish slave, you strumpet**,"...
(Egerton 1939, vol. 1, 149)

(5) This made Hsi-men Ch'ing very angry. "**You strumpet**," he shouted, "why don't you take yourself off? We are talking, but nobody asked you to put in your word."
(Egerton 1939, vol. 1, 197)

(6) "**You old bitch**," Wu Sung cried. "I know everything ... "I will kill **you** first," he said to Golden Lotus, "and then **this old bitch**."
(Egerton 1939, vol. 4, 193)

In TT1, the referents for women are couched in equally pejorative terms with the exception of "表子," which is neutralized as "new girl" in (1). Instances such as "shameless hussy," "you whore," "you thievish slave," "you strumpet," and "old bitch" retain the abusive nature of the original expressions. The English renderings in Table 4.2 maintain pejorative undertones when addressing female characters. Tellingly, TT1 reflects gender stereotypes, exposing not only the concept of female inferiority but also the misogyny present in the original. An average reader are likely to perceive stereotyped depictions of female characters in the provided passages from TT1.

As shown in Table 4.3, TT2 consistently incorporates gender stereotyping. It translates all the nameless referents to female characters using equivalent terms to convey the intended meaning of the source text. For example, the strategy of employing terms like "tart," "shameless perverted whore," "lousy whore," and "old pig and dog" to reproduce the original gender-derogatory expressions conveys the narrator's disdain for female characters. TT2's interpretation depicts female figures as inferior, echoing the portrayal in the Chinese text. It is worth noting that the patriarchal perspective of the implied author is more evident in Roy's version.

4.4.2 Use of Verse

In *Jin Ping Mei*, verse pervades the narrative. The intrusion of verse in prose narrative represents a distinctive characteristic of vernacular fiction in late imperial China (Chun 2009, 23). In his "Notes to the Reader" in *Pai'an jingqi* 拍案驚奇 (Slapping the Table in Amazement), Ling Mengchu 凌濛初 (1580-1644) argues that the many forms of verse in fictive texts could be likened to garlic and vinegar,

Table 4.3

---

(1) "To tell the truth," interposed Blabbermouth Sun, "this new **tart** that Brother's taken up with isn't even an inhabitant of the quarter. She's an outsider who doesn't give a fuck for the insiders."
(Roy 1993, vol. 1, 309)

(2) "So that **shameless perverted whore** had such hot pants she couldn't wait to get married, did she? And now he comes home and vents his spleen on us."
(Roy 1993, vol. 1, 365)

(3) "**You whore!** It is said that you're really intelligent, but I don't know what sort of a heart you have, so I'm going to take a look at it."
(Roy 2013, vol. 5, 128)

(4) Hsi-men Ch'ing had overheard everything she said. He came back in and struck her several additional blows with his fist, cursing as he did so, "**You lousy slave of a whore!** ...
(Roy 1993, vol. 1, 211)

(5) When Hsi-men Ch'ing heard these words, he was enraged and cursed at her, saying, "**You lousy whore!** Mind your own business. While we're talking here, for you to: Stick your beak in and wag your tongue, is completely out of place."
(Roy 2006, vol. 3, 11)

(6) "**Old pig and dog** that you are!" ejaculated Wu Sung, "I know all about it ... I will first carve up **this whore** and then proceed to kill you, **old pig and dog that you are.**"
(Roy 2013, vol. 5, 127)

Table 4.4 ST

---

(1) 水性從來是女流 背夫常與外人偷
金蓮心愛西門慶 淫蕩春心不自由
(Xiao 2003, chap. 3, 37)

(2) 轎內坐著浪滛婦 後邊跟著老牽頭
(Xiao 2003, chap. 9, 74)

(3) 正是為人莫作婦人身。百年苦樂由他人。
(Xiao 2003, chap. 12, 102)

(4) 正是蛇入筒中曲性在。鳥飛籠輕便飛騰。
(Xiao 2003, chap. 80, 813)

---

acting as seasonings for the narrative (Ling 1991, as quoted in Chun 2009, 23). Despite their hackneyed language, the verses inserted into *Jin Ping Mei* serve not merely as seasonings but as vehicles for the implied author or narrator's comments on fictional characters, offering the reader a key for interpreting their actions.

The examples in Table 4.4 comprises a few lines of verse extracted from the source text. The patronizing language used implies the omniscient narrator's stance and attitude toward female characters, suggesting strong biases against women. A subtle undertone of misogyny is conveyed, as realized by the meaning of the lines. As Catherine Emmott puts it, "In reading narrative texts, we imagine worlds inhabited by individuals who can be assumed to behave, physically and

Table 4.5 TT1

(1) [omitted]
(2) [omitted]
(3) [omitted]
(4) [omitted]

psychologically, in ways which reflect our real-life experiences of being situated in the real world" (1997, 58).

As one reads the Chinese lines riddled with sexism, sensitive readers may readily perceive the pronounced sexist stance in the narrative, linking these stereo-typical images of women to situations in the real word. Sexism, according to Wilma Pyle, suggests attitudes and actions that relegate women to a passive and inferior status (Pyle 1976, 116). The narrator here paints women as wicked, flawed, and immoral due to infidelity to their husbands and indifference to morality and law, as stipulated by the neo-Confucianist ethical system. An insightful reader of these lines can observe the prevailing gender stereotypes of neo-Confucianist society.

In Table 4.5, it is noticeable that all the verses in the source text are omitted from TT1. These omissions seriously impoverish the meaning as well as the structural integrity of the novel. The worldview of the omniscient narrator becomes invisible for the target audience. The male-centric or female-marginal clues furnished by the implied author are not mirrored in translation, as Egerton expurgates most of the passages in verse in his translation of *Jin Ping Mei*, aside from the omissions under discussion. According to my own statistics, there are one hundred pre-*hui* poems (namely, poems appearing before every chapter) throughout the novel, and sixty-two are deleted from Egerton's translation. It is fair to say that Egerton's deletion method apparently masks stereotypical images of women in the narrative, mitigating their social and moral inferiority in the translation. Yet, as indicated in the previous chapter, Egerton (1939, vii) himself views these poems as dull and gibberish even when turned into English, which also undermines the stylistic effect of the novel in English.

In contrast, TT2 preserves all the verse passages, thereby conveying the implied author's attitudes towards female characters. The biases or prejudices against female characters in the source narrative are reflected in the translation, enabling target readers to perceive a male-dominant world where women are demeaned and easily condemned for disloyalty and misconduct. Furthermore, TT2 also conveys to readers a male chauvinist worldview, echoing the prevailing neo-Confucianist attitudes towards women's conduct. Ultimately, the narratorial voice remains androcentric in TT2.

4.4.3 Visual Cues

In *Jin Ping Mei*, the novelist extensively employs visual cues to reveal the personal characteristics of his personages. As noted by Jonathan Culpeper (2014, 221),

Table 4.6 TT2

(1) It has always been the nature of women to be like water;
    Behind their husbands' backs they betray them with other men.
    In her heart Chin-lien hankers after Hsi-men Ch'ing;
    Once her desires are aroused, she can no longer control them.
    (Roy 1993, vol. 1, 77)
(2) Inside the sedan chair there sits
       a wanton whore;
    While tagging at her heels there follows
       an old procuress.
    (Roy 1993, vol. 1, 171)
(3) If you're going to be a human being, don't be a woman; Or your every joy and
    sorrow will be dependent on another.
    (Roy 1993, vol. 1, 233–239)
(4) If a serpent is confined in a tube,
       its sinuosity will remain;
    If a bird is released from its cage,
       it will resume its flight.
    (Roy 2011, vol. 4, 683)

Table 4.7 ST

(1) 那婆娘也把眼來偷睃西門慶。又低著頭。只做生活。
    (Xiao 2003, chap. 3, 37)
(2) 只見那婦人穿著一件素淡衣裳。白喬鬆髻。從裏面假哭出來。那婦
    人虛掩著淚眼道。說不得的苦。我夫心疼症候。幾個日子。便把命
    丟了。撇得奴好苦。
    (Xiao 2003, chap. 6, 53)
(3) 婦人黑影裡抽身。鑽入他房內更不答話。解開裙子。仰臥在炕上。
    (Xiao 2003, chap. 80, 810)

"visual or appearance cues such as stature, clothing, facial expression, and posture play a key role in person perception and characterization." The examples presented in Table 4.7 illustrate depictions of the female protagonist, Pan Jinlian, portraying her in vividly visualized scenes for the reader's imaginative gaze.

As Table 4.7 illustrates, Jinlian's kinesthetic features, specifically her body movements, vividly reflect her easy virtue. Culpeper explains that body movements and postures can suggest or cement characterization (Culpeper 2014, 224). In ST (1), the verb "偷睃" suggests the lascivious nature of Jinlian yearning to marry Ximen Qing. A wanton image of Jinlian, along with her sensual desire, is subtly communicated via her bodily movements. In the English versions, it is noticeable that TT1 misses this subtlety by using a neutral term "coyly" to modify the phrasal verb "looked up," which sacrifices the contemptuous tone present in the source text. TT2, nonetheless, renders "偷睃" as "stole surreptitious glances at," aptly capturing the narrator's pejorative attitude to the skittish Jinlian, meant to be understood as immoral, mischievous, impudent, and ill-behaved.

Table 4.8 TT1

---

(1) She looked up at him **coyly**, then bowed her head again and went on with her sewing.
   (Egerton 1939, vol. 1, 62)
(2) Golden Lotus, wearing plain clothes, with a white covering on her head, sobbed **as though her heart were breaking**… . "My sorrow is greater than I can bear," Golden Lotus said, drying her eyes. "My husband suffered from his heart and, after only a few days' illness, he died and left me inconsolable."
   (Egerton 1939, vol. 1, 88)
(3) … and Golden Lotus **ran through** the darkness to her room. They did not utter a word but undressed and lay down on the bed.
   (Egerton 1939, vol. 4, 108)

Table 4.9 TT2

---

(1) … and she, too, **stole surreptitious glances at** him. … but again, she merely lowered her head and continued to sew.
   (Roy 1993, vol. 3, 78)
(2) At this point he caught sight of the woman who came out from the interior of the house dressed in plain white clothes, with a white paper cap over her chignon, **feigning tears**. … The woman **pretended to wipe away her tears**, saying, "I can't tell you how terrible it is. My husband was stricken with heart trouble and in only a few days lost his life, just like that. It's really terrible to be so bereaved."
   (Roy 1993, vol. 3, 115)
(3) The woman, **concealing herself in the shadows, slipped inside** behind him, and: Without saying another word, unfastened her skirt, reclined face up on the k'ang …
   (Roy 2013, vol. 5, 673)

In ST (2), Jinlian's disloyalty, unchastity, and treachery after the death of her husband, Wu Da, are skillfully conveyed through her body movements and facial expressions. Both "假哭" and "虛掩著淚眼" serve as visual cues suggesting that Jinlian does not genuinely care about her husband's death. The narrator's negative attitude towards Jinlian's hypocrisy and mercilessness is evident. In TT1, the visual features "假哭" and "虛掩著淚眼" are rendered as "sobbed as though her heart were breaking" and "drying her eyes," respectively. Despite potential irony, neither "假" nor "虛掩" is reflected in the translation, altering the portrayal of Jinlian's character. Her falsity and deception, as evidenced by her actions, are downplayed. In TT2, the translation consistently emphasizes female-derogatory referents. Moreover, the visual cues "假哭" and "虛掩著淚眼" are rendered as "feigning tears" and "pretended to wipe away her tears," respectively, pointedly conveying Jinlian's unchastity and betrayal of her dead husband. Hence, a stereotyped image of a femme fatale is discursively recreated and made transparent to the reader. As Culpeper (2014, 223) suggests, a character's gait can significantly influence how they are perceived by the audience. In ST (3) in Table 4.7, Jinlian's gait is depicted by the verb "鑽入," which graphically conveys her unchastity and promiscuity.

Further, such a gait also characterizes Jinlian as timorous and powerless in the polygamous Ximen household. In the English texts, TT1 has "ran through the darkness to her room" for "鑽入," which fails to capture Jinlian's slyness and surreptitiousness in committing an immoral act. The implied author's contempt for this wanton woman is not manifested in the translation. By contrast, TT2 reflects the narrator's negative attitude towards Jinlian's ravenous sexual desire. TT2 renders "鑽入" as "concealing herself in the shadows, slipped inside behind him," which closely aligns with the Chinese original in depicting Jinlian's mien and movements. The verbs "concealing" and "slipped" allude to Jinlian's loose morals and impudence. The gender stereotypes present in the source narrative are discursively reconstituted in the translation.

4.4.4 Dehumanization

The dehumanizing portrayal of women in *Jin Ping Mei* appears to be an integral part of the novel's aesthetic construction. This is particularly evident in the depiction of the lead female protagonist, Pan Jinlian, who is often likened to various types of animals or objects, especially in her sexual relationships with Ximen Qing and other male characters. Jinlian is portrayed as willing to go to great lengths and do anything for Ximen Qing to win his love and favor within the household. Several examples illustrating this association with different animal images are presented in Table 4.10.

In ST (1), Jinlian is stigmatized as a horse during her intimate moments with Ximen Qing. In ST (2), she is depicted as a cat while committing adultery with her cicisbeo, Chen Jingji. In ST (3), Jinlian is reduced to a mouse hiding in Dame Wang's house after being purchased by the latter for less than one hundred taels of silver. In ST (4), Jinlian is degraded to a fox, a loaded image in the history of classical Chinese tales (Huntington 2003, 7). According to Victoria Cass, women in Ming conceptions of the feminine are unlikely to evade association with the supernatural (Cass 1997, 73). Beautiful and seductive women are often linked to supernatural beings, such as cats, snakes, and foxes.

Table 4.10 ST

---

(1) 叫春梅篩酒過來。在牀前執壺而立。將燭移在牀背板上。教婦人馬爬在他面前。
(Xiao 2003, chap. 18, 157)

(2) 猛然抬起頭来。見了經濟。就是个貓兒見了魚鮮飯。
(Xiao 2003, chap. 57, 517)

(3) 你身軀兒小。膽兒大。嘴兒尖。忒潑皮。見了人藏藏躲躲。耳邊廂叫叫唧唧。攪混人半夜三更不睡。
(Xiao 2003, chap. 86, 857)

(4) 月娘當下羞赧而退。回到後邊。向玉樓眾人說道。如今這屋裡。亂世為王。九條尾狐狸精出世。
(Xiao 2003, chap. 26, 228)

Table 4.11 TT1

(1) He called Plum Blossom to heat some wine and come and stand beside the bed to hold the wine jar. He set the candlestick beside the bed and told Golden Lotus to **go down on all fours before him**. (Egerton 1939, vol. 1, 257)
(2) When she saw him, it was as though **a cat suddenly espied a fish**. (Egerton 1939, vol. 3, 47)
(3) The **rat** is small. But bolder than it looks, Hungry and eager, ready for any prank. When anyone appears, It beats retreat and hides. Its scufflings in the depth of night disturb good honest slumberers. (Egerton 1939, vol. 4, 179)
(4) "What a cantankerous fellow the master of the house is," she said to Tower of Jade and the others. "There is **a nine-tailed fox** at work somewhere. ... (Egerton 1939, vol. 1, 359)

Table 4.12 TT2

(2) 3) **Your body is small**, but your daring is great; Your muzzle is pointed, and prone to mischief. On seeing anyone, you hide yourself away; But the squeaks you create can still be heard. You disturb one's sleep in the middle of the night. (Roy 2013, vol. 5, 107)
(4) All that Yueh-niang could do was to retire in confusion and go back to the rear compound, where she said to Meng Yu-lou and the others, "Right now in this household: Chaos is king. The **nine-tailed fox** fairy has appeared in the world ... (Roy 2001, vol. 2, 106)

The fox, in particular, appears as the most common female shapeshifter, a demon capable of metamorphosizing into different living things, as reflected in fictive writings in late imperial China. Notably, Jinlian is likened to a fox-spirit assuming supernatural powers, such as witchcraft, to allure and then destroy men. The frequent connection to animals implies "a gender-related social and cultural hierarchy in a patriarchal and patrilineal society" (Zhang 2015, 73).

In Table 4.11 and Table 4.12, the English versions effectively recreate the disparaging animalistic imagery linked to Jinlian, providing readers in the target language with a glimpse into the male-centric world portrayed in the narrative and enabling them to conjure stereotypical images of female characters. Apart from being likened to an animal, the protagonist, Jinlian, experiences dehumanization by being associated with various objects, including sex toys and commodities. Hence, translation readers have equal access to the dehumanization as portrayed in the original Chinese text.

In Table 4.13, the example vividly portrays Jinlian played with and tortured by her husband, Ximen Qing, for their sexual pleasure. In this scene, Jinlian is

Table 4.13 ST

西門慶道。小油嘴。看我投個肉壼。名喚金蟬打銀鵝。你瞧。若打中
一彈。我吃一鐘酒。
(Xiao 2003, chap. 27, 244)

Table 4.14 TTs

TT1	TT2
"Now," Hsi-men said, "watch me. I'm going to play Flying Arrows with **a living target**. The game is called Striking the silver Swan with a Golden Ball. Watch! If I hit the mark at the first shot, I shall treat myself to a cup of wine." (Egerton 1939, vol. 1, 385)	"Little oily mouth," said Hsi-men Ch'ing, "you can look on as I play a game of 'pitching into **the fleshly pot**.' This variation is called 'Shooting the Silver Goose with a Golden Pellet.' You watch; for every pellet that hits the target I'll drink a cup of wine." (Roy 2001, vol. 2, 145)

trivialized as a "肉壼," signaling a pot made of "human flesh." Ximen throws plums into the pot, which is *ipso facto* Jinlian's vagina. The mention of Pitch Pot, a popular game in traditional Chinese society, further accentuates this dehumanizing act. Ximen takes Jinlian's sexual organ as the pot, transforming the game into a thrilling and sexually alluring experience. Obviously, Jinlian is degraded to a sexual toy for her husband in this scene, with a markedly misogynous tone underlying the narrative.

As shown in Table 4.14, TT1 described "肉壼" as "a living target," a choice that seems to neutralize the explicit nature of the term and perhaps downplays the sexual dynamics inherent in the original. On the other hand, TT2 adopts a foreignizing approach by translating "肉壼" as "fleshly pot." This choice maintains a closer fidelity to the ST, capturing the essence of the term in a more literal manner. The term "fleshly pot" not only retains the sexual connotations but also introduces a vivid and evocative image. This visual effect helps the target audience in conjuring a more explicit mental picture of Ximen's sexual pleasure, thereby emphasizing the objectification of Jinlian in this context. The decision to use "fleshly pot" in TT2 contributes to the effective portrayal of Jinlian's inferior status and passivity as Ximen's concubine. By preserving the explicit nature of the term, the translation ensures that the power dynamics and objectification inherent in the original text are conveyed to the target audience. This choice not only reflects the commitment to linguistic and cultural faithfulness but also underscores the translator's awareness of the impact that specific language choices can have on the overall portrayal of characters and relationships within the narrative.

In Table 4.15, the narrative voice portrays Jinlian as merchandise to be bought, sold, and discarded by the whim of wealthy men in a male-oriented society. Born into a poor tailor's family, her mother sells her at the age of nine to a wealthy

Table 4.15 ST

小名叫做金蓮。娘家姓潘。原是南關外潘裁的女兒。賣在張大戶家。
學彈唱。後因大戶年老。打發出來。不要武大一文錢。白白與了他
為妻。

(Xiao 2003, chap. 3, 31)

Table 4.16 TTs

TT1	TT2
Her surname is P'an, and her personal name, Golden Lotus. Her father was P'an Ts'ai, who used to live by the South Gate. Originally, she **was sold to** Master Chang, and at his house she learned to sing and play. When Chang was very old, he made **a present** of her to Wu Ta. (Egerton 1939, vol. 1, 52)	After his death she **was sold into** the household of Mr. Chang, the well-to-do merchant, where she learned to play musical instruments and sing. Later, because Mr. Chang was getting along in years, he released her from the terms of her contract and gave her to Wu the Elder as wife **without demanding a candareen in return**. (Roy 1993, vol. 1, 65)

household following her father's death. Subsequently, she is given by her second master to the ugly dwarf, Wu Da, without cost. Before meeting her ultimate demise at the hands of Wu Song, Jinlian is transferred by Yueniang, the legal wife of Ximen Qing, to Dame Wang. Finally, Dame Wang sells Jinlian to Wu Song for about a hundred taels of silver. Throughout the story, Jinlian lacks freedom of choice in marriage and control over her own destiny. Instead, she is treated as a commodity, falling victim to a male-dominant society.

In Table 4.16, the gender stereotypes at play in the ST are more or less reflected in TT1, although it takes liberties to render his text concise and fluent. TT2 is stylistically quite different from TT1, with lexical choices that align more closely with the Chinese original. To illustrate, TT2 uses the phrase "he released her from the terms of her contract and gave her to Wu the Elder as wife without demanding a candareen in return" for "打發出來。不要武大一文錢。白白與了他為妻." In so doing, TT2 persists with a foreignizing method to capture all the nuanced details of the ST. The dehumanizing approach to characterizing Jinlian as merchandise is well reflected in the target text, and the idea of women's subservience remains the same in Roy's version as the ST.

4.4.5 Use of Special Narrative Categories

In *Jin Ping Mei*, the female characters' actions and attitudes are often made clear to the reader through their thought presentation. Geoffrey Leech and Mick Short remind us that different modes of thought presentation can "report what the character thinks" and "render the character's immediate experience or consciousness

Table 4.17 ST

這婦人一心只想著西門慶。那里來理會武大做多做少。這婦人巴不得他出去了。便踅過王婆茶坊裡來。等西門慶。
(Xiao 2003, chap. 5, 47)

Table 4.18 TTs

TT1	TT2
Golden Lotus was so taken up with her thoughts of Hsi-men Ch'ing that she did not notice how many cakes he made. She **waited impatiently** until he had gone out and then **went to** the tea shop to wait for her lover. (Egerton 1939, vol. 1, 78)	The woman was too preoccupied with Hsi-men Ch'ing to notice how many wheat cakes he made. … The woman **could hardly wait** until he was out the door before **slipping over to** Dame Wang's teashop to wait for Hsi-men Ch'ing. (Roy 1993, vol. 1, 99)

of those thoughts" (2007, 270). By manifesting what is in the minds of female characters, the narrator tends to convey his own attitudes or pass value judgments on them. The following examples demonstrate negative comments on female characters by revealing their inner thoughts or presenting their inner world.

In Table 4.17, the source passage conveys an inner feminine perspective, offering a glimpse into the intimate thoughts and desires of Jinlian. The sentence "這婦人巴不得他出去了。便踅過王婆茶坊裡來" serves as a poignant expression of Jinlian's yearning for the departure of her husband. Expressions like "巴不得" and "踅過" convey a sense of eagerness and anticipation, highlighting the depth of Jinlian's desire for a clandestine affair with Ximen Qing. Importantly, the sentence operates as a third-person narration of Pan Jinlian's inner thoughts, revealing her deep longing to go out and rendezvous with Ximen Qing. Simultaneously, the passage carries an implicit layer of judgment through the omniscient narrator. It implies the narrator's disapproval of the female protagonist's actions, suggesting a moral stance against her perceived treachery and wantonness. This nuanced approach contributes to the richness of the narrative and prompts readers to reflect on the female character's motivation while considering the larger cultural and moral context in which the story unfolds.

Table 4.18 shows the nuanced disparities between the two translations, shedding light on the intricacies of conveying Jinlian's emotions. TT1 has "impatiently" and "went to" for the lexical items "巴不得" and "踅過," imparting a direct interpretation of Jinlian's sentiments. This choice creates a sense of urgency, yet it may fall short of capturing the deep yearning embedded in her emotions. In contrast, TT2 employs more evocative phrases such as "could hardly wait" and "slipping over," showcasing a heightened ability to capture the narrator's ironic or satirical tone. The expression "could hardly wait" adeptly conveys the impatience inherent in Jinlian's emotional state, while the verbal phrase "slipping over" introduces a

Table 4.19 ST

那婦人想起蔣竹山說的话来。西門慶是打老婆的班頭。降婦女的領袖。思量我那世裡晦氣。今日大睜眼。又撞入火坑裡來了。越發煩惱痛哭起來。 (Xiao 2003, chap. 19, 169)

Table 4.20 TTs

TT1	TT2
The Lady of the Vase remembered that Ch'iang Chu-shan had told her of Hsi-men's prowess as a wife beater and **wondered what misdeed in a former existence had brought her to such a pass that day.** She sobbed more loudly. (Egerton 1939, vol. 1, 274)	Li Ping-erh remembered what Chiang Chu-shan had told her, that Hsi-men Ch'ing was: The foreman of the wife-beaters, The leader of the lotharios. **"What did I ever do in a previous incarnation to deserve such a fate?" she thought to herself.** "Today, with my eyes wide open, I've plunged right into the fiery pit all over again." The more upset she became the harder she cried. (Roy 1993, vol. 1, 397)

layer of dramatic irony. This implies a deeper awareness on the part of the narrator regarding the potential consequences or the nature of Jinlian's thoughts and actions. This treatment vividly portrays Jinlian's emotional state, emphasizing her intense longing for her lover, Ximen Qing. The same pattern in translational choices is evident in the next example:

The example in Table 4.19 relates to Li Ping'er, another female protagonist, whose inner thoughts are directed reported by the narrator. The example dramatizes Li Ping'er's fear of her husband, Ximen Qing, who is adept at manipulating and punishing women. According to Keith McMahon (1995, 16), late imperial Chinese novels depict a world dominated by polygamists who occupy the highest positions in society, and their conduct of desire – sexual debauchery – is considered the most authoritative. In *Jin Ping Mei*, the Ximen household typifies such a world. In this instance, the depiction of Li Ping'er's inner world serves as a poignant lens through which the pervasive theme of women's vulnerability and submissiveness within a patriarchal polygamous household is underscored. The narrative delves into the intricate layers of Li Ping'er's thoughts, unveiling a landscape dominated by societal structures that relegate women to positions of fragility and subservience. The nuanced exploration of Li Ping'er's psyche not only illuminates her personal struggles but also serves as a microcosm reflecting broader societal norms that perpetuate gender inequality in the novelist's day.

In TT1, the portrayal of Li Ping'er's sense of inferiority is subtly conveyed using an introductory reporting clause. This serves to temper the depiction of Li Ping'er's fragile nature and her apprehension about her husband's authority. By using this mode of thought presentation, TT1 mitigates the strength of the gender stereotypes inherent in the original narrator's perspective. Conversely, in TT2, Li Ping'er's psychological state and the rhetoric of her own inferiority are brought to life through direct thought presentation, resembling a poignant soliloquy. This narrative technique allows readers to perceive the depth of Li Ping'er's timorous and powerless nature as she engages in an internal dialogue. TT2 artfully unveils this female character's vulnerability as she grapples with her emotions and insecurities. As a concubine, Li Ping'er's submissive demeanor towards Ximen Qing becomes more evident in TT2. The direct thought presentation illuminates the nuances of her internal struggles and the complexities of her relationship with her husband, offering readers a deeper understanding of the challenges she faces as a woman in a society that imposes rigid expectations on gender roles. In short, the choice of thought presentation in the English texts significantly shapes the reader's perception of Li Ping'er's character and the social dynamics at play. TT1's indirect mode downplays the impact, while TT2's direct approach heightens the emotional intensity, providing a nuanced exploration of gender roles and power dynamics within the narrative. The same holds true of the following example:

As the head of the household, Ximen Qing is formidable and demanding, acting as a ruler who is seldom satisfied. His interactions with the women in the family reveal a dark and cruel side, marked by extreme actions in response to his changing moods. In moments of contentment, he often labels his women as strumpets. When angered, Ximen Qing resorts to a brutal display of power, ordering the stripping and subsequent beating of his women with a horsewhip. This reflects not only physical violence but also a demeaning exercise of dominance. Despite the cruelty in his actions, there is an undeniable allure about Ximen Qing. His charisma and power make him a figure difficult to resist, even for those who endure the brunt of his harsh treatment. The complex dynamics at play in Ximen Qing's relationships with women hint at the intricate power structures embedded in late Ming society. The description in Table 4.21 illustrates Ximen Qing's unbridled sexual assertiveness, wherein he fulfils his fantasies through violent means in the presence of his concubine. This depiction offers readers a glimpse into the prevailing attitudes of late Ming society, where the preservation and assertion of male authority in both the familial and societal spheres were paramount. Ximen Qing's behaviour, though extreme, aligns with a broader cultural framework that normalized and even celebrated such expressions of dominance. The example in Table 4.21 serves

Table 4.21 ST

拿張小椅兒坐在院內。花架兒底下。取了一根馬鞭子。拏在手裡。喝令滛婦脫了衣裳跪著。
(Xiao 2003, chap. 12, 100)

as a microcosm of the larger societal norms, showcasing the complex interplay of power, gender dynamics, and the accepted norms of the time.

In Table 4.22, the English texts contribute to the overall richness of the narrative, offering readers different perspectives on the portrayal of gender roles and power dynamics within the story. Specifically, TT1 opts for indirect modes of thought presentation, which possibly gives a more subdued portrayal of the characters and their relationships. This subtler approach could temper the impact of gender stereotypes or provide a more restrained interpretation of power dynamics within the narrative. The downplaying effect might also result in a less emphatic portrayal of the societal norms and tensions at play. By comparison, TT2 offers a more immediate and explicit portrayal of Ximen Qing's interactions with Jinlian through direct speech and thought presentation. Much like the source passage, TT2 doesn't evade the androcentric elements embedded in the narrative. The explicit portrayal of Ximen Qing's speech and thoughts exhibits the persistence of stereotypes, providing a vivid picture of a society steeped in androcentrism. Through this linguistic fidelity to the ST, TT2 maintains the cultural nuances and power dynamics inherent in the late Ming narrative, providing the target reader with a nuanced understanding of the complexities of gender roles and the patriarchal norms prevalent in the depicted society.

In Table 4.23, the example illustrates that after being interrogated by her husband, Ximen Qing, Jinlian has no option but to accept Ximen's punishment and maltreatment willingly. The narrator presents Jinlian's thoughts and actions in a trivial yet forceful manner, showcasing the heroine's lowly position and powerlessness in relation to the male protagonist, the ruler of the household. Ximen Qing symbolizes familial authority and male power, reducing his women to the status of passive objects. In this context, Ximen Qing has just returned from a brothel, and

Table 4.22 TTs

TT1	TT2
He took a small chair, went out, and sat in the courtyard in a shady place. Then he **took a horse whip**, and **made the woman take off her clothes and kneel before him**. (Egerton 1939, vol. 1, 164)	Then he got himself a small chair, sat down in the courtyard underneath the flower arbor, **pulled out a riding crop**, and, brandishing it in his hand, **commanded, "Whore! Take off your clothes and get down on your knees."** (Roy 1993, vol. 1, 236)

Table 4.23 ST

潘金蓮自知理虧。不敢不跪。到是真箇脫去了上下衣服。跪在面前。低垂粉面。不敢出一聲兒。
(Xiao 2003, chap. 12, 100)

Table 4.24 TTs

TT1	TT2
She bowed her white face, but did not dare to make a sound. (Egerton 1939, vol. 1, 164)	The woman, troubled as she was **by a bad conscience, did not dare to disobey**. She actually took off all her clothes, above and below, and knelt down before him: **Hanging her powdered face in shame, not daring to utter a sound.** (Roy 1993, vol. 1, 236)

he can't bear Jinlian's affair. This situation underscores a double standard: men can pursue sexual gratification and engage in infidelity freely, but women are subject to punishment for similar transgressions. Ximen Qing is only briefly criticized by the narrator and other characters in the story, while Jinlian is portrayed as the evil, unfaithful woman who seduced other men and brought shame to the household. The issue of the double standard regarding the transgression of desire is brought to the fore in this passage. Jinlian's suffering draws attention to the unequal power relations infused with patriarchal hypocrisy.

Table 4.24 illustrates that TT1 significantly detracts from the ST by omitting numerous details reported by the narrator. TT1 opts to present only selective aspects of Jinlian's thoughts and actions. This transformation contributes to the weakening of gender stereotypes in the translation. The selective presentation alters the portrayal of Jinlian for the target readers, who might perceive Jinlian differently, as her obedience and docility in submitting to Ximen's power are downplayed. Conversely, TT2 fully communicates the idea of Jinlian's subordinate status to male power. The juxtaposition of her inner thoughts against the backdrop of the patriarchal polygamous household is unveiled in the translation, adding depth and poignancy to the narrative. This invites readers to perceive the complex intersections of gender, power, and social expectations. The decision to include complete narrative details presents the target reader with a female figure who is distinctly socially inferior and reliant on men to survive within the household. This depiction reflects the broader male-dominated society, offering a microcosm of the androcentric thinking underlying the surface of the story. By remaining faithful to the original portrayal of gender dynamics, TT2 ensures that the target reader confronts the stark realities of a society where women's roles are subservient and dependent on male authority.

4.4.6 Stereotyping Femininity Through Foregrounding

Foregrounding is an essential literary device in stylizing poetic or fictitious texts. It serves to guide a proper interpretation of fictive characterization. Culpeper (2014, 129) contends that in literary texts, elements characterized by unexpectedness and unusualness contribute to salience through deliberate deviation from linguistic norms and conventions. G. W. Cook explains that foregrounding may also arise

Table 4.25 ST

這個老婆属馬的。小金蓮兩歲。今年二十四歲了。生的黄白淨面。身
子兒不肥不瘦。模樣兒不短不長。比金蓮腳還小些兒。性明敏善機
變。會粧餙。龍江虎浪。就是嘲漢子的班頭。壞家風的領袖。[1]
(Xiao 2003, chap. 22, 194)

---

from "discourse deviation," meaning the breaking of "the expectations that readers
form on the basis of their general knowledge of the world, or their world schemata"
in their interacting with the language of literary texts (as quoted in Culpeper 2014,
132). In Table 4.25, the narrator introduces the female character Song Huilian in
a quite unconventional way. The narrative takes an unexpected turn by initially
presenting her in a positive light, only to reveal a contrasting or somewhat negative perspective towards the end of the passage. This serves to shock the reader
by unveiling the woman's "true nature" towards the conclusion of the lengthy
description. The narrator's attitude shifts abruptly from positive to negative, and
the foregrounded aspects can bring about a surprising change in the reader's perception of Song Huilian's character. The subtle irony embedded in the narrative
suggests a stereotypical image of women.

Specifically, the narrator introduces Huilian, Ximen Qing's mistress, in meticulous detail. A battery of adjectives is used to deliver the narrator's judgmental view
on the female character – presented as attractive yet far from perfect. The glowing
delineation of Huilian's physical appearance, personal qualities, and moral failings
not only reflects the narrator's critical stance but also hints at a satirical attitude
towards the character. The use of glowing language to describe Huilian's attributes
and flaws creates a nuanced portrayal that sways between admiration and critique. This stylistic choice serves to emphasize the complexity of her character,
presenting her as a multi-dimensional figure. Particular noteworthy is the adversa-
tive conjunction "就是," which characterizes Huilian as a woman who is "嘲漢子
的班頭。壞家風的領袖," clearly conveying a misogynistic innuendo.

The English texts in Table 4.26 adeptly retain the narrator's sardonic tone, faithfully reproducing Huilian's flaws and merits of appearance and character. The
depiction of her physical attributes, signaling feminine allure or seductive beauty,
conveys the narrator's misogyny through seemingly positive evaluative words,
despite the preservation of derogatory references to the female character, reinforcing the narrator's androcentric stance. Yet a closer contrastive reading reveals that
the lexical and syntactic differences may offer the target reader of each translation a different perception of Huilian's character. In TT2, the negative portrayal of
the licentious Huilian, referred to as a seductress and home breaker, comes much
closer to the ST. Even subtle decisions on the level of word usage and sentence
construction can influence readers' perceptions of individual characters. By incorporating these linguistic nuances and using indentation, TT2 evokes a similar conception of Huilian, who turns out to be unchaste and promiscuous, as depicted
in the ST. The same is true of the following example concerning another female
character, Lady Lin.

Table 4.26 TTs

TT1	TT2
Wistaria was twenty-four years old, two years younger than Golden Lotus. she had a clean white skin, and her body was admirably proportioned, not too tall and not too short, neither too plump nor too slender. Her feet were even tinier than those of Golden Lotus. She was intelligent and wide awake, and had excellent taste in self-adornment. **But she was indeed a captain among those who dally with men and a leader of those who disturb the harmony of households.** (Egerton 1939, vol. 1, 311)	This woman was born in the year of the horse and was two years younger than Chin-lien, which made her twenty-five years old that year. She possessed: A clear off-white complexion. Her figure was neither plump nor thin; Her stature was neither short nor tall. Her bound feet were even smaller than Chin-lien's. She was: **Clever by nature, Highly adaptable, Adept at adorning herself, As able at making waves as a dragon or tiger;** **In fact: A champion among seductresses, A leader of the homebreakers.** (Roy 2001, vol. 2, 31)

Table 4.27 ST

婦人頭上戴著金絲翠葉　兒。身穿白綾寬紬袄兒。沉香色。遍地金粧
　花段子鶴氅。大紅宮錦寬襴裙子。老鸛白綾高底扣花鞋兒。是個綺
　閣中好色的嬌娘。深閨內合毬的菩薩。²
(Xiao 2003, chap. 69, 654)

Similarly, in Table 4.27, the narrator dedicates considerable attention to describing Lady Lin 林太太, a woman from a local aristocratic family with a husband holding a high official position in Qinghe county. The initial part of this passage describes Lady Lin as elegant, dignified, and graceful, creating an impression of physical beauty befitting the aristocracy. However, toward the end of the passage, the narrative takes an unexpected turn, revealing Lady Lin as far from dignified or decent. The ironical tone is foregrounded using two paradoxical collocations "好色的嬌娘" and "合毬的菩薩." The contrastive phrases "好色" and "嬌娘" create a literary oxymoron, revealing a paradox. By the same logic, the phrases "合毬" and "菩薩" form another oxymoron that reinforces the narrator's critical stance, contributing to the overall satirical tone of the narrative. The narrative becomes a commentary on social expectations, moral judgments, and gender roles. The satirical attitude embedded in the portrayal of Lady Lin adds depth to the narrative, prompting a critical examination of the female characters and the sociocultural context in which they exist. Evidently, the narrator exposes Lady Lin as a veritable lascivious whore, employing an ironic effect that comes into full play.

Table 4.28 TTs

TT1	TT2
Lady Lin wore a headdress of gold thread and jade, a full gown of white silk, and a coat of figured satin, with a gold design upon an incense-colored background. Her skirt was of the scarlet satin worn by ladies of the court, and her white silk shoes were high heeled. **She was, indeed, an exquisite woman of the embroidered chamber, a goddess who, as it were, made sacrifice of her body for the love of men.** (Egerton 1939, vol. 3, 258)	On the woman's head, she wore a headdress of gold filigree enhanced with emerald leaves. On her body, she wore a wide-sleeved jacket of white satin, over a brocaded, aloeswood-colored, crane-decorated robe of figured satin, and a wide-bordered skirt of palace-style crimson brocade. On her feet, she wore shoes of raven-hued fabric with embroidered patterns, and high white satin heels. **Manifestly, she was:** **An alluring and lascivious female inhabitant of ostentatious chambers; A veritable bodhisattva of coition, dwelling in her sequestered bower**. (Roy 2011, vol. 4, 253)

Table 4.28 illustrates notable differences between the two English versions. In TT1, the intended ironic effect of the ST is compromised, since the image of Lady Lin is transformed into that of "an exquisite woman" and "a goddess," thereby downplaying the narrator's judgmental view. This transformation leads to a shift in the reader's identification with the female character, shaping her as a woman willing to make a personal sacrifice for true love rather than one of easy virtue. This choice introduces a romantic undertone in the depiction of Lady Lin, a departure from the original ironic intent. On the other hand, TT2 stays closer to the ST, bringing out a similar, if not the same, satirical effect through collocations such as "an alluring and lascivious" and "a veritable bodhisattva of coition." These nuanced linguistic choices reproduce the misogynistic tone derived from the narrative, ensuring that the original's satirical and critical stance are manifested in the target text. The differences between the two translations underscore the impact of translational choices on the overall tone and interpretation of the narrative. While TT1 introduces a romanticized perspective, TT2 foregrounds satirical or misogynistic undertones through discursive nuances and special stylistic means, such as indentation.

4.5 Discussion

This chapter has conducted an in-depth analysis of gendered discourse in *Jin Ping Mei*, a profoundly misogynistic novel, and its English translations. The aim was to compare salient passages from the novel and its English translations that convey sexism and gender stereotypes, examining the extent of differences in the representation of gendered discourse between the two translations. The findings indicate that both translators have considered gender matters and their impact on the reader's perception of the story. This is evident in their discursive strategies employed to address various forms of gendered language in the source text. The translators' discursive strategies generally align with the target literary, cultural, and linguistic norms at play in their respective historical contexts.

However, it has been suggested that Egerton significantly intervenes in the source text, opting to renegotiate various stereotypes of female characters based on his own interpretation of the novel. This discursive intervention brings about a noticeable shift in the re-coding of gender in the target text. The original narrator's misogynistic tone is weakened in the translation. Passages involving visual cues, naming biases, verses, and thought presentations of female characters are either refashioned or omitted entirely, resulting in a target text that is less extreme in its portrayal of women. Thus, Egerton's translation does not aim to fully recapture the sexism or stereotypes present in the Chinese original. This reductive and transformative approach is influenced by the target literary and cultural norms that motivate the translator's choice.

As a rule, translators often adapt or manipulate source texts to align with mainstream ideologies and meet the expectations of target readers (Lefevere 1992, 39; Chesterman 1997, 64). In Egerton's translation, this approach results in conveying sexist and misogynist undertones somewhat differently in the target text, often in subtle ways. This translational choice aims to make the text more palatable to a broader audience, especially to female readers. Egerton's treatment of the misogynist narratives and gender stereotypes in the source text aligns closely with the target-cultural context of the 1920s and '30s. Britain during the first decades of the twentieth century remained a male-dominated society with sexist and misogynistic tendencies, albeit not as extreme as the late Ming portrayed in *Jin Ping Mei*, a text from sixteenth-century China. In the interwar years, women in Britain remained marginalized and undervalued, lacking equal rights compared to men (Dyhouse 1989; Glew 2016, 236). Matters such as access to education, equal employment, equal pay, economic autonomy, and free health care were distant from the lives of most women, especially those from lower classes (Dyhouse 1989; Glew 2016, 236). It was not uncommon for employers to advise women to quit their jobs after they were married before the 1940s. Few married women worked outside the home before 1939, as society largely accepted conventional gender roles, viewing men as the primary breadwinners (Glew 2016, 236). The official media regularly featured articles to encourage women to stay home and fulfill traditional feminine duties (Holmes 2018, 94). In short, sexism, misogyny, and gender inequality were characteristic of British society during that period. Gendered biases and masculinist misogyny were pervasive in British society, becoming central features of literary works by both male and female authors, including Eliot, Pound, Woolf, and Joseph Conrad (1857–1924). For instance, in *Jacob's Room* (1922), Woolf critiqued misogyny and triumphal androcentrism displayed by the male protagonist Jacob. His overt misogynistic attitudes, rooted in sexist power structures, and his male-dominated experience of intellectual life, are scrutinized (Ferrall and

McNeill 2018, 58). This influence extended to a number of other women writers who became engaged with the popular culture prevalent in that period. Gender matters found expression in novels and films.

As stated in Chapter 3, Britain during the interwar era witnessed unprecedented growth in mass consumerism and leisure entertainment industry (Skillen 2012, 750). Films and novels consumed by British audiences were closely tied to pressing issues related to economy, class, gender, sexuality, and nation that emerged after the Great War (Grandy 2016, 3). Reading fiction emerged as one of the most popular leisure activities for Britons during this period, leading to the establishment of a particular form of reading culture, middlebrow reading culture, alongside the growth of the democratization and commercialization of literature (Humble 2013, 100). As discussed earlier, the middlebrow novel enjoyed widespread popularity, catering to the cultural desires of broad audiences (Humble 2004, 13). Importantly, middlebrow fiction was skillfully plotted, featuring themes on domestic scenes, everyday lives, love, marriage, and ordinary aspirations (Holmes 2018, 13). Characterized as a gendered phenomenon shedding light on "the texture of women's lives," this type of novel was primarily consumed by female readers, especially middle-class women, given that paid employment for married women was discouraged and this allowed them ample leisure time for indulging in extensive reading (Beauman 2008, 7; Holmes 2018, 12). Many male writers also engaged in specific kinds of writing about femininity, often centering on domestic themes and associated with sentimentality (Marshik et al. 2018, 10). As a matter of fact, women comprised the majority of the British reading public in the interwar years, and female readers were recognized as a lucrative consumer market (Bloom 2021, 51; Brown 2015, 8). Little wonder, then, that middlebrow novels placed women's experience at the center of the narrative, attracting readers through "skillful characterization, effective plotting, and the creation of compelling fictional worlds" (Holmes 2018, 96–98). Clearly, gender, sexual identities, and domesticity were the prime concern of middlebrow fiction for its imagined readers (Humble 2004, 5). As a distinctive literary form, this type of novel enjoyed widespread appeal, circulating quickly among the general reading public in 1920s and '30s Britain (Holmes 2018, 124). It played a crucial role in (re)negotiating societal structures and gender identities in Britain during the interwar era, meeting both commercial and readerly expectations (Humble 2013, 110). These middlebrow novels were amusing yet serious, easily accessible, and permeated with cultural value.

It is therefore tempting to associate Egerton's middlebrow strategy in handling gender matters in *Jin Ping Mei* with this specific cultural context of interwar Britain. His renegotiation of gender stereotypes and patriarchal values during translation aligns with the expectations of the general reading public. By choosing to preserve but nonetheless soften misogynistic narratives, Egerton seeks to integrate the original Chinese story into the middlebrow canon and adapt to the tastes of contemporary readership. Importantly, *Jin Ping Mei* predominantly deals with conventionally feminine or domestic subjects such as everyday life, marriage, family, gender, romance, and sexuality. The novel ipso facto shares several similarities with the middlebrow novels that dominated the British book market between the wars. Popular middlebrow literature was not a minority interest, as it constituted a large proportion of novels published in Britain in the interwar years (Holmes 2018, 12). Egerton's decision-making aimed to achieve homogeneity and great accessibility in his translation. As previously mentioned, his choice of using the name of the lead heroine, Golden Lotus, as the title of his translation indicate his acute awareness of the popularity of feminine middlebrow culture at the time. Thus, it is fair to assert that Egerton's translation of the gender aspects of *Jin Ping Mei* serves an instrumental purpose by fostering communication with the target readers. According to Christiane Nord, "an instrumental translation is intended to fulfil a new communicative purpose in the target culture without the recipient being conscious of reading or hearing a text which, in a different form, was used before in a different communicative action" (Shuttleworth and Cowie 1997, 43).

Notably, the original sexist tones and gender stereotypes are mitigated, modified, or transformed in Egerton's translation, yet still meaningfully reproduced in a way that sensitive readers might perceive the underlying sexist and misogynistic tone of the story retold in English. The rendition of female characters' names (for example, Jinlian becomes Golden Lotus, Yulou becomes Tower of Jade, Chunmei becomes Plum Blossom, and so forth) adds a dimension to the misogynistic tone of the novel. This aligns with previous studies suggesting that Western translators tend to objectify women when translating the names of female characters in traditional Chinese literary texts (Qi 2018). The instrumental nature of the translation contributes to minimizing sharp differences in gender values across cultures, thereby improving its acceptability in the target culture. By freeing the original text from its potentially offensive dimension, it renders the text translated from past cultures more palatable to modern audiences attuned to gender politics. Egerton's translation introduces a different literary image of *Jin Ping Mei* in a new literary context to the British readership. In a word, Egerton's treatment of sexist discourse and gender stereotypes in translation could be seen as a repackaging of the source text's patriarchal worldview for mainstream readers of his time.

By comparison, Roy undertook his translation of *Jin Ping Mei* at the turn of the millennium, amidst a post-feminist landscape where gender equality and changing patriarchal values were emphasized, despite the ongoing efforts of gender-aware feminist translators to reduce androcentrism and deconstruct patriarchal values inscribed in works of literature by male writers. Paradoxically, in this study, it has been revealed that Roy's translation shows few "interventionist moves" (Simon 1996, 13). Unlike feminist/female translators, he refuses to adapt or readjust a misogynist text grounded in neo-Confucianist Chinese culture for the target readership. Rather, Roy strictly adheres to the principles of extreme "accuracy" and fidelity to the original text, not omitting or altering anything related to gender. It is worth noting that Roy undertook his translation in a postfeminist era. In the post-feminist world, feminism is effectively diminished or dismantled and postfeminist discourses are often simply statements of anti-feminism. Bonnie Dow (1996, 86) argues that a definite shift has occurred in society and culture, a "backlash" against feminist goals and ideas. This backlash suggests hostility towards or rejection of feminist ideals, aiming to downplay women's liberation and relegate them to subordinate roles of a bygone era. Thus, the postfeminist world can be seen as an era of "retro-sexism," which undermines the need for feminist theory and action (Whelehan 2000, 11). It was for this very reason that feminist literary criticism became particularly vibrant in the 1980s, with publications such as Hazel Carby's *Reconstructing Womanhood: The Emergence of the Afro-American Woman Novelist* (1989) standing out as representative feminist texts. Roy crafted his translation in such a postfeminist context. His translation reproduces the ethical values, sexist tones, misogynistic ideology, and gender stereotypes of the source text, aligning with the feminist agenda of emphasizing gender oppression as a universal problem. Hence, his *Plum* can be used as fine reading material to remind feminists in the post-feminist era of the ongoing need to fight for women's rights. Roy's approach aligns with the principles of documentary translation, which involves a faithful reproduction of the source text, prioritizing formal correspondence. It serves, as Nord notes, as a means of informing the reader about the exact content of the source text without significantly transforming or adapting the target text to the target situation in either functional or communicative terms (Palumbo 2009, 38). Following a documentary policy, Roy consciously delves into the intricacies of gendered discourse inscribed in the source work. As a researcher-cum-translator, Roy demonstrates a keen awareness of the ideas, beliefs, and values prevailing in late Ming society. His unmistakable inclination towards foregrounding gender stereotypes and the deeply ingrained patriarchal system contributes to the heterogeneity and exoticism of the target text, bringing its readers closer to a different, unfamiliar time and space. Roy's approach necessarily offers a set of gender values and ethics mirroring those of the original text, albeit resonating with the postfeminist discourse of his own society. This strategy might position his text with a hermeneutics of the past, particularly for readers hesitant to diminish their understanding of premodern text, history, and culture, emphasizing the importance of a critical revaluation of gender roles in history.

As Christopher Larkosh highlights in *Re-Engendering Translation*, "the mediating or re-engendering acts such as quotation or translation can mean at times actually setting aside one's own understandings of self, and in doing so, creating an institutional space for others to speak and trace out divergent understandings of identity and alterity" (2011, 4). The so-called re-engendering of the source text in translation may entail endorsing faithful re-presentation. The Roy translation continually invites its intended readers to perceive a patriarchal world governed by neo-Confucianist stereotypes and biases against women. It confronts the reader with a truthful picture of *Jin Ping Mei* as a socially significant and "realistic" novel written in the late Ming, where neo-Confucianist ideology and androcentrism penetrated almost all aspects of social life, even though this ideology was somewhat challenged by other philosophical thoughts during the time. Robert Hegel, in his essay "Teaching China as a Global Culture," emphasizes that "we must be faithful translators who can demonstrate *both* the familiarity *and* the foreignness of the originals as we recreate China in our own language" (Hegel 2008, 21; original emphasis). In this light, cultural and historical "truth" could be better acknowledged through faithful translation or acceptance of literary works in the original forms, even though truly or entirely faithful translation is hardly attainable and remains somewhat elusive. In like manner, Sandra Bermann and Michael Wood (2005, 7) state that with more refined, sensitive cultural and linguistic translations, the globalized world would become more hospitable. It follows that a sensitive cultural translation that captures the subtleties of the original text and manifests the essence of a tradition would contribute to facilitating cross-cultural dialogue and understanding.

Arguably, Roy's choice to preserve subtleties of gender portrayal, as demonstrated in the above analysis, seems ethically grounded, offering a modern-day audience a fuller picture of the androcentrism and patriarchal values portrayed in the late Ming novel.

4.6 Concluding Remarks

This chapter has shown that the literary representation of gender matters, including sexist discourse and stereotypes against women, has far-reaching implications for several aspects of *belles-lettres* translation. These implications encompass the reconstruction of female images, the alteration of fictional themes, and the overall atmosphere of the story. Gender stereotypes carry important political and cultural meanings in every community and era. The investigation of gendered aspects in *Jin Ping Mei* and their interlingual transfer serves as a tool for understanding gender-related issues in late imperial China, the historical contexts in which the translated texts were created, and the discursive mediation in the translation process. This study posits that the exploration of gender in literary translation illuminates the dynamic encounters between two different cultures. As Steiner would have it, "no two historical epochs, no two social classes, no two localities use words and syntax to signify exactly the same things, to send identical signs of valuation and inference" (Steiner 1992, 47). Translation, as both process and product, becomes a site that casts illuminating light on the evolution of the inscription of gender in literary texts. In agreement with Pierre Zobermman (2014, 252), it is argued that whether the translator chooses to re-engender the source text by revising its gendered discourse or reproduces such discourse by maintaining the system of the original, translation is always context-bound, dependent upon an awareness of gender politics in both the context of the source text and that of the target text. By addressing the reframing and reconstruction of gendered narratives in English translations, the chapter has contributed to the broader discourse on the role of translation in shaping cultural perspectives and navigating gender dynamics in literary works. By shedding light on the gendered dimensions within works like *Jin Ping Mei*, it is hoped that this book will inspire further studies exploring the nuanced gendered discourse embedded in traditional Chinese fictional works and the intricate dynamics that arise during the process of translating such narratives across different national and cultural contexts. This endeavor can further enrich our understanding of historical perspectives on gender roles and relationships within transnational contexts. The next chapter moves to a discussion on sexually themed narratives within *Jin Ping Mei*. It aims to uncover how these sensitive and titillating themes are treated in translation and explore how the nuances of erotic narratives are either maintained or transformed in the process of transposing them into different historical, cultural, and linguistic contexts.

Notes

1 In the Chongzhen edition (namely, Egerton's source text), the expression "這個老婆属馬的" appears as "這個婦人," and "龍江虎浪" is deleted.
2 In the Chongzhen edition, the expression "扣花" is deleted, and the expression "合毬" is changed to "施屄."

References

Arcos, Irene Rodríguez. 2017. "Translation and Ideology: The Construction of Identity in Magazines Aimed at Women." In *Translation, Ideology and Gender*, edited by Carmen Camus Camus, Cristina Gómez Castro, and Julia T. Williams Camus, 155–177. Newcastle: Cambridge Scholars Publishing.

Beauman, Nicola. 2008. *A Very Great Profession: The Women's Novel 1914–1939*. London: Persephone.

Bengoechea, Mercedes. 2014. "Feminist Translation? No Way! Spanish Specialised Translators' Disinterest in Feminist Translation." *Women's Studies International Forum* 42: 94–103.

Bermann, Sandra, and Michael Wood. 2005. *Nation, Language, and the Ethics of Translation*. Princeton, NJ: Princeton University Press.

Birge, Bettine. 2003. "Women and Confucianism from Song to Ming: The Institutionalization of Patrilineality." In *The Song-Yuan-Ming Transition in Chinese History*, edited by Paul Jakov Smith, and Richard Von Glahn, 212–240. Leiden: Brill.

Bloom, Clive. 2021. *Bestsellers: Popular Fiction Since 1900*. Cham: Springer.

Booth, Wayne C. 1983. *The Rhetoric of Fiction*. Chicago: The University of Chicago Press.

Breen, Margaret Sönser. 2011. "Gender and Translation: Writing as Resistance in Primo Levi's Se questo è un uomo." *European Legacy* 16 (2): 147–165.

Brown, Erica. 2015. *Comedy and the Feminine Middlebrow Novel: Elizabeth von Arnim and Elizabeth Taylor: Elizabeth von Arnim and Elizabeth Taylor*. London: Routledge.

Campbell, Emma. 2019. "Translating Gender in Thirteenth-Century French Cross-Dressing Narratives: La Vie de Sainte Euphrosine and Le Roman de Silence." *Journal of Medieval and Early Modern Studies* 49 (2): 232–264.

Cass, Victoria B. 1997. "Feng Menglong and the Late-Ming Articulation of Sentiment." *CHINOPERL* 20 (1): 71–84.

Chesterman, Andrew. 1997. *Memes of Translation: The Spread of Ideas in Translation Theory*. Amsterdam: John Benjamins.

Chien, Ying-ying. 1988. "Sexuality and Power: A Feminist Reading of Chin P'ing Mei." *Tamkang Review*, XIX: 607–629.

Chun, Mei. 2009. "Garlic and Vinegar: The Narrative Significance of Verse in 'The Pearl Shirt Reencountered'." *Chinese Literature: Essays, Articles, Reviews* 31: 23–43.

Croll, Elisabeth. 1978. *Feminism and Socialism in China*. London: Routledge and Kegan Paul.

Cua, Antonio S., ed. 2003. *Encyclopedia of Chinese Philosophy*. New York: Routledge.

Culpeper, Jonathan. 2014. *Language and Characterisation: People in Plays and Other Texts*. London: Routledge.

Dauncey, Sarah. 2003. "Bonding, Benevolence, Barter, and Bribery: Images of Female Gift Exchange in the Jin Ping Mei." *Nan nü* 5 (2): 203–239.

De Heredia, María Pérez L. 2016. "Translating Gender Stereotypes: An Overview on Global Telefiction." *Altre Modernità*, February, 166–181.

De Marco, Marcella. 2012. *Audiovisual Translation Through a Gender Lens*. Leiden: Brill.

Ding, Naifei. 2002. *Obscene Things: Sexual Politics in Jin Ping Mei*. Durham: Duke University Press.

Dow, Bonnie J. 1996. *Prime-Time Feminism: Television, Media Culture, and the Women's Movement Since 1970*. Philadelphia: University of Pennsylvania Press.

Drury, Annmarie. 2015. *Translation as Transformation in Victorian Poetry*. Cambridge: Cambridge University Press.

Dyhouse, Carol. 1989. *Feminism and the Family in England, 1880–1939*. Oxford: Basil Blackwell.

Ebrey, Patricia Buckley. 2003. *Women and the Family in Chinese History*. London: Routledge.

Egerton, Clement. 1939. *The Golden Lotus*. 4 vols. London: George Routledge and Sons, Ltd.

Emmott, Catherine. 1997. *Narrative Comprehension: A Discourse Perspective*. Oxford: Oxford University Press.

Ettner, Charles. 2015. "In Chinese, Men and Women are Equal-or-Women and Men are Equal?" In *Gender Across Languages: Volume 2*, edited by Marlis Hellinger, and Heiko Motschenbacher, 29–55. Amsterdam and Philadelphia: John Benjamins.

Ferrall, Charles, and Dougal McNeill. 2018. *British Literature in Transition: 1920–1940 Futility and Anarchy*. Cambridge: Cambridge University Press.

Fore, Steve. 1993. "Tales of Recombinant Femininity: The Reincarnation of the Chin P'ing Mei, and the Politics of Melodrama in Hong Kong." *Journal of Film and Video* 45 (4): 57–70.

Glew, Helen. 2016. *Gender, Rhetoric and Regulation: Women's Work in the Civil Service and the London County Council, 1900–1955*. Manchester: Manchester University Press.

Godard, Barbara. 1990. "Theorising Feminist Theory/Translation." In *Translation, History and Culture*, edited by Susan Bassnett, and Andre Lefevere, 87–96. London and New York: Pinter.

Grandy, Christine. 2016. *Heroes and Happy Endings: Class, Gender, and Nation in Popular Film and Fiction in Interwar Britain*. Manchester: Manchester University Press.

Hanan, Patrick. 1961. "A Landmark of the Chinese Novel." *University of Toronto Quarterly* 30 (3): 325–335.

Harvey, Keith. 1998. "Translating Camp Talk: Gay Identities and Cultural Transfer." *The Translator* 4 (2): 295–320.

He, Jianjun. 2007. "Burning Incense at Night: A Reading of Wu Yueniang in 'Jin Ping Mei'." *Chinese Literature: Essays, Articles, Reviews* 29: 85–103.

Hegel, Robert E. 1998. *Reading Illustrated Fiction in Late Imperial China*. Stanford: Stanford University Press.

Hegel, Robert E. 2008. "Teaching China as a Global Culture." *Tamkang Review* 38 (2): 9–23.

Hellinger, Marlis, and Heiko Motschenbacher, eds. 2015. *Gender across Languages: Volume 2*. Amsterdam and Philadelphia: John Benjamins.

Holmes, Diana. 2018. *Middlebrow Matters: Women's Reading and the Literary Canon in France Since the Belle Époque*. Liverpool: Liverpool University Press.

Hsia, Chih-tsing. 1968. *The Classic Chinese Novel: A Critical Introduction*. New York: Columbia University Press.

Humble, Nicola. 2004. *The Feminine Middlebrow Novel, 1920s to 1950s: Class, Domesticity and Bohemianism*. Oxford: Oxford University Press.

Humble, Nicola. 2013. "The Feminine Middlebrow Novel." In *The History of British Women's Writing, 1920–1945*, edited by Maroula Joannou, 97–111. London: Palgrave Macmillan.

Huntington, Rania. 2003. *Alien Kind: Foxes and Late Imperial Chinese Narrative*. Cambridge, Mass: Harvard University Asia Center#

Ko, Dorothy. 1995. *Teachers of the Inner Chambers: Women and Culture in Seventeenth-Century China*. Stanford: Stanford University Press.

Lähdesmäki, Tuuli. 2010. *Gender, Nation, Narration-Critical Readings of Cultural Phenomenon*. Jyvaskyla: Jyvaskyla University Printing House.

Larkosh, Christopher. 2011. *Re-Engendering Translation: Transcultural Practice, Gender, Sexuality and the Politics of Alterity*. Manchester: St. Jerome Publishing.

Lee, Jackie F. K. 2015. "Chinese Proverbs: How are Women and Men Represented?" *Multidisciplinary Journal of Gender Studies* 4 (1): 559–585.

Lefevere, André. 1992. *Translation, Rewriting, and Manipulation of Literary Fame*. London: Routledge.

Leonardi, Vanessa. 2017. "Gender, Language and Translation in the Health Sciences: Gender Biases in Medical Textbooks." In *Translation, Ideology and Gender*, edited by Carmen Camus Camus, Cristina Gómez Castro, and Julia T. Williams Camus, 8–32. Newcastle: Cambridge Scholars Publishing.

Ling, Mengchu. 1991. *Pai'an jingqi*. Beijing: Renmin wenxue.

Marshik, Celia, Allison Pease, Gayle Rogers, and Sean Latham. 2018. *Modernism, Sex, and Gender*. London: Bloomsbury Publishing.

McMahon, Keith. 1987. "Eroticism in Late Ming, Early Qing Fiction: The Beauteous Realm and the Sexual Battlefield." *T'oung Pao*, Second Series, 73 (4/5): 220.

McMahon, Keith. 1995. *Misers, Shrews, and Polygamists*. Durham: Duke University Press.

McMahon, Keith. 2003. "Obscene Things: Sexual Politics in Jin Ping Mei." *Harvard Journal of Asiatic Studies* 63 (2): 500–507.

Palumbo, Giuseppe. 2009. *Key Terms in Translation Studies*. London: Continuum.

Pyle, Wilma J. 1976. "Sexism in Children's Literature." *Theory Into Practice* 15 (2): 116–119.

Qi, Lintao. 2018. *Jin Ping Mei English Translations*. London: Routledge.

Rimmon-Kenan, Shlomith. 2002. *Narrative Fiction*. London and New York: Routledge.

Romaine, Suzanne. 1999. *Communicating Gender*. Mahwah, NJ: Lawrence Erlbaum Associates.

Roy, David T. 1993. *The Plum in the Golden Vase or, Chin P'ing Mei* (vol. 1). Princeton, NJ: Princeton University Press.

Roy, David T. 2001. *The Plum in the Golden Vase or, Chin P'ing Mei* (vol. 2). Princeton, NJ: Princeton University Press.

Roy, David T. 2006. *The Plum in the Golden Vase or, Chin P'ing Mei* (vol. 3). Princeton, NJ: Princeton University Press.

Roy, David T. 2011. *The Plum in the Golden Vase or, Chin P'ing Mei* (vol. 4). Princeton, NJ: Princeton University Press.

Roy, David T. 2013. *The Plum in the Golden Vase or, Chin P'ing Mei* (vol. 5). Princeton, NJ: Princeton University Press.

Shuttleworth, Mark, and Moira Cowie. 1997. *Dictionary of Translation Studies*. Manchester: St. Jerome.

Simon, Shery. 1996. *Gender in Translation -Cultural Identity and the Politics of Transmission*. London and New York: Routledge.

Skillen, Fiona. 2012. "Woman and the Sport Fetish: Modernity, Consumerism and Sports Participation in Interwar Britain." *The International Journal of the History of Sport* 29 (5): 750–765.

Steiner, George. 1992. *After Babel: Aspects of Language and Translation*. Oxford: Oxford University Press.

Szonyi, Michael. 2017. *A Companion to Chinese History*. Chichester: John Wiley & Sons, Ltd.

von Flotow, Luise. 1997. *Translation and Gender-Translating in the "Era of Feminism."* London and New York: Routledge.

Von Flotow, Luise, ed. 2011. *Translating Women*. Ottawa: University of Ottawa Press.

Wang, Yunhong, Yu Xinbing, and Chen Qing. 2019. "Translation and Negotiation of Gender Stereotypes: Metamorphosis of Female Characters in the English Version of a Chinese Classical Novel." *Perspectives* 28 (5): 702–716.

Wee, Shu-min. 2009. "Prison or Power: Feminine Sexuality in Jin Ping Mei and Mudan ting." In *Women and Men, Love and Power: Parameters of Chinese Fiction and Drama*, edited by Victor H. Mair, 35–51. Philadelphia: University of Pennsylvania.

Whelehan, Imelda. 2000. *Overloaded: Popular Culture and the Future of Feminism*. London: The Women's Press Ltd.

Xiao Xiao Sheng of Lanling 蘭陵笑笑生. 1963. *Jin Ping Mei cihua* (facsimile edition) 金瓶梅詞話. Fukuoka: Daian Co., Ltd.

Xiao Xiao Sheng of Lanling 蘭陵笑笑生. 2003. *Xinke xiuxiang piping Jin Ping Mei* 新刻繡像批評金瓶梅. Singapore: South Ocean Publishing.

Yang, Cheng, and Zhu Jianping. 2017. "The Transformation of Tan Chun's Character in David Hawkes's The Story of the Stone: A Cognitive Salience Theory Perspective." *Journal of Shanghai International Studies University* 40 (1): 91–99.

Zhang, Hong. 2015. "Reality and Representation: Social Control and Gender Relations in Mandarin Chinese Proverbs." In *Gender Across Languages: Volume 2*, edited by Marlis Hellinger, and Heiko Motschenbacher, 73–80. Amsterdam and Philadelphia: John Benjamins.

Zoberman, Pierre. 2014. "'Homme' peut-il vouloir dire 'Femme'?: Gender and Translation in Seventeenth-Century French Moral Literature." *Comparative Literature Studies* 51 (2): 231–252.

5 Re-narrating Desire

Translation of Sexuality and Erotic
Sensations/Swaying Between Titillation
and Repression

5.1 Introduction

As mentioned previously, *Jin Ping Mei* represents the first full-length Ming vernacular novel dedicated to portraying the private lives of its main characters. Within
the novel, readers are exposed to a multitude of forms depicting individual private
desires within their complete social context (Huang 2001, 59). The novel is rife
with sexual imagery and blatant depictions of sensual pleasures, to the extent that it
faced the possibility of being burned by Ming literati after its initial appearance. In
effect, the sexual content, an integral component of *Jin Ping Mei*'s narrative, intricately intertwines with fictional themes related to sensual desire and self-cultivation.
Nevertheless, when the novel undergoes translation into a different language, a
dilemma arises regarding whether to transpose such content in the target text or
not. Determining how far sexual-related content could or should be conveyed in
translation becomes a hard nut to crack. The translation of sexual-related elements in narrative prose raises important questions about the legal and moral limits
set by different cultures at different historical moments. This chapter sets out to
examine the treatment of *Jin Ping Mei*'s amorous narratives in Egerton's and Roy's
English renderings. The time gap between the two translations invites close critical
attention to the social contexts in which they were produced and received. In the
early twentieth century, Britain witnessed an extraordinary proliferation of sexual
discourses, influenced by sexological ideas propagated by figures such as Havelock
Ellis (1859-1939) and Edward Carpenter (1844-1929). The psychoanalytical theories of Sigmund Freud's (1856–1939) played a significant role in shaping these
discourses.[1] During this period, the nation became sex-obsessed, with a surge in
medical, popular, and literary discussions surrounding sexuality (Baldick 2004, 364;
Wolfe 2011, 12). Sex and sexual desire were regarded as fundamental to human
experience and identity. Representations of explicit sexual acts and same-sex desire
proliferated in tabloids, magazines, and novels, making such content widely accessible to the mass reading public (Marshik et al. 2018, 51). The representation of sex
was not merely a departure from the rigid bourgeois morality that associated sexuality with shame and privacy but, importantly, it was seen as a form of liberation
and modernity (Marshik et al. 2018, 55). This overt interest in sexuality became
the hallmark of modernity in Britain. It was notably manifested by a certain section

DOI: 10.4324/9781003472674-5

of the cultural elite, exemplified by groups such as the Bloomsbury Group.[2] This trend co-existed – and at times came into conflict – with the mainstream literary and legal culture, which was influenced by Victorian moral norms (Avery 2018, 17). The widespread concern about sexual matters among writers and intellectuals, prompted Britain to impose strict censorship on domestic and foreign literature dealing with sex and eroticism. The aim was to prevent such content from contaminating individual minds and corrupting society (Heath, 2010, 65). The attempts to censor literature featuring transgressive ideas and subversive values, including the celebration of (homo)sexuality, sadism, masochism, fetishism, voyeurism, exhibitionism, and sexual inversion, were driven by a desire to eliminate potential harmful effects on people's thoughts and behavior (ibid.). However, these efforts also suggested an unwillingness to tolerate unconventional ideas and views considered contrary to prevailing norms or established authorities. Evidently, there exists a conflict of values during this period, involving the arts and the press, knowledge and culture, and, fundamentally, the tension between public and private spheres (Moore 2016). This underscores literature's profound engagement with and sociopolitical influence on intimacy and subjective identity.

Indeed, there was tight control of domestic and foreign literature featuring sex and eroticism in Britain, as the obscene was strictly regulated to purify the Empire (Heath 2010, 65; Weeks 2018, 24). This took place not only within legal proceedings but also through censorship's authority in regulating the production, distribution, and consumption of cultural products. It dictated which forms of meaning were deemed legitimate within the literary realm (Moore 2016). According to Jeffery Weeks, "there was indeed a reign of euphemism and of ostensible delicacy which prevented, for instance, the novel from being too explicit, bowdlerized Shakespeare's plays, alluded to prostitution as the 'social evil' and gonorrhea and syphilis as the 'social diseases'" (2018, 24). References to sex, sensuality, bodily functions, human body, and indecent, coarse language in literary texts were generally unacceptable to the then dominant ideology of moral uprightness and delicacy characterized by linguistic prudishness. The 1857 Obscene Publications Act, also known as Lord Campbell's Act, and the watershed 1868 Hicklin judgment defined obscenity as the potential "to deprave and corrupt those whose minds are open to such immoral influence," allowing the British government and magistrates to "ban and destroy texts and images considered dirty, obscene, and indecent" (Jaillant 2017, 49; Sigel 2011; Zaragoza Ninet and Llopis Mestre 2021, 41). However, by the turn of the twenty-first century, sex and sensuality were no longer seriously policed or controlled but rather openly talked about and widely accepted in most Western cultures (Gill 2012, 484). In Brian McNair's (2002) words, Western society had already become a "striptease culture" preoccupied with more permissive sexual attitudes. This changing contextual background to the two translations scrutinized here has important implications for understanding the translation and reception of *Jin Ping Mei* in the Anglophone world.

By examining the treatment of sexual-related content in different translations of *Jin Ping Mei*, I argue that the two translations diverge significantly, involving important implications related to politics, ethics, and ideology that deserve critical attention. As José Santaemilia has noted, the translation of the language of sexuality is "always a risqué political act, which is entirely subservient to sociohistorical and ideological influences" (Santaemilia 2014, 125). This is primarily because translators always re-creates "under pressure of different constraints, ideological, poetical, economical etc., typical of the culture to which he/she belongs" (Álvarez and Vidal 1996, 5). Viewed through this prism, this chapter aims to compare the representation of sex in the source and target texts, describe its treatment in English renderings, and assess the potential results of the translators' individual strategies. Specifically, the chapter asks the following questions: How are sexual-related narratives in *Jin Ping Mei* handled in English translations? Do the target texts convey the same sexual urgency or erotic quality as the Chinese original? Do the two translations raise issues of decorum or (self-)censorship? If so, does censorship only serve to suppress sex and erotism in literature? By answering these questions, the chapter will offer a deeper understanding of the translation of the representation of sex in *Jin Ping Mei* and provide critical insights into the reception and metamorphosis of the novel in the receiving culture.

The remainder of the chapter is structured in the following manner. It begins by contextualizing the depiction of sex and erotic sensations in *Jin Ping Mei*, situating the novel within its literary and cultural context. Following this, the chapter provides a meticulous analysis of various forms of sexually provocative narratives in the English translations. Subsequently, it offers an in-depth analysis of the procedures employed by the translators in handling sexually charged passages. Moving forward, it discusses the potential factors motivating the translators' choices. Finally, the chapter concludes with some closing remarks.

5.2   The Unfolding of Sexuality and Erotic Sensations within *Jin Ping Mei*

The late Ming times were a period marked by "confusion and anxiety," characterized by "political failures, economic boom, rapid urbanization, social fluidity, and cultural flowering" (Brook 1998, 154; Mote 2000, 769). Due to political weakness, many talented men of letters and intellectuals displayed diminished interest in pursuing status within the imperial court, instead focusing on endeavors outside the political realm. This led to a taste or preference for lighter literary forms, such as colloquial novels, which experienced a surge in composition and publication during the late Ming (Birch 1978, 8; Hegel 1998, 11; Mote 2000, 770). Partially influenced by the philosophical thought of Wang Yangming's 王陽明 (1472–1529) and his followers, many intellectuals began scrutinizing the autonomy of the self, advocating for the spontaneous expression of human emotions and the fulfilment of individual desires. This challenged the conventional role of *tianli*, or heavenly principle, dictated by orthodox neo-Confucianism (Plaks 1987, 20; Hammond 2015, 12). This intellectual shift in the late Ming contributed to a period of "cultural brilliance, innovative ideas and endless pleasure" (Brook 1998, 153), making it one of the great ages in Chinese literary theory and criticism. Notably, literary criticism reached unprecedented heights, especially in the last years of the Ming dynasty when the literary landscape was divided into the archaist and individualist schools (Chou 1988, 1). The former, championed by Wang Shizhen 王世貞 (1526–90), advocated the imitation of ancient works, such as Qin-Han (221 BC–220 AD) prose and High Tang (650–755) poetry, while denigrating popular forms of literature and vernacular novels as trivial and undignified. The latter, led by the Yuan brothers from the Gong'an School, insisted on maintaining a strong connection between literary works and everyday life, particularly the lives of common people (Waley 1939, xviii).

The leader of the Gong'an School, Yuan Hongdao 袁宏道 (1568–1610), advocated for individuality, the expression of genuine emotion, and freedom of style in literary creation (Chou 1988, 44). According to him, one's personal nature, spirit, and true feelings could only be authentically revealed when expressed freely, unrestrained by convention. Yuan emphasized innate sensibility and spontaneity in literary creation, firmly believing that literature must express one's intent (Chou 1988, 43). In the preface to a poetry collection by his younger brother Yuan Zhongdao 袁中道 (1570–1626), for instance, Yuan Hongdao spoke of the exhilarating moment when his brother's emotions engaged with an external scene, transforming and compelling him to record the experience in mind (Eifring 2004, 25). Yuan Hongdao highlighted the significance of finding an outlet for deep feelings, whether it be through chess, sexuality, courtesans, or creative writing (ibid.). His ideas aligned with those of Li Zhi 李贄 (1527–1602), an iconoclastic thinker who emphasized the free expression of feelings and the satisfaction of desires as essential to human nature (Lee 2012, 47–65; see also Handler-Spitz 2017). Li Zhi also celebrated moral and spiritual authenticity, dismissing hypocrisy and challenging neo-Confucianism's emphasis on *tianli*. Both Li Zhi and the Gong'an School exerted great influence on Ming literature, particularly in popular vernacular works and other art forms (Epstein 2001, 75–76). Expressionistic features emerged in literary essay and poetry, a tendency towards abstraction was observed in graphic arts, and new dramatic literature resonated with humor and pathos. Most notably, eroticism and cardinal desire became important themes (Mote 2000, 770). The recognition of emotions and innate desires as an inherent part of human nature and the aesthetic pursuit of sensualism during the late Ming era were evident in a trend among writers to treat the human body, emotions, desire, and sensuality with a more relaxed attitude in their works (Chou 1988, 3; Huang 2001, 6; van Gulik 2003, 288). The intertwining of eroticism and cardinal desire provided writers with a platform to explore the depths of human experience, offering contemporary audiences a reflective mirror through which they could contemplate their own desires and aspirations (ibid.). Given that drama and fiction were deemed as peripheral and less respectable genres, writers working in them were free to indulge in the previously unconventional topic of love and lust. Thus, romantic sentiments, physical desire, and sensual pleasure became prominent motifs in late Ming popular literature, exemplified by works such as the drama *Mudan ting* 牡丹亭 (Peony Pavilion) and the novel *Jin Ping Mei*.[3] The main difference is that the former foregrounds romantic love, while the latter tends to celebrate erotic and physical love.

Doubtless, *Jin Ping Mei* reflects the trend toward self-expression in literature characteristic of the late Ming. The novel presents a detailed account of the intimate relations among members of a wealthy merchant's family. The meticulous depiction of everyday life in the work aligns with the philosophy of the Gong'an School, asserting that literature must maintain a close link to real life. In *Jin Ping Mei*, readers are confronted with realistic descriptions of sensual pleasure and sexual indulgence by the characters. The author seems uninhibited in dealing with sex, describing the sensual desire, libidinal love, and almost every sexual act of both male and female protagonists in graphic detail (van Gulik 2003).

As mentioned earlier, *Jin Ping Mei* has been controversial and misunderstood for most of its existence, primarily due to its blatant sexual descriptions. However, it is worth noting that sexually provocative passages constitute less than two percent of the work and are heavily outweighed by aesthetic, moral, and philosophical concerns. Late Ming literary theorists perceived the novel as a work of great value. Yuan Hongdao recognized the moral teachings inscribed in the narrative and the serious meanings hidden beneath the graphic portrayal of sex (Chou 1988, 56; Huo 1988, 708). In another instance, Yuan praised its merits instead of criticizing its candid treatment of sex, as seen in the 1617 preface written by Nongzhuke to the novel (Fang 1986, 166). Another preface by Xinxinzi argues that the novelist sought to express his views on the manners and morals of his time, hoping that the novel would contribute to improving public morality (ibid., 165). Furthermore, Niangong's postscript to the novel assumes the novelist's motive to be disclosing the ugly, dark side of society and claims that those who treat the book as pornography are missing its true intention, which arises from the theme of karmic retribution inscribed in the story (ibid., 167). The novelist himself remarks in the opening chapter of the novel that he aims to warn readers against striving for worldly enjoyments, such as material wealth and sexual indulgence. Nonetheless, contradictory intentions are apparent throughout the novel, as it contains a lot of titillation masquerading as moral superiority. This is by no means surprising because creative writing enables the writer to escape awareness of fantasy relatively near the surface by "creating a production from which they can distance themselves" (Person et al. 1995, 75). In the act of creative writing, the writer will tend to "externalize and actualize aspects of his self and object representations," along with their interaction as they "exist in the relevant unconscious fantasy" (ibid.). These aspects will be projected into the characters the writer portrays in his work; a process well recognized by Freud (ibid.). In any event, it is commonsensical that the reader's interpretation of the text may not align with the way intended by its producer, as they can read against the grain as well as with it.

Perhaps more interesting is the tension that runs through the novel between the narrator's endorsement of the characters' efforts towards personal fulfilment and his firm condemnation of their transgressions. Significantly, didactic remarks are routinely observed after scenes of sexual engagement in the novel. Ian P. McGreal states that what matters here is the author's view of sex as "natural and gratifying," yet also the "origin of evil" (McGreal 1996, 134). In fact, the narrator's depictions of sex carry a moralistic tone, and the theme of karmic retribution echoes throughout the story. The bold, unabashed depiction of sensual desire is essential to the novel's naked representation of a decadent society (Liu 1966, 235). In defense of *Jin Ping*

Mei against accusations of pornography, Gaetan Brulotte and John Phillips point out that "the lascivious and selfish characters die prematurely, violating in most instances the Confucian dictum to procreate" (Brulotte and Phillips 2006, 699). Ding Naifei (2002) then harbors a different view. By interpreting the novel as both obscene and deeply moral, she sees the combination of elements not as a paradox but rather as a unity: "an obscene morality and a moral obscenity" (Ding 2002, 19). All this shows that the representation of sex in *Jin Ping Mei* needs to be interpreted not only from the perspective of the novelist's intents but also within the changing intellectual atmosphere of the late Ming. In any case, the novel's "moral tendencies and ideological subscriptions" should not be overlooked because "its Confucianist concern and Buddhist message are too obvious to ignore" (Xiao 2022, 46). This chimes with Hegel's assumption that the novel seems to "reassert traditional orthodox Confucianism over the more liberal intellectual currents of its time" (Hegel 1998, 39). The depiction of sex in *Jin Ping Mei* could even be considered "dirt for art's sake," as it carries important aesthetic and ethical implications. As Woolf cogently points out,

> There can be no doubt that books fall in respect of indecency into two classes. There are books written, published and sold with the object of causing pleasure or corruption by means of their indecency [...] There are others whose indecency is not the object of the book but incidental to some other purpose – scientific, social, aesthetic, on the writer's part.
>
> (as quoted in Kendrick 1987, 196)

In this perspective, *Jin Ping Mei* must belong to the latter category because its indecency is calculated, and its aim is to provide a window on the manners, morals, politics, and lifestyles of the late Ming period. According to Berthold Laufer,

> As an artistic production this work belongs among the highest of its class. That the novel is immoral must be flatly denied. It is as little immoral as any work of Zola or Ibsen, and it is a work of art from the hand of a master, who knows his fellow-men thoroughly and depicts them with their passions as they are, not as some humbug or hypocrite thinks they ought to be.
>
> (as quoted in Egerton's archival documents)

As a well-known critic of the 1930s, Laufer spoke highly of *Jin Ping Mei*. His comment largely affirmed the novel's canonical status as a literary classic in Western Europe. Nonetheless, one might suspect that the novelist wants readers to think that the book belongs to the second category, as he cares about his own respectability. However, in some sense, his moralizing is mostly just symbolic, and his true intent is a celebration of pleasures, as can be discerned through reading between the lines. This brings to mind McMahon's observation in *Causality and Containment in Seventeenth-Century Chinese Fiction*, where he characterizes the fiction writer as a "moralist" as well as a "trickster" (McMahon 1988, 1). This draws attention to the dual role played by these writers. Identifying the vernacular fiction writer as a moralist suggests an inherent ethical dimension in their story-telling. In this role, the writer imparts moral lessons or reflections on social values through the narrative. The didactic aspect serves as a guiding force, aiming at influencing readers' perspectives and potentially encouraging them to reflect on their own behavior. By characterizing the fiction writer as a trickster, it introduces playful elements and artful deception into the narrative. The trickster figure is known for cunning and clever strategies, often challenging conventional norms and expectations (ibid.). The trickster element adds a layer of complexity and unpre-dictability to the storytelling, engaging readers in a dynamic and intellectually stimulating experience. Hence, a paradox emerges from the co-existence of these seemingly contrasting roles within the same narrative framework. On one hand, the writer engages with intimate desires, portraying the complexities of human relationships and emotions. On the other hand, didactic remarks are interwoven into the narrative, aiming to instruct and caution readers about social norms and moral considerations. This paradox highlights the rich and multifaceted nature of the storytelling tradition, where vernacular fiction serves not only as entertainment but also as a vehicle for moral reflection and social commentary.

Having understood the cultural and intellectual background regarding the candid treatment of sex and sensuality in *Jin Ping Mei*, this chapter aims to inves-tigate how this candid depiction is managed in Egerton's and Roy's English translations. This exploration is useful for investigating the "translation effect," which refers to "the visible and verifiable changes a text undergoes in translation and the effect this has on its reception in a new culture" (von Flotow 2000, 14). To this end, the chapter involves examining what has been added, deleted, or rewritten in the two translations regarding the handling of amorous narratives. As Román Álvarez and M. C. A. Vidal (1996, 5) put it, behind every one of the translator's selections, "there is a voluntary act that reveals his history and the socio-political milieu that surrounds him." The practice of addition, deletion, and rewriting is linked to the absences and silences in a (translated) text, and this is intricately tied to the operation of ideology (Eagleton 1976, 34). It is the ideological context in which translators operate that determines what can be said and cannot be said in the literary field. Moreover, in the case of translating and analyzing the paradox-ical narratives within the novel, recognizing and preserving the duality becomes a critical task for the translator. Balancing the intimate and didactic aspects while conveying the nuances of the novelist's dual role requires a keen understanding of cultural subtleties and a nuanced approach to language. The following two sections will try to illustrate these points by analyzing and discussing sexual-related narratives in English translation.

5.3 Analysis of Sexuality and Erotic Sensations in Translation

The two English translations, *Lotus* and *Plum*, appear rather different in their representations of sex and sensual desire described in *Jin Ping Mei*. In Egerton's translation, graphic sexual descriptions are not entirely absent but replaced instead by numerous Latin passages on several occasions. Quite the opposite, Roy's translation features numerous blatant depictions of sexual desire. In the introduction to *Lotus*, the translator stated that readers "would be exasperated to find occasional long passages in Latin, and he felt sorry about these as there was nothing else to do" (Egerton 1939, viii). Egerton originally intended to provide a complete translation of *Jin Ping Mei* to contemporary readers, stating that "if the book was to be produced at all, it must be produced in its entirety." However, he lamented that "it could not all go into English" (ibid.). As a result, the translation takes the form of a hybrid text, incorporating numerous Latin portions throughout the work.

Recently, scholarly attention has been paid to the treatment of the novel's juicy, amorous passages in English translation. Several studies have demonstrated the presence of Latin passages in Egerton's translation regarding the handling of sexually explicit material in the novel (Luo 2014; Qi 2016; Liang 2017; Qi 2018; Qi 2021). These studies have revealed the patronage system for Egerton's translation published in 1939, highlighting that the Latin renderings were not done by Egerton himself but by a third party working in classical studies in Britain during the 1930s. furthermore, these studies demonstrate that the appearance of Latin texts in Egerton's version was a result of censorship mechanisms. Building upon these previous insights, this chapter aims to shed more light on the representation of sexuality in translations of *Jin Ping Mei* by examining the translators' choices within the broader historical context. It also seeks to explore the potential impact of these choices on the translated texts and their readers. As far as my purpose is not to dispute but rather to expand the critical reach of prior research, the discussion will delve into sexually related narratives (for example, homosexual and heterosexual depictions) in translation and critically analyze the influence of Latin passages induced by censorship on the reader. The analysis in this chapter is supported by the translators' archival material and their statements on their own work, as illustrated in the peritext accompanying each translation, including the translator's notes.

Before discussion of the translation of sexual-related content in *Jin Ping Mei*, it is important to clarify that Egerton did not steer clear of identifiable erotic content in the novel; rather, he rendered them in English before publication in 1939. A close examination of the translator's archival materials confirms that the Latinized portions in Egerton's version were contributed by the British philologist and translator Frederick Adam Wright (1869–1946). Wright, who served as a Professor of Classics at the University of London, had many of his own writings published by George Routledge and Sons, Ltd., the same publisher that released Egerton's *Lotus* in 1939. Whereas Egerton himself was proficient in several languages, including Latin, he didn't consider employing Latin to render sexually explicit passages in the Chinese novel. In contrast to the German version of the novel, which omitted around 250,000 words from the original, including explicit content, without acknowledging these deletions, as revealed in a letter dated 3 July 1939, Egerton endeavored to incorporate sexual-related content – spanning homosexual, heterosexual, and sadomasochistic subjects – to varying degrees in his translation for a contemporary readership. There are at least three likely reasons behind Egerton's choice.

Firstly, Egerton possessed an open-minded attitude toward sex and sexuality, evident in his 1914 book, *The Future of Education*, where he expounded the import-ance of sex education. The open-mindedness exhibited by Egerton in addressing the topic of sex education suggests a departure from the prevailing norms of the time. His willingness to engage with a subject often deemed sensitive or subversive demonstrates a commitment to breaking down social taboos and fostering a more enlightened approach to sex education. Egerton's open-minded attitude toward sexuality represented a commendable departure from the normative views of his time. Emphasizing the importance of sex and/in education, Egerton contributed to a progressive discourse on human sexuality, aligning with the perspectives that persisted in shaping contemporary discussions on education and sexuality. Egerton's attitude towards sex education also aligned with the progressive ideas of modernist writers, members of the Bloomsbury Group, Malinowski, and, par-ticularly, Freud during the early twentieth century. As previously mentioned, they recognized sexuality as a legitimate and important aspect of human life, reflecting a modern and progressive mindset that fostered a more enlightened society. It can be assumed that Egerton had a clear understanding of the subject of sex in *Jin Ping Mei*. In his view, the novelist set out to depict the rise to fame and for-tune and the subsequent disintegration of a typical household during a period of exceptionally corrupt Chinese officialdom. To expose this corruption, the novelist spared no detail, whether in public or private life. Egerton contended that such details, described in the plainest of language, were, essential to the story as they revealed shades of character (Egerton 1939, vol.1, vii). Respecting the thematical concerns of the Chinese original, Egerton believed that his translation, *Lotus*, must be produced in its entirety if it was to be produced at all. Hence, Egerton essentially retained all the sexually provocative passages in his translation.

Secondly, another motive for Egerton's choice of translating *Jin Ping Mei* in the 1920s was his belief that the book served as a rich source of psychological and cultural material. To understand this choice, we can trace the intellectual impact of Friedrich Nietzsche's (1844–1900) philosophy of morality and modern art, as well as Freud's psychoanalytical theories of repression, on the discourse of sex in Egerton's time. Notably, a few of Sigmund Freud's works had been translated into English before the Great War, significantly influencing British intellectual cul-ture. In the aftermath of post-War years, concerns such as shell shock, war trauma, and bereavement gained prominence in the public sphere, leading to the rapid dis-semination of psychological ideas throughout British intellectual life (McHale and Stevenson 2006, 78). Eliot's *The Waste Land* (1922) and Woolf's *Mrs Dalloway* (1925), for instance, stood as defining expression of post-War disillusionment. In one sense, the first decades of the twentieth century were the Freudian age in Britain (Baldick 2004, 365). This period saw a notable dissemination of sexual discourses in popular culture and creative writing. The growing departure from Victorian reticence and euphemism in sexual matters marked a fully modern experience. Progressive intellectuals regarded any restraint on the libido as an outdated and unhealthy attitude, a continuation of Victorian repression (McHale and Stevenson 2006, 79). The contemporary discourse on sexuality and gender affected not only the personal lives of a wide range of writers, but their perception of desiring subjects and their ideas about literary experimentation (Moddelmog 2014, 270). Renowned writers and poets such as Joyce, Lawrence, Pound, E. M. Forster, Eliot, Norah James (1896–1979), and Richard Aldington (1892–1962) attempted to incorporate forbidden subjects into their literary creation. They viewed literary representations of the sexualized body and obscenity as a pathway to new understandings of art and subjectivity – exploring the unknown areas of the self; however, these endeavors often resulted in their works being banned, bowdlerized, or available only in foreign editions (Baldick 2004, 368; Potter 2013, 7). In 1915, despite Lawrence's rejection of Freudian interpretation, his novel, *Sons and Lovers* (1913), was subjected to such analysis. George Bataille (1897–1962) in his work, *Story of the Eye* (1928), illustrated that obscene images could serve as surrogates for repressed childhood experiences involving a fragile father and a traumatized mother; Bataille advocated for opening up writing to the loose, perverse, or destabilized subject (Potter 2013, 8). Additionally, many autobiographers openly recounted and exposed their obsessive engagement in sexual abnormality in their works. A remarkable example is T. E. Lawrence's (1888–1935) *Seven Pillars of Wisdom* (1926), which extensively explores the author's own homosexual experiences (Baldick 2004, 371). The literature of the 1920s and 1930s in Britain was saturated with allusions to psychological ideas. Many writers emphasized that literary representations of sexuality were an individual's right to free speech; they shared a common desire to connect psychoanalytical ideas of repression and psychic control with the contemporary political discourses on free speech and individual rights (Potter 2013, 6). Indeed, a conspicuous feature of the modernist period in Britain was the overt interest in human body, sexuality, and sensuality. Prominent writers like Joyce, Lawrence, and Woolf actively argued for normalizing discussions of sex and sensuality in their works (Marshik et al. 2018, 51). As a writer of the time, Egerton was not immune to the widespread influence brought about by Freudianism and sexological theories in the British literary scene. Having experienced the Great War, his interest in psychoanalysis came as no surprise. He may have believed that his work, *Lotus*, could serve as an ideal object for psychoanalysis, apart from providing a pleasurable reading.

Finally, as previously mentioned, Egerton's decision to translate sexual passages in *Jin Ping Mei* was likely influenced by his association with Lao She. As noted in Chapter 1, both Egerton and Lao She resided in the same flat, St James Gardens, in London for several years during the 1920s when Lao She served as a Lecturer in Chinese at the University of London (UoL). Lao She played a significant role in assisting Egerton during the translation process. In the Translator's Note, Egerton writes that "without the untiring and generously given help of Mr. C. C. Shu, I should never have dared to undertake such a task" and "I shall always be grateful to him" (1939, viii). During their collaboration, Egerton and Lao She contributed a series of public lectures in the autumn of 1926 at UoL, focusing on Oriental and African poetry, as well as tales of ancient China (Witchard 2012, 77–79). Lao She talked of the moral and ethical aspects of Tang romances, a genre that paved the way for the development of *Jin Ping Mei* and other Ming works (ibid.). According to Lao She, the intense interest in sex and sensuality during the Tang dynasty (618–907) was intricately linked to the burgeoning literary insight into the complexities of the human psyche (ibid.). In his discussions, Lao She highlighted how accounts of love, passion, and sensuality in literary works explored the "hidden desires and fears of the collective and individual self" (ibid.). Lao She's ideas on sex and sexuality in classic Chinese literature resonated with the intellectual trend in the British literary scene, especially the Bloomsbury Group's open attitudes toward sex in the early twentieth century (Baldick 2004, 365). In his lectures, Lao She conveyed the idea that classic Chinese narratives, such as Tang love tales, marked a milestone in the advancement toward modern notions of characterization in literary narrative. Lao She also asserted that the formal significance of traditional Chinese novels bore similarities to the modernist literary style or theme in the West (Witchard 2012, 82). As an admirer of the modernist writer James Joyce, Lao She held a high regard for Joyce's *Ulysses*, a banned (for indecency) book that every Londoner in the 1920s was eager to acquire. Lao She and Egerton were regular customers at the Ulysses Bookshop near the British Museum, where they engaged in discussions about Joyce's work (ibid., 81). Thus, it could be assumed that Egerton's translation of sexual-related content in *Jin Ping Mei* was likely influenced by Lao She's critical insight into the modern facets of "old" Chinese narratives, which also encompassed modernist themes.

It is my contention that the treatment of sexually provocative passages in Egerton's case can be understood as a result of social mores, ideologies, and literary norms on the receiving end, rather than conscious decisions on the translator's part. Moreover, this treatment brings about an unintended rhetorical effect of erotic narratives in the Egerton translation. I will discuss this aspect later in this chapter. Although Egerton himself didn't translate sexually explicit passages into Latin, he was involved in the task. As will be demonstrated presently, Egerton agreed to do so and signed a contract with his publisher, demonstrating a clear consciousness of this choice. In a sense, Egerton assumed the role of an indirect translator, overseeing and exerting influence over the rendering of amorous passages into Latin. Through negotiations with the publisher and the final concession and decision to Latinize, rather than eliminate, sexually explicit passages, Egerton's translation achieves final publishability via this particular stylistic means. The published translation strikes a balance between maintaining the narrative integrity and cultural nuances of the original text while also aligning with the moral and social norms of the receiving culture. This strategic decision, a compromise in some sense, involving different agents, reflects the multifaceted nature of translatorship, involving not only linguistic considerations but also cultural, ethical, and political-ideological factors. In his study of nineteenth-century English translations of Boccaccio's *Decameron*, Guyda Armstrong (2014) demonstrates that managing erotic content within the constraints of print publishing has historically been problematic for translators and their editors. A constant conflict exists between the desire to reveal and the necessity to conceal in these translations. The erotic passages, presented as French-language insertions in English translations of Boccaccio's tales, both mask and reveal censored obscenities, allowing for a degree of titillation for the

British audience. Armstrong argues that the very "Frenchness" is used editorially not merely to censor but, in fact, to amplify or foreground the erotic content of the translated book from the Italian. This calls to mind the paradox of literary and cultural censorship. According to Michael Holquist (1994), censorship tends to cultivate sophisticated readers who, when confronted with censored text, must fill in the gaps with their critical interpretations of what was excluded or suppressed, engaging in a process of reading between the lines. As noted by Hazel Tafadzwa Ngoshi (2023), repression and censorship play a fundamentally constitutive role in shaping or even enabling dissenting or subversive discourse. Paradoxically, the very content that authorities attempt to censor or -exclude often becomes more popular, catalyzing specific discourses. Judith Butler (2021) elucidates that censorship, even when implemented through legal channels, does not inevitably lead to complete or total subjectification, nor does it effectively restrict the social realm of permissible discourse. Rather than eradicating dissenting voices, censorship inherently draws attention to that which is intended to be deemed unspeakable or unrepresentable (Butler 2021, 132). Put differently, the control over the unspeakable or dissenting voices is not merely an act of censoring or silencing. Instead, it *redoubles* or amplifies the elements it seeks to suppress, achieving constraint merely through this paradoxical *redoubling* or amplification (Butler 2021, 131; original emphasis). Consequently, prohibition brings certain types of speech to the forefront that it intends to limit, thereby prompting discourse that should have been suppressed (ibid.). Butler's insights resonate with post-structuralist perspectives, emphasizing the constitutive or productive capacity of regulation. In *The History of Sexuality* (Volume 1), Michel Foucault (1926-84) expounds that "rather than a massive censorship, beginning with the verbal proprieties imposed by the Age of Reason, what was involved was a regulated and polymorphous incitement to discourse" (1978, 34). The paradoxical power of prohibition lies in its ability to bring forth, or interpolate, that which would otherwise remain unnamable or unspeakable (Moore 2016). In line with this view, Leo Strauss maintains that writers can employ flexible strategies to thwart and elude censorship, and no form of censorship can completely and effectively extinguish heterodox modes of expression (Strauss 1988; van den Abbeele 1997, 3; Ngoshi 2021, 814). Building on these perspectives, the present chapter will try to demonstrate that, as a case of literary (self)censorship, the decision to include Latin insertions in Egerton's translation of *Jin Ping Mei*, while seemingly circumventing or concealing erotic content, also, de facto, serves to amplify the sexual expression in the translated book. It can produce, rather than simply suppress, literary meaning, provoking a reading between the lines and creating a level of titillation among the book's readership.

In the subsequent part of this section, the chapter will first scrutinize how sexual content in the novel is rendered in English translations. The analysis will focus on chosen passages, selected almost at random, to emphasize noteworthy distinctions between the two translations. This examination specifically encompasses areas such as sexually suggestive elements, depictions of homosexuality, descriptions of heterosexual encounters, and sexual portrayals accompanied by narrative commentary. Subsequently, the chapter will explore the translators' decisions by contextualizing their works within their immediate sociocultural surroundings and investigating the potential implications of their choices.

5.3.1 Sexually Suggestive Elements

The tendency prevalent in Chinese culture to address sex or sexual desire euphemistically is evident in the poetic treatment of specific lexical items, such as *fenghua xueyue* 風花雪月 (flower in gentle wind and snow under the moon) and *yunyu* 雲雨 (cloud and rain) (Kao 1994, 173). *Jin Ping Mei* features numerous euphemisms and sexual innuendos to suggest love and sexual acts, as exemplified in the following examples:

(1)

ST:
不想婦人。曾在西門慶手裡。狂風驟雨都經過的。往往幹事不稱其意。
(Xiao 2003, chap. 19, 163)

TT1:
But Hsi-men Ch'ing had been **a more strenuous lover**, and Chiang failed to come up to her expectations …
(Egerton 1939, vol. 1, 265)

TT2:
What he failed to realize, however, was that the woman had already experienced every kind of: **Violent storm and sudden downpour at the hands of Hsi-men Ch'ing**, so that his inexperienced efforts often left her unsatisfied.
(Roy 1993, vol. 1, 385)

In (1), the fixed expression "狂風驟雨" is a metaphor for making love. TT1 doesn't directly render it but paraphrases it as "a more strenuous lover," which is intelligible but sacrifices the rhetorical effect of the ST. TT2, on the other hand, renders it as "Violent storm and sudden downpour." While this literal transfer effectively preserves the sexual metaphor, it increases the difficulty of comprehension for non-specialist readers unfamiliar with traditional Chinese culture.

(2)

ST:
西門慶。見婦人好風月。一徑要打動他。
(Xiao 2003, chap. 38, 341)

TT1:
Hsi-men Ch'ing had discovered that she was **well skilled in the arts of love**, and was anxious to show her that he himself was no mean performer.
(Egerton 1939, vol. 2, 157)

TT2:

Hsi-men Ch'ing was aware that the woman **was fond of the game of breeze and moonlight** and was anxious to see what he could do to arouse her.
(Roy 2001, vol. 2, 387)

In (2), the expression "好風月" in the ST carries sexual connotations. It is paraphrased as "well skilled in the arts of love" in TT1, which reveals the connotative sense. In TT2, however, it is replaced with "fond of the game of breeze and moonlight," indicating a commitment to maintain the literal meaning. This strategy has the effect of sometimes making the meaning less straightforward, although the vivid imagery is retained.

(3)

ST:

西門慶且不與他雲雨。明知婦人。第一好品簫。于是坐在青紗帳內。
(Xiao 2003, chap. 10, 86)

TT1:

But Hsi-men Ch'ing **would not allow her to go too fast**.
(Egerton 1939, vol. 1, 142–143)

TT2:

Hsi-men Ch'ing, however, did not proceed directly to **the clouds and rain**.
(Roy 1993, vol. 1, 201)

The term "雲雨" in (3) is a recurring motif in classical Chinese literature, symbolizing the intimate act of sexual intercourse between men and women. This metaphorical connotation, rich in cultural significance, may not be widely recognized by readers familiar with the source culture. In TT1, the term is skilfully paraphrased as "would not allow her to go too fast," a rendering that maintains the essence of the metaphor while ensuring accessibility for the target audience. This choice facilitates understanding for readers unacquainted with the intricacies of the original metaphor. In contrast, in TT2, "雲雨" is translated more literally as "clouds and rain." This faithful adherence to the original metaphor preserves the cultural nuance and symbolism embedded in the term, providing a more accurate representation of the source metaphor. However, this fidelity poses a challenge for ordinary readers who may need to decipher the meaning within the given context.

(4)

ST:

唗的西門慶。潑心頓　　。弔過身子。兩個幹後庭花。[4]
(Xiao 2003, chap. 38, 342)

TT1:
Tum Hsi-men cupidine iterum flagrans mulierem subvertit et in postico florem temptabat.
(Egerton 1939, vol. 2, 157)

TT2:
Turning her over, he set out, with her cooperation, to **pluck the flower in her rear courtyard**.
(Roy 2001, vol. 2, 389)

In (4), the term "後庭花" originally refers to the flower *celosia cristata*, originating from the title of the Chinese poem *Yushu houtinghua* (Flowers in the Backyard) by Chen Shubao 陳叔寶 (553–604). The renowned Tang poet, Du Mu 杜牧 (803–52), quoted this title in his poem *Bo Qinhuai* (Mooring at Qinghuai River) to express sorrow about a dynastic crisis. Over time, the meaning of "後庭花" has been extended, metaphorically representing the anus. In TT2, "pluck the flower in her rear courtyard" is used for the metaphorical expression "幹後庭花," providing a word-for-word transfer that arguably produces a strong exotic flavor. Yet this literal transfer may not evoke the sexual image directly in the minds of target readers, lacking a clear association with sexual acts. On the other hand, in TT1, the expression "幹後庭花" is rendered in Latin, making the colloquial register formal and unintelligible. This approach screens the dramatic love scene from view for the target reader, obscuring the meaning of the passage. Nonetheless, the use of Latin may spark the reader's curiosity, leading them to consult a dictionary to unveil the intended meaning.

5.3.2 Depiction of Homosexuality

Homosexuality remains a taboo topic in Chinese society; paradoxically, however, a variety of frank depictions of it can be found in traditional Chinese literature. Late imperial China, in particular, witnessed the emergence of numerous erotic texts centered around homosexuality. Wu Cuncun notes that in the late imperial period, "male-love became so fashionable as to cause the overshadowing of female brothels by male homosexual brothels in the capital city" (Wu 2004, 3). Classical novels, such as *Honglou meng* and *Jin Ping Mei*, also include scenes describing homosexual love. While the latter's homosexual scenes are outnumbered by heterosexual depictions, homoerotic scenes are not uncommon in the novel. The following is a typical instance where a homosexual scene is narrated at length.

(5)

ST:
那經濟推睡着不理他。他把那話弄得硬硬的。直豎一條棍。抹了些唾津在頭上往他糞門裡只一頂。原來經濟在冷舖中。被花子飛天鬼侯林兒弄過的。眼子大了。那話不覺就進去了。這經濟口中不言。心內暗道。這廝合敗。他討得十方便益。多了。把我不知當做甚麼人兒。也來報伏。
與他箇甜頭兒。且教他在我手內納些敗缺銀錢。[5]
(Xiao 2003, chap. 93, 920)

TT1:
Adversus alterius monachi ventrem Ching-chi dorsum suum pressit nec quidquam
amplius dixit quasi dormiret. Tum alterius penis rigidus fit et hastae similis surgit.
Sputum in isto onit et irruit. Dum Ching-chi apud mendicos devertit, duo socci
anum male usi ita tetenderunt ut via iam facilis monacho esset. Ching-chi still said
nothing. "This fellow will fall into my hands," he thought. "He doesn't know who
I am and he can't do me much harm. I will let him have a taste and then I will get
hold of his money."
(Egerton 1939, vol. 4, 275)

TT2:
Ch'en Ching-chi pretended to be asleep and paid no attention to him, but he went
on to manipulate his organ until it rose up as hard and straight as a stick, rubbed
some saliva on the head of his glans, and proceeded to thrust it into his anus. It so
happens that when Ch'en Ching-chi had been residing in the homeless shelter, the
beggar boss Hou Lin, whose nickname was Flying Demon, had sodomized him,
so that his anus was already enlarged. As a result, Chin Tsung-ming's organ had
penetrated him before he knew it.

As for Ch'en Ching-chi:
    From his mouth no word was uttered, but
    In his heart he thought to himself,

"This rascal is asking for it; he is trying to take such egregious advantage of me.
Who does he take me for? I'll give him something to savor in return and thereby
make him pay for his fun."
(Roy 2013, vol. 5, 262)

The narrative language in (5) is extremely frank and blunt in its description of homosexual sex involving two male characters, Chen Jingji 陳經濟 and Jin Zongming
金宗明. This narrative style evokes the works of the sixteenth-century French
novelist François Rabelais. As described by Bakhtin (1984) in *Rabelais and His
World*, Rabelais's novels exhibit a carnivalesque obsession with sensuality, bodily
apertures, and sexual organs, symbolizing a sense of irrepressible freedom and
vitality. While *Jin Ping Mei* shares these obsessions, its focus on bodily functions
serves different intentions. In this scene, Chen Jingji is depicted as willing to sacrifice his body for economic gains, given his homeless and stone-broke situation
at that point. The use of sex for material benefits is a recurring theme in the world
of *Jin Ping Mei*, where sex is often connected with themes of competition, materialism, economy, and aggression (Satyendra 1993, 95). In fact, the novel devotes
no less attention to sex than it does to money, showcasing a fascination with both
aspects of human experience (Lu 2021, 86). Chen Jinji's case here is illustrative,

and his homosexual act is by no means solely driven by love or affection but simply for money and material favors to address his awkward situation after the collapse of the Ximen household.

In the English texts, one can observe two distinct tendencies in dealing with the racy homosexual scene. Instead of eliminating or replacing the obscenities with euphemisms, Egerton's version creates a secret code (namely, Latin passages) that produces an effect of defamiliarization or a point of tension, making the reader pause and infer the meaning from the context, namely reading between the lines. The code-switching between English and Latin in TT1 hides obscene, barbaric, and disgusting elements. Without a doubt, the theme of homosexuality is tamed or repressed in TT1, suggesting a conservative attitude towards this subject. Yet on the other hand, TT1 could also induce the "plaisir du texte" of the sophisticated reader, who might be allured by the strange code (namely, Latin portions) to explore what it represents. In contrast, TT2 preserves this subject matter, describing homosexual acts vividly. The translating language is as bold and unabashed as the original in portraying male fantasies. Evidently, readers of TT2 can easily perceive the tangible, interactive relationship between sex and money as revealed in the depiction of the homosexual scene.

5.3.3 *Depiction of Heterosexual Encounters*

The author of *Jin Ping Mei* spares no ink in describing the characters' everyday life, including, of course, their sexual life. However, the novelist tends to depict the characters' sexual escapades luridly and negatively. While there are numerous descriptions of sex, sensuality, incest, sadomasochism in the novel, few pertain to the sublimation of sexual love (Liu 1966, 235; Huang 2018). The depiction of sex in *Jin Ping Mei* exhibits "a sheer pursuit of carnal desire and sensual pleasure" that is devoid of "spiritual and affectional communication between man and woman" (Huang 2018, 213; see also McMahon 2019, 35). In fact, sexual adventures delineated in the novel often entail physical pain or psychological trauma for female characters submissive to the male protagonist while pursuing sexual pleasure. Insightful readers could perceive hierarchy, inequality, objectification, and even violence instead of intimacy and affection involved in sexual depictions in the novel. Thus, descriptions of sex in *Jin Ping Mei* often present female characters in unattractive or undesirable ways, portraying women simply as passive objects of the male protagonist's sexual urges. This recalls *Sexual Politics*, in which Kate Millett (2000) argues that all sex, including sexual representations, is political, as it always involves sexism and unequal power dynamics entrenched in seemingly minor sexual details, as demonstrated in the previous chapter. The following example may illustrate how such depictions are treated in the translations.

(6)

ST:
那話直抵牝中。只顧揉搓。沒口子叫親達達。罷了。五兒的死了。須臾。一陣昏迷。舌尖冰冷。泄訖一度西門慶覺牝中一股熱氣。直透丹田。心中翕翕然美快。不可言也。已而滛津溢出。

婦人一連丟了兩遭。身子亦覺稍倦。西門慶只是佯佯不採。暗想胡僧之
藥通神。[6]
(Xiao 2003, chap. 51, 459)

TT1:
Tum leniter susurrabat "deliciaemeae, aut finem facies aut moriar." Mox languit;
lingua quasi gelu frogida fuit; e muliere suci amoris fundebantur. Hsi-men sensit
calidum esse cunnum; iecur ipsius ferbuit et supra modum gaudebat. ... Suci rusus
effluxerunt et tandem lassari incepit. His-men Ch'ing was undaunted. He could
only marvel at the medicine which the Indian Monk had given him.
(Egerton 1939, vol. 2, 338)

TT2:
His organ had penetrated all the way to the interior of her vagina, as he continued
kneading away at her. "My own daddy!" she cried out inarticulately. "That's
enough. Your Fivey is dying."

    A moment afterwards:
      She swooned completely away,
      The tip of her tongue became ice-cold, and
      She gave way to an orgasm.

Hsi-men Ch'ing became aware of a wave of warmth within her vagina that
penetrated all the way to his cinnabar field, while in his heart, he felt a melting sen-
sation the pleasure of which was indescribable. ...
    The woman had two orgasms in a row and began to feel somewhat fatigued, but
Hsi-men Ch'ing:
      Feigning total indifference, thought to himself, "This medication of the
Indian Monk's is truly supernatural."
(Roy 2006, vol. 3, 240)

In (6), the male dominance involved in the sexual spectacle is evident in the ST.
The female protagonist Pan Jinlian is objectified as she is portrayed as the object of
Ximen to fulfil his sensual passion. Their physical contact is not explicitly tender
and gentle but instead mechanical and unsatisfying. The sexual intercourse involves
a lack of reciprocity, as Ximen always ignores the wishes of the woman and treats
her as a sexual toy for his own insatiable carnal desire. Perhaps for Ximen, his
partner's sexual pleasure may not be that important, as she is only a sexual object
to prove his sexual potency or male-centered carnalism. While Pan Jinlian gives
way to orgasm, she, in fact, suffers more from trauma and injury than pleasure.
As the narrative progresses, she even feels as if she was dying and pleads Ximen
to stop immediately. She becomes faint and extremely fatigued, but Ximen simply
disregards her feelings, as shown by "只是佯佯不採," immersing himself instead
in the indescribable pleasure generated by the aphrodisiacs administered by the
Indian monk. In TT1, the strategic inclusion of Latin passages serves to obscure
explicit descriptions of sexual encounters, creating a layer of discretion that shields
the reader from explicit content while tantalizingly veiling the narrative's sexual

fantasies. This deliberate use of a "secret code" heightens intrigue, encouraging readers to delve deeper into the text to unravel the concealed meanings behind the Latin expressions. TT2, however, reproduces every single detail of the sexual scene and reveals both the tone and feel of the narrative presented in the original. For instance, Pan Jinlian's suffering induced by sexual intercourse is neatly reflected by such expressions as "Your Fivey is dying," "She swooned completely away," and "tongue became ice-cold." Moreover, Roy has "Feigning total indifference" for "佯佯不採," which aptly reveals Ximen's indifference to his women. By repackaging sex, women, and male-centered carnalism in the same way as the original text, TT2 revels in a similarly bawdy, erotic, and transgressive celebration of the physical.

5.3.4 Sexual Portrayals Accompanied by Narratorial Commentary

In *Jin Ping Mei*, depictions of sex are often accompanied by the narrator's commentary. Narratorial commentary focuses on the characters' indecent, transgressive behavior and appears intended to steer the reader's perceptions of the story and characters. According to Seymour Chatman, narrative commentary entails the expression of the narrator's feelings or personal opinions and a comparison between "story elements and outside-world facts or universal truths" (1978, 228). By engaging in dialogue with the reader, the narrator communicates a moral vision and shapes the reader's responses to the text by shifting perspectives and adding depth. Yet such narratorial intrusions in *Jin Ping Mei* have come in for much criticism on account of their alleged moral censure. Critics such as C. T. Hsia contend that the author of *Jin Ping Mei* is "the stern moralist who seizes every opportunity to condemn adultery and debauchery, but by the very fact he takes so many pains to describe the sexual act belies the attitude of moral censure" (1968, 185). I do not disagree with the claim, as moral admonition can be used as a pretense to justify indulgence in the realistic, frank portrayal of sex and the erotic. One can certainly observe a contradiction between the narrator's moral pronouncements and his own obsession with describing characters' sexual behaviors or private desires throughout the work. It is the very contradictions and ambivalence dramatized in the text that constitute the appeal of *Jin Ping Mei*, as they coincide with the perplexing phenomenon of late Ming culture (Huang 2001, 67; Zhang 2023, 337). In any case, the narrator, by intruding on descriptive narrative and remarking on courses of events and characters, presents commentary that has the potential to shape and shift the reader's interpretation and perception of the story and characters. Thus, commentary has artistic function that detaches and distances to make the reader more capable of active participation in the text. The following example will suffice:

(7)

ST:
兩個對面坐着椅子。春梅便在後邊推車。三人串作一處。但見
一個不顧夫主名分。一個那管上下尊卑。一個氣的吁吁。猶如牛吼柳影。[7]
(Xiao 2003, chap. 83, 835)

TT1:
Golden Lotus and Ch'en Ching-chi were plunging and rearing, and Plum Blossom, behind the young man, was rendering every assistance in her power, and in this way the three worked together.
(Egerton 1939, vol. 4, 146)

TT2:
[…] two of them going at it while seated on facing chairs, while Ch'un-mei stood behind Ch'en Ching-chi propelling him forward like a cart. Behold:
　　One of them shows total disregard
　　　　for the status of her husband;
　　The other does not discriminate between
　　　　above and below, exalted or humble.
　　One of them, panting for all he is worth,
　　　　Sounds like an ox snoring in the willow's shade.
(Roy 2013, vol. 5, 51)

In (7), the Chinese passage vividly depicts a clandestine love affair among three characters in the Ximen household. The erotic activities are described in graphic detail, as seen in expressions such as "赤着身子, 後邊推車," and "三人串作一處." It evokes a disturbing attraction and even pleasure but also feeds into a sense of repulsion. The sexual scene is a typical instance where the female protagonist engages in incest with her husband's son-in-law. *Jin Ping Mei* contains several instances of incest, with almost every member of the Ximen family being guilty in some way of incest understood as "the muddling of proper relations that is the Confucian form of incest" (Lu 2008, 184). In the ST, the narrator makes value judgments about the characters' promiscuity and laxity of morals. Using poetic sentences guided by the narratological marker "但見," the narrator metes out bitter sarcasm on the characters' adulterous and incestuous acts. Both English texts have reproduced the objectionable scene with the same force and tone as the original. However, the narrator's comment is omitted from Egerton's text, perhaps because it takes a poetic form. In fact, most of the poems in the novel, as discussed in Chapter 4, are left out in Egerton's translation, considered gibberish, and their deletion does not affect the plot development (Egerton 1939, vol.1, vii). Yet the absence of narrative comment deprives the translation's reader of the opportunity to perceive the moral censure inscribed in the narrative. In Roy's version, narratorial commentary is preserved and made prominent in the text, giving the reader access to the moral, didactic tone of the narrator's voice. A full translation is essential for the reader to perceive the narrator's attitude toward the characters' immoral, transgressive behavior, as they will receive due punishment later in the story. Thus, the twin goals of entertaining and educating are preserved in Roy's text.

(8)

ST:

這婦人趴伏在他身上。用朱唇吞裹其龜頭。只顧往來不已。又勒勾約一
頓飯時。那管中之精猛然一股邊將出來。猶水銀之瀉筒中相似。忙用口
接嚥不及。只顧流將起來。初時還是精液。往後盡是血水出來。在無個
收救。西門慶已昏迷去。四肢不收。婦人也慌了。急取紅棗與他吃下
去。精盡繼之以血。血盡出其冷氣而已。良久方止。
看官聽說。一己精神有限。天下色慾無窮。又曰嗜欲深者。其天機淺。
西門慶自知。貪淫樂色。更不知油枯燈盡體竭人亡。[8]
(Xiao 2003, chap. 79, 795)

TT1:

Se flexit illa et labris rubris caput mentulae huc illuc movens suxit. Subito semen
album effunditur, quasi argentum vivum, quod in ore cepit nec potuit satis celeriter
sorbere. Primo sane semenerat, mox cruor fiebat sineintermissione fluens. Hsi-
men Ch'ing had fainted and his limbs were stiff outstretched. Golden Lotus was
frightened. She hastily gave him some red dates. Semen secutus est sanguis,
sanguinem gelidus aer. …
Readers, there is a limit to our energy, but none to our desires. A man who sets no
bounds to his passion cannot live more than a short time. Hsi-men had given himself to the enjoyment of women, and he did not realize that he was like a lantern
whose oil is exhausted and whose light is failing. Now his seed was used up, there
was nothing in store for him but death.
(Egerton 1939, vol. 4, 85)

TT2:

He told her to suck it, and so she crouched over his body, engulfed his turtle head
with her ruby lips, and proceeded to move it:

    Back and forth without stopping.
She continued for as much time as it would take to eat a meal, until the semen in his
urethra spurted out en masse like mercury pouring into a bucket. She tried to catch
it in her mouth and swallow it but she wasn't quick enough.

    The emission went on and on. At first it was semen but it soon changed to blood.
There was no stopping it. Hsi-men Ch'ing had fainted and his four limbs lay inert.
In a state of panic the woman put a red date into his mouth and he swallowed it.
When the flow of semen ceased, it was followed by blood; when the flow of blood
stopped, nothing came out but a discharge of cold air. It was some time before this
came to an end. …

    Gentle reader take note:
        The vitality of the individual is finite, but
        The prurience in this world is unlimited.
It has also been said that:
        Where desires and cravings are deep,
        The Heavenly impulse is shallow.

Hsi-men Ch'ing sought only his own sexual gratification but did not realize that:
 When its oil is used up the lamp goes out;
 When his marrow is drained a man will die.
(Roy 2011, vol. 4, 639)

Similarly, narrative commentary in (8) immediately follows the titillating account of the male and female protagonists' sexual escapades. The narratological marker "看官聽說" directs readers' attention to the narrator's voice, inviting them to participate in interpreting the preceding narrative. It tells the reader that indulgence in sensual pleasure could ultimately lead to the ruin of one's life, cautioning against uninhibited cravings for sex. Thus, a didactic overtone is brought to the fore. In the English texts, explicit references to sex and bodily functions, such as "龜頭," "管中之精," "精液," or whatever, are rendered in Latin in TT1. As stated above, these Latinized portions may protect the reader from accessing indecent or objectionable content, while simultaneously adding a mystic, or even "seductive" dimension to the text, tantalizing the reader. In other words, this technique not only maintains a level of decorum and tastefulness in the portrayal of intimate scenes but also adds an element of intellectual engagement for the reader. It invites them to embark on a journey of interpretation and discovery as they navigate the intricacies of the narrative's clandestine language. Notably, the narrative commentary in this instance is not expurgated but instead preserved in TT1. Commentaries introduced by the narrative marker "readers" are not uncommon in nineteenth century British novels such as George Eliot's fictional works. Hence, the apparent moral vision is transmitted in the target text, which delivers moral, philosophical instructions to the reader, much like the original. In TT2, both graphic depictions of sex (namely, words like "suck," "turtle," "semen," "urethra," and the like.) and narratorial commentary are fully transposed in the target text. As in the previous example, TT2 makes sustained use of literal translation to foreground the voice or the continued presence of the narrator, bringing the reader into dialogue with him. Both the narrative focus on the characters' transgression and the emphasis on moral inculcation are consistently reconfigured in the target text.

5.4 Discussion

The descriptive analysis in this chapter reveals that the two translations exhibit divergent tendencies in reproducing "private desires" in *Jin Ping Mei*. The Egerton translation appears puritanical, as sexual-related content, such as homosexual depictions, is largely tamed or toned down. This includes shifts ranging from omission and mitigation to adapting indecent terms or rendering them in a "secret code," namely Latin. It seems that restraint and propriety take precedence over the depiction of sexual realities, rendering the novel less transgressive for the reader in a different cultural milieu. However, narratorial commentary is often omitted, which somehow obscures the narrator's voice or dialogue with the reader in the text. The translational choice in the Egerton translation helps sanitize the text, heighten its register, and distance it from the characteristic features of an erotic novel. Hence, it contributes to altering the reader's perception of the story.

Yet it is worth taking a more nuanced view of the taming of sexual depictions in Egerton's translation, particularly regarding the use of Latin. The occurrence of Latin sections itself could become an instrument of titillation and seduction, as titillation, in general, depends on what is obscured as what is revealed. It could become a mystery for the reader to uncover, a veil that can be lifted if the reader is prepared to make the conscious effort. Because of the strategy adopted, Latin itself has been sexualized. As the saying goes, the more it tries to hide, the more it is exposed. Latin ipso facto becomes like "a red light" outside a brothel, signaling that there is something taboo (namely, sex and erotism) going on inside and inviting the reader to imagine what that might be. Through the Borgesian looking glass, the act of suppressing erotic scenes and descriptions deemed indecent and objectionable ipso facto affirms the representation of sex in the translated text, making it even more obscene and, consequently, sexualized. This is because more (namely, in the form of tantalizing trails) is left to the reader's curiosity and imagination, showcasing the vicarious joys of prohibition (Levine 2013, 51). From a psychoanalytical point of view, the reader may produce a strong desire to unravel the Latin elements, and this desire is promptly met by an external prohibition against touching erotic material. Such prohibition can never abolish the desire to touch but merely represses it and banishes it into the unconscious. In fact, the reader driven by the unconscious, is constantly wishing to perform the act of touching and views it as their supreme enjoyment (Freud 2001, 34–36). In this respect, the Latinization present in Egerton's text has the magical power for arousing temptation or producing an alluring or desiring effect precisely because it foregrounds the consciousness of prohibition and transgression. Accordingly, it can be assumed that sex becomes a more prominent theme in Egerton's *Lotus* due to the appearance of Latin chunks. Put differently, the use of Latin to police representations of grossness and lewdness falls flat in a way as it might instead reinforce the tension between prohibition and temptation. It may, in fact, serve to impress, tease, manipulate, and tantalize the (voyeuristic) reader if they choose to read Egerton's text. As Roland Barthes (1915–80) has it, there are texts that seek to titillate and seduce the reader but simultaneously aim to escape this desired possession (Barthes 1975). For Egerton's version, its Latin texts seemingly conceal or repress sex and the erotic impulse but nonetheless lead to the sexualization of the translation, acting as important thematic clues to the perceptive reader.

In comparison, Roy's version does not baulk at any sexual discourse or raise any issues of decorum or self-censorship. Rather, the translation retains all sexually suggestive and explicit references, conveying the same sexual frankness as the original. Still, narrative commentary is fully preserved in translation, reproducing the tension between fascination and repulsion, pleasure and danger. All of this contributes to representing the subversive implications of the plot and characterization, as well as the novel's didactic and titillating effects. For a faithful representation of the "private desires" depicted in the Chinese original, the translation's reader can consistently perceive the tension between titillation and moral censure and get a glimpse of what some scholars have called "the revalorization of individual desire" (Plaks 1987, 20) and of the ambivalent attitudes toward such desire among literati during the late Ming. In this sense, the reading effect and the relationship between reader and author should be similar in both cases. The different treatment of the representation of sex in the two translations can be attributable to several factors. Generally, distinct translative intentions and the changing culturohistorical circumstances are deemed most significant in shaping the two translations regarding the representation of sexual-related narratives. The following discussion will elaborate on these.

Egerton was motivated by an ethos of introducing to contemporary readers an oriental classic featuring a fascinating story about a villainous merchant and his love-affairs. Stories of this type, featuring romance, love-interests, villainous characters, marriage, and gender roles, were quite popular among audiences in interwar Britain (Grandy 2016, xiv). As a writer and translator, Egerton strove to offer his contemporary readers a "complete" translation of *Jin Ping Mei*. Therefore, he maintained, though to a varying degree, sexual depictions in his translation so that the book could be produced in its entirety. Yet the book could not all go into English for it contains embarrassing passages featuring the mildness of sexual content (Egerton 1939, vol.1, viii). So, most of the sexual passages were turned into Latin to become suitable for publication. In one sense, such treatment of sexual material helped improve the image of the novel in the receiving culture. This needs to be viewed in relation to the pivotal historical and aesthetic moment when Egerton performed his task. Within any context, the translator is influenced by "a series of constraints [...] typical of the culture to which he belongs" (Álvarez and Vidal 1996, 5) and his or her "translation is therefore always enmeshed in a set of power relations that exist in both the source and target contexts" (Bassnett and Lefevere 1998, 137). Edwin Gentzler and Maria Tymoczko explain that "translation is not simply an act of faithful reproduction but, rather, a deliberate and conscious act of selection, assemblage, structuration, and fabrication – and even, in some cases, of falsification, refusal of information, counterfeiting, and the creation of secret codes" (Gentzler and Tymoczko 2002, xxi). Viewed through this prism, it seems necessary to understand why there is a secret code such as Latin scattered in Egerton's text, which are textual signals of poetological intervention or conscious manipulation. Márta Minier is right to state that a translation as a metatext reflects "how an individual culture and translator perceives and constructs within its own boundaries the foreignness of another culture" (2006, 120). Minier stresses that this metatext informs "a great deal about contemporaneous discourse in a receiving community" (2006, 120). The treatment of sexuality in Egerton's translation reveals contemporaneous discourses or a set of values in the target culture regarding literary depictions of sex. The Latin passages present provide evidence of textual reformulation, translational agents' assumptions about their assumed readerships, and the poetic norms and ideological imperatives that manoeuvre translated literature to meet social expectations.

Let us not forget that it was common practice for erotic passages of a book to be left in the original or put into Greek, French, and Latin, with the rest rendered into English in Britain (Perrin 1969, 23). For instance, when Giovanni Boccaccio's (1313–75) *Decameron* was translated into English in the nineteenth century, obscene passages in extremely indecent stories were either left in Italian or rendered in French (Billiani 2014, 214). Similarly, in English translations of Marquis de Sade's (1740–1814) works in the 1950s, pornographic passages were left in French (Wyngaard 2013, 317). In this regard, Egerton's translation of *Jin Ping Mei* is no exception. According to Theo Hermans (2019, 427), the practice of substituting explicitly sexual passages with Latin or French in English translations contributes to covering up perceived indecency for an average audience, but it could allow cultural elites (namely, readers who could read Latin or French but are supposed to be immune to the danger of moral corruption) the access to the amorous detail. This was, as Lise Jaillant aptly describes it, the so-called double moral standard that prevailed in early twentieth century Britain, since complete texts, or prohibited contents, could be enjoyed by the "ripe scholars" (Jaillant 2017, 23). While Latin segments might be accessible to cultural elites, such as upper-class readers, they could be challenging for a certain average audience. This should be of great significance for public morality, considering the notable growth in reading habits in Britain in the interwar years. Most readers during the time were from working-class communities, enjoying fiction reading (namely, historical romance novels) and cinema-going as their primary leisure activities (James 2010, 204). The switching from one language to the other in Egerton's translation was somewhat "progressive," adapting to the target cultural needs and moral discipline, and promoting a desired image of fiction as a major form of popular culture among the audiences targeted in the interwar period.

As mentioned earlier, Britain in the early twentieth century witnessed the appearance of a number of new or experimental texts by modernist and avant-garde writers. These writers displayed deliberate transgression of moral conventions and intense interest in exploring the human body. Bodies, especially sexualized obscene bodies that deliberately transgressed legal and religious taboos, and colloquial dirty words (for example, fucks, sluts, and bitches) were pervasive in modernist texts like *Ulysses* (Potter 2013, 4). Such literary trends towards direct representations of sexuality led to the rise in legal prosecutions of "indecent" literature. Literary representations of sexuality were highly regulated or controlled on account of the 1857 Obscene Publications Act, because they could corrupt the minds of the mass audience, especially the young and impressionable (ibid.). According to Rachel Potter (2013, 2), 1900–1940 represented one of the most severely controlled periods in the history of literary expression in Britain. A book would be considered to have the tendency to corrupt the mind of the mass readership even if only a small extract from it concerned obscenity. Christopher Hilliard (2021, 34) maintains that official concern about offensive books reflected a desire to stabilize British society after the First World War and to maintain national security. The home secretary William Joynson-Hicks (1865–1932), a very prudish, puritanical official, led a campaign to censor indecent and obscene cultural products prevalent in metropolitan life in the 1920s (Jaillant 2017, 50). Moreover, the "Indecent Books" debate (1926) between home secretary William Joynson-Hicks and MP Joseph Kenworthy (1886–1953) in London expressed a deep concern over obscenity as well as the distribution of sexually suggestive books (ibid.). Controversies over works by Lawrence and Joyce fueled popular interest and facilitated sales of their other less subversive works (Jaillant 2017, 51). Many controversial works of the time became targets of censorship either in Britain or in the U.S., such as *Ulysses*, *Lady Chatterley's Lover*, *The Well of Loneliness*, and so on (Bradshaw and Potter 2013, 72). Joyce's *Ulysses* was banned in Britain and in other English-speaking countries; Lawrence even prepared three versions of his *Lady Chatterley's Lover* to respond to the censors of obscenity with each more sexually explicit than the previous one (Sigel 2011, 61). Radclyffe Hall's (1880–1943) *The Well of Loneliness* was banned for homosexual themes incongruent with British social expectations of gender and norms of sexuality during the interwar years (Kent 1999, 290). E. M. Forster's *Maurice* was published posthumously in the 1970s for its homosexual topics, which failed to fit with the ideal of normative heterosexuality. The rapid growth of reading rates in the general population during the interwar period reinforced the perception by British authorities of "a need to protect innocent readers, particularly young people, the lower classes, and women" (Jaillant 2017, 23). Library authorities across Britain advocated the purchase of "good" books, namely books with an educational and uplifting character, to "improve the reading habits of the lower social classes" and to "maintain a healthy public interest in popular literature" (ibid., 85). As Jaillant puts it, it was not unusual for British publishers to refuse to print certain books and to bowdlerize texts for fear of being accused of spreading obscenity (Jaillant 2017, 52). Censorship took various forms, such as excising particular representations and promoting others, and could be implemented by both governmental and non-governmental agencies (Sigel 2011, 67). Organizations like the London Public Morality Council were supported by the government to take strict measures to censor books with obscenity and indecency (ibid.). In 1930, the organization acted as the deputy of the government for public censorship and strengthened the laws against obscene literature. According to statistics, about sixty cases of legal proceedings occurred in Britain between 1935 and 1936, and sentences for obscenity included months of hard labor or imprisonment (Sigel 2011, 73). Censorship of literature in interwar Britain contributed to constructing popular narratives deemed both healthy and entertaining for a mass audience.

Egerton carried out his translation project during the 1920s and 1930s. His London-based commercial publisher George Routledge and Sons Ltd. was certainly mindful of the laws against objectionable books. The exchange of letters shows that the publisher initially rejected Egerton's *Lotus* because it contains abundant depictions of sex and erotism and would not pass the censor.[9] A letter dated 31 January 1937 states that the translation could not be published unless Egerton allowed the publisher to put small parts (namely, sexually explicit passages) of the book into Latin. A telegraph dated 16 July 1939 reveals that a small part (depictions of sex) of Egerton's translation needed to be put into Latin; otherwise, it would not pass the censor. Other letters from the same archive illustrate that Egerton was then advised to modify obscene passages, and an agreement was finally reached that satisfied the demands of the publisher.[10] Significantly, a letter of 16 August 1939 indicates that Egerton's translation was rejected for publication in New York due to the near certainty of difficulties with the censor.[11] The treatment of sexuality in translation in Egerton's case brings attention to the relationship between power and knowledge production. For Michel Foucault , power produces knowledge and that both knowledge and power imply one another. Power, being both prohibitive and productive, infiltrates all facets of our social lives, which "induces pleasure, forms knowledge, produces discourse" (Foucault 1980, 119). Power also means the "exercise of re-presentation through the medium of language, and linguistic re-presentation of reality has the power to construct identities and to serve the interests of institutions," such as the defense of public morality (Claramonte 2018, 80). The notion of power informs us that translation could be understood as an ethical or political activity involving manipulation and intervention. Emerging in the context of a cultural climate that deemed sex in literature as transgressive, Egerton's translation shows clear traces of self-censorship exercised both by Egerton himself and by an invisible translator, F. A. Wright, who was invited to put many sexual passages into Latin, as shown in the archival documents.[12] For instance, the frank depiction of homosexual sex was Latinized in the Egerton translation to fit with the spirit of the times when a normative masculine ideal was promoted through the endorsement of heterosexuality. The ultimate goal was to get the translation published and to reduce the risk of displeasing or offending the censors because of the content of the work. However, as Lintao Qi (2016; 2018; 2021) and others have noted, all the Latin passages in Egerton's translation were put into English in the 1970s when the new Obscene Publications Bills (1958) was in force in Britain. Several other erotic novels like *Lolita* and *Lady Chatterley's Lover* also became publishable in full length in the 1970s. Qi (2021) suggests that the back-translation of Latin into English in Egerton's *Lotus* reflects the changing picture of the Anglo-American censorship system. In fact, this back-translation also reflects the changing literary culture and the increasing open-mindedness or liberal attitude toward literary representations of sexuality within the target literary context. However, this does not indicate that literary censorship does not work any longer. In certain Western countries like New Zealand, government-appointed censors still oversee and regulate sensitive publications. A notable example is the temporary national ban imposed on the young adult novel *Into the River* by Ted Dawes (1950-) in New Zealand in 2015. Despite being subject to an interim restriction, the ban paradoxically resulted in increased sales.

Significantly, while censorship may lead to a compromised text, it may also produce "unintended" interpretations when insightful or shrewd readers read between the lines. According to Annabel Patterson, the act of censorship would mean that "provocation is given, or signification promoted, by some kind of signal in the text itself" and "confers a greater importance on the prohibited views than they would otherwise have had" (1984, 56). One must bear in mind that a thing that is censored or forbidden with the greatest emphasis must be a thing that is desired (Freud 2001, 81). Hence, the very act of censorship per se can serve, in some way, as a signal or cue to the reader, directing them just where to look for prohibited views. For instance, both Britain and the United States witnessed tight control and censorship of novels and poems for their representation of sex and erotism during the first decades of the twentieth century; however, writers became more interested than ever before in incorporating discussions of the human body, sexuality, and individual psyche in literature. As Rachel Potter (2013) postulates, rather than curtailing the writing of obscenity and sensuality in this period, censorship, however, seemed to stimulate writers to explore it further by linking it to the author's defending rights of free speech and sexual liberation. This might be the result of the arousal of *psychological reactance*, which, according to James M. Olson and Victoria M. Esses (2016, 279), suggests a motivation to restore the threatened freedom induced by prohibition or censorship. Since censorship entails restricted access to certain information or limited expression of ideas, it easily triggers psychological reactance. Once it spurs such reactance, interest in or curiosity about the restricted or censored information might become stronger to individuals, motivating them to seek out the information or change their attitudes (often favorable) towards the prohibited message (ibid., 280). Following this logic, the Latin segments in Egerton's translation might play such a role in directing or stimulating sophisticated readers to look for their exact meaning, which, as articulated previously, contributes to the activation of the secret code and makes sexual discourse in the text all the more prominent. Put differently, the arcane code evokes taboo, and as such, it may stir readers' curiosity or bring them pleasure to unveil the true meaning of that code. As Georges Bataille indicates, "in human terms the taboo never makes an appearance without suggesting sexual pleasure, nor does the pleasure without evoking the taboo" (1986, 108). Hence, Latinized elements ipso facto constitute an immediate cause of the noticeable sexualization of Egerton's translation. True enough, literary censorship could somehow contribute to titillating the readers who may create a somatic response to the censored or banned material since human bodies "often react to language use that seems different, deviant, somehow 'wrong,' with anxiety signals" (Robinson 1991, 10). Viewed in this light, the censored version of Egerton's translation should possess much more appeal and temptation than the "normalized" version in which the mysterious code (Latin portions) were erased and back-translated into English in 1972. It is worth noting that a series of literary persecution cases in Egerton's time, including Radclyffe Hall's *The Well of Loneliness (1928)*, Lawrence's *The Rainbow* (1915) and *Lady Chatterley's Lover* (1928), as well as Joyce's *Ulysses* (1922). These works faced public trials for containing disruptive or subversive subjects. The sensational trials ipso facto played the role of incitement, pushing the boundaries of sexual expression depicted in these modernist works into the public view (Doan 2001; Marshik 2006; Ladenson 2007). These works, along with their portrayed dissenting themes, might not have gained such fame in the twentieth century without severe censorship due to the permeation of (homo)sexual themes into their narratives. The trials not only generated audience interest and reaction but also produced literary and social meaning. Noticeably, the trial of Hall's *The Well of Loneliness* ultimately brought the male or female homosexual as a widely known type into British public culture. This recalls Butler's analysis of the attempt to curtail homosexuality in the military, which paradoxically leads to a heightened visibility of the issue (Butler

2021, 131). The term "homosexuality" emerges not just within the regulations as the targeted discourse but also resurfaces in public discussions regarding its legitimacy and fairness. The act of censorship not only evokes the public discourse on homosexuality that it aims to contain but also actively participating in the construction of a representation of homosexuality.

Unlike Egerton, Roy performed his translation task in a cultural context that considered sexual topics natural and agreeable without incurring repulsion. The translator's archive, especially correspondences with his editors, reveals that Roy's publisher, Princeton University Press, barely censored or regulated his translation but allowed the translator great autonomy in terms of representing sex and eroticism in the text.[13] Carlitz notes that "we own a great debt to the publisher for staying totally away from trying to censor or micromanage Roy's translation" (personal communication, December 4, 2021). As a matter of fact, sexuality, erotism, and sensual desire are commonplace in modern culture. The rise of the new social movements since the 1960s has paved the way for diverse sexual subjects (for example, women, gays, lesbians, sado-masochists, transgendered people, and so forth.) to perform on the stage of human history and make claims to rights and justice (Weeks 2011, 7). Still, sex and sexuality have become more and more visible, and more explicit in mainstream Western culture, becoming a trend since the 1990s (Attwood 2006, 82). As Karen Boyle puts it, sex has largely been normalized within mainstream culture in the twenty-first century (Boyle 2008, 35). Sex and pornography can be produced and distributed through a plethora of media platforms like television, internet, advertisement, films, social media, or whatever, providing people with the means to derive enjoyment from consuming these imaged or visual products. Immersed in such a cultural milieu, creative writers, publishers, and readers would certainly find it quite normal and acceptable to read sex-related material in but not limited to literary genres. Little wonder that close textual analysis shows no indications of (self-)censorship for Roy's text when it comes to dealing with sexual subjects in translation. Rather, the translator adheres scrupulously to the source text to render sexually suggestive/explicit references, including the most objectionable ones. In almost all cases, he strives to represent sexuality as graphically as the original author does, and the depiction of every sex act is preserved or even reinforced on some occasions in the translation. The main tactic used is the literal or word-for-word transfer, reflecting an effort to find exact English equivalents. As a researcher-cum-translator, Roy sticks to his own translation philosophy: to translate everything in the source text (Roy 1993, xlviii). His task of retranslating *Jin Ping Mei* was chiefly motivated by, in Venuti's words, his "personal appreciation and understanding of the foreign text, regardless of transindividual factors" (2004, 30). So, sex scenes of various kinds are not circumvented but rendered into English in a straightforward way, so much so that certain passages become obscure or exotic only because they are too close to the original text. In addition to sexual depictions, narratorial commentary is consistently represented in the translation, and so the tension between moral inculcation and titillation in the novel is aptly revealed. In a word, Roy's translation allows its readers full access to the "private desires" of the novel's major characters and widens their perception about the relaxed attitude toward sex and the open fascination with sensual desire in late Ming China, known for its confusions of pleasure.

5.5 Concluding Remarks

This chapter has shown that translators exhibit divergent tendencies when dealing with the representation of sexuality in *Jin Ping Mei*. It has also revealed that sexually suggestive language, homosexual scenes, heterosexual spectacles, and narratorial commentary are more fully preserved in Roy's translation compared to Egerton's translation. This difference can be attributed primarily to the changing nature of political, ethical, and moral constraints in the receiving culture. The chapter further demonstrates that suppression (namely, mitigation, omission, and euphemizing) is not the universal norm abided by translators while handling erotic narratives in literary translation. Instead, translators' decision-making can be informed and shaped by the assumed acceptability or commensurability of sexuality in the target-cultural community. The chapter suggests that translators may not have the final say in shaping the ultimate translation products due to power relations involved in the translation process. Significantly, while (self-)censorship and moral regulation are crucial factors shaping Egerton's choices, they simultaneously contribute to enhancing the novel's image in the receiving culture, appealing to a broader audience. However, (self-)censorship, as seen in the form of Latinization in the Egerton example, may foreground what has been concealed, namely the subject of sex, and, in turn, stimulate the reader's curiosity or reading impulse. As such, (self-)censorship is not merely a prohibitive and defensive act to manage the moral and ethical impact of fictional narratives on targeted readers; it can have a titillating, inviting, or even impulsive effect on the reader, who might be enticed by the arcane or uncanny codes inscribed in the text. Therefore, the chapter affirms poststructuralist perspectives, including Butler's and Foucault's insights on regulation and censorship, demonstrating how what is censored can paradoxically be brought to light and made visible to the public. It also reveals the tension between the translator's desire for sexual expression and the symbolic pressure exerted by the social field, which results in a compromised work. In the case of Roy's version, however, the faithful rendering, shaped by the assumed acceptability of literary representations of sexuality in the target culture, historicizes and exoticizes the foreign work for envisaged readers. Finally, the chapter demonstrates that literary representations of sex and sensual desires within translational and transnational contexts should be a privileged locus for understanding the difference between societies and cultures. Each culture has its moral and ethical limits, justifying the contingent, temporal, and provisional (re)framings of sexual discourse in the source and target texts. In brief, this chapter has provided a nuanced and in-depth study of translation and literary censorship concerning the literary representation of sex and erotic sensations. It demonstrates the dialectics and paradoxes involved in regulating and policing the representation of sex and erotic sensations within both literature and translation. It offers readers a thought-provoking exploration of the complexities, implications, and potential results of translating subversive themes of sexuality and eroticism within different historical circumstances.

Notes

1 Sigmund Freud was an Austrian neurologist and psychoanalyst, whose studies were translated by James Strachery (1887–1967), a Bloomsbury psychoanalyst, and published by Hogarth Press run by Virginia Woolf and her husband Leonard Woolf (1880–1969) in the early decades of the twentieth century, during which Freud's ideas were in wide circulation amongst many British novelists and poets writing in English, including W. H. Auden, H. D., James Joyce, E. M. Forster (1879–1970), D. H. Lawrence (1885–1930), among others.

2 The Bloomsbury Group was organized by influential figures such as E. M. Foster, Lytton Strachey, and Leonard Woolf, who showed a sustained interest in sexuality as an ideological site for contesting old artistic and political values while craving for new ones. Through experimental writings, they made significant contributions to British modernist culture in the first decades of the twentieth century. For more details on the Bloomsbury Group, see Derek Ryan and Stephen Ross, *The Handbook to the Bloomsbury Group* (London: Bloomsbury Academic, 2018).

3 *Peony Pavilion* was written by the late Ming dramatist Tang Xianzu 湯顯祖 (1550–1616) in 1598. It has been acclaimed as one of the greatest *chuanqi* 傳奇 (legendary) plays ever written in premodern China. It features an amazing story about how the heroine Du Liniang 杜麗娘 longs for romantic love, or the cult of *qing* 情, until she dies and how she comes to life again due to the power of *qing*.

4 The expression "弔過身子" appears as "調過身子" in the Chongzhen edition and the meaning remains unchanged.

5 In the Chongzhen edition, the expression "便益" appears as "便宜;" the expression "敗缺" appears as "銀錢." Yet the meaning keeps the same.

6 In the Chongzhe edition, the expression "佯佯不採" appears as "洋洋不睬."

7 In the Chongzhen edition, the expression "對面坐着椅子" appears as "一往一來;" the expression "便在後邊推車" appears as "又在後邊推送;" the passage "一個氣的吁吁。猶如牛吼柳影。一個嬌聲噎噎。猶似鶯囀花間" is cut out.

8 In the Chongzhen edition, the expression "自知" appears as "只;" the expression "油枯燈盡" appears as "油盡燈滅."

9 The publisher's archival records are housed in the Special Collections, University of Reading, UK.

10 A letter from managing director to Egerton, 26 February 1937, informs that Egerton and the director reached an agreement on publishing *The Golden Lotus*, allowing small part of sexual passages in the book to appear in a foreign language, that is, Latin.

11 A telegraph dated 16 August 1939 shows that *The Golden Lotus* was rejected for publication in New York.

12 Letters to Professor F. A. Wright indicate that the Latin passages were not provided by Egerton himself but by Wright.

13 All the publisher's archival records about David Roy's translation of *Jin Ping Mei* are collected in the Special Collections Research Center, University of Chicago Library. Besides, Roy's notecards, index cards, personal and professional files, press reviews and interviews with scholars and news reporters are also collected in the Center.

References

Álvarez, Román, and M. Carmen Africa Vidal, eds. 1996. *Translation, Power, Subversion*. Clevedon: Multilingual Matters.

Attwood, Feona. 2006. "Sexed Up: Theorizing the Sexualization of Culture." *Sexualities* 9 (1): 77–94.

Avery, Todd. 2018. "Bloomsbury and Sexuality." In *The Handbook to the Bloomsbury Group*, edited by Derek Ryan, and Stephen Ross, 17–29. London: Bloomsbury Publishing Plc.

Bakhtin, Mikhail M. 1984. *Rabelais and His World*. Bloomington: Indiana University Press.

Baldick, Chris. 2004. *Oxford English Literary History, Volume 10 The Modern Movement, 1910–1940*. Oxford: Oxford University Press.

Barthes, Roland. 1975. *La Plaisir du Texte/The Pleasure of the Text*. New York: Hill and Wang.

Bassnett, Susan, and André Lefevere, eds.1998. *Constructing Cultures: Essays on Literary Translation*. Clevedon: Multilingual Matters.

Bataille, Georges. 1986. *Death and Sensuality*. New York: Walker and Company.

Billiani, Francesca, ed. 2014. *Modes of Censorship: National Contexts and Diverse Media*. London: Routledge.

Birch, Cyril. 1978. *Stories from a Ming Collection*. Westport: Greenwood Press.

Boyle, Karen. 2008. "Courting Consumers and Legitimating Exploitation: The Representation of Commercial Sex in Television Documentaries." *Feminist Media Studies* 8 (1): 35–50.

Bradshaw, David, and Rachel Potter, eds. 2013. *Prudes on the Prowl: Fiction and Obscenity in England, 1850 to the Present Day*. Oxford: Oxford University Press.

Brook, Timothy. 1998. *The Confusions of Pleasure: Commerce and Culture in Ming China*. Berkeley: University of California Press.

Brulotte, Gaetan, and John Phillips. 2006. *Encyclopedia of Erotic Literature*. New York: Routledge.

Butler, Judith. 2021. *Excitable Speech: A Politics of the Performative*. London and New York: Routledge.

Chatman, Seymour Benjamin. 1978. *Story and Discourse: Narrative Structure in Fiction and Film*. Ithaca, NY: Cornell University Press.

Chou, Chih-p'ing. 1988. *Yüan Hung-tao and the Kung-an School*. Cambridge: Cambridge University Press.

Claramonte, Ma Carmen África Vidal. 2018. "Power." In *The Routledge Handbook of Translation and Culture*, edited by Sue-Ann Harding, and Ovidi Carbonell Cortés, 79–96. London and New York: Routledge.

Ding, Naifei. 2002. *Obscene Things: Sexual Politics in Jin Ping Mei*. Durham: Duke University Press.

Doan, Laura. 2001. *Fashioning Sapphism: The Origins of a Modern English Lesbian Culture*. New York: Columbia University Press.

Eagleton, Terry. 1976. *Marxism and Literary Criticism*. Berkeley and Los Angeles: University of California Press.

Egerton, Clement. 1939. *The Golden Lotus*. 4 vols. London: George Routledge and Sons, Ltd.

Eifring, Halvor. 2004. *Love and Emotions in Traditional Chinese Literature*. Leiden: Brill.

Epstein, Maram. 2001. *Competing Discourses: Orthodoxy, Authenticity, and Engendered Meanings in Late Imperial Chinese Fiction*. Cambridge, MA: Harvard University Asia Center.

Fang Ming 方銘. 1986. *Jin Ping Mei ziliao huilu* 金瓶梅資料匯錄 (Collected Materials on *Jin Ping Mei*). Hefei: Huangshan shushe.

Foucault, Michel. 1978. *The History of Sexuality* (vol. 1). Translated by Robert Hurley. London: Random House.

Foucault, Michel. 1980. *Power/Knowledge. Selected Interviews and Other Writings 1972–1977*. New York: Pantheon Books.

Freud, Sigmund. 2001. *Totem and Taboo*. London and New York: Routledge.

Gill, Rosalind. 2012. "The Sexualisation of Culture?" *Social and Personality Psychology Compass* 6 (7): 483–498.

Grandy, Christine. 2016. *Heroes and Happy Endings: Class, Gender, and Nation in Popular Film and Fiction in Interwar Britain*. Manchester: Manchester University Press.

Guyda Armstrong. 2014. "Eroticism *à la française*: Text, Image, and Display in Nineteenth-Century English Translations of Boccaccio's *Decameron*." *Word & Image* 30 (3): 194–212.

Hammond, Kenneth J. 2015. "All that is Solid Melts into Air: Wang Shizhen, *Jinpingmei*, and the Taizhou School." *Ming Studies* 71: 11–22.

Handler-Spitz, Rivi. 2017. *Symptoms of an Unruly Age: Li Zhi and Cultures of Early Modernity*. Seattle and London: University of Washington Press.

Heath, Deana. 2010. *Purifying Empire: Obscenity and the Politics of Moral Regulation in Britain, India and Australia*. Cambridge: Cambridge University Press.

Hegel, Robert E. 1998. *Reading Illustrated Fiction in Late Imperial China*. Stanford: Stanford University Press.

Hermans, Theo. 2019. "Positioning." In *Routledge Encyclopedia of Translation Studies*, edited by Mona Baker, and Gabriela Saldanha, 423–428. London: Routledge.

Hilliard, Christopher. 2021. *A Matter of Obscenity: The Politics of Censorship in Modern England*. Princeton, NJ: Princeton University Press.

Hsia, Chih-tsing. 1968. *The Classic Chinese Novel: A Critical Introduction*. New York: Columbia University Press.

Holquist, Michael. 1994. "Introduction: Corrupt Originals: The Paradox of Censorship." *PLMA* 109 (1): 14–25.

Huang, Martin W. 2001. *Desire and Fictional Narrative in Late Imperial China*. Cambridge, MA: Harvard University Press.

Huang, Yonglin. 2018. *Narrative of Chinese and Western Popular Fiction*. Singapore: Springer.

Huo Songlin 霍松林. 1988. *Zhongguo gudian xiaoshuo liuda mingzhu jianshang cidian* 中國古典小說六大名著鑒賞辭典 *(Anatomy of Six Chinese Classical Novels)*. Xi'an: Huayue wenyi chubanshe.

Jaillant, Lise. 2017. *Cheap Modernism: Expanding Markets, Publishers' Series and the Avant-Garde*. Edinburgh: Edinburgh University Press.

James, Robert. 2010. *Popular Culture and Working-class Taste in Britain, 1930–39: A Round of Cheap Diversions?* Manchester: Manchester University Press.

Kao, George. 1994. "Euphemism: Its Interpretation and Translation." In *Translation and Interpreting: Bridging East and West*, edited by Richard K. Seymour, and Ching-chih Liu, 171–179. Honolulu: University of Hawai'i Press.

Ken McMahon, Keith. 1988. *Causality and Containment in Seventeenth-Century Chinese Fiction*. Boston: Brill.

Kendrick, Walter M. 1987. *The Secret Museum: Pornography in Modern Culture*. New York: Viking.

Kent, Susan Kingsley. 1999. *Gender and Power in Britain 1640–1990*. London and New York: Routledge.

Ladenson, Elisabeth. 2007. *Dirt for Art's Sake: Books on Trial from Madame Bovary to Lolita*. New York: Cornell University Press.

Lee, Pauline C. 2012. *Li Zhi, Confucianism, and the Virtue of Desire*. Albany: SUNY Press.

Levine, Suzanne Jill. 2013. "Borges on Translation." In *The Cambridge Companion to Jorge Luis Borges*, edited by Edwin Williamson, 43–55. Cambridge: Cambridge University Press.

Liang, Wayne Wen-Chun. 2017. "Translating Chinese Erotic Literature: A Case Study of the English Translations of Jin Ping Mei." *SPECTRUM: NCUE Studies in Language, Literature, Translation* 15 (1): 1–20.

Liu, Wu-chi.1966. *An Introduction of Chinese Literature*. Bloomington: Indiana University Press.

Lu, Tina. 2008. *Accidental Incest, Filial Cannibalism, and Other Peculiar Encounters in Late Imperial Chinese Literature*. Cambridge, MA: Harvard University Press.

Lu, Tina. 2021. "Slavery and Genre in The Plum in the Golden Vase." *Harvard Journal of Asiatic Studies* 81 (1&2): 85–108.

Luo, Junjie. 2014. "Translating Jin Ping Mei: A Preliminary Comparison of The Golden Lotus and The Plum in the Golden Vase." *Perspectives: Studies in Translatology* 22 (1): 56–74.

Marshik, Celia. 2006. *British Modernism and Censorship*. Cambridge: Cambridge University Press.

Marshik, Celia, Allison Pease, Gayle Rogers, and Sean Latham. 2018. *Modernism, Sex, and Gender*. London: Bloomsbury Publishing.

McGreal, Ian P. 1996. *Great Literature of the Eastern World: The Major of Prose, Poetry and Drama from China, Japan, Korea and the Middle East*. New York: Harper Collins Publishers.

McHale, Brian, and Randall Stevenson, eds. 2006. *The Edinburgh Companion to Twentieth-Century Literatures in English*. Edinburgh: Edinburgh University Press.

McMahon, Keith. 2019. "The Art of the Bedchamber and Jin Ping Mei." *Nan Nü* 21 (1): 1–37.

McNair, Brian. 2002. *Striptease Culture: Sex, Media and the Democratization of Desire*. London: Routledge.

Millett, Kate. 2000. *Sexual Politics*. Urbana and Chicago: University of Illinois Press.

Minier, Márta. 2006. "Linguistic Inventions, Culture-Specific Terms and Intertexts in the Hungarian Translations of *Harry Potter*." In *No Child is an Island: The Case of Children's Literature in Translation*, edited by P. Pinsent, 119–137. Lichfield, England: Pied Piper.

Moddlemog, Debra A. 2014. Modernism and Sexology. *Literature Compass* 11 (4): 267–278.

Moore, Nicole. 2016. "Censorship." *Oxford Research Encyclopedia of Literature.* Accessed 27 Dec. 2023. https://oxfordre.com/literature/view/10.1093/acrefore/9780190201 098.001.0001/acrefore-9780190201098-e-71

Mote, Frederick W. 2000. *Imperial China 900–1800*. Cambridge, MA: Harvard University Press.

Ngoshi, Hazel Tafadzwa. 2021. "Repression, Literary Dissent and the Paradox of Censorship in Zimbabwe." *Journal of Southern African Studies* 47 (5): 799–815.

Olson, James M, and Victoria M. Esses. 2016. "The Social Psychology of Censorship." In *Interpreting Censorship in Canada*, edited by Klaus Petersen, and Allan C. Hutchinson, 268–289. Toronto: University of Toronto Press.

Perrin, Noel. 1969. *Dr Bowdler's Legacy: A History of Expurgated Books in England and America*. London: Macmillan.

Person, Ethel Spector, Peter Fonagy, and Servulo Augusto Figueira. 1995. *On Freud's "Creative Writers and Day-Dreaming."* New Haven: Yale University Press.

Plaks, Andrew H. 1987. *The Four Masterworks of the Ming Novel: Ssu Ta Ch'i-Shu*. Princeton, N.J: Princeton University Press.

Potter, Rachel. 2013. *Obscene Modernism: Literary Censorship and Experiment 1900–1940*. Oxford: Oxford University Press.

Qi, Lintao. 2016. "Agents of Latin: An Archival Research on Clement Egerton's English Translation of Jin Ping Mei." *Target* 28 (1): 42–60.

Qi, Lintao. 2018. *Jin Ping Mei English Translations*. London: Routledge.

Qi, Lintao. 2021. "Translating Sexuality in the Context of Anglo-American Censorship: The Case of Jin Ping Mei." *Translation and Interpreting Studies* 16 (3): 416–433.

Robinson, Douglas. 1991. *The Translator's Turn*. Baltimore: JHU Press.

Roy, David T. 1993. *The Plum in the Golden Vase or, Chin P'ing Mei* (vol. 1). Princeton, NJ: Princeton University Press.

Roy, David T. 2001. *The Plum in the Golden Vase or, Chin P'ing Mei* (vol. 2). Princeton, NJ: Princeton University Press.

Roy, David T. 2006. *The Plum in the Golden Vase or, Chin P'ing Mei* (vol. 3). Princeton, NJ: Princeton University Press.

Roy, David T. 2011. *The Plum in the Golden Vase or, Chin P'ing Mei* (vol. 4). Princeton, NJ: Princeton University Press.

Roy, David T. 2013. *The Plum in the Golden Vase or, Chin P'ing Mei* (vol. 5). Princeton, NJ: Princeton University Press.

Ryan, Derek, and Stephen Ross. 2018. *The Handbook to the Bloomsbury Group*. London: Bloomsbury Academic.

Santaemilia, José. 2014. "The Sex of Translation/the Translation of Sex: Fanny Hill in Spanish." In *Gender, Sex and Translation: The Manipulation of Identities*, edited by José Santaemilia, 117–136. Manchester: St. Jerome.

Satyendra, Indira. 1993. "Metaphors of the Body: The Sexual Economy of the Chin P'ing Mei tz'u-hua." *Chinese Literature: Essays, Articles, Reviews* 15: 85–97.

Sigel, Lisa Z. 2011. "Censorship in Inter-War Britain: Obscenity, Spectacle, and the Workings of the Liberal State." *Journal of Social History* 45 (1): 61–83.

Special Collections, Library of the University of Chicago, The David Roy Archive.

Special Collections, University of Reading, Routledge & Kegan Paul Archive.

Strauss, Leo. 1988. *Persecution and the Art of Writing*. Chicago and London: University of Chicago Press.

Tymoczko, Maria, and Edwin Gentzler. 2002. *Translation and Power*. Amherst: University of Massachusetts Press.

van den Abbeele, Georges. 1997. "The Persecution of Writing: Revisiting Strauss and Censorship." *Diacritics* 27 (2): 3–17.

Van Gulik, Robert Han. 2003. *Sexual Life in Ancient China: A Preliminary survey of Chinese Sex and Society from ca. 1500 B.C. Till 1644 A.D.* Leiden: Brill.

Venuti, Lawrence. 2004. "Retranslation: The Creation of Value." *Bucknell Review* 47 (1): 25–38.

von Flotow, Luise. 2000. "Translation Effects: How Beauvoir talks sex in English." In *Contingent Loves. Simone de Beauvoir and Sexuality*, edited by Melanie Hawthorne, 13–33. Richmond, VA: University of Virginia Press.

Waley, Arthur. 1939. "Introduction." In *Chin P'ing Mei: The Adventurous History of Hsi Men and His Six Wives*, translated by Bernard Miall, vii–xviii. London: John Lane.

Weeks, Jeffrey. 2011. *The Languages of Sexuality*. Abingdon, Oxon: Routledge.

Weeks, Jeffrey. 2018. *Sex, Politics and Society: The Regulation of Sexuality Since 1800*. London: Routledge.

Witchard, Anne. 2012. *Lao She in London*. Hong Kong: Hong Kong University Press.

Wolfe, Jesse. 2011. *Bloomsbury, Modernism, and the Reinvention of Intimacy*. Cambridge: Cambridge University Press.

Wu, Cuncun. 2004. *Homoerotic Sensibilities in Late Imperial China*. London: Routledge.

Wyngaard, Amy S. 2013. "Translating Sade: The Grove Press Editions, 1953–1968." *Romanic Review* 104 (3): 313–331.

Xiao Xiao Sheng of Lanling 蘭陵笑笑生. 1963. *Jin Ping Mei cihua* (facsimile edition) 金瓶梅詞話. Fukuoka: Daian Co., Ltd.

Xiao Xiao Sheng of Lanling 蘭陵笑笑生. 2003. *Xinke xiuxiang piping Jin Ping Mei* 新刻繡像批評金瓶梅. Singapore: South Ocean Publishing.

Xiao, Jiwei. 2022. *Telling Detail: Chinese Fiction, World Literature*. New York: Routledge.

Zaragoza Ninet, Gora, and Sara Llopis Mestre. 2021. "The Unlit Lamp (1924): Translation, Reception and Censorship." *Language and Intercultural Communication* 21 (1): 37–54.

Zhang, Longxi. 2023. *A History of Chinese Literature*. New York: Routledge.

6   Conclusion

Translating as a Hermeneutic Act is an Infinite Task

This study systematically compares *Jin Ping Mei* and its two full-length English translations. The analysis is conducted within the framework of descriptive translation studies, incorporating extratextual cultural, societal, and historical variables into the examination of translational phenomena. The investigation allows for an in-depth exploration of the English translations of *Jin Ping Mei* from cultural, literary, linguistic, and sociohistorical perspectives. Building upon prior *Jin Ping Mei* scholarship, this study focuses on several previously underexplored areas, including the treatment of culturemes, narratorial voices, gendered narratives, and literary representations of sexuality in the two translations of *Jin Ping Mei*. Such a multi-perspective approach has provided a stereoscopic view of the novel and its English renderings. The primary objective of the comparative analysis has been to unveil each translator's translatorial behavior (namely, textualizing choices) and extratextual contingencies (namely, literary currents, ideology, readers' expectations, and so forth) that might have influenced their decision-making during translation. Chapter 1 has described how each translator came to (re)translate *Jin Ping Mei*, what they said about their work, and how their immediate social milieus influenced their translational decisions. In Chapters 2 to 5, the two translations of *Jin Ping Mei* have been thoroughly compared vis-à-vis the original in relation to the four aspects mentioned above. In each of these four main Chapters, the study has aimed to relate its findings to the literary, cultural, political, and sociohistorical context of each translation, identifying significant influences upon the translators and accounting for the observed translational shifts.

To the best of my knowledge, this study is the first to conduct stereoscopic readings of *Jin Ping Mei* and its two full-length English translations in the English-speaking world, focusing on the representation of late Ming culture, narratological elements, gender matters, and (homo)sexual subjects. This selection highlights some of the most characteristic features of *Jin Ping Mei*, including its cultural specificity rooted in late Ming China, animated narrative language and idiosyncratic narrative style, gendered narratives, and sexual-related narratives. In particular, this study represents the first in-depth and systematic investigation into how representations of late Ming culture and the narrative voice in *Jin Ping Mei* are carried over in English renderings. Additionally, it is the initial effort to examine how and to what

DOI: 10.4324/9781003472674-6

extent the gendered narratives of *Jin Ping Mei* are represented within a different societal context, (namely, early twentieth-century Britain), where gender norms and patriarchal relations differed significantly from those of late Ming China. More nuanced differences between the two translations have emerged from the in-depth analysis carried out in this study. Translation, as a decision-making process across languages and cultures, involves a myriad of complex, dynamic, and multifaceted factors – ethical, cultural, sociopolitical, historical, ideological, and subjective. The study demonstrates that the two English translations, *Lotus* and *Plum*, offer distinct representations of the salient features of *Jin Ping Mei*. These differences are influenced to varying degrees by the translators' translational purposes, professional backgrounds (namely, a writer versus a researcher), attitudes toward the art and poetics of the original, levels of aesthetic acuity, literary imagination, *re-creativity*, habitual use of (literary) language, the expectations of their targeted readership, and, most importantly, the different literary, cultural, and sociopolitical environments in which they crafted their translations.

Furthermore, the study confirms that extratextual factors exert a significant influence, albeit to varying degrees, on the decisions made by translators. These influences not only constrain their choices but also serve as motivators, prompting them to respond to the target culture (for example, ideology, poetic norms, cultural needs, readers' horizons of expectation, critical trends, and the like) in self-reflective and creative ways. Translation, as a literary and aesthetic practice, is far from ideologically neutral but is rather shaped by its own purpose, historical contingencies, cultural norms, and the receptive environment. Qualities such as perceived faithfulness or infidelity depend on translational norms, needs, and principles existing within the target culture, as well as on the translators' attitudes towards, and understanding of the source text and culture.

Overall, then, the approaches of the two English-language translators to translating *Jin Ping Mei* largely mirror broader differences between the cultural and historical contexts in which they wrote their translations. A related factor concerns differences we might anticipate between a writer-translator and a researcher-translator translating the same source work. As the study has shown, a researcher-translator's intention, professional background, working environment, and proficiency in the source language and culture differ significantly from those of a writer-translator. Consequently, a researcher-translator, especially one with a strong grasp of the source language, as evidenced in this study, tends to prioritize the integrity, identity, full substance, and historico-cultural specificity of the original work, to lean towards source-oriented translation strategies, and to emphasize the academic, ethnographical, and pedagogical value of translation. The resulting translation is characterized by literality and all-round fidelity, often at the expense of beauty, brevity, smoothness, naturalness, and easy accessibility and readability. Readers are confronted with unnecessary barriers or frustration due to their own preconceptions and cultural presuppositions when encountering these types of translations. The translations' outlandish, defamiliarizing, and exhaustive nature gives them the semblance of the work of a religious interpreter rather than that of a literary translator. On the other hand, a writer-translator, especially one lacking adequate knowledge of the source language but possessing a strong literary reimagination, connoisseurship, and creative mind, is more likely to appropriate or refashion the original work to respond to the literary, cultural, socio-political, and commercial concerns of their own era. They prioritize the actual needs of the target readership and meet the horizon of their expectations. This dynamic approach enables a more creative, relevant, and critical (mis)interpretation of the original, challenging traditional notions of fidelity and the presumed authority of the original. Unconstrained by reverence for the source work, they take great liberties to remodel, transform, and upgrade it into a desirable or reader-friendly (namely, aesthetically pleasing or culturally appropriate for the general reading public) form, or into their own aesthetic prose. They also see translation as an active and productive engagement with foreign works, recognizing it as both a creative and critical act, as well as a significant force for literary change, experimentation, and innovation. Emphasizing the generative and transformative role of translation, they perceive it as a potent catalyst for literary reimagination and recreation within their immediate context. Typically, translation of this nature involves the use of familiar concepts, associations, and literary borrowings from existing genres, antecedent art forms, and themes to decipher and re-encode unfamiliar situations through the familiar language of the target reader. As a result, the translations become readily acceptable by most publishers and easily accessible to the general reading public (Venuti 1995, 1; Venuti 2008). They bring about temporal and spatial displacements, emphasizing shifts in both readership and the immediate receptor cultural milieu. Thus, they achieve a better fusion of horizons with the envisaged readers, ensuring a smooth, pleasurable reading experience without encountering unnaturalness or peculiarities, such as wordy prose or tumescence. This dynamic and creative approach finds its best exemplification in the translation of numerous Chinese poems, novels, and plays into European languages. Examples include Jean Pierre Abel Rémusat's (1788–1832) *Iu-kiao-li* (1826), Thomas Percy's *Pleasing History* (1761), Arthur Murphy's (1727–1805) drama *The Orphan of China* (1756), H. A. Giles's *Strange Stories from a Chinese Studio* (1880), Waley's *Monkey*, and Pound's *Cathay*, Hawkes and Minford's *Story of the Stone*, and, of course, Egerton's *Lotus*, among others. By prioritizing the spirit, tone, mood, and aestheticism of the original over exactitude or interlinear transfer, this adaptive, re-creative, and transformative approach proves relevant and instrumental in cultivating a more favorable reception and appreciation of Chinese literature in the Western world. This is particularly because translated works face constant challenges in finding interested readers, unlike fiction originally written in the target language, such as English. Additionally, the stark difference may also arise from the fact that Roy's *Plum* is a retranslation of *Jin Ping Mei*.[1] His attempt is to reveal the "true value" (which varies from translator to translator) of the novel and its significance not only to Chinese literature but also to world literature. J. W. Goethe (1749–1832) viewed world literature as translated literature that sparks new thoughts and brings into the target literary repertoire new forms and fresh possibilities of linguacultural expression (Strich 1971, 7–13). Goethe also asserts that in retranslation, "the goal [...] is to achieve a perfect identity with the original" both in form and content (Robinson

2014, 224). It has been suggested that Roy's retranslation aimed to achieve a perfect identity with the original in content, if not as much in form or genre or tone. In a way, Roy's retranslation of *Jin Ping Mei* has enriched and rejuvenated both source and target literary systems, affording the novel a new lease of life during globalized literary exchanges. The two different translations of *Jin Ping Mei* are somewhat in competition, in Venuti's (2004) words, although they may complement each other and enrich interpretations of the novel in the target culture. Notably, while Roy mentioned Egerton's translation in passing in the paratexts of his own translation, there appears to be no direct reference to Egerton's work in the actual translation. This is evident in the stark difference in the deployment of translation strategies. Although Roy also acknowledged André Levy's French version of the same novel, there is little or no evidence that Roy consulted Egerton's translation during the course of his project. Perhaps Roy didn't want to work in Egerton's shadow while translating, especially given their shared status as English-language translators. It seems that he aimed to sidestep the influence of previous English versions, possibly to overcome what Harold Bloom's (1997) terms the "anxiety of influence" during the translation process. This situation is reminiscent of Edward Seidensticker's (1921–2007) retranslation of *Genji monogatari*, published in 1976. Seidensticker, a noted scholar and translator of Japanese literature, was best known for his retranslation of *Genji*. Prior to his retranslation, Waley's version, *The Tale of Genji*, had been circulating and widely read in the West for decades. In *Genji Days*, Seidensticker acknowledged that his version would certainly be compared to Waley's by others, but he intentionally avoided taking another look at Waley's version to prevent overt influence or, perhaps, out of fear (as quoted in de Gruchy 2003, 133). It appears that the anxiety of influence could be a significant factor influencing literary retranslators.

Arguably, the two translations of *Jin Ping Mei* occupy different positions in the target literary system. Egerton's *Lotus* became popular and underwent multiple reprints, owing to its inherent qualities that resonate with his contemporary readers, who saw it as a novel of their time, and also due to the intellectual trend for Chinese literature and culture in early twentieth-century Europe. Notably, it has sustained interest among twenty-first-century readers, having experienced two reprints since the turn of the century, in 2011 and most recently in 2023. By the time Roy wrote his *Plum* some forty years later, *Jin Ping Mei* had already been known to English-language audiences for decades. Roy utilized the *cihua* edition as a base text to justify his motivation for retranslation and his method of translating. His *Plum* was mainly received and reviewed by sinologists and specialist readers in an educational setting and is currently consumed by professional readers, scholars, and students of traditional Chinese literature. Consequently, the two translations leave distinct impressions on readers in terms of artistic performance and aesthetic sensibility: one is creative, transformative, and reads like an English novel in its own right; the other is serious and strongly academically oriented. All in all, the Egerton translation offers us Egerton's reading of *Jin Ping Mei*, nurtured by Egerton's time, while the Roy translation provides us with Roy's interpretation in his institutional or pedagogical setting. The two translators approached the novel with different interpretive experiences, dispositions, and aesthetic concerns. They viewed it from within different historical contexts and came at it from the perspectives of different interpretive traditions. Their translations not only engage in dialogue with the Chinese original but also involve a dialogical polemic, whether overt or covert, with each other. In this way, they not only sustain the "afterlife" of the original but also compete to maintain readers' interest in the story of *Jin Ping Mei* in the Western context. However, both translations cannot be claimed as "definite" or "complete" versions of *Jin Ping Mei*. According to Schleiermacher and Gadamer, a truly complete or entirely faithful translation is impossible and unattainable due to the fundamental gulf between the source and target languages, as this barrier cannot be entirely overcome (Altman and Coe 2013, 103; George and van der Heiden 2022, 155). As Benjamin (2021) observes, within all languages and linguistic creations, there exists something beyond what can be expressed – something that eludes communication and re-presentation. Translation inevitably involves both loss and gain and capturing every aspect of the original is an unattainable goal. Even in a dense scholarly translation fortified with a wealth of paratextual devices, not all the information of the original text can be realized or captured with accuracy or absolute fidelity (Tymoczko 2014, 50). Translation is inherently a hermeneutic project, marked perpetually by imperfection. The hermeneutic or interpretive experience of translation always entails renunciation – emphasizing some features of the original at the expense of others – since the translator is not in the position to express all dimensions of the source text in an adequate or apprehensible way (George and van der Heiden 2022, 157). Thus, any translation can merely represent partial features or meanings of the original as it is always designed for a different audience or adapted to align with particular poetics or ideologies in a new language and cultural setting. Translation is de facto a refracted text that maintains a metonymic relationship with the original (Tymoczko 2014, 42). Translation is an ongoing, never-ending process where the features and meanings of the original are both revealed and concealed through various interpretations within various historical contexts. This is primarily due to the inherent subjectivity and diversity in interpretation, the dynamic interplay between languages, cultures, and the pursuit for a deeper, distinct understanding of the original, and the constant negotiation between fidelity to the original and the need to make the translation relevant, accessible and meaningful to the target readership. In a nutshell, translating is, at best, an understanding of another person's utterance, and this understanding is an infinite task, given its historical conditioning and constant state of flux (Eckert 1984; Parris 2015, 31). Each translator brings their own background, biases, unconscious fantasies, and personal/collective experiences to the translating/interpreting process, contributing to the perpetual unfolding and understanding of meaning (Parris 2015). Each translation is a snapshot in time, capturing a specific interpretation, but it remains open to new insights, changing perspectives, and evolving linguistic and cultural landscapes (George and van der Heiden 2022). In brief, translation serves as the medium through which the original work endures or survives in the target culture, and the original is shaped by how it is interpreted and continues to be interpreted via (re) translation. Consequently, as long as there is interest in *Jin Ping Mei* and a literary market for it, there is always room for future versions in various forms.

Despite the achievements made in this book, it can, at best, be counted as one case study of English translations of classical Chinese novels. As any research serves as "a stepping stone for further development" (Toury 1995, xiii) in a certain field, this book paves the way for future research. There is still room for exploring other aspects of *Jin Ping Mei* in translation that have not been addressed in this book, such as modality, intertextuality, explicitation, cult of *qing*, irony, emotions, (im)politeness features, and conceptual metaphor. To enhance the data sampling process for descriptive analysis, the use of corpus tools and techniques (for example, WordSmith Tools) could be beneficial. Thus, a corpus-based study of *Jin Ping Mei* in English translation holds promise for future projects. Additionally, further research could employ reader-response theory, using questionnaires to gauge English-language readers responses. This approach could help assess the effects of translational choices made by different translators of *Jin Ping Mei* on the reception and perception of each translation in the English-reading community.

The methodological framework employed in this project is replicable and can serve as a foundation for critical analyses of various literary works and their translations across diverse genres and language pairs. Additionally, it holds potential as a guide for aspiring translation practitioners before embarking on translation projects. It is firmly believed that delving into cultural representations, narratological elements, gender dynamics, and subversive themes related to sexuality and eroticism within sophisticated literary works can empower literary translators. Such an exploration enables them to reflect upon their choices and strategies, providing critical insights during the translation process. In conclusion, no research can claim finality, given our unending thirst for knowledge and the varying perspectives that different researchers bring to the same research object.

Note

1 The stark difference between the two translations also arises from the fact that they are based on different recensions of the Chinese original, as previously mentioned in Chapter 1.

References

Altman, Matthew C., and Coe, Cynthia D. 2013. *The Fractured Self in Freud and German Philosophy*. New York: Palgrave Macmillan.

Benjamin, Walter. (1923) 2021. "The Task of the Translator." In *The Translation Studies Reader*, edited by Lawrence Venuti, 89–97. London and New York: Routledge.

Bloom, Harold. (1973) 1997. *The Anxiety of Influence: A Theory of Poetry*. Oxford: Oxford University Press.

De Gruchy, John Walter. 2003. *Orienting Arthur Waley: Japonism, Orientalism, and the Creation of Japanese Literature in English*. Honolulu: University of Hawaii Press.

Eckert, Michael. 1984. "Hermeneutics in the Classroom: An Application of Reception Theory." *CEA Critic* 46 (3/4): 5–16.

George, Theodore, and van der Heiden, Gert-Jan. 2022. *The Gadamerian Mind*. London and New York: Routledge.

Parris, David Paul. 2015. *Reading the Bible with Giants: How 2000 Years of Biblical Interpretation Can Shed New Light on Old Texts*. Eugene, Oregon: Cascade Books.

Robinson, Douglas. 2014. *Western Translation Theory from Herodotus to Nietzche*. London and New York: Routledge.

Strich, Fritz. 1971. *Goethe and World Literature*. Westport, Conn: Greenwood Press.

Toury, Gideon. 1995. *Descriptive Translation Studies and Beyond*. Amsterdam: John Benjamins.

Tymoczko, Maria. 2014. *Translation in a Postcolonial Context: Early Irish Literature in English Translation*. London and New York: Routledge.

Venuti, Lawrence. 2004. "Retranslation: The Creation of Value." *Bucknell Review* 47 (1): 25–38.

Venuti, Lawrence. 2008. *The Translator's Invisibility: A History of Translation*. London and New York: Routledge.

Index